Classical Subjects Creatively Taught

LATIN
Alive!
BOOK 1

Karen Moore
Gaylan DuBose

Latin Alive! Book 1 Teacher's Edition
© Classical Academic Press®, 2008
Version 3.0

ISBN: 978-1-60051-055-7

Classical Academic Press
515 S. 32nd Street
Camp Hill, PA 17011

www.ClassicalAcademicPress.com

Proofreader: Anthony Thomas
Cover, illustrations, and design by: Rob Baddorf

PGP.08.20

Latin Alive! Book 1

Table of Contents

Unit Six

Unit Seven

Appendices

Preface

We have written this text just for you, the preteen preparing to begin the dialectic stage of learning (the School of Logic). Whether you are beginning to study Latin for the first time or have studied some Latin in the grammar school, we have created this textbook for you. As the fourth Latin text published by Classical Academic Press, this text will review all the grammar you learned in the *Latin for Children* Primer Series. Now that you are older and can read and think better, the text will teach you much more about how to use what you have learned. For beginners, this text will leave no stone unturned. We will teach you all the basics of the language. For all students this text is the first in a series that will prepare you to read, understand, even construe Latin texts, which represent some of the greatest literature ever written.

What you will find inside:

- **Pronunciation** – The first chapter begins with a thorough lesson on classical pronunciation. This includes important rules on syllabication and accent.
- **Glossaries** – Each chapter begins with a vocabulary and English derivatives. There is also a complete alphabetical glossary in the back for all of these vocabulary words.
- **Grammar Lessons** – The sections in each chapter provide clear, concise, and complete grammatical instruction written just as we teach in our classrooms. Grammatical exercises follow each lesson to help you practice what you have just learned.
- **Sentence Translation** – These exercises appear toward the end of each chapter. They will help you apply what you have practiced in the grammatical exercises and prepare you for the chapter reading to follow.
- **Chapter Readings** – Latin stories about the Roman monarchy and republic end each chapter. We based many of these on the stories of Livy.
- **Unit Review Chapters** – Each unit concludes with a review chapter designed to review the previous lessons. The Unit Review Chapters resemble the format of the reading comprehension portion of the National Latin Exam and the multiple choice section of the Advanced Placement Exam. We intentionally designed these unit reviews to increase reading comprehension skills.
- **Reading Helps** – Each reading whether in a regular chapter or a Unit Review Chapter contains the following helps:
  - Character lists describe the characters that will appear in each story.
  - An extra glossary for unfamiliar words in the text. Each word appears in *italics* in the Latin text. This will allow you to see which words you can expect help on.
  - We have provided the translation for some phrases appearing in bold type at the end of the passage. This feature allows us to introduce you to classical idioms and expressions that frequently appear in Latin literature.
  - Reading comprehension questions in both Latin and English follow each reading.
- **Historical Context** – The Latin readings in this text tell of the history and culture of the Roman people from the Trojan War to the death of Julius Caesar. In addition to these Latin passages, each Unit Review Chapter begins with a historical passage written in English. These provide opportunities for us to communicate more about the people, places, and events that surround the stories you are reading. We are

honored to have Christopher Schlect, historian and Academic Dean of New St. Andrew's College, as a contributing writer on several of these pieces.

- **Bonus Material –** In addition to all of the above we have provided a combination of the following segments in each chapter to supplement your lessons.
  - o <u>Colloquāmur</u> – Improve your command of Latin by increasing your oral proficiency. These activities appear regularly throughout the text and offer practical and sometimes entertaining ways to apply your Latin skills in and out of the classroom.
  - o <u>Derivative Detective</u> – Build your English vocabulary through these activities that demonstrate how we can trace modern words back to an ancient vocabulary.
  - o <u>Culture Corner</u> – Learn more about the Romans, their lives, their history, and their traditions using these windows into the past.
  - o <u>Latin Americana?</u> – No, this is not an oxymoron. Each chapter features one of the national or state mottoes which regularly appear on official insignia. In addition, we offer several opportunities for the student to see how classical history and civilization have shaped our world.

NOTE TO TEACHERS AND PARENTS:

Like *Latin for Children*, this text includes clear, concise, and complete grammatical instruction, making it user-friendly for the novice Latin teacher. As seen in the list of features above it also incorporates a great number of exercises and additional activities, making a supplemental text quite unnecessary. We have, however, created a teacher's edition for this text in order to aid you in the classroom. This edition includes not only answers and translations, but also teacher tips, tests, and additional classroom projects accumulated from our combined experience of more than fifty years of teaching.

It is our hope that you will enjoy learning Latin with this textbook as much as we have enjoyed creating it for you.

S.D.G.

Karen Moore and Gaylan DuBose

Introduction for Teachers

ATTENTION TEACHERS:

This manual is intended to provide you with as much support as possible in order to assist you during the course of this text. For that reason this manual supplies you with much more than an answer key. Inside you will find:

- Descriptions of the history and symbolism of the U.S. national and state seals that are featured at the beginning of each chapter.
- Further explanations on some of the more complex grammar lessons
- Teacher tips for conveying ideas or to warn of common student pitfalls
- Additional exercises for further practice
- Supplemental worksheets for declining nouns and adjectives, conjugating verbs, and parsing verbs
- Suggested projects in each unit review chapter based on the history and culture lessons presented
- Unit tests

Should you have any questions for which this manual does not supply an answer, please submit them via Ask the Magister on the Classical Academic Press website at www.classicalacademicpress.com/ask-the-magister. There we will provide you with the answers you need. It is our desire to support you in your endeavor to introduce students to the fascinating world of Latin.

Before You Begin: Please do read through the teacher guide before creating your lesson plans. For those students who have studied Latin via *Latin for Children* or another Latin primer, some chapters may contain review material that need not be reviewed. Others may contain material that may appear to be review, but does contain new concepts and important information the students have not yet learned. The scope and sequence of this text is designed to serve students new to Latin, while at the same time to provide further insight and challenges for "veterans" of any grammar school series. The text also contains a great wealth of supplemental material. Not everyone will have time to fit it all in, so pick and choose what you feel will serve your classroom the best. The following are a few teacher tips that will be useful throughout the text:

Great Seals: Each chapter begins with a chapter maxim taken from one of the U.S. national and state mottoes. This guide provides additional insight into the great seals which often display these mottoes. Many seals not only display a Latin motto but also use images that hearken back to the ancient civilizations of Greece and Rome. Understanding the influence behind these mottoes and seals demonstrates how relevant Latin still remains to our modern culture. Teachers may want to consider using the "Latin Across America" geography project in the appendix to help integrate a little geography and American history into their Latin classrooms. These mottoes also make great bonus questions on chapter quizzes or unit tests.

Oral Practice: Although Latin is no longer spoken in most settings, a student has much to gain from oral practice. First and foremost, countless studies have proven that the more senses used to learn something, the better one will retain it. Oral practice provides another creative (and often diverting) means to reinforce the lessons in this text. Second, by training students how to communicate Latin orally (i.e. speak), bypassing the pen and paper, we are training their minds to process other foreign languages in the same manner—by speaking.

This text provides a number of helps and exercises to make this an obtainable goal for any classroom. First, chapter one begins with an in-depth lesson on the pronunciation of the Latin language. Each chapter reinforces this first series of lessons by asking students to mark the appropriate pronunciation for each one of their vocabulary words. This exercise will also prepare students for the Latin poetry that they will read in later texts. It is highly beneficial for the students and/or teacher to read the Latin in this text aloud at every opportunity.

It is important to not only include scripted Latin for oral practice, but some more natural conversation as well. Get students to think (or speak) on their feet. Many chapters provide a bonus segment called **Colloquāmur** (Let's Talk). These segments provide a wide variety of ways to practice Latin aloud in a conversational manner. These exercises can include social Latin (polite Roman conversation), grammar practice (how to have a classroom discussion on grammar in Latin), and even a few topics for nature studies. On a more academic note, each chapter reading also concludes with a set of reading comprehension questions in Latin. While the students may complete these in writing, the questions provide another opportunity for great Latin conversation. Such exercises greatly affirm the student's confidence in Latin.

Practice, Practice, Practice: The teacher will notice that each time the text introduces a new noun declension, verb conjugation, or verb tense the following exercise immediately asks students to decline/conjugate a new set of words. Students cannot practice these forms enough – orally or in writing. This text provides a set of reproducible declension, conjugation, and verb parsing worksheets to provide a uniform structure for these exercises. Often the authors of this text have suggested additions to these practices that may help students better imbed new grammar concepts.

Parsing & Labeling Sentences: Most of the sentence translation exercises ask students to "parse and label" sentences. A math teacher would never accept final answers to mathematical problems when the students had failed to show their work. Likewise, Latin students ought to regularly practice analyzing the grammatical structure of a sentence. In the beginning with simple sentences this direction is pretty straight forward. Students can use the same abbreviations and symbols as in their English classes. (If the English teacher is different from the Latin teacher, be sure that the two find common ground on how to label sentences. This will prevent confusion for the students.) As syntax becomes more complex the labeling will begin to differ from what students might use in their English classes. For example, English uses prepositional phrases much more than Latin. So teachers may want to identify a particular ablative word by its construction instead (such as "manner"). Teachers and students can use the labels demonstrated in this text, or come up with another method that better suits their own classroom. Just be consistent.

The text does not ask students to parse the Latin readings featured at the conclusion to each chapter and in the unit reviews. Here students must begin learning to leave the analytical behind, trust in the skills they have learned, and read the Latin.

Latin Passages: Beginning with the fourth chapter, each chapter contains a Latin reading. In chapters 4 through 6 the readings consist of individual numbered sentences that as a group tell a bit about the Trojan War. The text presents these first readings in this manner as a means to prepare students gradually for translating longer passages in paragraph form. Beginning with the first unit review chapter students will begin translating paragraphs about the Romans. Most of these readings are inspired by *Ab Urbe Condita* (*From the Founding of the City*) by Titus Livius, usually known in English as Livy. By allowing students the opportunity to read about the great exploits and heroes of the Roman Republic, we believe students should gain a great understanding of the people who spoke this ancient language. The best way to learn any language is in the context of the culture and history of those who spoke it. By studying the Roman Republic in this text, students will also gain a deeper understanding of and appreciation for the American Republic.

It is the goal of this text series to begin training students to read original Latin texts, unadapted from the author's pen. There is, however, a great bridge to cross from modern English to ancient Latin texts. So it is worth emphasizing that the majority of the passages in this text are "inspired by" Livy's writings. The authors have studied Livy's records of the events and people mentioned in his text, and based these passages upon those records. Whenever possible, Livy's vocabulary and phrasing have been retained. Often, however, it is necessary to adapt and re-write portions to bring them within the student's capability. As the text progresses the passages will gradually grow closer to what might be considered "real Latin."

In *Latin Alive! Book 2* the passages will no longer be inspired by Latin authors, but adapted straight from the author's text. The authors will tinker with the original Latin only as much as is necessary to bring the text within the student's reach. By that time, however, the students will have mastered a great deal more of the language, and will require less adaptation. In *Latin Alive! Book 3* students will reach the goal of reading original Latin texts, just as the original author wrote them.

Reading Aids: In order to assist the students as they begin learning to read Latin, the text provides several reading aides or tips for each passage. Most readings begin with a list of characters. This will help students distinguish whom or what the proper nouns represent. When students encounter in the Latin readings words they have not yet learned, those words can be found in one of three places: in the reading glossary, in the alphabetical glossary at the back of the book (see p. 255), or in a good Latin dictionary. While each reading will review much of the vocabulary the students have learned, additional vocabulary for the stories has been provided. Many of the new words or grammatical structures not introduced in preceding chapters will appear in the reading glossary that follows the passage. Such words appear in *italics* within the passage itself in order to alert students to the fact that the word is glossed. New words that do not appear in the reading glossary may be found in the alphabetical glossary or in a Latin dictionary. Some words in later passages are underlined. An example might be the Latin word honor, which means "honor." The underlined "eye" Latin words are not included in the glossary. These words resemble their English counterparts so closely that we ask students to use their "eye" Latin to discern the meaning. Other phrases in the passage may appear in **bold type**. These are usually phrases that contain grammar too difficult for most students to grasp, and the full translation is provided immediately following the passage. They are included for a couple of reasons. First, many are constructions or actual phrases that appear in Latin Literature. Since it is our goal to train students for reading original Latin Literature we feel it best to begin acquainting them with such constructions early in their studies. In some cases, the text will also provide explanations for the grammar exemplified in bold type. Second, these phrases are included in this format because the meaning and translation add a great deal to the story. The authors could simply find no better way to express those thoughts or ideas while remaining true to Latin.

Reading Comprehension: As students increase their translating skills they need to learn to read for comprehension. A series of reading comprehension questions follow each chapter reading. While these can serve as a written assignment, they also provide a tremendous opportunity for class conversation about the passage. Several chapters also provide an additional group discussion question in English. Often this question will prompt a discussion comparing or contrasting the history and culture of America with that of Rome. Encourage students whenever possible to cite a portion of the Latin passage as they make their observations. This skill will serve them well as they prepare for writing assignments in other classes, making speeches, participating in debates, or even preparing for the Latin Advanced Placement Exam.

Unit Reviews: The text includes seven unit review chapters. The focus of each chapter is to build the student's reading skills. Each unit review features a story (also based on the history or culture of Rome) that reviews the vocabulary and grammar concepts learned in the preceding chapters. The story is followed by a series of multiple choice questions. The format of the story and the questions that follow is similar to that one might see on the National Latin Exam or the Advanced Placement Exam. For students who desire to take one of these exams this will prove excellent practice.

Generally, the students should follow these steps to success for reading comprehension exercises.
- Read the English title. (It is often a clue to the theme or content of the reading.)
- Read the Latin text all the way through without any attempt at translation.
- Read the questions in order to know what to look for in the reading.
- Read the selection again, translating carefully. In order to get as close to the original as possible, it is good for students to read each text in Latin word order, understanding the possible functions of each word before moving on to the next. This will help students avoid thinking about Latin as English and will enable them to begin to see the purpose for an author's choice of word order.
- Go back and begin answering the questions.

Assessments: The teacher's guide includes seven unit tests. These tests should be taken upon completion of the corresponding unit review chapters. The unit tests not only assess the grammar the student has learned, but also the student's ability to apply that grammar to a reading passage.

This guide does not include chapter quizzes, but a separate *Latin Alive! Book 1 Test Packet* is available for purchase at ClassicalAcademicPress.com. The test packet includes a set of comprehensive, standardized tests designed to supplement *Latin Alive! Book 1*. It is an excellent and helpful resource for teachers and parents. The downloadable packet includes a weekly test for each chapter, a complete answer key, and suggested scoring based on a 100-point system. Choose between three licenses (1–3, 4–9, or 10+ students).

Oral quizzes (much like an English spelling quiz) are a good way to continue to develop auditory proficiency. Teachers should give the first form from the vocabulary list (e.g. nominative singular for nouns and adjectives or first principal part for verbs). The student should then write that word and the necessary forms and meanings that follow. Teachers may want to add a bonus question taken from the chapter maxims or perhaps from the Culture Corner segments. Such bonus questions are a great way to encourage students to read and learn these items.

Supplemental Lessons: In an appendix at the back of this text the authors have included several projects that have been favorites in their classes. They include the following:
- Latin Across America – incorporate American geography with the state mottoes
- Tempus Fugit – build a timeline for the Roman Republic incorporating the people and events students will read about in this text
- Roman Calendar – learn about the history of the Roman Calendar and how little it differs from the one we use today, then create your own
- Archaeology – create your own archeological dig

Thank you for choosing *Latin Alive!* for your classroom. It is our hope that this series will lead you and your students on a wonderful voyage of discovery into the world of Latin.

Blessings,
Karen Moore and Gaylan DuBose

Here is a handy chart of all the abbreviations used in the parsing and labeling exercises throughout the book.

Abbreviation	Meaning
Sing.	Singular
Pl.	Plural
Pf.	Perfect
Imp.	Imperfect
Fut.	Future
FP	Future Perfect
Pres.	Present
Pluperf.	Pluperfect

Ē plūribus ūnum

One from many

—Motto on the United States of America Great Seal [A]

This phrase is adapted from Pseudo-Vergil's *Morētum*, 1.104.

"*color est ē plūribus ūnus*"

[A]Charles Tomson was the principal designer for the Great Seal, adopted by Congress on June 20, 1782. He gave the following explanations for the symbolism of the design:

- The shield is composed of 13 stripes representing the 13 colonies joined into one single body, the Congress of the U.S.
- The shield is borne on the breast of the American Eagle alone representing that the U.S. ought to rely on her own virtue.
- The olive branch and arrows represent the power of peace and war which is vested in Congress alone.
- The constellation of 13 stars above the eagle represents the new country (13 states) taking its place in the universe among other sovereign powers.

Chapter 1

- Latin alphabet
- pronunciation
  - syllabication
  - accent
- sentence structure

Latin has for many years carried with it a sense of foreboding. Many perceive Latin as a difficult course of study, much too difficult for any but the most intelligent and adept of students. However, this is simply not the case. The fact is that many boys and girls of various nationalities and backgrounds have studied this language over the centuries. If you take up the biographies of many men and women of reputation, including the founding fathers of America, you will find that they had quite a bit of training in Latin as youths, some in the small one-room schoolhouses of the backwoods. The truth is that English is actually much harder to learn than Latin. Compared to English, Latin is simple. Before you laugh at this remark, take the Roman point of view. Let us suppose that a young Roman boy named Marcus decided to take up the study of English. How would he, a native speaker of Latin, find this modern language?

SECTION 1. Alphabet

Marcus's first lesson would of course be the alphabet. Here he would be relieved to find great common ground, for our alphabets are very similar. The earliest writings we possess in the Latin alphabet date from the sixth century BC. The Latin alphabet was adapted primarily from that of the Etruscans, a people who inhabited central Italy prior to the Romans, and consisted initially of only 20 letters:

A B C D E F G H I L M N O P Q R S T V X

The letters *K*, *Y*, and *Z* were added from the Greek alphabet later when Romans wanted to adapt Greek words to the Latin language. The letters *J*, *U*, and *W* were added at a much later stage also for the purposes of adapting other languages. The letter *J* became the consonant form of *I*, *U* is the vowel form of *V*, and *W* was introduced as a "double-u" (or double-v) to make a clear distinction between the sounds we know today as 'v' and 'w.' With these additions, the Latin alphabet, also called the Roman alphabet, has come today to be the most widely used alphabetic writing system in the world. So, Marcus need only learn a couple of new letters in order to obtain a complete understanding of the modern day alphabet. As for you, you needn't learn any, but only learn to live without a few.

1

The final form of the alphabet in Latin was:

A B C D E F G H I K L M N O P Q R S T U V X Y Z
a b c d e f g h i k l m n o p q r s t u v x y z

SECTION 2. Pronunciation

While the alphabet will pose little or no problem for our Roman friend, Marcus, phonics will be a great obstacle. The twenty-six letters that create the modern English alphabet can make seventy-two different phonetic sounds!

Let's start with vowels. Surely you have noticed in the English language how challenging it can be to know how to pronounce a vowel or group of vowels. We sometimes even have homophones (words with identical spellings) that are pronounced two different ways (e.g., **pre**sent and pre**sent**) and others that are spelled differently but pronounced identically (e.g., to, too, and two)!

Latin vowels are much more consistent. For the time being, assume that the consonants are pronounced just as they are in English. Your teacher will help you if there are any unusual ones.

Vowels in Latin consist of the typical *a, e, i, o, u.* They are either long or short by nature. Thus, each vowel has two and only two sounds. Unlike English, long vowels in Latin are often clearly marked by a macron (from the Greek word *makros*, meaning "long").

SHORT	LATIN EXAMPLE	LONG	LATIN EXAMPLE
a as in **a**like [uh]	*casa*	**ā** as in f**a**ther [ah]	*stāre*
e as in p**e**t [eh]	*memoria*	**ē** as in th**ey** [ey]	*cēna* [key-nuh]
i as in p**i**t [ih]	*inter*	**ī** as in mach**i**ne [ee]	*īre*
o as in b**ou**ght [aw]	*bonus*	**ō** as in h**o**se [oh]	*errō*
u as in p**u**t [ù]	*Marcus*	**ū** as in r**u**de [oo]	*lūdus*
y as in p**i**t [ih] [B]	*thymum*	**ȳ** as in mach**ī**ne [ee]	*Lȳdia*

[B] The letter *y* was only used to represent Greek words (along with the letters *k* and *z*).

Exercise 1. Pronounce the following words aloud. [C]

1. pater — **puh-tehr**
2. māter — **mah-tehr**
3. sinō — **sih-noh**
4. sīvī — **see-wee**
5. ōrdō — **ohr-doh**
6. potior — **paw-tee-awr**
7. est — **ehst**
8. ēst — **eyst**
9. uxor — **ùk-sawr**
10. ūsus — **oo-sùs**
11. syllaba — **sihl-luh-buh**
12. sȳcophanta — **see-caw-puhn-tuh**

[C] You may want to demonstrate some of these for students. For others, you may want to see how they do and give gentle correction as needed. It is highly advisable that you practice these well before presenting them to your students so that you are able to guide them.

Now let's look at consonants. Look at the following list of English words and read them aloud.

cat	apple	rock
city	ant	rope
chorus	avocado	love
charade	aviator	loose

Can you make one general rule for the sounds produced by each of the letters *c*, *a*, or *o*? There are phonetic rules for each of these letters, but they are numerous and there are many exceptions to almost all of them.

Marcus will most likely feel quite overwhelmed and even a bit frustrated by the numerous phonic rules he must learn. His native Latin is much simpler and very easy to understand. Each consonant produces only one sound when on its own. Most are identical to our modern pronunciation, but there are a few variations that you should learn.

Students do not need to know the definitions of the Latin examples, but we are including them here for you in anticipation of curious minds.

CONSONANT	PHONETIC RULE	LATIN EXAMPLE	
c	always hard as in **c**at, never soft as in **c**ent	cantō cēna	I sing / dinner
g	always hard as in **g**oat, never soft as in **g**entle	glōria genus	glory / birth
i (j)	as a consonant when it is an initial vowel before another vowel *or* when it is between two vowels, pronounced as the *y* in **y**ellow[1]	iam Iūppiter	now / Jupiter
r	often rolled as in Spanish or Italian	rēctus	straight
s	always like the *s* in **s**it, never like the *z* sound in plea**s**e	semper senātus	always / senate
t	always like the *t* in **t**able, never like the *sh* sound in na**t**ion	teneō ratiō	I hold / reason
v	sounds like the *w* in **w**ine	vīnum victōria	wine / victory
x	sounds like the *x* in o**x**, not the *gz* in e**x**ert	nox rēx	night / king

[D]You may want to demonstrate for students the pronunciation of some of these words. For other words, you may want to see how students do on their own and give gentle correction as needed.

Exercise 2. Pronounce these words aloud.[D]

1. cīvitās — **kee**-wih-tahs
2. interrogātiō — ihn-tehr-roh-**gah**-tee-oh
3. casa — **kuh**-suh
4. vēritās — **wey**-rih-tahs
5. vinculum — **wihn**-kŭ-lŭm
6. exercitās — ek-**sehr**-kih-tahs
7. uxor — **uhk**-sohr
8. gravitās — **grah**-wih-tahs
9. genus — **geh**-nŭs
10. ēsurgō — ey-**sŭr**-goh
11. iungō — **yŭng**-goh

In English, when two consonants appear together their sound can change in a myriad of different ways. Take for instance the common pairing of *th*.

then   **th**eatre   goa**th**erd

___

1. **Exception:** The *i* is a consonant in compound words when it is a consonant uncompounded (e.g., *adiŭvō* from *ad* + *iŭvō*), where the *i* is a consonant in both instances.

Once again, Marcus will be overwhelmed. He must learn another set of rules in order to know how to pronounce the consonant blend 'th' in varying settings. Latin is simple. On most occasions that two consonants appear together, you will pronounce each one with its individual sound as prescribed above. There are a few consonant blends, but unlike English, each blend has one assigned sound that never varies.

CONSONANT BLEND	PHONETIC RULE	LATIN EXAMPLE	
bs, bt	**b** sounds like **p**	urbs (urps) obtineō (op-TIN-e-oh)	city I hold
gu, qu	sounds like **gw, qw** as in pen**gu**in and **qu**art (The **u** is considered a consonant here, not a vowel.)	lingua quod	tongue, language because
ng	sounds like *ng* as in a**ng**le (You hear an *ng* sound followed by a *g* sound) not like a**ng**el or si**ng**.	lingua	tongue, language
gn	sounds like *gn* or *ngn* as in ma**gn**et or a**nn**ual	magnus	big, great
ch	each sound pronounced individually like **ch**orus, not like ba**ch**elor	charta Chaos	paper, document Chaos
th	each sound pronounced individually like goa**th**erd, not like **th**en or **th**eatre	thymum theātrum	thyme theatre
ph	each sound pronounced individually like u**p h**ill, though most people pronounce it *f* as in **ph**ilosophy [E]	philosophia Orpheus	philosophy Orpheus
double consonants [F]	pronounced as two individually distinct sounds with a slight pause between them	ecce (EC-ce) puella (pu-EL-la)	look girl

[E] The correct classical pronunciation is an aspirated *p*; however, medieval, ecclesiastical, neoclassical, and modern pronunciations all use the *f* sound. Either pronunciation is acceptable, and students will likely encounter both throughout their Latin journey.

[F] The double-consonants *ch*, *th*, and *ph* are used almost solely to represent Greek words. A common exception would seem to be *pulcher* which is Latin in origin.

Exercise 3. Pronounce the following words aloud. [G]

1. obstat — **awp**-stuht
2. obtulī — **awp**-tŭ-lee
3. anguis — **uhng**-gwihs
4. sanguen — **suhng**-gwehn
5. pulcher — **pu'l**-kehr
6. architectus — uhrkh-ih-**tehk**-tŭs
7. philosophia — fih-loh-**soh**-fee-uh
8. theātrum — teh-**a**-trŭm
9. quisque — **kwihs**-kweh
10. cūrō — **koo**-roh
11. currō — **cŭr**-roh
12. sumus — **sŭ**-mŭs
13. summus — **sŭm**-mŭs

[G] You may want to demonstrate for students the pronunciation of some of these words. For other words, you may want to see how students do on their own and give gentle correction as needed.

Finally, there are a few combinations of vowels that are pronounced together. These diphthongs are two vowels blended together to create one sound. Latin has only six diphthongs. The most common diphthongs, and the only ones you will usually have to worry about, are *ae, au,* and *oe.* You will occasionally encounter *ei* and *ui.* Very infrequently, you may come across *eu* as a diphthong, but only in words such as the interjection *heu* (given as an example in the table on p. 5) and in words coming from Greek in which *eu* is always a diphthong.

	DIPHTHONG	PRONUNCIATION	LATIN EXAMPLE	
This symbol indicates that there is more information in the Teacher's Pages at the end of the chapter. In this instance it indicates that note H is located there.	ae	sounds like the **ai** in **aisle**	fēminae, aequus	**women, equal**
	au	sounds like the **ou** in **out**	laudō, auctor	**I praise, author**
	ei	sounds like the **eigh** in w**eigh**	deinde	**then**
	eu[2]	pronounced **eh-oo**	heu	**alas**
	oe	sounds like the **oi** in c**oil**	proelium	**battle**
	ui[H] TE	pronounced oo-ee as in t**wee**t	huic, cui	**to this, to whom**

Exercise 4. Pronounce the following words aloud.

1. caedō **kae**-doh
2. hui* **hui**
3. poena **poe**-nuh
4. heu* **heu**

5. ei* **ei**
6. seu* **seu**
7. audiō **au**-dee-oh

*The diphthongs marked with an asterisk are very rare. The diphthongs not so marked are very common diphthongs.

The various sounds produced by the consonants and vowels in Latin total forty different phonetic sounds. Compare this to the seventy-two sounds produced by the English language and you can begin to see why Latin could be considered the easier of the two. However, there is still more to consider in learning how to pronounce words correctly. So, while Marcus continues to learn his seventy-two new sounds, we will turn to syllabication.

SECTION 3. Syllabication[1] TE

The term "syllable" is used to refer to a unit of a word that consists of a single, uninterrupted sound formed by a vowel, diphthong, or by a consonant-vowel combination. **Syllabication** is the act of dividing a word into its individual syllables. With English this can be tricky because there are often letters that remain silent. However, in Latin there are no silent letters, so any given Latin word will have as many syllables as it has vowels or diphthongs. There are three main rules of syllabication and a couple of more-complicated rules that occur in unusual circumstances. Our suggestion is that you memorize the first three rules, and then refer to the other rules when you need them, until they become second nature.

Main Rules: Divide

1. Before the last of two or more consonants:
   pu-el-la   ter-ra
   ar-ma   temp-tō
   (but phi-lo-so-phi-a because, remember, *ph* is considered a single consonant)

2. Between two vowels or a vowel and a diphthong (never divide a diphthong):
   Cha-os   proe-li-um

3. Before a single consonant:
   me-mo-ri-a   fē-mi-nae

Special Rules:

4. Before a stop + liquid combination, except if it is caused by the addition of a prefix to the word:
   pu-**bli**-ca (but **ad-lā**-tus according to the exception)[3]

5. After the letter *x*. Though it is technically two consonants, it is indivisible in writing, so we divide after it:
   ex-i-ti-um   ex-e-ō

---

2. Essentially, it is safe to assume that all combinations of *e* and *u* are two syllables.

3. A *stop* is a consonant whose sound cannot be sustained. For example, you can sustain or extend the sound of *f* or *v* or *s*, but once you make the *d* or *t* sound, it is over: the sound automatically stops. Liquids are the letters *l* and *r*. *Tr* is an example of a stop + liquid combination.

6. Before *s* + a stop, if the *s* is preceded by a consonant:
mōn-stro   ad-scrip-tum

It is easy to tell long syllables in Latin, and it will be important to know how to do so in order to properly accent words. Syllables are long when they contain a long vowel (marked by a macron), a diphthong, or a short vowel followed by two consonants. Otherwise, they are usually short. Recognizing the length of a syllable will become particularly important when reading poetry later on.

Caveat Discipulus (Let the Student Beware): The length of the syllable does not change the length of the vowel. You should still pronounce short vowels according to the phonetic rules you have just learned. The length of the syllable will affect how you accent the words, as you will soon learn in Section 4.

Exercise 5. Practice dividing the following Latin words into syllables and mark the length of the syllables. ᴶ

1. dominus
2. annus
3. cōnsilium
4. theātrum
5. ager
6. oppidum
7. victōria
8. audiō

SECTION 4. Accent ᴷ

Accent is the vocal emphasis placed on a particular syllable of a word. As usual English complicates rules for pronunciation. Consider the following examples paying particular attention to the underlined words.

> We will present the present to the birthday girl. They object to the object of the speech.

The underlined homonyms are spelled the same, yet each one is pronounced differently. Why? Certainly Marcus or any other student attempting to learn English would be quite puzzled by this. Latin on the other hand accents words in a uniform manner. The rules for accent are as follows:

ᴷNotā Bene: The last syllable is referred to as the *ultimā*, meaning "last" in Latin. The next to last syllable is called the penult (almost last). The syllable third from the end is known as the antepenult (before the almost last).

Hint: Think in terms of the penult having a gravitational pull. If it is long the "gravity" pulls the accent close to it. If it is short, then there is a lack of gravity as on the moon, and the accent floats away to the third position. There is, however, an invisible force field on the other side of the antepenult, so the accent cannot float past that syllable.

1. In words of two syllables always accent the first syllable: **aúc-tor, naú-ta**
2. In words of more than two syllables accent the penult when it is long: **for-tū́-na, im-pe-rā́-tor**
3. Otherwise, accent the antepenult syllable: **fḗ-mi-na, aú-di-ō**

Exercise 6. Return to exercise 5 and practice accenting the words that you have already broken down into syllables.

SECTION 5. Sentence Structure

There are three common ways to communicate meaning in a language: 1) word order, 2) function words, which express the relationship between words (articles, prepositions, helping verbs, etc.), 3) inflection. English relies mainly on word order and function words to communicate meaning, but Latin relies mainly on inflection. In an English sentence we can distinguish between the subject and the object by the order in which they appear.

> Greece attacks Troy.

It is clear in this sentence who is doing the attacking (the subject), and who is receiving the attacking (the object). If we were to reverse the word order, the outcome would be quite different.

Troy attacks Greece.

Greece is now the object of the verb; they are no longer doing the attacking, but are on the receiving end. This makes a big difference to the Greeks! Latin's word order is much looser than English, so it relies on the use of inflection to communicate meaning. Inflection (from the Latin *īnflectere*, to change, warp) is the changing of a word's form by the addition of an affix. We often use inflection in English to indicate the difference between singular and plural:

ENGLISH:	sailor	sailors	lord	lords
LATIN:	nauta	nautae	dominus	dominī

Latin does the same. However, it also uses inflection to express the relationship between words in the same sentence.

Trōiam Graecia oppugnat.   Graecia Trōiam oppugnat.   Graecia oppugnat Trōiam.

Each of the above sentences means the same thing, "Greece attacks Troy," even though the word order is different. It is the ending that indicates the subject, object, and verb, not the order of the words. English can further define the relationship between words by adding a number of function words:

Troops sail from Greece, and will attack the town of Troy.
Cōpiae ā Graeciā nāvigant, et oppidum Trōiae oppugnābunt.

You can see clearly from this example that while Latin does use a few function words (et, ā), it relies mostly on inflection, i.e., the changing of endings to define the relationship between the words of this more complex sentence. In the sentence above, for example, the ending *-ae* on *Trōiae* is what is translated "of" in the English phrase "of Troy," while the ending *-bunt* on *oppugnābunt* is translated "will" in the English phrase "will attack."

It would appear that on account of the simplicity of this ancient language, students learning Latin are already well ahead of Marcus and his English studies. So, now that we have completed our introduction to the Latin language, we will bid him farewell and begin the study of Latin grammar.

Exercise 7. Define the following terms using complete sentences.

1. Diphthong
2. Syllabication
3. Accent
4. Function words
5. Inflection

Notā Bene (Note Well):
Although we have given you some helpful rules regarding pronunciation, syllabification and accent, there will occasionally be some exceptions to these rules (as with English rules). These exceptions will be rare, however, and there is no need to list all possible exceptions for you now.

Once Marcus has completed the tedious process of learning all the rules for pronouncing and spelling English words, he will be delighted to find how similar many of them are to Latin. In fact, there are many Latin words that have been adopted into the English language without any change in spelling at all. The only challenge is that they are often pronounced differently in Latin.

Exercise 8. Study the following list of Latin words. Divide them according to the rules of syllabication and accent them appropriately, then practice reading them aloud.

1. animal
2. clāmor
3. honor
4. genus
5. horror
6. toga
7. status
8. paenīnsula
9. interim
10. neuter
11. poēta
12. ulterior
13. arēna
14. herba
15. firmus
16. gladiātor
17. atrium
18. candidātus
19. ergō
20. forma

Culture Corner: Roman Names

Most people today have three names: first, middle, and last (or surname).

e.g. Michael Richard Moore

Have you ever thought about the purposes that each of your names serves? Your last name (Moore) signifies the family to which you belong. Often either your first or middle name is inherited from a parent or ancestor. In this example Richard is a name inherited from this boy's father and grandfather. The first name is often one chosen just for you. It sets you apart from the other members of your family. Your parents may have chosen this name based on how it sounds or what it means.

Generally your friends and family call you by your first name (Michael), unless you have a nickname or preference for your middle name. Your middle name is reduced to an initial on most documents (Michael R. Moore). Rarely does anyone call you by both your first and middle name (Michael Richard) or by all three names except in formal situations such as graduation, or when your mother catches you in some mischief.

Roman names are somewhat similar. Roman boys also had three names: praenōmen, nōmen, cognōmen.

e.g. Gāius Jūlius Caesar

The cognōmen (Caesar) was similar to our surname. It identified the family to which that person belongs. The nōmen (Jūlius) was usually inherited from the father. This was the case with both boys and girls. The son of Jūlius Caesar would also be called Jūlius, and his daughter would be called Jūlia. This was the name by which you were most often addressed publicly. Girls, would you like to inherit your father's name? The praenōmen was your own unique name. Only your family and closest friends would address you with this name. The praenōmen was the name often reduced to an abbreviation: G. Jūlius Caesar.

Our name us-ually does not change, except in the instance of marriage. The Romans, however, sometimes changed or added an agnōmen to recognize certain accomplishments in a man's life. For example, Publius Cornēlius Scīpiō won the Second Punic War against Carthage (a country in North Africa), and was rewarded with the agnōmen "Āfricānus." He is known in history as Scipio Africanus.

You can Latinize your own name using some of the phonetic sounds you learned in this chapter. Girls' names usually end in –a, and boys' names usually end in –us. Michael Richard Moore, for example, would be *Michael Richardus Morus*. You can also read the *Colloquāmur* section to choose an authentic Latin name for yourself.[L]

[L]A further note:

Students might also be interested to know that girls generally had only one name (nōmen), which was the feminine form of their father's name. So the daughter of Cornēlius would be Cornēlia. The daughter of Jūlius would be Jūlia. If a man had more than one daughter the following additions were made:

1st daughter – Cornēlia Māior (Older Cornelia)

2nd daughter – Cornēlia Minor (Younger Cornelia)

3rd daughter – Cornēlia Tertia (Third Cornelia)

It is often fun to ask the girls in your class what their Roman name might be according to this tradition.

Colloquāmur (Let's Talk)

Did you know that many of our modern names come from those used by the Romans or their Latin-speaking successors? Use the list below to see if you can find the origin of your name or choose another Roman name for yourself. Then use the conversation guide to introduce yourself to your classmates. Don't forget to pronounce them correctly!

BOYS:	
Albertus	Laurentius
Antōnius	Leō
Bernardus	Leonardus
Carolus	Ludovīcus
Chrīstophorus	Mārcus
Cornēlius	Martīnus
Dominicus	Michael
Eduardus	Pātricius
Ferdinandus	Paulus
Francīscus	Petrus
Frederīcus	Philippus
Gregorius	Raymundus
Gulielmus	Robertus
Henrīcus	Rūfus
Iacōbus	Silvester
Ioannes	Stephanus
Iōsēphus	Timotheus
Iūlius	Victor
Iūstīnus	

GIRLS:	
Aemilia	Margarīta
Agatha	Marīa
Alma	Monica
Anastasia	Pātricia
Angela	Paula
Anna	Paulīna
Barbara	Roberta
Caecilia	Rosa
Catharīna	Stella
Chrīstīna	Terēsia
Clāra	Ursula
Deana	Vēra
Dorothēa	Vēronica
Flōra	Victōria
Flōrentia	Viōla
Iūlia	Virginia
Iūliāna	Vīviāna
Lūcia	

Salvē, nōmen mihi est _____.　　Hello, my name is _____.
Quid nōmen tibi est?　　What is your name?

ᴴIn Latin, a combination of vowels is only considered a diphthong if the individual vowels have no macrons. Therefore, the letter combination *ui* is not a diphthong when the *u* is part of the combination *qu* (e.g., *quis*) nor if it precedes another vowel, in which case the *i* is acting as a consonant (e.g., *cūius* => *cūjus*). In cases in which the *i* is acting like a consonant and is preceded by a vowel, the vowel will be long (e.g., *māior*, *pēius*).

ᴵ*Notā Bene* (Note Well), from p. 5: Please note that we are talking about syllable length and not vowel length. A long syllable can contain a short vowel, as in the case of the short vowel followed by two consonants. Just because a syllable is marked long does *not* mean that the vowel will become long. Such is the case with *oppidum* in exercise 1, #6. The *o* is short, but the syllable is long because of the double consonant that follows. The length of the syllable does not change how you pronounce vowels. It will instead affect how you accent the words, as you will see in Section 4.

Exercise 5

1. dominus   dŏ-mĭ-nŭs
2. annus   ān-nŭs
3. cōnsilium cōn-sĭ-lĭ-ŭm
4. theātrum   thĕ-āt-rŭm*

5. ager   ă-gĕr
6. oppidum   ōp-pĭ-dŭm
7. victōria   vīc-tō-rĭ-ă
8. audiō   au-dĭ-ō

*Notā Bene: Since the *a* is followed by a mute (*t*) plus a liquid (*r*), the vowel may be either long or short depending upon what the writer has decided during the composition of the line. The same might be true, for example, for the *a* in *atrium* or *atrox*.

ᴶIf your students need more practice with syllabication, have them syllabify words from the previous four exercises. The answers can be found below. Do not feel the need to have students be too meticulous when dealing with the difficult words.

Extra Syllabication Practice

Exercise 1.

1. pa-ter
2. mā-ter
3. si-nō
4. sī-vī
5. ōr-dō
6. po-ti-or
7. est
8. ēst
9. u-xor
10. ū-sus
11. syl-laba
12. sȳ-co-phan-ta

Exercise 2.

1. cī-vi-tās
2. in-ter-ro-gā-ti-ō
3. ca-sa
4. vē-ri-tās
5. vin-cu-lum
6. e-xer-ci-tās
7. u-xor
8. gra-vi-tās
9. ge-nus
10. ē-sur-gō
11. iun-gō

The combination *ng* is also tricky, but because it makes two distinct sounds, we will divide *n* from *g*.

Exercise 3.

1. ob-stat
2. ob-tu-lī
3. an-guis
4. san-guen
5. pul-cher
6. ar-chi-tec-tus
7. phi-lo-so-phi-a

> When words are compounded, it is customary to divide between the compounds; in addition, *st* is often felt to constitute one unit in syllabication.

> The letters *ch* are considered a single consonant for the purpose of syllabication.

> The letters *ph* are considered a single consonant for the purpose of syllabication.

8. the-ā-trum
9. quis-que
10. cū-rō
11. cur-rō
12. su-mus
13. sum-mus

> The letter combinations *th* and *'tr* are considered a single consonant for the purpose of syllabication.

Exercise 4.

1. cae-dō
2. hui
3. poe-na
4. heu
5. ei
6. seu
7. au-di-ō

Exercise 6

1. dominus	dŏ-mĭ-nŭs	5. ager	ă-gĕr
2. annus	ắn-nŭs	6. oppidum	ŏp-pĭ-dŭm
3. cōnsilium	cōn-sĭ-lĭ-ŭm	7. victōria	vīc-tŏ́-rĭ-ă
4. theātrum	thĕ-ắt-rŭm	8. audiō	áu-dĭ-ō

Exercise 7

1. Diphthong   Diphthongs are two vowels blended together to create one sound.
2. Syllabication   Syllabication is the act of dividing a word in order to reveal its individual syllables.
3. Accent   Accent is the vocal emphasis placed on a particular syllable of a word.
4. Function words   Function words express the relationship between other words.
5. Inflection   Inflection is the changing of a word's form by the addition of an affix.

Exercise 8

1. animal	á-ni-mal	11. poēta	po-ḗ-ta
2. clāmor	clá-mor	12. ulterior	ul-té-ri-or
3. honor	hó-nor	13. arēna	a-rḗ-na
4. genus	gé-nus	14. herba	hér-ba
5. horror	hór-ror	15. firmus	fír-mus
6. toga	tó-ga	16. gladiātor	gla-di-ắ-tor
7. status	stá-tus	17. atrium	á-tri-um
8. paenīnsula	pae-nī́n-su-la	18. candidātus	can-di-dắ-tus
9. interim	ín-te-rim	19. ergō	ér-gō
10. neuter	neú-ter	20. forma	fór-ma

Annuit coeptīs.

He has favored our undertakings.[A]

—Reverse side of the seal of the United States

[A]Charles Tomson was the principal designer for the Great Seal, adopted by Congress on June 20, 1782. He gave the following explanations for the symbolism of the design.

- The pyramid is a symbol of strength.
- The eye over the pyramid and the motto *annuit coeptis* refer to the interposition of God on behalf of the American Cause.
- The date in Roman numerals is 1776, a reference to the signing of the Declaration of Independence.
- The words *novus ordo seclorum* (a new order of the ages) refer to the beginning of a new American Era.

Chapter 2

- verbs
  - principal parts
- 1st conjugation, present tense
  - tense, person, number

VOCABULARY

VERBS			
LATIN	ENGLISH	DERIVATIVES
amō, amāre, amāvī, amātum	to love, like	(amorous)
cantō, cantāre, cantāvī, cantātum	to sing	(chant, cantata)
labōrō, labōrāre, labōrāvī, labōrātum	to work	(labor)
nāvigō, nāvigāre, nāvigāvī, nāvigātum	to sail	(navigate, navigation)
oppugnō, oppugnāre, oppugnāvī, oppugnātum	to attack	(pugnacious)
ADVERB			
nōn	not	(nonsense)

TE **Exercise 1.** Using the rules for syllabication and accent that you have learned, write out the syllables and accents for the vocabulary words above. Then practice pronouncing them aloud.[B]

SECTION 6. Principal Parts

Verbs are the central part of any sentence. In English you cannot have a complete sentence without a verb. In Latin you can have a complete sentence that consists of nothing more than a single verb. In fact, when translating any Latin sentence, it is advisable to find and translate the verb first. So, it is very important that you begin your study of Latin by learning how to recognize and translate verbs.

[B]This exercise is repeated for each chapter vocabulary list. The purpose is to prepare students for oratory and the reading of poetry in later texts. You may not wish to repeat this exercise for every single chapter.

Every Latin verb has with it a set of principal parts. Principal parts are the forms of the verb that are considered basic and from which you create all other forms of the verb. In English, the principal parts are as follows:

1. present infinitive .... to *love* .... *to sing*
2. 3rd person present tense .... *(he) loves* .... *(he) sings*
3. preterit (simple past) .... *loved* .... *sang*
4. past participle .... *loved* .... *sung*

The principal parts of Latin verbs are categorically similar:

1. 1st person present .... *amō – I love* .... *cantō – I sing*
2. present infinitive .... *amāre – to love* .... *cantāre – to sing*
3. 1st person perfect (simple past) ..... *amāvī – I loved* .... *cantāvī – I sang*
4. past participle (supine) .... *amātum – loved* .... *cantātum – sung*

It is worth noting that although both use the same basic forms to comprise their principal parts, Latin is much more consistent in the pattern these forms follow.

The first principal part is used to list and locate words in a Latin dictionary. The remaining three principal parts form various verb tenses. For now we will only use the first two principal parts. You should take care, however, to memorize all of them now as a complete verb set. Latin has its share of irregular verbs also, and some verbs alter their stem in the last few principal parts. You will save yourself a great deal of work later if you memorize them as part of your vocabulary list now.

Section 7. First Conjugation

Remember, the TE symbol indicates that there is more information in the Teacher's Pages at the end of the chapter.

A **conjugation** is a group of verbs that share similar patterns for their endings. Consider your family as an example. Each member in your family is a unique individual, and each one is different in his or her own way. However, your family also tends to share similar characteristics in appearance and personality. Each conjugation is a family of verbs. Each verb is a little different, but each verb within a conjugation tends to have the same set of endings and follow the same rules for changing those endings as the rest of its family members. There are four different conjugations, or groups of verbs. For now we will focus only on the first. You can always recognize the first conjugation by the second principal part which ends in **-āre**. It is from this form that a verb forms its stem:

> **2nd principal part – re = verb stem**
> amā/re = amā
> cantā/re = cantā

TE **Exercise 2.** Following the examples of *amāre* and *cantāre* identify the stem for each of the verbs in the vocabulary list of this section.

Section 8. Present Tense and Personal Endings

Now that you know how to identify a verb's stem, it is time to learn how to apply a set of endings in order to create a sentence. To **conjugate** a verb is to list a verb with its endings. The verb **amāre** is conjugated below with its personal endings. The personal endings of a verb demonstrate two important characteristics: number and person.

PERSON	SINGULAR	PLURAL
1	*am-ō* I love	*amā-mus* we love
2	*amā-s* you love	*amā-tis* you (pl.) love
3	*ama-t* he/she/it loves	*ama-nt* they love

Number reveals *how many* are doing the action. There are two options for number: singular and plural.

Singular: I love.   Plural: We love.

Person reveals *who* is doing the action. There are three options for person.[C]

1st person, the speaker is doing the action:
I love.   We love.

2nd person, the person spoken to is doing the action:
You love.   You (pl.) love.

3rd person, another person is being spoken about:
He/She/It loves.   They love.

> [C]Fun Chant:
> I'm Number 1,
> 2 is You,
> He is 3.

[TE] **Exercise 3.** Following the example of *amāre*, conjugate the verbs *cantāre* and *nāvigāre*. Take care to notice where the macra (long marks) appear.[D]

A third characteristic of all verbs is tense. **Tense** tells the time of the action taking place. The present tense describes action that is happening right now. In English there are three different ways to indicate action in the present tense.

simple present:	I love
present progressive:	I am loving
present emphatic:	I do love

> [D]If you wish, there is a reproducible conjugation worksheet included with this guide. You may use it for this exercise and even add other verbs to the assignment. The more students practice this routine orally and in writing the better they will imbed the pattern.

Fortunately for us, Latin has only one present tense form—that shown in the chart you have just seen. As a result, one present tense Latin verb can be translated in three different ways.

amō =	I love.	I am loving.	I do love.
cantat =	She sings.	He is singing.	It does sing.

Notā Bene: To change a Latin verb from declarative (making a statement) to interrogative (asking a question) simply add the suffix *-ne*.[E]

cantat**ne** =   Does she sing?... Is he singing?   Does it sing?

> [E]You may want to add more oral examples to practice the concept. Students will apply this concept in the following exercise.

[TE] **Exercise 4.** Identify the person and number of the following Latin sentences. Then, where possible, translate them into English in three different ways.

Example: amās **2nd person, singular: you love, you are loving, you do love**

1. Cantāmus.
2. Oppugnāsne?
3. Non nāvigant.
4. Labōrātis.

5. Nāvigatne?
6. Nōn oppugnō.

 Exercise 5. Identify the person and number of these English sentences, then translate them into Latin.

Example: I am singing.   **1st person, singular: cantō**

1. I sail.
2. You (s.) do not work.
3. Are they attacking?
4. She loves.
5. We do sing.
6. You (pl.) are not sailing.

"Eye" Latin

Some words look the same in Latin and in English. When you can tell the meaning of a Latin word because it looks just like or nearly like an English word, you are using "eye" Latin.

Using "eye" Latin, tell the meanings of *Trōia*, *circus*, *Rōma*, *maximum*, *māior*, and *plūs*.[F]

Troy, circus, Rome, maximum, major, plus

[F]These Latin words look nearly like the English words: Troy, circus, Rome, maximum, major, and plus. The Latin words actually mean: Troy, circus (race course), Rome, greatest, greater/bigger, and more. Discuss with your students how the English derivatives can help us arrive at the meaning of these words.

Colloquāmur (Let's Talk)

TE Use the following questions and responses to review the characteristics of some Latin verbs. Use some "eye" Latin to figure out what the responses mean.

interrogātiō:	Cūius est numerī?	What number is it?
respōnsum:	Singulāriter est.	
	Plūrāliter est.	

interrogātiō:	Cūius est persōnae?	What person is it?
respōnsum:	Est prīmae persōnae.	
	Est secundae persōnae.	
	Est tertiae persōnae.	

The sentences above use the interrogative pronoun *cūius* to signify a question the same way English uses interrogative pronouns such as *who, whose, what,* etc. Another way to ask questions in Latin is to add the suffix *-ne* to the end of a verb just as we did in exercises 4 and 5. These types of questions expect the answer **yes** (*sīc est*) or **no** (*minimē*). Try testing your knowledge of Latin verbs with some yes/no questions.

interrogātiō:	Estne singulāriter?	Estne plūrāliter?
respōnsum:	Sīc est!	Minimē!

interrogātiō:	Estne prīmae persōnae?	
	Estne secundae persōnae?	
	Estne tertiae persōnae?	
respōnsum:	Sīc est!	Minimē!

Chapter 2 Teacher's Pages

Exercise 1

a-mō, a-mā-re, a-mā-vī, a-mā-tum
can-tō, can-tā-re, can-tā-vī, can-tā-tum
la-bō-rō, la-bō-rā-re, la-bō-rā-vī, la-bō-rā-tum
nā-vi-gō, nā-vi-gā-re, nā-vi-gā-vī, nā-vi-gā-tum
op-pug-nō, op-pug-nā-re, op-pug-nā-vī, op-pug-nā-tum
nōn

Exercise 2

amā   cantā   labōrā   nāvigā   oppugnā

Exercise 3

CANTĀRE

cantō (I sing, I am singing, I do sing)*	**cantāmus** (we sing, we are singing, we do sing)
cantās (you sing, you are singing, you do sing)	**cantātis** (you all sing, you all are singing, you all do sing)
cantat (he/she/it sings, he/she/it is singing, he/she/it does sing)	**cantant** (they sing, they are singing, they do sing)

NĀVIGĀRE

nāvigo (I sail, I am sailing, I do sail)	**nāvigāmus** (we sail, we am sailing, we do sail)
nāvigās (you sail, you are sailing, you do sail)	**nāvigātis** (you all sail, you all are sailing, you all do sail)
nāvigat (he/she/it sails, he/she/it is sailing, he/she/it does sail)	**nāvigant** (they sail, they are sailing, they do sail)

*Depending on their own preference, teachers may want to require for conjugation exercises that students supply only one English translation rather than all three.

You may want to point out to students the macron over the *ō* in the ending of the first-person singular, as well as the *ā* of the ending for the second-person singular, first-person plural, and second-person plural. For now, students should just memorize this. Later, when they are comfortable with conjugating verbs, you may want to explain that the vowel in an ending is long except before a final *-m*, *-r*, or *-t*, and before any *-nt-*. For example, consider the following forms: *amem, amēs, amet, amētur, ament, amentur, amor.* (Students have not yet learned the preceding forms, but those forms illustrate well the lengths of the vowels before the endings.)

Exercise 4

1. Cantāmus.   1st person, plural: We sing. We are singing. We do sing.
2. Oppugnāsne?   2nd person, sing.: Do you attack? Are you attacking?
3. Non nāvigant.   3rd person, pl.: They are not sailing. They do not sail.
4. Labōrātis.   2nd person, pl.: You work. You are working. You do work.

5. Nāvigatne?   3rd person, sing.: Is he sailing? Does he sail?

6. Nōn oppugnō.   1st person, sing.: I do not attack. I am not attacking.

Numbers 3 and 6 use the negative *nōn*, and will not translate well in the simple present. Two answers are acceptable for these exercises.

For exercise 4, #2, notice that there are only two translations. In English, when a statement is turned into a question, the word "do" is added automatically, so there is no special distinction between simple and emphatic.

Exercise 5

1. I sail.   1st person, sing.: Nāvigō.

2. You (s.) do not work.   2nd person, sing.: Nōn labōrās.

3. Are they attacking?   3rd person, pl.: Oppugnantne?

4. She loves.   3rd person, sing.: Amat.

5. We do sing.   1st person, pl.: Cantāmus.

6. You (pl.) are not sailing. 2nd person, pl.: Nōn nāvigātis.

These are complete sentences so it would be advisable to require punctuation and capitalization if you wish to reinforce English grammar skills.

Colloquāmur!

Interrogātiō:	Cūius est numerī?	What number is it?
Respōnsum:	Singulāriter est.	It is singular.
	Plūrāliter est.	It is plural.
Interrogātiō:	Cūius est persōnae?	What person is it?
Respōnsum:	Est prīmae persōnae.	It is first person.
	Est secundae persōnae.	It is second person.
	Est tertiae persōnae.	It is third person.

Novus Ordō Seclōrum
A New Order of the Ages
—Reverse of the seal of the United States[A]

Chapter 3

- present system
  - present
  - future
  - imperfect

VOCABULARY

	LATIN	ENGLISH	DERIVATIVES
VERBS			
ambulō, ambulāre, ambulāvī, ambulātum	to walk	(perambulator, ambulance)
arō, arāre, arāvī, arātum	to plow	(arable)
habitō, habitāre, habitāvī, habitātum	to live, dwell	(habitat)
portō, portāre, portāvī, portātum	to carry	(portable)
rogō, rogāre, rogāvī, rogātum	to ask	(interrogation)
rēgnō, rēgnāre, rēgnāvī, rēgnātum	to rule	(reign, regnant)
vocō, vocāre, vocāvī, vocātum	to call	(vocal, vocation)
CONJUNCTIONS			
et	and	(et cetera)
aut	or	

Exercise 1. Using the rules for syllabication and accent that you have learned, write out the syllables and accents for the vocabulary words above. Then practice pronouncing them aloud.

SECTION 9. Tense

Another important characteristic that every verb has is tense. The verb's tense indicates at what time the action takes place. Latin has six verb tenses. This chapter will focus on the present, imperfect, and future tenses. These three tenses make up what we call the present system.

This is because they all use the present stem!

First, let us quickly review the present tense. The present tense describes action that is happening right now. In English there are three different ways to indicate action in the present tense.

simple present: She sings.
present progressive: She is singing.
present emphatic: She does sing.

The present tense is formed by simply finding the stem of a verb (2nd principal part minus *re*) and adding the personal endings.

PERSON	SINGULAR	PLURAL
1	-m/ō*	-mus
2	-s	-tis
3	-t	-nt

Notā Bene (*Note Well*):
The first person singular ending is most often -ō, however in some cases (such as the imperfect tense) an -m appears instead.

Exercise 2. Translate the following present tense verbs into Latin or English.

1. Vocat.
2. Habitās.
3. Ambulat aut nāvigat.
4. Arātisne?
5. He does work.
6. We ask.
7. Are they calling?
8. I rule and they work.

In English we often indicate tense by the addition of a helping verb.

present: She **is** singing.
imperfect: She **was** singing.
future: She **will** sing.

Instead of adding a separate word as in English, Latin adds a tense marker between the stem and the personal endings, which you have already learned. A tense marker is a letter or letters that signal a change in tense. The formula for forming any verb tense is quite simple:

stem (2nd pp – re) + tense marker + personal endings

Section 10. Future Tense

The future tense of first conjugation verbs uses the tense marker -bi-. The 'i' drops out before the vowel ending -ō, and changes to a -u- before the consonant ending -nt. Notice that the stem vowel -ā- remains long throughout.

stem: **amā/re** + future tense marker: **bi** + personal endings

PERSON	SINGULAR	PLURAL
1	amā-**b**-ō I will love	amā-**bi**-mus we will love
2	amā-**bi**-s you will love	amā-**bi**-tis you (pl.) will love
3	amā-**bi**-t he/she/it will love	amā-**bu**-nt they will love

In Latin there is only one way to express future action. However, English has a couple of options. Either of these are acceptable when translating:

simple future: I will love
progressive future: I will be loving

Exercise 3. Identify the person and number of the following future tense verbs. Then translate in two different ways.

1. rogābis
2. habitābimus
3. rēgnābit
4. vocābunt
5. arābitis
6. ambulābō

SECTION 11. Imperfect Tense

The imperfect tense uses the marker -ba-. Notice that the first person singular uses the ending -m instead of the more common vowel -ō. This is because the -a- from the tense marker and the -ō in the ending blend together and become indistinguishable. This linguistic change is the same reason that the -ā- drops out before the -ō in the first person singular of the present tense. Notice that just as with the future tense the stem vowel -ā- remains long throughout. The -ba- is long in the first person plural and in the second person, the same pattern seen in the present tense in the previous chapter.

stem: **amā/re** + imperfect tense marker: **ba** + personal endings

PERSON	SINGULAR	PLURAL
1	amā-**ba**-m I was loving	amā-**bā**-mus we were loving
2	amā-**bā**-s you were loving	amā-**bā**-tis you (pl.) were loving
3	amā-**ba**-t he/she/it was loving	amā-**ba**-nt they were loving

Notā Bene (Note Well):
Notice that the macra (long marks) on the endings are on the same positions as they were in the present tense: 1st person plural, 2nd person singular and plural.

Long ago the word perfect (derived from the Latin *perfectus*, finished) meant "complete, finished." If an object or a task has been truly completed well, then you cannot improve upon it; it is perfect. If the same task is *im*perfect, then it is *not* completed. The imperfect tense, therefore, is used to describe past actions that are not known to be complete or were ongoing for a long period of time. The true English equivalent for the Latin imperfect tense is the past progressive. However, the simple past tense can also be used on some occasions.[B]

past progressive: I was loving, I used to love, I kept on loving
simple past: I loved

Exercise 4. Identify the person and number of the following imperfect tense verbs. Then translate in two different ways.

1. rogābās
2. habitābāmus
3. rēgnābat
4. vocābant
5. arābātis
6. ambulābam

Exercise 5. To parse (from the Latin *pars*, part) a verb is to identify all of its parts. Parse each of the following verbs identifying their tense, person, and number. Then translate them into English.

LATIN	TENSE	PERSON	NUMBER	TRANSLATION
habitābam	Imp.	1	Sing.	I was living
rogābis				
ambulant				
rēgnābāmus				
vocābō				
labōrātis				
portābat				

Exercise 6. Identify the person, number, and tense of the following English sentences. Then, translate into Latin.

1. We were singing.
2. I will walk and sing.
3. You (pl.) were not plowing.
4. It sails.
5. Will she rule?

[B]Encourage students to stick with the past progressive translation as much as possible. This will help them distinguish this tense from the perfect tense that they will learn later on. (Almost always, if not always, there will be an imperfect tense verb on the National Latin Exam, and the answer for that item usually if not always includes "was" or "used to.")

Derivative Detective

Nōn came directly into English in such words as *nonsense*. Seeing that *sequence* comes from a Latin word meaning "follow," what do you think a *nōn sequitur* is?

Nauta gives us such words as *astronaut* and *nautical*. Nautical miles are measured in knots, though *knot* does not come from *nauta*.

Use your language detective skills and your dictionaries to find some more English words that use *nōn* and *nauta*.

Colloquāmur (Let's Talk)

Use the following questions and responses to review the parsing exercise above. Use some "eye" Latin to figure out what the responses mean.

interrogātiō:	Cūius est numerī?	What number is it?
respōnsum:	Singulāriter est.	
	Plūrāliter est.	
interrogātiō:	Cūius est persōnae?	What person is it?
respōnsum:	Est prīmae persōnae.	
	Est secundae persōnae.	
	Est tertiae persōnae.	
interrogātiō:	Cūius est temporis?	What tense (time) is it?
respōnsum:	Est praesentis.	
	Est imperfectī.	
	Est futūrī.	

Chapter 3 Teacher's Pages

Exercise 1

am-bu-lō, am-bu-lā-re, am-bu-lā-vī, am-bu-lā-tum
a-rō, a-rā-re, a-rā-vī, a-rā-tum
ha-bi-tō, ha-bi-tā-re, ha-bi-tā-vī, ha-bi-tā-tum
por-tō, por-tā-re, por-tā-vī, por-tā-tum
ro-gō, ro-gā-re, ro-gā-vī, ro-gā-tum
reg-nō, reg-nā-re, reg-nā-vī, reg-nā-tum
vo-cō, vo-cā-re, vo-cā-vī, vo-cā-tum
et
aut

Exercise 2

1. Vocat.	He calls. He is calling. He does call.
2. Habitās.	You are living. You do live. You live.
3. Ambulat aut nāvigat.	He walks or sails. He is walking or sailing. He does . . .
4. Arātisne?	Are you (pl.) plowing? Do you plow?
5. He does work.	Labōrat.
6. We ask.	Rogāmus.
7. Are they calling?	Vocantne?
8. I rule and they work.	Regnō et labōrant.

Remember that there are three options for translating the present tense into English. Encourage students to use a variety of translations.

Exercise 3

1. rogābis	2, S	You (s.) will ask.	You will be asking.
2. habitābimus	1, P	We will live.	We will be living.
3. rēgnābit	3, S	He will rule.	He will be ruling.
4. vocābunt	3, P	They will call.	They will be calling.
5. arābitis	2, P	You (pl.) will plow.	You will be plowing.
6. ambulābō	1, S	I will walk.	I will be walking.

Exercise 4

1. rogābās	2, S	You (s.) were asking.	You used to ask.
2. habitābāmus	1, P	We were living.	We began to live.
3. rēgnābat	3, S	He was ruling.	He kept on ruling.
4. vocābant	3, P	They were calling.	They began to call.
5. arābātis	2, P	You (pl.) were plowing.	You used to plow.
6. ambulābam	1, S	I was walking.	I kept on walking.

Remember there is a variety of ways to translate this tense. Encourage students to use more than two in these exercises.

Exercise 5

LATIN	TENSE	PERSON	NUMBER	TRANSLATION
habitābam	Imp.	1	Sing.	I was living
rogābis	Fut.	2	Sing	You will ask
ambulant	Pres.	3	Pl.	They walk
rēgnābāmus	Imp.	1	Pl.	We were ruling
vocābō	Fut.	1	Sing.	I will call
labōrātis	Pres.	2	Pl.	You (pl.) are working
portābat	Imp.	3	Sing.	He was carrying

There is a reproducible parsing worksheet included in this guide. You may wish to have students copy their work onto that sheet. You can also use it to add some more parsing practice if you wish.

Exercise 6

1. We were singing.   1, Pl., Imperfect   Cantābāmus.
2. I will walk and sing.   1, Sing., Future   Ambulābō et cantābō.
3. You (pl.) were not plowing. 2, Pl., Imperfect   Nōn arābātis.
4. It sails.   3, Sing., Present   Nāvigat.
5. Will she rule?   3, Sing., Future   Regnābitne?

Colloquāmur!

Interrogātiō:	Cūius est numerī?	What number is it?
Respōnsum:	Singulāriter est.	It is singular.
	Plūrāliter est.	It is plural.
Interrogātiō:	Cūius est persōnae?	What person is it?
Respōnsum:	Est prīmae persōnae.	It is first person.
	Est secundae persōnae.	It is second person.
	Est tertiae persōnae.	It is third person.
Interrogātiō:	Cūius est temporis?	What tense (time) is it?
Respōnsum:	Est praesentis.	It is present.
	Est imperfectī.	It is imperfect.
	Est futūrī.	It is future.

You can also use the yes/no questions with –ne that we introduced in the last chapter!

DISTRICT OF COLUMBIA

Iūstitia omnibus
Justice for all
—District of Columbia ^A

Chapter 4

- first declension nouns: case, number, gender
- nominative case
  - subject
  - predicate

VOCABULARY

NOUNS		
LATIN	ENGLISH	DERIVATIVES
agricola, agricolae, m.	farmer	(agriculture)
fēmina, fēminae, f.	woman	(feminine)
Graecia, Graeciae, f.	Greece	(Grecian)
incola, incolae, m.	settler	
īnsula, īnsulae, f.	island	(insulate)
nauta, nautae, m.	sailor	(nautical)
pātria, pātriae, f.	fatherland, country	(patriot)
poēta, poētae, m.	poet	(poet)
puella, puellae, f.	girl	
rēgīna, rēgīnae, f.	queen	
terra, terrae, f.	earth, land	(terrain)
Trōia, Trōiae, f.	Troy (a city-state in Asia Minor)	(Troy, Trojan)
ADJECTIVE		
pulcher, pulchra, pulchrum	beautiful	(pulchritude)

TE **Exercise 1.** Using the rules for syllabication and accent that you have learned, write out the syllables and accents for the vocabulary words above. Then practice pronouncing them aloud.

Just as with English, a Latin noun (from Latin *nōmen*, name) is a word that names a person, place, thing, or idea. When a Latin noun is listed in a dictionary it provides three pieces of information: the nominative singular, the genitive singular, and the gender. The first form, called nominative (also from Latin *nōmen*) is the means used to list, or name, words in a dictionary. The second form, the genitive (from Latin *genus*, origin, kind or family) is used to find the stem of the noun and to determine the declension, or noun family, to which it belongs. To find the stem of a noun, simply look at the genitive singular form and remove the ending -ae. The genitive also reveals which declension or family of nouns from which this word originates. The final abbreviation is a reference to the noun's gender, since it is not always evident by the noun's endings. We will discuss each of these forms in more detail in this section.

Exercise 2. Identify the stem for each of the nouns in the vocabulary list above.

Example: fēmina, fēminae   stem = fēmin/ae

You have learned that verbs are divided up into families or groups called conjugations. Nouns also have families or groups that share similar characteristics and behavior patterns. A **declension** is a group of nouns that share a common set of inflected endings, which we call case endings. There are five declensions in Latin, but for now we will focus only on the first declension. All nouns that belong to the first declension have a genitive singular that ends in -ae. Therefore it is very important that you memorize the genitive singular of each noun provided in the vocabulary list, so you can easily recognize them as first declension nouns.

All Latin nouns have three characteristics: case, number, and gender. There are three **genders**: masculine, feminine, and neuter. In English the gender of a noun is determined by its sex. All female things are feminine, male things are masculine, and everything that is neither male nor female must be neuter (from the Latin *neuter*, neither). In Latin, however, the noun's gender does not necessarily match the gender of the object it describes. Nouns describing a female person (e.g. girl, woman, queen, Helen) are generally feminine. Nouns describing a male person (e.g. boy, man, king, sailor) are generally masculine. However, if an object has neither gender (e.g. table, tree, town) Latin may classify the noun in any of the three genders. Therefore, the best way to learn the gender of a Latin noun is simply to memorize it. Fortunately, most nouns of the first declension will be feminine in gender. There are a few first declension nouns that are masculine because they refer specifically to men, or what would have clearly been a man's office in ancient Rome. The most common masculine words of the first declension can be remembered by the acronym **PAIN.** ᴮ

ᴮThere are also *scrība* (the scribe), *pīrāta* (the pirate), *bibliopōla* (the bookseller), *aurīga* (the charioteer), and *āthlētā* (the athlete). There are probably others, too; however, these four are the ones students most often encounter.

Poēta	**A**gricola	**I**ncola	**N**auta
(poet)	(farmer)	(settler)	(sailor)

Number simply indicates whether a noun is singular (one) or plural (more than one).

nauta = sailor   nautae = sailors

fēmina = woman   fēminae = women

Notice how English can be inconsistent with the way it pluralizes a noun. Latin, on the other hand, is extremely consistent.

Exercise 3. Using the above examples of **nauta** and **fēmina**, make the following Latin nouns plural:

Example: | **nauta** = sailor | **nautae** = sailors

1. **īnsula** = island   _____ = islands
2. **rēgīna** = queen   _____ = queens
3. **poēta** = poet   _____ = poets
4. **puella** = girl   _____ = girls
5. **agricola** = farmer   _____ = farmers

Case is the form of a noun, pronoun, or its modifier that reveals its job, or how it functions, in a sentence. In Latin, there are five main cases.* The chart below identifies these cases and the jobs assigned them. It also declines the noun fēmina (woman) along with the appropriate meanings for each case. To **decline** a noun is to list a noun with all of the case endings that belong to its declension. Before you decline a noun, however, you must first identify its stem.

stem: fēmin/ae				
	ENDINGS		**FEMININE**	
CASE	**SING.**	**PLURAL**	**SINGULAR**	**PLURAL**
NOMINATIVE SUBJECT, PREDICATE	-a	-ae	fēmin-a the woman	fēmin-ae the women
GENITIVE POSSESSION	-ae	-ārum	fēmin-ae of the woman	fēmin-ārum of the women
DATIVE INDIRECT OBJECT	-ae	-īs	fēmin-ae to/for the woman	fēmin-īs to/for the women
ACCUSATIVE DIRECT OBJECT, OBJECT PREPOSITION	-am	-ās	fēmin-am the woman	fēmin-ās the women
ABLATIVE OBJECT PREPOSITION	-ā	-īs	fēmin-ā by/with/from the woman	fēmin-īs by/with/from the women

Notā Bene: There are two additional cases known as the vocative, which generally has the same forms as the nominative, and the locative. These cases, however, are much less common and you will learn them later.[c]

 Exercise 4. Following the pattern of *fēmina*, decline *nauta* and *puella*.

[c]The locative is not taught until *Latin Alive! Book Two*.

SECTION 13. Nominative Case [D]

The nominative case (from the Latin *nōmen*, name) is often referred to as the naming case. It is for us learning the language a point of reference or identification for every Latin noun, for it is the standard form used to list Latin words in the dictionary. More importantly, it is the case that 'names' the subject of the sentence. For example:

Graecia Trōiam oppugnat.   Greece attacks Troy.

Quis Trōiam oppugnat? Graecia.   Who attacks Troy? Greece.

[D]A reproducible declension worksheet is included with this guide. You may use it for exercise 4 and even add other nouns to the assignment. The more students practice this routine orally and in writing the better they will imbed the pattern.

It is evident by the nominative ending -a that Greece is the subject, the one attacking Troy.

Exercise 5. Look at the nominative endings in the chart above. Underline the subject(s) in each of the following sentences. Do not translate.

1. Agricola terram arat.
2. Nautae ad terram nāvigant.
3. Hecuba in oppidō habitat.
4. Fēmina et puella cantant.

In addition to identifying the subject of the sentence, the nominative case is also used to identify the predicate noun or adjective. A **predicate nominative** (from Latin *praedicāre,* to declare) is a noun or adjective that renames the subject. Generally predicate nominatives will follow linking verbs such as *est* (is) and *sunt* (are). For example:

Helena est rēgīna.	Helen is a queen.
Quis est Helena? Est rēgīna.	Who is Helen? She is a queen.
Helena est pulchra.	Helen is beautiful.
Quis est pulchra? Helena est pulchra.	Who is beautiful? Helen is beautiful.

In the above examples you see that both the subjects and predicate nominatives share the same ending. Since the predicate nominative is simply referring to or renaming the subject, it is fitting that they both use the nominative case. Generally the subject will appear before the predicate nominative in a sentence, so it will be easy to tell the two apart.

Exercise 6. Underline the subject(s) and circle the predicate nominative(s) in each of the following sentences.

1. Hecuba est rēgīna.
2. Puella nōn est rēgīna.
3. Agricola et nauta nōn fēminae sunt.
4. Īnsulae sunt pulchrae.

Caveat Discipulus (Let the Student Beware): When translating Latin verbs in a sentence with a separate subject noun, it is important to remember that it is not necessary to include the English personal pronoun alongside the subject. This would make for bad English.ᴱ

LATIN	BAD ENGLISH	GOOD ENGLISH
Helena amat.	Helen she loves.	Helen loves.
Nautae nāvigant.	The sailors they are sailing.	The sailors are sailing.

ᴱIf you would like additional translating practice, encourage students to compose their own Latin sentences. Allow them to be as creative as they wish. The class can exchange papers or work through the new sentences together as a group.

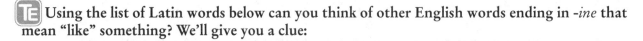

GREECE AND TROY

1. Trōia *est pātria.*

2. Trōia est in Āsiā; Trōia nōn est īnsula.

3. Rēx *Prismus* regnat.

4. *Hecuba* est rēgīna.

5. *Helena in terrā, nōmine* Graeciā, habitat.

6. *Helena* et Hecuba rēgīnae sunt.

7. *Helena* fēmina pulchra est.

8. *Paris in pātriā, nōmine* Trōiā, habitat.

GLOSSARY

rēx .... king
in pātriā .... in a country
Prismus .... Priam (the king of Troy, father of Paris)
Hecuba .... Hecuba (the queen of Troy, wife of Priam)
in terrā .... in a land
nōmine .... called
Helena .... Helen (the queen of Sparta)
Paris .... Paris (a Trojan prince)

Culture Corner

Troy was a city in Asia Minor, in what is today Turkey. The Greeks and Trojans fought a war at Troy for ten years. We know this war as the Trojan War. You will learn more about this war and its aftermath as you study the readings and the Culture Corner sections in this book.

Derivative Detective

A derivative is a word in one language that comes from another language. More than 60 percent of English words we use every day are Latin derivatives. The Latin word *fēmina* gives us the English word *feminine*, which means "like a woman."

 Using the list of Latin words below can you think of other English words ending in *-ine* that mean "like" something? We'll give you a clue:

Bōs, bovis = Bovine, like a cow
Canis
Equus
Fēles
Porcus

Piscis
Aquila

How many more can you come up with on your own?

Colloquāmur (Let's Talk)

Here are a few more phrases that can be used in your Latin class and beyond.

Sī placet.	Please.
Grātiās tibi agō.	Thank you (sing.)
Grātiās vōbīs agō.	Thank you (pl.)
Omnēs surgite.	Everyone rise.
Omnēs sedēte.	Everyone sit down.
Aperīte librōs.	Open the books.
Claudite librōs.	Close the books.
Distribuite chartās.	Pass/Hand out/Distribute the papers.
Intellegisne hōc?	Do you understand this?
sīc est	yes [F]
minimē	no

[F] The Spanish word sí (yes) is derived from *sīc.*

Chapter 4 Teacher's Pages

Exercise 1

a-gri-co-la, a-gri-co-lae, m.
fē-mi-na, fē-mi-nae, f.
Grae-ci-a, Grae-ci-ae, f.
in-co-la, in-co-lae, m.
īn-su-la, īn-su-lae, f.
nau-ta, nau-tae, m.
pā-tri-a, pā-tri-ae, f.

po-ē-ta, po-ē-tae, m.
pu-el-la, pu-el-lae, f.
rē-gī-na, rē-gī-nae, f.
ter-ra, ter-rae, f.
Trō-i-a, Trō-i-ae, f.
pul-cher, pul-chra, pul-chrum

Exercise 2

agricola, agricolae	agricol	pātria, pātriae	pātri
fēmina, fēminae	fēmin	poēta, poētae	poēt
Graecia, Graeciae	Graeci	puella, puellae	puell
incola, incolae	incol	rēgīna, rēgīnae	rēgīn
īnsula, īnsulae	īnsul	terra, terrae	terr
nauta, nautae	naut	Trōia, Trōiae	Trōi

Exercise 3

īnsulae = islands
rēgīnae = queens
poētae = poets
puellae = girls
agricolae = farmers

Exercise 4

NAUTA	SINGULAR	PLURAL
Nominative	**nauta** (the sailor)	**nautae** (the sailors)
Genitive	**nautae** (of the sailor, the sailor's)	**nautārum** (of the sailors, the sailors')
Dative	**nautae** (to/for the sailor)	**nautīs** (to/for the sailors)
Accusative	**nautam** (the sailor)	**nautās** (the sailors)
Ablative	**nautā** (by/with/from the sailor)	**nautīs** (by/with/from the sailors)

PUELLA	SINGULAR	PLURAL
Nominative	**puella** (the girl)	**puellae** (the girls)
Genitive	**puellae** (of the girl, the girl's)	**puellārum** (of the girls, the girls')
Dative	**puellae** (to/for the girl)	**puellīs** (to/for the girls)
Accusative	**puellam** (the girl)	**puellās** (the girls)
Ablative	**puellā** (by/with/from the girl)	**puellīs** (by/with/from the girlst)

Exercise 5

1. Agricola terram arat.
2. Nautae ad terram nāvigant.
3. Hecuba in oppidō habitat.
4. Fēmina et puella cantant.

Exercise 6

1. Hecuba est (rēgīna)
2. Puella nōn est (rēgīna)
3. Agricola et nauta nōn (fēminae) sunt.
4. Īnsulae sunt (pulchrae.)

Translation

1. Troy is a country.
2. Troy is in Asia; Troy is not an island.
3. King Priam rules.
4. Hecuba is the queen.
5. Helen lives in a land, called Greece.
6. Helen and Hecuba are queens.
7. Helen is a beautiful woman.
8. Paris lives in a country called Troy.

Derivative Detective

Canis = Canine, like a dog

Equus = Equine, like a horse

Felis = Feline, like a cat

Porcus = Porcine, like a pig

Piscis = Piscine, like a fish

Aquila = Aquiline, like an eagle

Others:

Ovis = Ovine, like a sheep

Vulpis = Vulpine, like a fox

Elephantus = Elephantine, like an elephant
(Chryselephantine means "made of gold and ivory.")

Lupus = Lupine, like a wolf

Taurus = Taurine, like a bull

Audēmus jūra nostra dēfendere.
We dare to defend our rights.

—Official Alabama State Coat of Arms[A]

[A]Alabama officially adopted this coat of arms in 1939. The original design, however, was created in 1923 by B. J. Tieman, New York, an authority on heraldry.

Chapter 5

The coat of arms consists of the five flags which have flown over Alabama: France, Spain, Britain, the Confederacy, and the U.S. The ship that sails over the top is the *Baldine*, which Iberville and Bienville sailed from France to settle a colony in 1699 near present day Mobile.

- transitive and intransitive verbs
- accusative case
  o direct object

VOCABULARY

NOUNS			
	amīca, amīcae, f.	friend (female friend)	(amicable)
	ancilla, ancillae, f.	maid-servant	(ancillary)
	cēna, cēnae, f.	dinner	(cenacle)
	culīna, culīnae, f.	kitchen	(culinary)
	fābula, fābulae, f.	story	(fable, fabulous)
	fīlia, fīliae, f.	daughter	(filial)
	pūpa, pūpae, f.	doll	(pupa)
	rosa, rosae, f.	rose	(rose)
	stella, stellae, f.	star	(stellar, constellation)
VERBS			
	aedificō, aedificāre, aedificāvī, aedificātum	to build	(edifice, edification)
	spectō, spectāre, spectāvī, spectātum	to look at, watch	(spectator, spectacle)

TE **Exercise 1.** Using the rules for syllabication and accent that you have learned, write out the syllables and accents for the vocabulary words above. Then practice pronouncing them aloud.

SECTION 14. Intransitive and Transitive Verbs

So far we have seen two different types of sentences. One type uses a nominative subject, a linking verb (**est, sunt**), and a predicate nominative.

Helena est rēgīna.   Helen is a queen.

The second type of sentence uses a nominative subject and what is called an intransitive verb.

Nautae nāvigant.   The sailors sail.

An **intransitive** verb does not require a direct object. The word in-trans-itive comes from the Latin words *trāns* (across) and *īre* ("to go"—eō, īre, iī/īvī, itum) along with the prefix *in* (not). The action of an intransitive verb does **not go across** to an object.

There are other verbs that often must take a direct object so that the sentence will present a clear complete thought to the reader. For example:

Rēgīna accūsat.   The queen accuses.

This sentence does not present a totally complete thought; it leaves us hanging. The queen accuses whom? The verb *accūsāre* usually is a transitive verb. A **transitive** verb requires a direct object. It describes an action that must **go across** to a direct object that can receive the verb's action.

Rēgīna puellam accūsat.   The queen accuses the girl.

There are also some verbs that can act as a transitive or intransitive depending on the context of the sentence.

Poēta cantat.   The poet sings.
Poēta carmen cantat.   The poet sings a song.

Exercise 2. Look at the lists of verbs in the vocabulary lists for chapters 2, 3, and 5. Determine which verbs are transitive, intransitive, and which can be both.

Hint: Use a Latin-English dictionary to help you.

SECTION 15. Accusative Case

The nominative case "names" the subject of the sentence: the person or thing who is doing the action of the verb. The accusative case gets its name from the Latin verb *accūsāre* (to accuse). This case shows who or what is receiving the action of the subject, much in the same way that the "accused" is receiving the charge or blame of the prosecution in a trial. Let's refer to the first declension set of case endings to see the inflected endings that signify the accusative case.

CASE	SINGULAR	PLURAL
Nominative Subject, Predicate	-a	-ae
Genitive Possession	-ae	-ārum
Dative Indirect Object	-ae	-īs
Accusative **Direct Object, Object** **Preposition**	**-am**	**-ās**
Ablative Object Preposition	-ā	-īs

27

 **Exercise 3.** Change the endings of the nominative nouns below to make them accusative. Take care to keep the number the same.

> Example: puella = puellam

1. nautae
2. ancilla
3. pūpae
4. rosae
5. stella
6. cēna

SECTION 16. Word Order

Latin does have a general word order: Subject – Object – Verb. However, Latin holds this order loosely and words can often be moved around for style and emphasis. Therefore, it is very important to look at the endings on every word before determining how to translate the sentence.

 Exercise 4.
A. Circle all endings in the sentences below.
B. Parse each word.
   verbs: person, number, tense; nouns: case, number, gender
C. Diagram the sentence labeling the subject, verb, direct object, or predicate.
D. Translate.

1. Jūlia est fīlia.

2. Jūlia pūpās portat.

3. Ancillae puellās spectābunt.

4. Adiuvābatne* Jūlia ancillam?

Notā Bene: Notice how the interrogative sentence (#4) moves the verb to the front. English does the same thing.

> Declarative: I do love chocolate.   Interrogative: Do you love chocolate?

 **Exercise 5.** Following the steps below, translate the English sentences into Latin.
A. Diagram the sentence.
B. Parse verbs and nouns.
C. Translate into Latin.

1. Flōra is a maid-servant.

2. Does Jūlia like Flōra?

3. Jūlia and Flōra are friends.

4. Jūlia was carrying a doll.

5. The girls look at the stars.

*Adiuvābatne is from the verb *adiuvō, adiuvāre, adiuvāvī, adiuvātum*: to help.

THE TROJAN WAR BEGINS

1. *Paris* Helenam amat.

2. Paris *ad Āsiam* Helenam portat.

3. *Priamus* et Hecuba fīliās *habent*.

4. Hecuba fīliās amat.

5. *Priamus rēx* rēgīnam amat.

6. *Priamus* nautās spectat.

7. Nautae sunt *Graecī*.

8. Graecia Trōiam oppugnat!

GLOSSARY

Paris .... Paris (a Trojan prince)
ad Āsiam .... to Asia (Troy is located in Asia Minor)
Priamus .... Priam (the king of Troy, father of Paris)
habent .... they have
rēx .... king
Graecī .... Greeks

Exercise A: Underline once all the intransitive verbs in the sentences above.

Exercise B: Underline twice all the transitive verbs in the sentences above.
Exercise C: Circle all the accusative nouns in the sentences above.

Culture Corner

Menelaus and Helen were the king and queen of Sparta, one of the mightiest cities of ancient Greece. Helen was a daughter of Zeus (king of the gods) and the most beautiful woman in the world. Paris was the son of King Priam and Queen Hecuba of Troy. While a guest in Menelaus' home, Paris fell in love with Helen, and took her home with him to Troy. King Menelaus and his brother Agamemnon, King of Athens, rallied the other kings of Greece and their armies. They sailed to Troy to bring back Helen, "the face that launched a thousand ships." Many poets have retold the events of the Trojan War. The most famous of them was the Greek poet Homer, who composed the *Iliad*.

Derivative Detective

Just for fun:
Write down a derivative for each word below.

amat, nauta, spectat

Hints: What do we call an actor who appears on stage not for money but just because he loves acting? What do we call citizens who go into space? What do we call such sports as football and baseball?

Colloquāmur (Let's Talk)

Use the following questions and responses to review the nouns in the sentences above. Use some "eye" Latin to figure out what the responses mean.

interrogātiō:	**Cūius est numerī?**	What number is it?
respōnsum:	**Singulāriter est.**	
	Plurāliter est.	
interrogātiō:	**Quō est cāsū?**	In what case is it?
respōnsum:	**Cāsū nōminātīvō est.**	
	Cāsū accūsātīvō est.	

Exercise 1

a-mī-ca, a-mī-cae, f.
an-cil-la, an-cil-lae, f.
cē-na, cē-nae, f.
cu-lī-na, cu-lī-nae, f.
fā-bu-la, fā-bu-lae, f.
fī-li-a, fī-li-ae, f.

pū-pa, pū-pae, f.
ro-sa, ro-sae, f.
stel-la, stel-lae, f.
ae-di-fi-cō, ae-di-fi-cā-re, ae-di-fi-cā-vī, ae-di-fi-cā-tum
spec-tō, spec-tā-re, spec-tā-vī, spec-tā-tum

Exercise 2

TRANSITIVE	INTRANSITIVE	BOTH
portō	ambulō	cantō
vocō		rēgnō
amō		labōrō
aedificiō		nāvigō
spectō		habitō
arō		
oppugnō		
rogō		

Exercise 3

1. nautae   nautās
2. ancilla   ancillam
3. pūpae   pūpās
4. rosae   rosās
5. stella   stellam
6. cēna   cēnam

Exercise 4

```
    S      LV    PrN
1. Jūlia   est   fīlia
   n/s/f  3/s/pr  n/s/f
   Julia is the daughter.
```

```
    S      DO      V
3. Ancillae   puellas    spectābunt
   n/p/f      ac/p/f     3/p/fut
   The maidservants will watch the girls.
```

```
    S      DO      V
2. Jūlia   pūpās   portat
   n/s/f  ac/p/f   3/s/pr
   Julia carries dolls.
```

```
     V         S        DO
4. Adiuvābatne   Jūlia    ancillam?
   3/s/imp       n/s/f    ac/s/f
   Was Julia helping the maidservant?
```

The abbreviations used for these exercises throughout the book are found on page xii of the teacher's introduction.

Exercise 5

```
     S    LV      PrN
1. Flōra  is a   maid-servant.
   n/s/f  3/s/pr n/s/f
   Flora est ancilla.
```

```
   HV    S     V     DO
2. Does Jūlia like  Flōra?
         n/s/f 3/s/pr ac/s/f
   Amatne Julia Floram?
```

```
     S    C    S    LV    PrN
3. Jūlia and Flōra are  friends.
   n/s/f      n/s/f 3/p/pr n/p/f
   Julia et Flora sunt amīcae.
```

```
     S      V        DO
4. Jūlia was carrying a doll.
   n/s/f  3/s/imp    ac/s/f
   Julia portābat pūpam.
```

```
     S      V        DO
5. The girls look at  the stars.
   n/p/f  3/p/pr     ac/p/f
   Puellae spectant stellās.
```

Remind students that an interrogative sentence should move the verb to the front and add the suffix -ne.

Translation

Paris loves Helen.

Paris carries Helen to Asia.

Priam and Hecuba have daughters.

Hecuba loves (her) daughters.*

King Priam loves (his) queen.*

Priam sees sailors.

The sailors are Greeks.

Greece attacks Troy!

*You have noticed by now that Latin does not use articles (e.g. the, a, an). These can be supplied by the student as needed. In a similar manner, Latin does not always supply the possessive pronouns (his, her, my, etc.) particularly when it should be obvious. Students may supply these as needed for a good English translation. Such will be the case in sentences #4 and 5.

Chapter Reading Exercises

1. *Paris* Helenam amat.

2. Paris *ad Asiam* Helenam portat.

3. *Priāmus* et Hecuba filiās habent.

4. Hecuba filiās amat.

5. *Priāmus rēx* rēgīnam amat.

6. *Priāmus* nautās spectat.

7. Nautae sunt *Graecī.*

8. Graecia Trōiam oppugnat!

There are no intransative verbs in this exercise.

Dītat Deus.
God enriches.
—Arizona state motto [A]

This motto is from Genesis 14:23 of the Vulgate Bible.

[A] Arizona became a state in 1912, the year depicted on its shield. The shield depicts the state's landscape, climate, and industry. Note particularly the rich and fertile fields on the right.

Chapter 6

- 2nd declension nouns
  - masculine and neuter
- dative case
  - indirect object
  - reference

VOCABULARY

Nouns			
ager, agrī, m.	field	(agriculture, agrarian)
amīcus, amīcī, m.	friend (male friend)	(amicable, amigo)
auxilium, auxiliī, n.	aid, help	(auxiliary)
bellum, bellī, n.	war	(belligerent, bellicose)
dōnum, dōnī, n.	gift	(donation)
equus, equī, m.	horse	(equestrian, equine)
germānus, germānī, m.	brother	(German, germane)
humus, humī, f.	ground	(humus)
līberī, līberōrum, m. pl.	children	
oppidum, oppidī, n.	town	
puer, puerī, m.	boy	(puerile, puerperal)
socius, sociī, m.	ally	(social)
vir, virī, m.	man	(virile)
Verbs			
*dō, dare, dedī, datum	to give	(donate)
monstrō, monstrāre, monstrāvī, monstrātum	to show	(demonstration)
narrō, narrāre, narrāvī, narrātum	to tell	(narrate, narrator)

| pugnō, pugnāre, pugnāvī, pugnātum | to fight | (pugnacious) |
| servō, servāre, servāvī, servātum | to take care of; guard, protect | (conserve) |

Notā Bene: The pattern for the principal parts changes slightly for some first conjugation verbs. Take care to memorize this new pattern.

TE **Exercise 1.** Using the rules for syllabication and accent that you have learned, write out the syllables and accents for the vocabulary words above. Then practice pronouncing them aloud.

SECTION 17. Second Declension

BSee Latin in Science on page 37 for an explanation as to why the names of trees are feminine.

As we learned in section twelve a **declension** is a group of nouns that share a common set of inflected case endings. The first declension consists primarily of feminine nouns and a few masculine nouns. The second declension does not include many feminine nouns, but consists of nouns that are either masculine or neuter. The most common feminine exceptions are the noun *humus* (ground) and the names of some trees such as *quercus* (oak).**B**

The second declension distinguishes itself from other declensions by its genitive singular ending, -ī. The genitive singular is unique for every declension and is always the form most reliable in determining to which declension a noun belongs. As you may recall, the genitive singular is also the form that reveals a noun's stem, the form to which all inflected endings are added. Simply drop the ending -ī from the genitive singular to find the stem of a second declension noun.

TE **Exercise 2.** Identify the stem for each of the nouns in the vocabulary list above.

Example: dōnum, dōnī **stem = dōn/ī**

By now you have certainly noticed that while the genitive endings are all very similar, the nominative endings vary quite a bit. This is due in part to the varying gender of the nouns. The neuter nouns all have a nominative singular that ends in -um. Masculine nouns end in -us or -r.

SECTION 18. Masculine

Just as all nouns that refer to female people are designated as feminine in Latin, so nouns referring to male people are designated masculine. There are a great many objects, however, such as *field* that do not have an obvious gender. So, it is important to memorize the gender of every noun that you learn. Most masculine nouns of the second declension are easily recognized by the nominative ending -us. However, there is a small group of masculine nouns that end in -r in the nominative singular. Whether they end in -r or -us in the nominative, the rest of the masculine endings are as follows:

Chapter 6

stem: amīc/ī				
	ENDINGS		**MASCULINE**	
CASE	SING.	PLURAL	SINGULAR	PLURAL
Nominative Subject, Predicate	-us/-r	-ī	amīc-**us** the friend	amīc-**ī** the friends
Genitive Possession	-ī	-ōrum	amīc-**ī** of the friend	amīc-**ōrum** of the friends
Dative Indirect Object	-ō	-īs	amīc-**ō** to/for the friend	amīc-**īs** to/for the friends
Accusative Direct Object, Object Preposition	-um	-ōs	amīc-**um** the friend	amīc-**ōs** the friends
Ablative Object Preposition	-ō	-īs	amīc-**ō** by/with/from the friend	amīc-**īs** by/with/from the friends

stem: agr/ī		
CASE	SINGULAR	PLURAL
Nominative Subject, Predicate	age**r** the field	agr-**ī** the fields
Genitive Possession	agr-**ī** of the field	agr-**ōrum** of the fields
Dative Indirect Object	agr-**ō** to/for the field	agr-**īs** to/for the fields
Accusative Direct Object, Object Preposition	agr-**um** the field	agr-**ōs** the fields
Ablative Object Preposition	agr-**ō** by/with/from the field	agr-**īs** by/with/from the fields

Notā Bene: The noun *ager* drops the e, but some nouns such as *puer* keep the e when declining. Take care to learn the genitive singular form in order to know which pattern a noun will follow.

[TE] **Exercise 3.** Following the pattern of *amīcus* and *ager*, decline *puer, vir,* and *equus.*

Notice that this new chart is in many ways very similar to the first declension. In many places the vowels *o* or *u* simply replace the familiar *a* of the first declension. Which cases seem similar? Which ones seem different?

The Latin word *neuter* means *neither.* It is a fitting title for this third gender for it describes objects that are neither masculine nor feminine. The neuter gender is therefore never used to name a person or animal. The second declension neuter endings are very similar to the masculine endings. In fact, there are only two cases that are different. Can you tell which cases are different in the declension of *dōnum*?

	ENDINGS		NEUTER	
CASE	SING.	PLURAL	SINGULAR	PLURAL
Nominative Subject, Predicate	-um	-a	dōn-**um** the gift	dōn-**a** the gifts
Genitive Possession	-ī	-ōrum	dōn-ī of the gift	dōn-ōrum of the gifts
Dative Indirect Object	-ō	-īs	dōn-ō to/for the gift	dōn-īs to/for the gifts
Accusative Direct Object, Object Preposition	-um	-a	dōn-**um** the gift	dōn-a the gifts
Ablative Object Preposition	-ō	-īs	dōn-ō by/with/from the gift	dōn-īs by/with/from the gifts

stem: **dōn/ī**

The neuter endings differ from the masculine only in the nominative and accusative cases. This brings us to a very important rule that applies to every neuter noun in every noun declension in Latin. **The neuter rule:** the neuter nominative and accusative endings are *always* the same, AND the nominative and accusative plural *always* end with a short **a.** Most second declension neuter nouns are recognizable by the nominative singular that ends in -um. However, there are a couple of notable exceptions:

pelagus, pelagī, n. sea
vulgus, vulgī, n. crowd   (sometimes masculine)

Exercise 4. Following the pattern of *dōnum*, decline *oppidum*.[c]

[c]Reminder: There is a declension worksheet for this exercise.

SECTION 20. Dative Case

A. Indirect Object

The dative case has many uses, and usually we can translate this case with the English prepositions "to" or "for." The two most frequent uses are the indirect object and dative of reference or interest. The name for the dative case is derived from the Latin word *dare* (to give), a very fitting verb since it is one that uses indirect objects in the dative case quite frequently.

An **indirect object** generally describes the object to which something is given, said, or done. It does not receive the action of the verb directly, but is nevertheless indirectly affected by it. For example:

The girl gives a gift **to the boy.**
The girl gives **the boy** a gift.

Notice that English does not have to use a prepositional phrase to indicate the indirect object. Often it relies on the word order to communicate the meaning. You can imagine that this might be confusing for someone learning English. Latin is much more consistent. Latin always puts the indirect object into the dative case.

Puella puerō dōnum dat.

 **Exercise 5.** Underline the indirect object in each of the English sentences below. Then translate each indirect object into Latin.

Example: The man gives a ball to the boys.   **puerīs**

1. He shows the field to the farmer.
2. The mother gives the daughter a doll.
3. Will you read a story to the boy?
4. The man entrusts his money to the friends.
5. The mother tells the children a story.
6. The man shows a friend the town.
7. The children feed apples to the horses.

B. Dative of Reference

Dative of reference, sometimes called a dative of interest, is in some ways similar to the indirect object. It also describes something which is not directly receiving the action of the verb, but is the object to which a statement refers.

They build a town for the allies.
They build the allies a town.

 **Exercise 6.** Following the steps provided, translate the sentences.
   A. Circle all endings in the sentences below.
   B. Parse each word: verbs = person, number, tense; nouns = case, number, gender
   C. Diagram the sentence labeling the subject, verb, direct object, or predicate.
   D. Translate.

1. Puerīs dōnum damus.

2. Virī oppidō aedificia aedificābant.

3. Puellīs fābulam narrābis.

4. Puer agrum amīcō monstrat.

5. Agricolae humum arātis.

6. Dabuntne sociī patriae auxilium?

 **Exercise 7.** Review the sentences in Exercise 6. Determine which sentences use indirect objects and which use the dative of reference.

THE TROJAN HORSE

1. *Menelāus* Helenam amat.
2. *Menelāus* et *Agamemnōn* sunt germānī.
3. *Agamemnōn* et sociī *Menelāō* auxilium dant.
4. Graecī et Trōiānī bellum *gerunt*.
5. Virī Helenae pugnābant.
6. Graecī equum aedificant, et *in equō cēlant*.
7. Trōiānī *in oppidum* equum portant.
8. Graecī Trōiam *cremant*.
9. Aenēas et Trōiānī *fugiunt*; *ad Ītaliam* nāvigābunt.
10. Graecī et Rōmānī līberīs fābulam narrant.

GLOSSARY

Menelāus .... Menelaus (King of Sparta, husband to Helen)
Agamemnōn .... Agamemnon (King of Athens, brother to Menelaus)
gerunt .... they wage, carry on
in equō .... in the horse
cēlō, cēlāre, cēlāvī, cēlātum ...... to hide
in oppidum .... into the town
cremō, cremāre .... to burn (to ashes)
Aenēas .... Aeneas (son-in-law of King Priam, destined to found the Roman race)
fugiunt .... they flee
ad Ītaliam .... to Italy

Culture Corner

Homer told about the Trojan War in the *Iliad*, an epic poem. A Roman poet who wrote about the Trojan War was Vergil, who wrote the *Aeneid*. Book II of the *Aeneid* contains the story of the Trojan horse. After the Greeks destroyed their city, Aeneas led the surviving Trojans to Italy.

The planet Venus was named for the Roman goddess of love and beauty. She was the mother of Aeneas, a prince of Troy and the hero of the *Aeneid*.

Latin in Science

Most nouns in the second declension are either masculine or neuter. Just as in the first declension, however, there are a few gender exceptions. Interestingly, many feminine nouns of the second declension name trees. Trees are feminine because the Romans believed that female spirits called dryads inhabited trees.

These Latin words have survived the ages through the scientific classification for trees. Landscape architects and gardeners still use these words every day. Use a Latin dictionary to discover which trees these words represent. You will find that a few of the common names for trees also derive from some of these words.

 quercus*ᴰ   iūniperus

ulmus   fīcus

cyparissus   prūnus

laurus   mālus

fraxinus   alnus

> ᴰSuggested Activity: Nature Walk
> Look up the names of a few more trees indigenous to your area. Then take a nature walk and practice identifying the trees by their Latin names.
> Quālis arbor est? What kind of tree is it?
> Est _____. It is a _____.

*Note that *quercus* is not a second declension noun, but actually a fourth declension noun.

Colloquāmur (Let's Talk)

Use the following questions and responses to review the nouns in the sentences above. Use some "eye" Latin to figure out what the responses mean.

interrogātiō:	Cūius est numerī?	What number is it?
respōnsum:	Singulāriter est.	
	Plūrāliter est.	

interrogātiō:	Quō est cāsū?	In what case is it?
respōnsum:	Cāsū nōminātīvō est.	
	Cāsū accūsātīvō est.	
	Cāsū datīvō est.	

Chapter 6 Teacher's Pages

Exercise 1

a-ger, a-grī, m.
a-mī-cus, a-mī-cī, m.
au-xi-li-um, au-xi-li-ī, n.
bel-lum, bel-lī, n.
dō-num, dō-nī, n.
e-quus, e-quī, m.
ger-mā-nus, ger-mā-nī, m.
hu-mus, hu-mī, f.
lī-be-rī, lī-be-rō-rum, m. pl.

op-pi-dum, op-pi-dī, n.
pu-er, pu-e-rī, m.
so-ci-us, so-ci-ī, m.
vir, vi-rī, m.
dō, da-re, de-dī, da-tum
mon-strō, mon-strā-re, mon-strā-vī, mon-strā-tum
nār-rō, nār-rā-re, nār-rā-vī, nār-rā-tum
pug-nō, pug-nā-re, pug-nā-vī, pug-nā-tum
ser-vō, ser-vā-re, ser-vā-vī, ser-vā-tum

Exercise 2

ager, agrī — agr/ī
amīcus, amīcī — amīc/ī
auxilium, auxiliī — auxili/ī
bellum, bellī — bell/ī
dōnum, dōnī — dōn/ī
equus, equī — equ/ī
germānus, germānī — germān/ī

humus, humī — hum/ī
līberī, līberōrum — līber/ōrum
oppidum, oppidī — oppid/ī
puer, puerī — puer/ī
socius, sociī — soci/ī
vir, virī — vir/ī

Exercise 3

CASE	SINGULAR	PLURAL	SINGULAR	PLURAL	SINGULAR	PLURAL
Nominative	puer	puer-ī	vir	vir-ī	equus	equ-ī
Genitive	puer-ī	puer-ōrum	vir-ī	vir-ōrum	equ-ī	equ-ōrum
Dative	puer-ō	puer-īs	vir-ō	vir-īs	equ-ō	equ-īs
Accusative	puer-um	puer-ōs	vir-um	vir-ōs	equ-um	equ-ōs
Ablative	puer-ō	puer-īs	vir-ō	vir-īs	equ-ō	equ-īs

Exercise 4

CASE	SINGULAR	PLURAL
Nominative	oppid-um	oppid-a
Genitive	oppid-ī	oppid-ōrum
Dative	oppid-ō	oppid-īs
Accusative	oppid-um	oppid-a
Ablative	oppid-ō	oppid-īs

Exercise 5

1. He shows the field <u>to the farmer</u>.   agricolae
2. The mother gives <u>the daughter</u> a doll.   fīliae
3. Will you read a story <u>to the boy</u>?   puerō
4. The man entrusts his money <u>to the friends</u>.   amīcīs
5. The mother tells <u>the children</u> a story.   līberīs
6. The man shows a <u>friend</u> the town.   amīcō/amīcae
7. The children feed apples <u>to the horses</u>.   equīs

Exercise 6

      IO   DO   V
1. Puerīs dōnum damus.
  d/p/m ac/s/n 1/p/pr
We give a gift to the boys.

      S   DR   DO   V
2. Virī oppidō aedificia aedificābant.
  n/p/m d/s/n   ac/p/n   3/p/imp
The men were building buildings for the town.

      IO   DO   V
3. Puellīs fābulam nārrābis.
  d/p/f   ac/s/f   2/s/fut
You will tell a story to the girls.

      S   DO   IO   V
4. Puer agrum amīcō monstrat.
  n/s/m ac/s/m d/s/m   3/s/pr
The boy shows the field to (his) friend.

      DR   DO   V
5. Agricolae humum arātis.
  d/s/m   ac/s/f   2/p/pr
You plow the ground for the farmer.

      V   S   IO   DO
6. Dabuntne sociī patriae auxilium?
  3/p/f   n/p/m   d/s/f   ac/s/n
Will the allies give help to the country?

Exercise 7

1. Puerīs dōnum damus.   IO
2. Virī oppidō aedificia aedificābant.   DR
3. Puellīs fābulam nārrābis.   IO
4. Puer agrum amīcō monstrat.   IO
5. Agricolae humum arātis.   DR
6. Dabuntne sociī patriae auxilium?   IO

Translation

1. Menelaus loves Helen.

2. Menelaus and Agamemenon are brothers.

3. Agamemnon and allies give help to Menelaus.

4. The Greeks and Trojans wage war.

5. The men were fighting for Helen.

6. The Greeks build a horse, and hide in the horse.

7. The Trojans carry the horse into the city.

8. The Greeks burn Troy.

9. Aeneas and the Trojans flee, they will sail to Italy.

10. The Greeks and Romans tell the story to (their) children.

Latin in Science

quercus	Oak	iūniperus	Juniper
ulmus	Elm	fīcus	Ficus (Fig Tree)
cyparissus	Cypress	prūnus	Plum Tree
laurus	Laurel	mālus	Apple Tree
fraxinus	Ash Tree	alnus	Alder

Notes

Unit 1 Reading

Reading and Review for Chapters 1–6

ABOUT THE READINGS FOR THIS TEXTBOOK

So far, you have been reading sentences designed to reinforce vocabulary and grammatical structures and to serve as an introduction to the skill of reading Latin and as a preparation for reading stories in Latin. The purpose has not been to tell a story or illustrate any theme but rather to give you an easy start in reading in a language other than your own.

From this point on, though, you will be reading stories about early Roman history. These stories are fascinating! We have adapted the stories you will read from the early chapters of a book called *Ab Urbe Condita* (*From the Founding of the City*) by Titus Līvius, usually known in English as Livy. Some scholars believe that Livy had no fixed goal in mind foār his history but rather that he "toiled on till his strength failed him . . . giving his history to the public in parts as [he completed them]." (B. O. Foster. *Livy: History of Rome, Books 1 –2.* Cambridge, Massachusetts. Harvard University Press. 2002. xv.)

Livy's work is complicated Latin reading, containing many different tenses and many examples of complex sentences and indirect discourse. We have simplified this work for you and have primarily used the historical present tense. The historical present tense makes historical writing vivid by writing about the past using the present tense. For example, we can write "Achilles <u>raises</u> his mighty sword" instead of "Achilles <u>raised</u> his mighty sword" even though we are describing a past action.

THE DESCENDANTS OF AENEAS
Gaylan DuBose

When Troy fell to the Greeks after ten years of fighting, Aenēas, along with his father and son, was among the very few Trojan leaders who escaped the burning city. He traveled over land and sea for years before finally arriving in Italy, the land of his destiny. Another Trojan, Antēnor, had also settled in Italy. Aeneas eventually arrived in Latium, the area of Italy where Rome was later to stand. The area was Latium, the language was Latīna, and the king was Latīnus. This king had a daughter named Lāvīnia, who was to marry a prince of a neighboring tribe, a man called Turnus; however, Aenēas married Lāvīnia; and this marriage led to war. The son of Aenēas, Ascanius (also known as Iūlus), settled at what we call Alba Longa. Rōmulus and Remus, along with the Julian clan, whose most famous member was Gāius Jūlius Caesar, were descendants of this man. Our stories begin with Rōmulus and Remus.

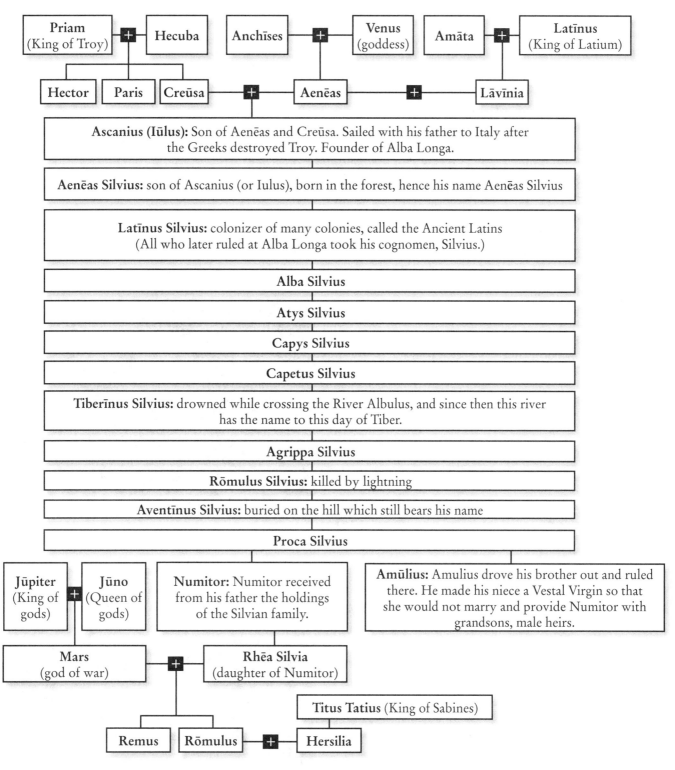

Ascanius (Iūlus): Son of Aenēas and Creūsa. Sailed with his father to Italy after the Greeks destroyed Troy. Founder of Alba Longa.

Aenēas Silvius: son of Ascanius (or Iulus), born in the forest, hence his name Aenēas Silvius

Latīnus Silvius: colonizer of many colonies, called the Ancient Latins (All who later ruled at Alba Longa took his cognomen, Silvius.)

Alba Silvius

Atys Silvius

Capys Silvius

Capetus Silvius

Tiberīnus Silvius: drowned while crossing the River Albulus, and since then this river has the name to this day of Tiber.

Agrippa Silvius

Rōmulus Silvius: killed by lightning

Aventīnus Silvius: buried on the hill which still bears his name

Proca Silvius

Jūpiter (King of gods) — **Jūno** (Queen of gods)

Numitor: Numitor received from his father the holdings of the Silvian family.

Amūlius: Amulius drove his brother out and ruled there. He made his niece a Vestal Virgin so that she would not marry and provide Numitor with grandsons, male heirs.

Mars (god of war)

Rhēa Silvia (daughter of Numitor)

Titus Tatius (King of Sabines)

Remus **Rōmulus** — **Hersilia**

(Tatius became a joint ruler with Rōmulus when the Sabine and Roman tribes intermarried. Upon the death of Titus Tatius, Rōmulus became sole king. Rōmulus, according to legend, was taken up in a chariot by his father, the god Mars. He was then deified as Rōmulus-Quīrinus. Hersilia grieved for her missing husband so greatly that Jūno deified her as well. The "mother" of the Romans was then worshipped as Hōra.)

THE BIRTH AND EARLY LIFE OF RŌMULUS AND REMUS [A]

CHARACTERS:

Rhēa Silvia – daughter of King Numitor and mother of Rōmulus and Remus
Vesta – goddess of the hearth
Mars – god of war
Rōmulus – legendary founder and first king of Rome
Remus – Rōmulus' twin brother

1.　　Rhēa Silvia est fīlia *rēgis. Quoque* ancilla deae Vestae est. Mars Rhēam Silviam
2.　*vīsitat*, et *mox* fēmina puerōs *geminōs parit. Pātruus Rhēae Silviae* iubet servum
3.　puerōs *in rīvum pōnere. Rīvus altus* est, et puerī *in* terram nāvigant. Lupa līberōs
4.　servat. Tum servus puerōs spectat et *ad casam* puerōs portat. Servus et
5.　*marīta* puerōs in *casā cūrant*.
6.　　*Ubi* puerī sunt virī, oppidum **aedificāre volunt**. Rōmulus mūrum aedificat.
7.　Rōmulus Remō mūrum mōnstrat. Remus *rīdet*. Remus est *īrātus*. Rōmulus
8.　Remum necat. Rōmulus oppidum aedificat. Rōmulus oppidum Rōmam *appellat*.
9.　Nunc Rōmulus est *rēx*.

———————

Notā Bene:
aedificāre volunt = they wish to build

GLOSSARY

rēgis	of a king
quoque, adv.	also
vīsitō, vīsitāre	to visit
mox, adv.	soon
geminus, ī, m.	twin
pareō, parēre	to give birth to
pātruus, pātruī, m.	paternal uncle (father's brother)
Rheae Silviae	of Rhea Silvia
iubeō, iubēre	to order
in	into
rīvus, ī, m.	river, stream
pōnere	to put, to place
altus, a, um, adj.	deep
lupa, ae, f.	a female wolf
ad, preposition + accusative	to
casa, ae, f.	house
marīta, marītae, f.	wife
cūrō, cūrāre	to care for
ubi, adv.	when
mūrus, mūrī, m.	wall
rīdeō, rīdēre	to laugh
īrātus	angry
necō, necāre	to kill
nunc, adv.	now
appellō, appellāre	to call, name
rēx, nominative, sing., m.	king

[A] The students should follow these steps to success for this reading comprehension exercise.
- Read the English title. (It is often a clue to the theme or content of the reading.)
- Read the Latin text all the way through without any attempt at translation.
- Read the questions in order to know what to look for in the reading.
- Read the selection again.
- Go back and begin answering the questions.

Translation:
Rhea Silvia is the daughter of the king. She is also a maidservant for the goddess Vesta. Mars visits Rhea Silvia, and soon the woman gives birth to boys, twins. The uncle of Rhea Silvia orders a servant to put the boys into the river. The river is deep, and the boys sail onto the land. A wolf guards the children. Then a servant sees the boys and carries them to his own house. The servant and his wife care for the boys in the house. When the boys are men, they want to build a town. Romulus builds a wall. Romulus shows the wall to Remus. Remus laughs. Romulus is angry. Romulus kills Remus. Romulus builds a town. Romulus calls the town Rome. Now Romulus is king.

1. According to this reading, besides being the daughter of a king, Rhēa Silvia was _____.
   a. the cousin of Aenēas
   b. the mother of twin boys
   c. a servant of Mars
   d. a goddess of a river

2. *Geminōs* in line 2 ___.
   a. means "twins"
   b. is an appositive
   c. is accusative
   d. all of the above

3. The verb *nāvigant* in line 3 implies that ___.
   a. there was a flood
   b. the babies were in something like a boat
   c. the river was nearly dry
   d. the babies had been thrown into the sea

4. Which family member below is not mentioned in the reading?
   a. uncle on the father's side
   b. husband
   c. wife
   d. grandfather

5. Which word or phrase below best characterizes the prevailing emotion between Rōmulus and Remus?
   a. brotherly love
   b. jealousy and anger
   c. anger followed by total remorse and loss
   d. sadness followed by joy

6. What is the case of *Vestae* in line 1?
   a. nominative
   b. dative
   c. accusative
   d. none of the above

7. Which of the following words serves as a direct object in line 6?
   a. casā
   b. puerī
   c. oppidum
   d. Rōmulus

8. What is the function of *Remō* in line 7?
   a. subject
   b. direct object
   c. predicate nominative
   d. indirect object

It is a great hope that someday you will take an Advanced Placement test in Latin. Preparation for AP tests must begin in the earliest stages of Latin and continue throughout your study of the language. These questions are of the type that you are likely to encounter on an AP test or the National Latin Exam at a higher level.

The Romans had more words for relatives than we do and also more exact words. This fact probably indicates that the Romans placed more value on the extended family than we do in America today. Remember that *familia* meant **everyone** who lived in the household, even slaves. [B]

> *pater* – father
> *māter* – mother
> *avus* – grandfather
> *avia* – grandmother
> *nepōs* – grandson
> *neptis* – granddaughter
> *pātruus* – a father's brother, a paternal uncle
> *amita* – a father's sister (Oddly, the Romans did not seem to use this term in the same way that we would use *aunt*, but consider the use of *pātruus* above. What may this tell you about Roman society?)
> *avunculus* – a mother's brother, a maternal uncle (This word means literally "little grandfather." How does this term signal a different relationship between a maternal and a paternal uncle?)
> *mātertera* – a mother's sister, a maternal aunt (This word literally means "ma-relative-relative; *māter* means just "ma-relative." What might a Roman child, like one of us today, first call his mother?)
> *patruēlis* – a cousin on the father's side (a male or a female cousin)
> *cōnsōbrīnus* and *consōbrīna* – a male and female cousin, respectively, on the mother's side

[B]Suggested Project:
Create your own Latin family tree using the Latin words provided above. You can include photographs of your family members, or draw pictures of them dressed as Romans!

AAn American eagle occupies the center of this seal. In his beak he holds a banner with the state motto **Regnat Populus** written upon it. On his breast is a shield which depicts a steamboat, a beehive next to a plow, and on the bottom stands a sheaf of wheat. In his talons he holds an olive branch and a bundle of arrows. On the left (near the peaceful olive branch) is the Angel of Mercy; on the right is the sword of justice. Above the eagle is the personification of Liberty surrounded by thirteen stars representing the thirteen original colonies. Liberty holds a wreath in her right hand. In her left hand is a long pole with a Phrygian cap, commonly referred to as a liberty cap. Roman slaves who had been emancipated often wore this cap as a symbol of their liberty and that of their children who were considered free citizens of the Roman Empire. The French Revolution adopted this piece of clothing as a symbol of liberty. Today the national emblem of France, Marianne, still wears the red cap on her head. This imagery inspired many in both North and South America. Several U.S. states as well as Latin American countries have included Liberty's pole and her Phrygian cap on their seals. Watch for these symbols in future chapters.

Rēgnat populus.
The people rule.
—Arkansas state motto A

Chapter 7

- adjectives of 1st and 2nd declension
  - agreement
- irregular verb *esse*
  - present system

VOCABULARY

NOUNS			
deus, deī, m.	god	(deity)	
flamma, flammae, f.	flame	(flammable, inflammatory)	
scūtum, scūtī, n.	shield	(scutes)	
signum, signī, n.	sign	(signal)	
templum, templī, n.	temple	(temple, Knights Templar)	
VERBS			
creō, creāre, creāvī, creātum	to create, make	(creation, creator)	
iuvō, iuvāre, iūvī, iūtum	to help	(aid, adjutant)	
optō, optāre, optāvī, optātum	to wish for, desire	(option, opt)	
saltō, saltāre, saltāvī, saltātum	to leap, dance		
sum, esse, fuī, futūrum	to be	(essence, future)	
ADJECTIVES			
aēneus, aēnea, aēneum	bronze		
bonus, bona, bonum	good	(bonus, bonafide)	
magnus, magna, magnum	big, great	(magnify, magnitude)	
multus, multa, multum	many	(multiply, multitude)	

pius, pia, pium	pious, devout (god-fearing)	(pious, piety)
sacer, sacra, sacrum	sacred, holy	(sacred)
tūtus, tūta, tūtum	protected, safe	
ADVERBS		
dum	while	
tum	then	
CONJUNCTION		
quoque	also	

Exercise 1. Using the rules for syllabication and accent that you have learned, write out the syllables and accents for the vocabulary words above. Then practice pronouncing them aloud.

SECTION 21. Adjectives

You have now learned all the forms for nouns of the first and second declension. What's more, you have also learned the forms for adjectives of the first and second declension. The word *adjective* comes from the Latin *adiectus*, meaning "an adding to." Adjectives are words used to modify or describe nouns, adding information about the person, place, thing, or idea to which they refer. In general adjectives tell us what kind, which one, or how many something/someone might be.

In English an adjective generally appears immediately before the noun that it modifies.

The **good farmer** ploughs a long ditch around the **wide field**.

Agricola bonus fossam circā **agrum lātum** longam arat.ᴮ

In English it is quite apparent to us that "good" is describing the farmer and not the ditch or the field because of its position in the sentence. In Latin adjectives generally follow the nouns they modify. However, because Latin holds word order loosely you cannot always depend on an adjective appearing immediately after its noun. In many cases an adjective may appear before the noun it modifies in order to create emphasis. On other occasions it may not appear next to its noun at all, but on the other side of the sentence. This arrangement can be a very effective syntactical tool as in the sentence above where the long ditch *(fossam longam)* actually does surround the wide field *(agrum lātum)* in the words of the sentence itself. It is therefore dependent upon the inflected endings of the adjectives to reveal which nouns they modify.

CASE	MASCULINE		FEMININE		NEUTER	
	Singular	Plural	Singular	Plural	Singular	Plural
Nom.	bon**us**	bon**ī**	bon**a**	bon**ae**	bon**um**	bon**a**
Gen.	bon**ī**	bon**ōrum**	bon**ae**	bon**ārum**	bon**ī**	bon**ōrum**
Dat.	bon**ō**	bon**īs**	bon**ae**	bon**īs**	bon**ō**	bon**īs**
Acc.	bon**um**	bon**ōs**	bon**am**	bon**ās**	bon**um**	bon**a**
Abl.	bon**ō**	bon**īs**	bon**ā**	bon**īs**	bon**ō**	bon**īs**

SECTION 22. Agreement

An adjective must agree with the noun it modifies in case, number, and gender. Adjectives are therefore quite like the chameleon. They are able to take on any ending of the first or second declension in order to obtain the appropriate gender for their noun. This is why all three nominative forms are listed as the dictionary entry for an adjective. In order to find the stem of an adjective look to the feminine form that always appears as the second entry. The masculine nominative sometimes varies, but the feminine will always reveal the true stem.

bonus, bon/a, bonum   pulcher, pulchr/a, pulchrum

Exercise 2. Identify the stems of the adjectives *longus* and *sacer.* Then, following the example of *bonus,* decline them in all three genders.

Caveat discipulus (Let the Student Beware): Although an adjective must agree with the noun it modifies in case, number, and gender, it may not always match that adjective in the appearance of its ending. This is particularly true of the PAIN nouns discussed in chapter four. Even though they have an ending that is typically feminine, they are masculine and only a masculine adjective can modify them as illustrated in the previous sentence with *agricola bonus*, the good farmer.

Exercise 3. Translate the adjectives and the nouns they modify into the designated case. Take care to make them agree in case, number, and gender.

Example: good farmer (nominative) = agricola bonus

1. good town (nominative)
2. pious boy (genitive)
3. bronze shields (dative)
4. big temple (ablative)
5. sacred flame (accusative)
6. safe signs (nominative)
7. many poets (accusative)

SECTION 23. Irregular verb: esse

English has quite a few verbs whose principal parts do not follow what is considered the usual format.

Regular:	Love	(he) loves	loved	loved
Irregular:	Sing	(he) sings	sang	sung
	Do	(he) does	did	done
	Be	(he) is	was	been

The list of irregular English verbs could go on *ad infīnītum*,[c] but the most notorious of these irregularities is the linking verb "to be." It is also the most common verb used. It should therefore be no surprise that the most common irregular verb in Latin is this same linking verb, *esse* (to be). The principal parts for this verb are indeed irregular:

sum, esse, fuī, futūrum

[c](to infinity)

You can form the stem for this verb in a similar manner to other verbs. Simply remove the ending -se from the infinitive (second principal part). The result is the irregular stem *es*. Add to this stem the familiar personal endings you have already learned and you will conjugate most of the present tense of *esse*—there are a few places where the stem changes. Can you come up with a rule for these irregularities?

PERSON	SINGULAR	PLURAL
1	**su-m** I am	**su-mus** we are
2	**e-s** you are	**es-tis** you (pl.) are
3	**es-t** he/she/it is	**su-nt** they are

Notā Bene:
- Notice that the personal endings in this chart are the same as those taught in section 2.

The stem of *esse* is a bit irregular. In the third person singular and the forms of the second person the stem is what you might expect: *es* (the first *s* in the second person singular is simply absorbed into the ending). In the third person plural and the forms of the first person, however, the stem changes to su-. At first this may seem quite strange. This linguistic change, however, is due to the sounds produced by the joining of the stem and the ending. The sounds produced by the letters *m* and *n* are called nasals because the sound is produced largely through the nasal passage. The sound produced by the stem es- followed by a nasal was not clearly distinguishable or pleasing to the Roman ear. Therefore, the es- changed to a su- when placed in front of a nasal.[D]

Try pronouncing these forms aloud: **esm, sum   esmus, sumus   esnt, sunt**
Which are easier to understand?

SECTION 24. Present system of *esse*

The imperfect and future tenses of *esse* are also irregular. Once again the endings are the same regular familiar endings. Even the vowel pattern of the tense markers is the same as the regular verbs. However, we now see -ra- instead of -ba- in the imperfect tense and -r- instead of -b- in the future tense.

PERSON	IMPERFECT		FUTURE	
	Singular	Plural	Singular	Plural
1	**eram** I was	**erāmus** we were	**erō** I will be	**erimus** we will be
2	**erās** you were	**erātis** you (pl.) were	**eris** you will be	**eritis** you (pl.) will be
3	**erat** he/she/it was	**erant** they were	**erit** he/she/it will be	**erunt** they will be

[D]Linguistic demo: Have students make the sounds 'mmm' and 'nnn.' Ask them where that sound is coming from. They should notice that they are not using their mouth at all, particularly on the 'm.' The sound is coming through their nasal passage (nose).

Exercise 4. Parse each of the following verbs identifying their tense, person, and number. Then translate them into English.

LATIN	TENSE	PERSON	NUMBER	TRANSLATION
eram	Imp.	1	Sing.	I was
eris				
sunt				
erāmus				
erō				
est				
erātis				
sum				
eritis				

SECTION 25. Translating esse: predicate review

Linking verbs such as *esse* in Latin or "to be" in English generally link a subject with a predicate. A predicate nominative (from Latin *praedicāre*, to declare) is a noun or an adjective that renames or refers to the subject. The predicate nominative in Latin must always be in the nominative case. If the predicate nominative is an adjective, it must agree with the subject in case, number, and gender.

Predicate nominative:	Vir est **agricola.**	The man is a **farmer.**
	Puella erit **rēgīna.**	The girl will be a **queen.**
Predicate adjective:	Agricola est **bonus.**	The farmer is **good.**
	Germānus erat **īrātus.**	The brother was **angry.**

Exercise 5. Underline the predicate nominative or predicate adjective for each sentence, then translate the complete predicate.

1. Agricola est bonus vir.

2. Eram pius puer.

3. Templum est sacrum quoque magnum.

4. Dum flamma ardet,* oppidum erit tūtum.

5. We will be good friends.

6. The sailors are not many.

7. They were good men and also god-fearing.

Ardet comes from *ardeō*, which means "to be on fire," or "to burn."

Chapter Reading ⓣⓔ

NUMA POMPILIUS

Rōmulus ruled Rome for thirty-seven years. One day he disappeared in a thundercloud. The Romans believed that the gods took him to the heavens. At this time the Sabines and Romans had been living together under his rule. The Romans and Sabines could agree on only one man to take the kingship—Numa Pompilius, a Sabine. Numa was a deeply pious man. He had a great respect for the gods and nature. Legend says that he married a nymph named Ēgeria, who imparted to him great wisdom. During the forty-three-year reign of Numa Pompilius Rome knew great peace and prosperity.

Numa Pompilius, *Sabīnus*, *secundus rēx Rōmae* est. Numa est vir bonus et pius. In oppidō *Curēs* habitat. Rōmānī *post mortem Rōmulī* Numam rēgem creāre optant quod est vir optimus. Numa *sīcut* Rōmulus deīs *pārēre* optat. **Sedēns in saxō, ad deōs ōrat ūnā cum augure.** *Iūppiter* signa dat; *itaque* Rōmānī Numam Pompilium *rēgem* dēclārant. Tum Numa sacrificat.

Numa templum *Iānī* aedificat. Templum *fieret* signum *bellī*. *Iānuīs apertīs,* Rōmānī bellum gerēbant; *iānuīs clausīs,* Rōmānī bellum nōn gerēbant et *pāx* erat. Numa quoque annum in *duodecim mēnsēs* dīvidit. *Diēs fāstōs* et *nefāstōs cōnstituit. Sacerdōtēs* creat. **Numa quoque multa sīcut sacerdōs agit.** *Rēx* Numa Pompilius quoque *virginēs Vestālēs* creat. Virginēs flammam sacram *cūrant.* Dum flamma sacra ardet, Rōma tūta erit. *Nōminat duodecim virōs Martī* sacrōs, et virī togam pictam gerunt et scūtum aēneum. Virī in viīs cantābant et saltābant. Uxor Numae erat Ēgeria, nympha. Numam iuvat esse *rēx* bonus Rōmae. Numa *trēs et quādrāgintā annōs* rēgnat.

Notā Bene:
Sedēns in saxō = Sitting on a rock, he prays to the gods along with the augur.
Numa quoque multa sīcut sacerdōs agit = Numa also does many things in the manner of a priest.

GLOSSARY

Numa Pompilius	the second king of Rome
Sabīnus, ī, m.	Sabine
secundus, a, um, adj.	second
rēx Rōmae	king of Rome
Curēs	Cures [the name of a town]
post mortem Rōmulī	after the death of Rōmulus
rēgem, accusative, sing.	king
optimus, a, um, adj.	best
sīcut	just as, like, in the manner of
pāreō, pārēre, + dative object	to obey
ūnā cum augure	along with the augur (priest)
ad, preposition + acc.	to
Iūppiter	Jupiter, the king of the Roman gods; the counterpart to the Greek Zeus
itaque, conj.	and so
Iānī	of Janus [Janus was the two-faced Roman god of doorways and beginnings. Our month of January is named for him.]
fieret	would become
bellī, genitive, sing., n.	of war
iānuīs apertīs	the doors having been opened; *i. e.,* when the doors were open
iānuīs clausīs	the doors having been closed; *i. e.,* when the doors were closed
pāx, nominative, sing., f.	peace

duodecim mēnsēs	twelve months
diēs fāstōs et nefāstōs	"good" and "bad" days [The word *fās* is difficult to translate. It most nearly means something according to the gods' will. *Nefās* would be, then, something against the gods' will.]
constituō, constituere	to establish, set up
sacerdōtēs, accusative plural...............	priests
virginēs Vestālēs, accusative plural.....	Vestal virgins
cūrō, āre...	to care for
nōminō, nōmināre	to appoint
Martī, dative of reference	for Mars
toga picta	*see Culture Corner*
uxor Numae	the wife of Numa
Ēgeria, ae, f.	Egeria
nympha, ae, f......................................	nymph (water deity)
trēs et quādrāgintā annōs....................	for forty-three years

Culture Corner: The Toga Picta and the Shield

The *toga picta* was a brightly colored toga. Some sources translate *picta* as "painted" while others state that the toga was embroidered with brightly colored thread. Later in Roman times, a triumphant general wore the *toga picta* during his triumphal procession.

The Romans believed that the original shield fell from Heaven. They made eleven exact copies of it to lessen the chance of it being stolen. It was shaped "rather like a violin."

Respondē Latīnē:

 1. Quis est Numa?

2. Quālis vir est Numa?

3. Quandō optant Numam rēgem creāre?

4. Cūr optant Numam rēgem creāre?

5. Quis signa dat?

6. Quid Numa aedificat?

7. Quī flammam sacram cūrant?

quis, quī = who?, quālis = what kind of?, quandō = when?, cūr = why?

ANSWER IN ENGLISH!

1. What conditions did the doors of the temple of Janus signify?

2. How did Numa Pompilius affect the Roman calendar?

3. What was unique about the wife of Numa Pompilius?

49

Culture Corner: The Olympians

The Romans were polytheistic, meaning that they believed in many gods. There were many minor deities such as nymphs (water spirits) and dryads (tree spirits). The Romans referred to the major gods as the Olympians because they dwelt on top of Mt. Olympus in Greece. There were, at various times, seventeen different deities considered Olympians; however, there were never more than twelve at a time. The Greeks and Romans named the planets after some of the Olympians, and we still call them by those names today.

The following deities were always considered Olympians. (Their Roman counterparts are in parentheses.)

Zeus (Jupiter) .... ruler of Mt. Olympus, sky god
Hera (Juno) .... wife of Zeus, queen of heaven and stars, goddess of marriage and fidelity
Poseidon (Neptune) .... god of the sea, rivers, springs, floods, and earthquakes
Ares (Mars) .... god of war
Hermes (Mercury) .... messenger of Zeus (Jupiter); god of thieves, travelers, and commerce
Hephaestus (Vulcan) .... blacksmith of the gods
Aphrodite (Venus) .... goddess of love and beauty
Athena (Minerva) .... goddess of wisdom, just warfare, arts and crafts
Apollo (Apollo) .... god of prophecy, healing, disease, music
Artemis (Diana) .... goddess of the hunt

THE VARIABLE DEITIES

Heracles (Hercules) .... son of Zeus and strongest man ever to have lived on earth
Hebe (Hebe) .... daughter of Zeus and Hera who waited upon the gods at Mt. Olympus
Helios (Sol) .... sun god
Hestia (Vesta) .... goddess of hearth and home
Demeter (Ceres) .... goddess of grain and agriculture
Dionysus (Bacchus) .... god of agriculture and wine
Hades (Pluto) .... god of the underworld
Persephone (Proserpina) .... daughter of Demeter, wife of Hades, queen of the underworld

- Hestia gave up her throne to Dionysus (god of agriculture) so that she could live upon earth with mankind.
- Persephone spends three months of each year in the Underworld. (Others say six months.)
- Demeter stayed away from Mt. Olympus when Persephone was in the Underworld.
- Hades, though he was one of the principal Greek gods, had his home in the Underworld.
- Helios gave up his throne to Apollo.
- Hebe was either replaced by Ganymede or gave up her throne to marry Heracles, q. v.
- Heracles became an Olympian upon his death.

Colloquāmur (Let's Talk)

The earliest Romans did not have the concept of a week; however, every ninth day was a market day. Later the Romans called the days of the week after the planets, which were named for their gods. These names influenced the days of the week as we know them today. Some are still called after the Roman names, others after the Norse equivalent.

Diēs Sōlis	= Sun's Day
Diēs Lūnae	= Moon's Day
Diēs Martis	= Mars' Day Norse Mythology: Tyr, god of war.
Diēs Mercuriī	= Mercury's Day Norse Mythology: Woden, cunning god
Diēs Iovis	= Iove's Day (Jupiter) Norse Mythology: Thor, god of thunder
Diēs Veneris	= Venus' Day Norse Mythology: Freya, goddess of love
Diēs Saturnī	= Saturn's Day

Use your knowledge about Roman weekdays and the tenses of *esse* to discuss the days of the week.[E]

Quid est hodiē?	What is today?
Quid erat herī?	What was yesterday?
Quid erit crās?	What will be tomorrow?

[E]In chapter 23 there will be a more in-depth lesson on the Roman Calendar and an optional class project. Practicing the days of the week now (and on a regular basis) will not only be a diverting class activity, but will also help students prepare for this future lesson.

Chapter 7 Teacher's Pages

Exercise 1

de-us, de-ī, m.
flam-ma, flam-mae, f.
scū-tum, scū-tī, n.
sig-num, sig-nī, n.
tem-plum, tem-plī, n.
cre-ō, cre-ā-re, cre-ā-vī, cre-ā-tum
iu-vō, iu-vā-re, iū-vī, iū-tum
op-tō, op-tā-re, op-tā-vī, op-tā-tum
sal-tō, sal-tā-re, sal-tā-vī, sal-tā-tum
sum, es-se, fu-ī, fu-tū-rum

a-ē-ne-us, a-ē-ne-a, a-ē-ne-um
bo-nus, bo-na, bo-num
mag-nus, mag-na, mag-num
mul-tus, mul-ta, mul-tum
pi-us, pi-a, pi-um
sa-cer, sa-cra, sa-crum
tū-tus, tū-ta, tū-tum
tum
quo-que

Exercise 2

longus, -a, -um   stem: long/a

	MASCULINE		FEMININE		NEUTER	
CASE	SINGULAR	PLURAL	SINGULAR	PLURAL	SINGULAR	PLURAL
Nominative	longus	longī	longa	longae	longum	longa
Genitive	longī	longōrum	longae	longārum	longī	longōrum
Dative	longō	longīs	longae	longīs	longō	longīs
Accusative	longum	longōs	longam	longās	longum	longa
Ablative	longō	longīs	longā	longīs	longō	longīs

sacer, -a, -um   stem: sacr/a

	MASCULINE		FEMININE		NEUTER	
CASE	SINGULAR	PLURAL	SINGULAR	PLURAL	SINGULAR	PLURAL
Nominative	sacer	sacrī	sacra	sacrae	sacrum	sacra
Genitive	sacrī	sacrōrum	sacrae	sacrārum	sacrī	sacrōrum
Dative	sacrō	sacrīs	sacrae	sacrīs	sacrō	sacrīs
Accusative	sacrum	sacrōs	sacram	sacrās	sacrum	sacra
Ablative	sacrō	sacrīs	sacrā	sacrīs	sacrō	sacrīs

Exercise 3

1. good town (nominative)   oppidum bonum
2. pious boy (genitive)   puerī piī
3. bronze shields (dative)   scūtīs aēneīs
4. big temple (ablative)   templō magnō
5. sacred flame (accusative)   flammam sacram
6. safe signs (nominative)   signa tūta
7. many poets (accusative)   poētās multōs

Exercise 4

LATIN	TENSE	PERSON	NUMBER	TRANSLATION
eram	Imp.	1	Sing.	I was
eris	Fut.	2	Sing.	You will be
sunt	Pres.	3	Pl.	They are
erāmus	Imp.	1	Pl.	We were
erō	Fut.	1	Sing.	I will be
est	Pres.	3	Sing.	He/she/it is
erātis	Imp.	2	Pl.	You were
sum	Pres.	1	Sing.	I am
eritis	Fut.	2	Pl.	You will be

Exercise 5

1. Agricola est bonus vir.   is a good man.
2. Eram pius puer.   was a pious boy.
3. Templum est sacrum quoque magnum.   is sacred and also great/big.
4. Dum flamma ardet, oppidum erit tūtum.   will be safe.
5. We will be good friends.   Erimus bonī amīcī/bōnae amīcae.
6. The sailors are not many.   nōn sunt multī.
7. They were good men and also god-fearing.   Erant bonī virī et piī quoque.

Translation

Numa Pompilius, a Sabine, is the second king of Rome. Numa is a good man and pious. He lives in the town Cures. The Romans after the death of Romulus wish to elect Numa king because he is the best man. Numa just as Romulus wishes to obey the gods. Sitting on a rock, he prays to the gods along with the augur. Jupiter gives signs; thus the Romans declare Numa Pompilius king. Then Numa makes sacrifices.

Numa builds a temple for Janus. The temple would become a sign of war. The doors having been opened, the Romans were waging war; the doors having been closed, the Romans were not waging war and there was peace. Numa also divides the year into twelve months. He establishes good and bad days. He creates priests. Numa also does many things in the manner of a priest. King Numa Pompilius also creates the Vestal Virgins. The Virgins care for the sacred flame. While the sacred flame burns, Rome will be safe. He names twelve men priests for Mars, and the men wear the toga picta and bronze shield. The men used to sing and dance in the streets. The wife of Numa was Egeria, a nymph. She helps Numa to be a good king for Rome. Numa rules three and forty (forty three) years.

Respondē Latīnē!

1. Quis est Numa?   Who is Numa?
   Numa secundus rēx Rōmae est.   Numa is the second king of Rome.

2. Quālis vir est Numa?   What kind of man is Numa?
   Numa est vir bonus et pius.   Numa is a good and pius man.

3. Quandō optant Numam rēgem creāre?   When do they wish to elect Numa king?
   Post mortem Rōmulī Numam rēgem creāre optant.   After the death of Romulus, they want to elect Numa king.

4. Cūr optant Numam rēgem creāre?   Why do they choose to elect Numa king?
   Numam rēgem creāre optant quod est vir optimus.   They want to elect Numa king because he is the best/ a very good man.

5. Quis signa dat?
Iuppiter signa dat.

Who gives signs?
Jupiter gives signs.

6. Quid Numa aedificat?
Numa templum Ianī aedificat.

What does Numa build?
Numa builds a temple of Janus.

7. Quī flammam sacram cūrant?
Virginēs Vestālēs flammam sacram cūrant.

Who cares for the sacred flame?
The Vestal Virgins care for the sacred flame.

ANSWER IN ENGLISH!

1. What conditions did the doors of the temple of Janus signify?
War and peace

2. How did Numa Pompilius affect the Roman calendar?
He created twelve months and added good and bad days.

3. What was unique about the wife of Numa Pompilius?
Egeria was a nymph (deity).

Notes

Major R.S. Garnett of the U.S. Army designed this seal, which California adopted at her Constitutional Convention in 1849. California became a state the following year. Minerva, Roman goddess of wisdom and war, is the principal figure on this shield. In her right hand she holds a spear. In front of her she holds her shield upon which you can see the

**Eureka!
I found it!**
—California state motto

Uttered by the Greek mathematician, Archimedes, upon discovering a method determining the purity of gold.

head of Medusa. At her feet stands the California grizzly bear, symbol of strength and independence. Minerva seems to watch over the work of a miner nearby digging for gold. A pan and rocker, common tools for those panning for gold, are just beside him. The many ships that sail in the background along the Sacramento River represent Califonia's commercial prosperity. The state motto is not Latin, but Greek, and refers to the excitement created by the California gold rush. This is the only state motto that is in Greek.

Chapter 8

- second conjugation
- perfect tense
  - principal part review

VOCABULARY

VERBS		
clāmō, āre, āvī, ātum	to shout	(clamor, exclaim)
dēsīderō, āre, āvī, ātum	to desire, wish	(desire)
exerceō, exercēre, exercuī, exercitum	to train	(exercise)
habeō, habēre, habuī, habitum	to have, hold; consider	(habit)
moneō, monēre, monuī, monitum	to warn	(admonish)
necō, āre, āvī, ātum	to kill	
parō, āre, āvī, ātum	to prepare, get ready	(preparation)
terreō, terrēre, terruī, territum	to scare, frighten	(terrify)
videō, vidēre, vīdī, vīsum	to see	(video, vision)
vulnerō, āre, āvī, ātum	to wound	(vulnerable)
ADJECTIVES		
laetus, a, um	happy	
validus, a, um	strong	(validity)
vīvus, a, um	living, alive	(vivacious)
vulnerātus, a, um	wounded	
ADVERBS		
deinde	then	
mox	soon	

Chapter 8

52

Exercise 1. Using the rules for syllabication and accent that you have learned, write out the syllables and accents for the vocabulary words above. Then practice pronouncing them aloud.

SECTION 26. Second Conjugation

As you learned in chapter 2, a **conjugation** is a group of verbs that share similar patterns for their endings. Up until now you have learned only first conjugation verbs. Each of these verbs followed a similar pattern with regard to their principal parts and the manner in which you conjugate them in the various tenses. The first conjugation can be recognized by the infinitive which ends in -āre. This infinitive appears only in first conjugation verbs.

The second conjugation has its own unique infinitive which ends in -ēre. It is the only conjugation that will have a long ē as part of the infinitive. You can identify the present stem of a second conjugation verb in the same way as the 1st conjugation. Simply drop the -re from the infinitive.

> **2nd principal part – re = verb stem**
> **habē/re = habē**
> **vidē/re = vidē**

Exercise 2. Identify the stem and conjugation of each of the verbs in the vocabulary list of this section.

In order to conjugate these verbs, simply add the same tense markers and personal endings as you did for the first conjugation. The only difference between these two conjugations is the stem vowel ē. Notice that in the first person singular of the present tense, the stem vowel remains. In the first conjugation the stem vowel ā was absorbed by the -ō ending.

Present Tense: I see, I am seeing, I do see
stem: **vidē/re** + personal endings

PERSON	SINGULAR	PLURAL
1	vide**ō**	vidē**mus**
2	vidē**s**	vidē**tis**
3	vide**t**	vide**nt**

Future Tense: I will see, I will be seeing
stem: **vidē/re** + future tense marker: **-bi-** + personal endings

PERSON	SINGULAR	PLURAL
1	vidē**bō**	vidē**bimus**
2	vidē**bis**	vidē**bitis**
3	vidē**bit**	vidē**bunt**

Imperfect Tense: I was seeing, I used to see
stem: **vidē/re** + imperfect tense marker: **-ba-** + personal endings

PERSON	SINGULAR	PLURAL
1	vidēbam	vidēbāmus
2	vidēbās	vidēbātis
3	vidēbat	vidēbant

ᴮReminder: You can use the conjugation worksheet for this exercise. You can change this up a little by asking students to conjugate one 2nd conjugation verb in all three tenses and one 1st conjugation verb in all three tenses. This will help them become accustomed to seeing both patterns.

TE **Exercise 3.** Following the example of *vidēre,* conjugate the verb *habēre* in all three tenses of the present system. Include the English translations. ᴮ

TE **Exercise 4.** Parse each of the following verbs identifying their tense, person, and number. Then translate them into English.

LATIN	TENSE	PERSON	NUMBER	TRANSLATION
habēbam	**Imp.**	**1**	**Sing.**	**I used to have**
exercet				
creābis				
monēbant				
optābō				
terrētis				
				We leap
				You (pl.) are scaring
				I will warn
				She shouts
				They used to see

SECTION 27. Perfect Tense

Most Latin verbs have four principal parts; some have only three. In chapter 2 the principal parts were explained as follows (Section 5):

1st person present	*amō – I love*	*habeō – I have*
present infinitive	*amāre – to love*	*habēre – to have*
1st person perfect (simple past)	*amāvī – I loved*	*habuī – I had*
past participle (supine)	*amātum – loved*	*habitum – had*

Up until now you have used only the first two principal parts; the first for reference, and the second to form the stem of the present system. The third principal part provides the stem for the tenses of the perfect system (perfect, pluperfect, and future perfect). In order to identify the perfect stem used to conjugate the various tenses of the perfect system, simply drop the final -ī from the third principal part.

3rd principal part – ī = perfect stem
amāv/ī = amāv
habu/ī = habu

Chapter 8

54

Exercise 5. Following the examples of *amāre* and *habēre* below, identify the perfect stem for each of the verbs in the vocabulary list of this chapter.

The perfect tense in Latin corresponds with the simple past or past emphatic in English.

> *amāvī = I loved, I have loved, I did love*
> *habuī = I had, I have had, I did have*

The perfect tense portrays a past action that has been completed *(perfectus)*, whereas the imperfect tense (Section 11) portrays a past action that was ongoing or incomplete *(imperfectus)*. In order to form the perfect tense simply add on this special set of personal endings to the perfect stem. The perfect tense is the only tense that uses this set of endings; therefore it should be fairly easy to identify. Even the irregular verbs such as *esse* are consistent in using this same set of endings.

PERSON	SINGULAR	PLURAL
1	habu-**ī** I had	habu-**imus** we had
2	habu-**istī** you had	habu-**istis** you (pl.) had
3	habu-**it** he/she/it had	habu-**ērunt** they had

Exercise 6. Following the example of *habēre* given above, conjugate *vidēre, esse,* and *labōrāre* in the perfect tense.

Exercise 7. Identify the person and number of the following perfect tense verbs. Then translate.

1. amāvistis
2. habuimus
3. fuēruntne?
4. nāvigāvit
5. parāvistī

6. I gave
7. Did he shout?
8. We called
9. They fought
10. You (pl.) built

Exercise 8. Parse, diagram, and translate the following sentences.

1. Multī puerī pugnāvērunt.

2. Puer exercēre parat.

3. Amīcus bonus sociōs monēbit.

4. Socius vulnerātus nōn erat laetus.

5. The happy men were shouting.

6. Did you see the great shield?

7. The girls did not want to exercise.

8. The friends have been good allies.

THE HORĀTIĪ AND THE CŪRIĀTIĪ

When Numa Pompilius, a religious man, died, Rome for a while had no king. Historians call such a period between kings an interregnum. Then the people declared Tullus Hostīlius king. According to the historian Livy, he reigned from 672–641 BC. Hostīlius was a warlike man who, according to Livy, "everywhere sought excuses for stirring up war." At this time, the Romans and the Albans were stealing each other's cattle. The king at Alba was Gāius Cluilius. Both kings sent ambassadors to the other side. Restitution was the demand of both groups of ambassadors. When the Albans refused, the Romans declared a state of war.

Soon after all this, Cluilius died and the Albans made Mettius Fufetius dictator. Tullus Hostīlius, inclined by nature to war and anticipating victory, was willing for the Romans to meet the Albans in battle. It was Tullus who, when the armies seemed stalemated over broken treaties, suggested that representatives from each army fight for the whole city-state. A set of triplet brothers from each group stepped forward.

Forte in ambōbus oppidīs erant germānī trigeminī. Nōmina Rōmānōrum erant Horātiī, Albānōrum Cūriātiī. Hostīlius et rēx Albānus dēsīderāvērunt germānōs trigeminōs prō ambōbus oppidīs pugnāre. Cōnsentiēbant.

Sex puerī prō virīs cucurrērunt et pugnāvērunt. Albānī duōs ē Rōmānīs mox necāvērunt. Albānī laetī clāmāvērunt. Rōmānus vīvus parāvit pugnāre Cūriātiōs, singulōs. Rōmānus cucurrit, et Albānī post eum cucurrērunt. Rōmānus ūnum ex Albānīs necāvit dum aliī procul fuērunt, deinde secundum. Clāmāvit, "Duōs germānōs Mānibus dedī; tertium . . . [Mānibus] causā bellī dabō." Cūriātius vulnerātus nōn erat validus, et Rōmānus tertium germānum necāvit. Hōc modō, Rōmānī victōrēs fuērunt.

GLOSSARY

forte	by chance
ambōbus	both
trigeminus, a, um, adj.	triplet
nōmina, nom., pl., n.	names
Rōmānōrum	of the Romans
Albānōrum	of the Albans
rēx, nominative, sing., m.	king
cōnsentiō, cōnsentīre	to consent, agree to
prō + ablative	in front of
sex, indeclinable adj.	six
currō, currere, cucurrī, cursum	to run
duōs ē + ablative	two of
singulōs	one at a time
post eum	after him
unum ex + ablative	one of
aliī	the others
procul, adv.	far, at a distance
secundus, a, um, adj.	second
prope, prep. + ablative	near
duo, dua, duo, adj.	two
Mānibus	to the Shades (spirits of the dead)
tertius, a, um, adj.	third
causā bellī	for the sake of war
hōc modō	in this way
victōrēs, nom., pl., m.	victors

Respondē Latīnē:

 1. Quī sunt trigeminī Rōmānī?

2. Quī sunt trigeminī Albānī?

3. Quid rēx Albānus dēsīderāvit?

4. Quid sex puerī fēcērunt?

quī = who?, quid = what?, quid fēcērunt = what did they do?

ANSWER IN ENGLISH!

1. How did the single Roman manage to defeat the three Alban brothers?

2. What did the Roman mean by the phrase "I give the brothers to the Shades?"

3. Who won the war as a result of the battle between the Horatii and the Curiatii?

Colloquāmur (Let's Talk)

Use the following questions and responses to review the parsing exercise above. Use some "eye" Latin to figure out what the responses mean.

interrogātiō:	Cūius est numerī?	What number is it?
respōnsum:	Singulāriter est.	
	Plūrāliter est.	

interrogātiō:	Cūius est persōnae?	What person is it?
respōnsum:	Est prīmae persōnae.	
	Est secundae persōnae.	
	Est tertiae persōnae.	

interrogātiō:	Cūius est temporis?	What tense (time) is it?
respōnsum:	Est praesentis.	
	Est imperfectī.	
	Est futūrī.	
	Est perfectī.	

More than 60% of our English vocabulary derives from Latin. Often these are the more elevated words in our dictionary. Knowing Latin and being familiar with its vocabulary will enable you to decipher the meaning of some pretty fancy speech. The two rules for detecting derivatives are 1) it must look similar to the Latin verb it derives from, and 2) it must have a meaning related to the Latin origin.

The following is a list of English words that derive from the Latin verbs in this chapter's vocabulary list. Figure out which verb each one derives from and make an educated guess as to its meaning. Then look up the word in an English dictionary and compose a sentence for each one.

terrific	internecine
evident	premonition
provide	parry
exhibit	deter
desideratum	revise

For Discussion:

How are the meanings of these derivatives related to their Latin origin?

Chapter 8 Teacher's Pages

Exercise 1

clā-mō, ā-re, ā-vī, ā-tum
dē-sī-de-rō, ā-re, ā-vī, ā-tum
ex-er-ce-ō, ex-er-cē-re, ex-er-cu-ī, ex-er-ci-tum
ha-be-ō, ha-bē-re, ha-bu-ī, ha-bi-tum
mo-ne-ō, mo-nē-re, mo-nu-ī, mo-ni-tum
ne-cō, ā-re, ā-vī, ā-tum
pa-rō, ā-re, ā-vī, ā-tum
ter-reō, ter-rē-re, ter-ru-ī, ter-ri-tum

vi-de-ō, vi-dē-re, vī-dī, vī-sum
vul-ne-rō, ā-re, ā-vī, ā-tum
lae-tus, a, um
va-li-dus, a, um
vī-vus, a, um
vul-ne-rā-tus, a, um dein-de
mox

Exercise 2

clāmō, āre, āvī, ātum
dēsīderō, āre, āvī, ātum
exerceō, exercēre, exercuī, exercitum
habeō, habēre, habuī, habitum
moneō, monēre, monuī, monitum
necō, āre, āvī, ātum
parō, āre, āvī, ātum
terreō, terrēre, terruī, territum
videō, vidēre, vīdī, vīsum
vulnerō, āre, āvī, ātum

clāmā/re—1st conjugation
desiderā/re—1st conjugation
exercē/re—2nd conjugation
habē/re—2nd conjugation
monē/re—2nd conjugation
necā/re—1st conjugation
parā/re—1st conjugation
terrē/re—2nd conjugation
vidē/re—2nd conjugation
vulnerā/re—1st conjugation

Exercise 3

PERSON	PRESENT		FUTURE		IMPERFECT	
	SINGULAR	PLURAL	SINGULAR	PLURAL	SINGULAR	PLURAL
1	*habeō* I have	*habēmus* we have	*habēbō* I will have	*habēbimus* we will have	*habēbam* I used to have	*habēbamus* you (pl.) used to have
2	*habēs* you have	*habētis* you (pl.) have	*habēbis* you will have	*habēbitis* you (pl.) will have	*habēbas* you used to have	*habēbatis* we used to have
3	*habet* he/she/it has	*habent* they have	*habēbit* he/she/it/will have	*habēbunt* they will have	*habēbat* he/she/it used to have	*habēbant* they used to have

Exercise 4

LATIN	TENSE	PERSON	NUMBER	TRANSLATION
habēbam	Imp.	1	Sing.	I used to have
exercet	Pres.	3	Sing.	He trains
creābis	Fut.	2	Sing.	You will create/elect

a

monēbant	Imp.	3	Pl.	They were warning
optābō	Fut.	1	Sing.	I will wish/desire
terrētis	Pres.	2	Pl.	You scare/frighten
saltāmus	Pres.	1	Pl.	We leap/dance
terrētis	Pres.	2	Pl.	You (pl.) are scaring
monēbō	Fut.	1	Sing.	I will warn
clāmat	Pres.	3	Sing.	She shouts
vidēbant	Imp.	3	Pl.	They used to see

Exercise 5

clāmō, āre, āvī, ātum	clāmāv/ī
dēsīderō, āre, āvī, ātum	dēsīderāv/ī
exerceō, exercēre, exercuī, exercitum	exercu/ī
habeō, habēre, habuī, habitum	habu/ī
moneō, monēre, monuī, monitum	monu/ī
necō, āre, āvī, ātum	necāv/ī
parō, āre, āvī, ātum	parāv/ī
terreō, terrēre, terruī, territum	terru/ī
videō, vidēre, vīdī, vīsum	vīd/ī
vulnerō, āre, āvī, ātum	vulnerāv/ī

Exercise 6

PRINCIPAL PART	videō, vidēre, vīdī, vīsum		sum, esse, fuī		labōrāre, āre, āvī, ātum	
PERFECT STEM	vīd/ī		fu/ī		labōrā/vī	
PERSON	SINGULAR	PLURAL	SINGULAR	PLURAL	SINGULAR	PLURAL
1	vīd-ī	vīd-imus	fu-ī	fu-imus	labōrāv-ī	labōrāv-imus
2	vīd-istī	vīd-istis	fu-istī	fu-istis	labōrāv-istī	labōrāv-istis
3	vīd-it	vīd-ērunt	fu-it	fu-ērunt	labōrāv-it	labōrāv-ērunt

Exercise 7

1. amāvistis	2, pl. –	you have loved, you loved
2. habuimus	1, pl. –	we have had, we had, we did have
3. fuēruntne?	3, pl. –	have they been? were they?
4. nāvigāvit	3, sing. –	he sailed, she has sailed, it did sail
5. parāvistī	2, sing. –	you have prepared, you prepared, you did prepare
6. I gave	1, sing. –	dedī
7. Did he shout?	3, sing. –	clāmāvitne?
8. We called	1, pl. –	vocāvimus
9. They fought	3, pl. –	pugnāvērunt
10. You (pl.) built	2, pl. –	aedificāvistis

Encourage a variety of translations. Remember: There is more than one way to skin a cat – and to translate these verbs into English.

Exercise 8

```
        Adj    S        V
```
1. Multī puerī pugnāvērunt.
```
   n/p/m n/p/m    3/p/perf
```
Many boys fought/have fought/did fight.

```
        S    Inf      V
```
2. Puer exercēre parat.
```
   n/s/m         3/s/pres
```
The boy prepares/is preparing/does prepare to train.

```
        S    Adj    DO       V
```
3. Amīcus bonus sociōs monēbit.
```
   n/s/m  n/s/m ac/p/m   3/s/f
```
The good friend will warn the allies.

```
        S       Adj     Adv   V      PrN
```
4. Socius vulnerātus nōn erat laetus.
```
   n/s/m    n/s/m         3/s/imp n/s/m
```
The wounded ally was not happy.

```
        Adj   S      V
```
5. The happy men were shouting.
```
   Laetī    virī   clāmābant.
   n/p/m   n/p/m    3/p/imp
```

```
        S    V       Adj   DO
```
6. Did you see the great shield?
```
   Vīdistīne magnum  scūtum?
   2/s/perf    ac/s/n    ac/s/n
```

```
        S       Adv  V   Inf
```
7. The girls did not want to exercise.
```
   Puellae exercēre nōn optāvērunt.
   n/p/f          3/p/perf
```

```
        S      V      Adj  PrN
```
8. The friends have been good allies.
```
   Amīcī fuērunt  bonī  sociī.
   n/p/m 3/p/perf n/p/m n/p/m
```

It sometimes helps students to underline an entire "verb phrase" as seen above in order to remind them that the helping verbs are a part of the main verb in Latin. They do not need to translate the English verbs separately.

Translation

By chance there were triplet brothers in both towns. The names of the Romans were Horatii, (the names) of the Albans (were) Curiatii. Hostilius and the Alban King desired the triplet brothers to fight on behalf of both towns. They agreed.

Six boys ran and fought on behalf of the men. The Albans soon killed two of the Romans. The happy Albans shouted. The living Roman prepared to fight the Curiatii, one at a time. The Roman ran, and the Albans ran after him. The Roman killed one of the Albans while the other was far off, then the second. He shouted, "I gave two brothers to the shades; I will give the third [to the Shades] for the sake of war." The wounded Curiatius was not strong, and the Roman killed the third brother. In this way, the Romans were the victors.

Respondē Latīnē!

1. Quī sunt trigeminī Rōmānī?
   Horātiī sunt trigeminī Rōmānī.

   Who are the triplet Romans?
   The Horātiī are the triplet Romans.

2. Quī sunt trigeminī Albānī?
   Cūriātiī sunt trigeminī Albānī.

   Who are the Alban triplets?
   The Cūriātiī are the Alban triplets.

3. Quid rēx Albānus dēsīderāvit?
   Albānus rēx dēsīderāvit germānos trigeminōs prō ambōbus oppidīs pugnāre.

   What did the Alban king desire?
   The Alban king desired the triplet brothers to fight on behalf of both cities.

4. Quid sex puerī fēcērunt?
   Sex puerī prō virīs pugnāvērunt.

   What did the six boys do?
   The six boys fought on behalf of the men.

ANSWER IN ENGLISH!

1. How did the single Roman manage to defeat the three Alban brothers?
   He ran and they ran after him, separating them out so he could fight each one individually.

2. What did the Roman mean by the phrase "I give the brothers to the Shades?"
   It means that he sent them to the spirits of the dead, or killed them.

3. Who won the war as a result of the battle between the Horatii and the Curiatii?
   The Romans won.

Derivative Detective

terrific	terreō	causing great fear
evident	videō	easy to see
provide	videō	to get ready beforehand
exhibit	habeō	to present
desideratum	dēsīderō	something needed
internecine	necō	harmful to both sides
premonition	moneō	warning in advance
parry	parō	to ward off or deflect
deter	terreō	to discourage
revise	videō	to read carefully

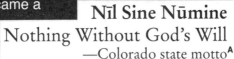

Nīl Sine Nūmine
Nothing Without God's Will
—Colorado state motto[A]

This phrase was drawn from Vergil's Aeneid, Book II, line 777. The Latin reads:
. . . nōn haec sine nūmine devum ēveniunt.

Chapter 9

- ablative case, uses without prepositions (by, with, from)
  - means/instrument
  - manner
  - separation

VOCABULARY

NOUNS

arma, armōrum, n. pl.	weapons, arms	(armor, arms)
carrus, carrī, m.	wagon, cart, chariot	(cart)
cōpiae, cōpiārum, f. pl.	troops	(copious)
frūmentum, frūmentī, n.	grain	
gaudium, gaudiī, n.	joy	
grātia, grātiae, f.	thanks, gratitude	(gratitude, grateful)
rēgia, rēgiae, f.	palace	(regal)
studium, studiī, n.	zeal, eagerness	(studious)

VERBS

careō, carēre, caruī, caritūrum (+ abl. of separation)	to be without, to be deprived of, want, lack; be free from	
līberō, līberāre, līberāvī, līberātum	to free	(liberate)
lūdificō, lūdificāre, lūdificāvī, lūdificātum	to fool	(ludicrous)
prohibeō, prohibēre, prohibuī, prohibitum	to keep (back), prevent	(prohibit)

ADJECTIVES

mortuus, a, um	dead	(mortuary)
optimus, a, um	best	(optimum)

ADVERBS

nunc	now	
ubī	when	

Exercise 1. Using the rules for syllabication and accent that you have learned, write out the syllables and accents for the vocabulary words above. Then practice pronouncing them aloud.

SECTION 28. The Ablative Case

The ablative case is generally easy to recognize when reading Latin. The singular form always consists of a single vowel, often long. The plural form is either -īs (as in the first and second declensions) or -ibus. While easy to recognize, this case sometimes proves more difficult to translate, for it may take on a wide variety of meanings. However, the use of the English prepositions "by, with, from" will often take care of the more common uses:

1. means / instrument

This construction indicates the "thing" *by* or *with* which something is accomplished. The Romans never used this construction for a person or animal. Using the phrase *by means of* is often a good way to recognize this construction.

Armīs **pugnant.**	They fight *with weapons.*
Carrō **frūmentum portāvit.**	He carried the grain *by (means of a) cart.*

2. manner

This construction expresses the manner or the attitude with which something was accomplished. When an adjective is included in this construction a Latin preposition is not needed.

Magnā Gratiā **ōrāmus.**	We pray *with great gratitude.*
Multō Gaudiō **clāmat.**	He shouts *with much joy.*

3. separation

This construction expresses that some person or thing is separated from another. The ablative of separation is commonly used with certain verbs meaning "to free," "to lack," and "to deprive."

Oppidō **cōpiās prohibuit.**	He kept the troops *from the town.*
Agrī frūmentīs **carent.**	The fields are lacking *grain.*

Exercise 2. Identify examples of separation, manner, and means in the reading below. Do not translate.

Ancus Marcius

The fourth king of Rome was Ancus Marcius, the grandson of Numa Pompilius. Like his grandfather, Ancus Marcius loved peace and ruled with great piety. Since Marcius was such a peaceful ruler, the neighboring tribe called the Latins began to plunder the country around Rome. The peaceful king immediately took his place at the head of the Roman army to defend his people from the Latins. The Romans fought with great valor and overcame the Latin tribe by the sword. The king took the prisoners with him back to Rome and allowed them to settle on the Aventine Hill.

Up until this time those who broke the law were banished from the city. Ancus Marcius built the first prison under the Capitoline Hill, known today as the Mamertine. It has only two rooms: one above and one below. You could reach the lower room only by a small opening in the floor. The prisoners remained in the lower room and their guard in the upper. It is thought that the Apostle Paul was kept prisoner here while he awaited trial in Rome.

In order to protect Rome from other enemies, Ancus Marcius built the first bridge across the Tiber called the Pōns Sublicius. The bridge joined Rome to the Jāniculum Hill. This bridge was built with wooden beams placed loosely together so that it might be taken apart quickly if an enemy were to attack. Mārcus also sought to protect the Romans' ability to trade by a secure route to the sea. He fought the tribes who lived between Rome and the sea, and took their lands from them. He then founded the port city of Ostia, which remained an important port of trade for Rome for centuries to come.

Exercise 3. Identify the case and function of the underlined words and phrases. Then translate the sentences into English.

1. Lūdificatne rēgīna fīliōs?

2. Virōs bonōs armīs necant.

3. Oppidum frūmentum cōpiīs dedit.

4. Cōpiae malum virum rēgiā prohibent.

5. Aedificābant templum Diānae.

6. Agricolam vir malus necāvit.

7. Sociī pātriae pugnāvērunt magnō studiō.

Exercise 4. Diagram the following English sentences, and then parse each word. Take care to identify the new ablative phrases you have learned. Then translate into Latin.

1. The farmer was without a wagon.

2. The troops will fight with arms.

3. We sing with thanks to God.

4. God will free men from evil.

5. Did the farmer train the horse with a cart?

6. He will build a temple with great joy.

Chapter Reading ^B

ᴮAs you translate through these stories with students watch for opportunities to reinforce constructions you have learned. Ask questions such as "Do you see an ablative of means?" or "What kind of construction do you see in this sentence?" or "How is this dative noun functioning here?"

SERVIUS TULLIUS: THE SIXTH KING OF ROME
CHARACTERS:
Servius Tullius – Sixth king of Rome
Tarquinius Priscus – Fifth king of Rome
Tanaquil – wife of Tarquinius Priscus, queen of Rome
Tarquinius Superbus – son of Tarquinius Priscus, son-in-law of Servius Tullius

Servius Tullius est *rēx Rōmae sextus*. Servius est *probābiliter* vir Latīnus, nōn Ētruscus. *Probābiliter* nōn est fīlius *servae*. Aedificat templum Diānae *in monte Aventīnō* magnō gaudiō.

Ubī Tarquinius Priscus, *quīntus rēx Rōmae*, periit, rēgīna Tanaquil **negat rēgem mortuum esse**. *Hōc modō* Tanaquil fīliōs *Tarquiniī lūdificat*. Fīliōs *Tarquiniī* rēgiā prohibet. Servius, nōn fīlius *Tarquiniī*, est *rēx* post Tarquinium Priscum.

Post multōs annōs fīliī *Tarquiniī* habent **uxōrēs, fīliās Serviī Tullī**. *Ūnus ē fīliīs* bonus est, *ūnus* malus. **Ūna ē fīliābus Tullī** bona est, *ūna* mala. *Duo* malī *duōs* bonōs armīs necant. Tum, malus fīlius malam fīliam **in mātrimōnium dūcit**. Servium Tullium vir malus necat, et fīlia *Serviī*, fēmina mala, carrō *super corpus* agit. Tarquinius malus nunc rēx est.

Notā Bene:

negat rēgem mortuum esse = denies that the king is dead

This is an advanced construction called indirect statement. You will learn about indirect statement later on. Briefly, an indirect statement tells what someone says without using a direct quotation. In English indirect statements often, but not always, begin with *that*. This indirect statement, then, may be translated as "[denies] that the king has died." *Negat* (denies) is not part of the indirect statement.

Direct Statement: [She] says, "The king has not died."
Indirect Statement: She denies that the king has died.

uxōrēs, filiās Servī Tullī = wives, the daughters of Servius Tullius (The daughters of Servius Tullius married the sons of Tarquinius Priscus.)
Ūna ē filiābus Tarquinī = One of the daughters of Tarquin
in mātrimōnium dūcit = marries; literally, "leads into matrimony"

GLOSSARY

rēx Rōmae	king of Rome
sextus, a, um, adj.	sixth
probābiliter, adv.	probably
Ētruscus, a, um, adj.	Etruscan
servae, genitive, sing., f.	of a slave woman
in monte Aventīnō	on the Aventine Hill
quīntus, a, um, adj.	fifth
periit	died
hōc modō	in this way
Tarquiniī, genitive, sing., nom....	of Tarquinius
uxor, nom., sing., fem.	wife
uxōrēs, filiās Serviī Tullī	[The daughters of Servius Tullius married the sons of Tarquinius Priscus.]
ūnus, a, um, numerical adj.	one
ē filiīs	out of the sons; hence, "one of the sons"
e filiābus	of the daughters
duo, dua, duo	numerical adj. two
Serviī, genitive, sing., m.	of Servius
super corpus	over or above the body
agō, agere	to drive

Respondē Latīnē:

1. Quis est sextus rēx Rōmae?

2. Cuī templum in monte rēx aedificat?

3. Quālis vir Servium Tullium necat?

4. Quis est rēx post Servium Tullium?

5. Lūdificābatne Tanaquil filiōs Tarquiniī?
(Hint: See *Colloquāmur* in chapter 2 for an answer to this question.)

quis = who?, cuī = for whom?, quālis = what kind of?

Colloquāmur (Let's Talk)

Use the following questions and responses to review the nouns in the sentences above. Use some "eye" Latin to figure out what the responses mean.

interrogātiō:	**Cūius est numerī?**	What number is it?
respōnsum:	**Singulāriter est.**	
	Plūrāliter est.	
interrogātiō:	**Quō est cāsū?**	In what case is it?
respōnsum:	**Cāsū nōminātīvō est.**	
	Cāsū accūsātīvō est.	
	Cāsū datīvō est.	
	Cāsū ablātīvō est.	

Culture Corner

The latter Kings of Rome were actually from the neighboring Etruscan tribe. The Romans adopted many Etruscan traditions including the *fascēs*, a symbol of the power and authority of the king. After the Romans expelled their last king, other leaders and magistrates continued to use the traditional symbol. Lictors, special attendants, would often carry it before them in processions.

The axe symbolizes the power of the king or state. It is bound to a bundle of rods, which symbolizes strength through the unity of many (*ē plūribus ūnum*). The binding of the rods is also meant to symbolize the restraint that must be exercised with the power of authority. The king, or later magistrate, might have his lictor unbind the rods to warn offenders that restraint was nearing an end.

You can see the *fascēs* today in many places across the United States of America. Colorado has placed this symbol in the middle of its seal. The *fascēs* appear on the Lincoln Memorial in Washington D.C., as well as President Lincoln's memorial at Gettysburg. The *fascēs* are present in the chambers of both the U.S. Senate and the House of Representatives. A Roman Centurion holding the *fascēs* adorns the front edifice of the Supreme Court. Why do you think these are appropriate places for this classical symbol?

Chapter 9 Teacher's Pages

Exercise 1

ar-ma, ar-mō-rum, n. pl.
car-rus, car-rī, m.
cō-pi-ae, cō-pi-ā-rum, f. pl.
frū-men-tum, frū-men-tī, n.
gau-di-um, gau-di-ī, n.
grā-ti-a, grā-ti-ae, f.
rē-gi-a, rē-gi-ae, f.
stu-di-um, stu-di-ī, n.

ca-re-ō, ca-rē-re, ca-ru-ī, ca-ri-tū-rum
lī-be-rō, lī-be-rā-re, lī-be-rā-vī, lī-be-rā-tum
lū-di-fi-cō, lū-di-fi-cā-re, lū-di-fi-cā-vī, lū-di-fi-cā-tum
pro-hi-be-ō, pro-hi-bē-re, pro-hi-bu-ī, pro-hi-bi-tum
mor-tu-us, a, um
op-ti-mus, a, um
nunc
u-bi

Exercise 2

with great piety. (manner)

from the Latins. (separation)

with great valor (manner)

by the sword. (means)

from the city. (separation)

by a small opening (means)

from other enemies (separation)

with wooden beams (means)

by a secure route (means)

from them. (separation)

Exercise 3

1. Lūdificatne rēgīna fīliōs?   accusative, direct object
   Does the queen fool the sons? Is the queen fooling . . .?

2. Virōs bonōs armīs necant.   ablative, means
   They kill the good men with (by means of) arms.

3. Oppidum frūmentum cōpiīs dedit.   dative, indirect object
   The town gave grain to the troops.

4. Cōpiae malum virum rēgiā prohibent.   ablative, separation
   The troops keep the bad man from the palace.

5. Aedificābant templum Diānae.   dative, reference
   They were building a temple for Diana.

6. Agricolam vir malus necāvit.   nominative, subject
   The bad man killed the farmer.

7. Sociī pātriae pugnāvērunt magnō studiō.   ablative, manner
   The allies fought with great zeal for the country.

Exercise 4

```
          S     V        AbS
```
1. The farmer was without a wagon.
   Agricola   carrō   carēbat.
   n/s/m   ab/s/m   3/s/imp

```
          S      V       AbMe
```
2. The troops will fight with arms.
   Cōpiae pugnābunt armīs.
   n/p/f   3/p/f   ab/p/n

```
        S    V    AbMa     DR
```
3. We <u>sing</u> with thanks to God.
   Cantāmus cum grātiīs Deō.
   1/p/p   ab/p/f d/s/m

```
      S      V    DO    AbS
```
4. God <u>will free</u> men from evil.
   Deus līberābit virōs   malō.
   n/s/m 3/s/f ac/p/m ab/s/m

```
              S    V    DO    AbMe
```
5. Did the farmer <u>train</u> the horse with a cart?
   Exercuitne agricola equum carrō?
   3/s/perf   n/s/m ac/s/m ab/s/m

```
      S    V     DO    AbMa
```
6. He <u>will build</u> a temple with great joy.
   Aedificābit templum magnō gaudiō.
   3/s/f   ac/s/n ab/s/n ab/s/n

Encourage students to underline the whole verb phrase as seen here in the answer key. This will help them to remember that the English helping verb is included within the Latin verb.

Translation

Servius Tullius is the sixth king of Rome. Servius is probably a Latin man, not an Etruscan. He is probably not the son of a slave. He builds a temple to Diana on the Aventine hill with great joy.

When Tarquinius Priscus, the fifth king of Rome died, queen Tanaquil denied that the king had died. In this way Tanaquil fools the sons of Tarquin. She keeps the sons of Tarquin from the palace. Servius, not the son of Tarquin, is king after Tarquinius Priscus.

After many years the sons of Tarquin have wives, the daughters of Servius Tullius. One of the sons is good, one bad. One of the daughters of Tullius is good, one bad. The two bad kill the two good with arms. Then, the bad son marries the bad daughter. The bad man kills Servius Tullius, and the daughter of Servius, the bad woman, drives over the body with a cart. The bad Tarquinius is now king.

Respondē Latīnē!

1. Quis est sextus rēx Rōmae? (Who is the sixth king of Rome?)
   Servius Tullius est rēx Rōmae sextus. Servius Tullius is the sixth king of Rome.

2. Cuī templum in monte rēx aedificat? (For whom does the king build a temple on the hill?)
   Aedificat templum Diānae. He builds a temple for Diana.

3. Quālis vir Servium Tullium necat? (What kind of a man kills Servius Tullius?)
   Servium Tullium vir malus necat. A bad man kills Servius Tullius.

4. Quis est rēx post Servium Tullium? (Who is king after Servius Tullius?)
   Malus Tarquinius est rēx. The bad Tarquin is king.

5. Lūdificābatne Tanaquil fīliōs Tarquiniī? (Does Tanaquil fool/trick the sons of Tarquin?)
   Sīc est! Yes! [lit., It is so!]

Unit 2 Reading

Reading and Review for Chapters 7–9

PART ONE
THE PATHS TO KINGSHIP
Gaylan DuBose

During the reign of Ancus Marcius, the fourth king at Rome, an Etruscan named Lucumo came to Rome to live. This Lucumo was the son of Demaratus of Corinth (a Greek city), and because of his parentage, he had little or no hope in gaining prominence among the Etruscans. Demaratus had two sons, Lucumo and Arruns. Only Lucumo survived his father. Demaratus died not knowing that he was to be a grandfather; and so he made no provisions in his will for any grandchildren. Therefore, when a grandson was born to the widow of Arruns, he received the name of Egerius. (This name derives from *egēre*—to be in need—and we could interpret it as something like "Penniless.") Lucumo was then heir to the whole estate of his father Demaratus.

The wealthy Lucumo married Tanaquil, "a woman of the most exalted birth, and not of a character lightly to endure a humbler rank . . . ," according to Livy. Tanaquil had the idea of moving out of Etruscan territory and into Rome. When the pair arrived at the Janiculum and were sitting in their covered wagon, an eagle descended and took Lucumo's cap from his head. The eagle rose noisily with the cap in its beak and then descended and placed the cap back on Lucumo's head. Tanaquil interpreted this omen to mean that Lucumo was the subject of divine approval. In Rome, Lucumo assumed the name of Lucius Tarquinius or, as Livy assumed, Lucius Tarquinius Priscus. As Lucius Tarquinius he became involved in the politics of Rome and even advised King Ancus.

King Ancus ruled for twenty-four years. Lucius Tarquinius had the king's two grown sons sent out of town on a hunting trip, and he successfully campaigned for the kingship. He was the first man to seek rule at Rome actively. Lucius Tarquinius Priscus led the Romans through much warfare.

Near the end of one war, there was living in the king's house a child named Servius Tullius. As this boy lay sleeping, his head burst into flames in the sight of many. Even the king and queen rushed to see this portent. When a servant tried to put out the flames, Queen Tanaquil insisted that the boy be allowed to remain asleep and that the flames not be doused. When Servius awoke on his own, the flames went out. Tanaquil interpreted this omen to mean that Servius would one day be a protector to her and Lucius's royal house. From that moment, Tanaquil began to look upon Servius Tullius as a son.

Lucius Tarquinius Priscus ruled about thirty-eight years. By the end of his reign, nearly everyone in Rome held Servius Tullius in high regard. The sons of the late King Ancus Marcius resented the reign of Lucius and the influence and popularity of Servius Tullius. These sons arranged the murder of Lucius

Tarquinius Priscus. There was an uproar among the witnesses of the axe murder; Tanaquil ordered the palace to be closed off. She ordered all the witnesses ejected. She summoned Servius Tullius and told him that he alone deserved to succeed Lucius Tarquinius. Tanaquil announced to the people that Lucius was badly wounded but not dead. She ordered the people to obey the commands of Servius Tullius while the king recovered, and Servius did render some judgments. When the authorities arrested the agents of murder hired by Ancus's sons, the sons went into voluntary exile.

PART TWO
THE REIGN AND DEATH OF SERVIUS TULLIUS

Servius Tullius knew that he must solidify and protect his power; therefore, he married his two daughters to Lucius and Arruns Tarquinius, the sons of Tarquinius Priscus. Lucius was of violent temper and great ambition; Arruns was of peaceful temper and little ambition. One daughter of Tullius was gentle; one was ruthless and ambitious. Each young man was married to the young woman opposite him in temperament. The headstrong Tullia turned from her gentle husband to his brother. She also despised her gentle sister. The spouses of the ruthless ones died suspiciously and close together, and the ruthless ones married. Tullia looked forward to another crime. She goaded her husband into action.

Lucius Tarquinius went about and drummed up support especially among the lesser families. He gave gifts. He bribed. When he judged the time right, he surrounded himself with armed men and sat down upon the throne, summoning all to come to see King Tarquinius at the senate house. While Lucius addressed the people, Servius Tullius came and challenged the man sitting upon the throne. Lucius, enraged and perhaps desperate, grabbed his father-in-law and threw him down the steps of the senate house. Stunned, the king tried to get home; but the henchmen of Lucius Tarquinius killed him on the way there.

Assured that her father was dead, Tullia drove to the senate house to be the first to greet her husband as king. On her way back home, seeing the corpse of her father, she drove her chariot over it. This action contaminated and defiled this already evil woman. It is said that bits of her father's flesh clung to the wheels of the chariot. Servius Tullius had ruled forty-four years. Then the tyrant Lucius Tarquinius, who afterwards received the name Superbus, ruled Rome.

PART THREE
EXPULSION OF THE TYRANT

CHARACTERS:

Tarquinius Superbus	– last king of Rome, who murdered his father-in-law Servius Tullius in order to be king. His character earned him the cognomen Superbus, "proud."
Sextus Tarquinius	– son of Tarquinius Superbus
Tarquinius Collātīnus	– Roman nobleman
Lūcrētia	– virtuous wife of Tarquinius Collatinus
Lūcius Iūnius Brūtus	– Roman nobleman, friend to Tarquinius Collatinus
Lars Porsenna	– king of the Etruscans, ally to Tarquinius Priscus
Mamilius Octāvius	– son-in-law to Tarquinius Superbus
Castor & Pollux	– deified twin brothers

POST ULTIMUM TYRANNUM: Tarquinium Superbum ᴀ

1.   *Ultimus tyrannus* Rōmae erat Tarquinius Superbus. Quod fīlius *tyrannī*, Sextus
2. Tarquinius, fēminae bonae, Lūcrētiae, *nocuit*, Rōmānī īrātī *tyrannum cum* familiā *ex*
3. oppidō armīs *expulērunt*. Rōmānī Sextum *Gabiī* necāvērunt, sed *pater* et germānī Sextī
4. *fūgērunt* ad alium oppidum. *Duo* virī, Brūtus et Collātīnus, erant nunc *cōnsulēs*.
5.   Tarquinius Superbus oppugnāvit Rōmānōs *prope* Silvam Arsiam. Pugna *minimē*
6. *significāns* erat. Tarquinius, *igitur, appropinquāvit* Larem Porsennam, rēgem *Clūsiō*.
7. Porsenna tyrannum adiuvābat. Rōmam nōn *cēpērunt* Tarquinius Superbus et Lars
8. Porsenna. Horātius, Mūcius, et Cloelia, *iuvenēs* Rōmānī, Rōmam servāre adiuvērunt.

9.   Quod Rōmānī Ētruscōs *ex* oppidō *expulērunt,* populī *aliī* in Ītaliā expellere Etruscōs
10. *temptābant. Fortūna* erat bona: Etruscōs *ex* oppidīs *expulērunt.* **Quā dē causā** *populī*
11. *quī* in Ītaliā habitābant erant validī.
12.   Tarquinius Superbus, *tamen, etiam vīvit!* *Fūgit tyrannus ad* Mamilium Octāvium.
13. Mamilius erat marītus *fīliae tyrannī.* Etruscī *cum* Tarquiniō et Mamiliō *prope* Lacum
14. Rēgillum magnō studiō pugnāvērunt. Latīnī adiuvābant Etruscōs in pugnā. Rōmānī
15. *superāvērunt.* Castor et Pollux, deī, Rōmānōs ad Rēgillum adiūvērunt. *Paucōs annōs*
16. *post* Tarquinius Superbus mortuus erat. *Post* Tarquinium Superbum, *ultimum*
17. *tyrannum* Rōmae, Rōmānī *propter scelera semper verbum* "*tyrannus*" aut "*rēx*"
18. dēplōrāvērunt; et *numquam iterum* erat rēx *Rōmae.*

_____

Notā Bene:
Quā dē causā = for this reason

GLOSSARY

post, prep. + acc.	after
ultimus, a, um, adj.	last
tyrannus, ī, m.	Use your "eye" Latin to decipher the meaning of this word.
noceō, nocēre, nocuī, nocitum, (+ dat. object)	to harm
cum, prep. + abl.	with
ex, prep. + abl.	out of, from
expellō, expellere, expulī, expulsum	to drive out, expel
Gabiī	at Gabia (town)
pater, nom., sing., m.	father
fugiō, fugere, fūgī, fugitum	to flee
ad, prep. + acc.	to, toward
alius, a, ud, adj.	other
duo, numerical adj.	two
cōnsulēs, nom., pl., m.	consuls (highest elected official)
prope, prep. + acc.	near
minimē, adv.	least
significāns	significant
igitur, adv.	therefore
appropinquō, āre, āvī, ātum	to approach
Clūsiō.	at Clusium
capiō, capere, cēpī, captum	to seize
iuvenēs, nom., pl., m./f.	youth, young people
temptō, āre, āvī, ātum	to try
fortūna, ae, f.	fortune
populī, nom., pl.	peoples
quī	who
tamen, conj.	nevertheless
etiam, adv.	also
vīvō, vīvere, vīxī, victum	to live
superō, āre, āvī, ātum	to overcome
fīliae tyrannī, genitive	of the tyrant's daughter
paucōs annōs	a few years (accusative of time)
propter, prep. + acc.	on account of, because of
scelera, acc., pl., n.	wicked deeds, crimes
semper, adv.	always

ᴬThe students should follow these steps to success for this reading comprehension exercise.
• Read the English title. (It is often a clue to the theme or content of the reading.)
• Read the Latin text all the way through without any attempt at translation.

• Read the questions in order to know what to look for in the reading.
• Read the selection again.
• Go back and begin answering the questions.

Suggested Project:
This unit begins an outline of Roman history that will extend throughout the text. In the appendix you will find a timeline project that students may begin now and continue throughout the year. This timeline will help students keep track of the historical context of their readings.

verbum, ī, n..word
dēplōrō, āre, āvī, ātum ....to deplore
numquam iterum..never again

Question & Answer

1. According to line 1, ___.
    a. the first king of Rome was Tarquinius Superbus
    b. Superbus was the son of the first king of Rome
    c. Superbus was the son of the last king of Rome
    d. Superbus was the last king of Rome *(circled)*

2. The writer has characterized Lucretia as ___.
    a. angry
    b. stoic
    c. good *(circled)*
    d. queenly

3. According to lines 3 and 4, ___.
    a. the Romans killed Sextus and Superbus
    b. the Romans killed Sextus but Superbus fled to Gabium
    c. the Romans killed Sextus but Superbus fled someplace else *(circled)*
    d. the Romans killed Superbus but Sextus fled somewhere else

4. What event in the reading took place in or near a forest?
    a. the death of Superbus
    b. a major battle
    c. an indecisive battle *(circled)*
    d. the utter defeat of the Etruscans

5. Which one of the following was important in saving Rome at the time of the story?
    a. Sextus
    b. Porsenna
    c. Mamilius
    d. Horātius *(circled)*

6. What was a result of the Romans' actions regarding the Etruscans upon other peoples of Italy, according to lines 10 and 11?
    a. The other peoples fell totally under Roman rule.
    b. The other peoples became strong. *(circled)*
    c. The other peoples did not try to throw off Etruscan rule.
    d. The other peoples tried to follow the Romans' example but were unsuccessful.

7. What relation was Mamilius to Tarquinius Superbus?
    a. Mamilius was the brother of Tarquinius.
    b. Mamilius was the son-in-law of Tarquinius. *(circled)*
    c. Mamilius was the cousin of Tarquinius.
    d. Mamilius was the son of Tarquinius.

8. Who are the gods mentioned in the reading?
    a. Cloelia and Horātius

It is a great hope that someday you will take an Advanced Placement (AP) test in Latin. Preparation for AP tests must begin in the earliest stages of Latin and continue throughout your study of the language. These questions are of the type that you are likely to encounter on an AP test or the National Latin Exam at a higher level.

b. Mūcius and Horātius

c. Castor and Pollux

d. Mucius and Cloelia

9. What line in the reading tells of Tarquinius' seeking help from the king of Clūsium?

a. line 6

b. line 15

c. line 12

d. line 6

10. According to the reading, Lūcius Tarquinius Superbus ___.

a. died at the hands of Brūtus

b. turned against Lars Porsena

c. died at the Battle of Lake Rēgillus

d. died a few years after the Battle of Lake Rēgillus

11. *Armīs* in line 3 is ___.

a. dative indirect object

b. dative of interest

c. ablative of means or instrument

d. ablative of manner

12. What is the tense of *erant* in line 4?

a. present

b. future

c. perfect

d. imperfect

13. What is the use of *bona* in line 10?

a. subject

b. predicate nominative

c. predicate adjective

d. direct object

14. What word in lines 15–18 is not in the perfect tense?

a. erat

b. adiūvērunt

c. dēplōrāvērunt

15. In what line is there an ablative of manner?

a. line 14

b. line 12

c. line 15

d. line 18

16. What word in this story is a synonym for *rex*?

a. consulēs

b. tyrannus

c. ultimus

d. marītus

TRANSLATION

The last king of Rome was Tarquinius Superbus. Because the son of the tyrant, Sextus Tarquinius, harmed a good woman, Lucretia, the angry Romans drove the tyrant with his family out of the city with weapons. The Romans killed Sextus at Gabia, but the father and brothers of Sextus fled to another town. Two men, Brutus and Collatinus, were now consuls.

Tarquinius Superbus attacked the Romans near Silva Arsia. The battle was the least significant. Tarquinius, therefore, approached Lars Porsenna, king at Clusius. Porsenna was helping the tyrant. Tarquinius Superbus and Lars Porsenna did not seize Rome. Horatius, Mucius, and Cloelia, Roman youths, helped to save Rome.

Because the Romans drove out the Etruscans from the town, the other people in Italy began to try to drive out the Etruscans. Fortune was good: they drove the Etruscans out of the towns. For this reason the people who were living in Italy were strong.

Tarquinius Superbus, nevertheless, also lived! The tyrant fled to Mamilium Octavium. Mamilius was the husband of the tyrant's daughter. The Etruscans with Tarquinius and Mamilius fought with great zeal near Lacus Regillus. The Latins were helping the Etruscans in battle. The Romans overcame. Castor and Pollux, gods, helped the Romans at Regillus. After a few years Tarquinius Superbus was dead. After Tarquinius Superbus, the last king of Rome, the Romans because of the wicked deeds always deplored the word "tyrant" or "king"; and never again was there a king of Rome.

For Discussion:

How was the expulsion of the Tarquins by Rome similar to the rejection of the British Monarchy by America during the Revolutionary War?

Quī trānstulit sustinet.
He who transplants sustains.
—Connecticut state motto^A

This motto is inspired by Psalms 79:3 of the Latin Vulgate Version of the Bible: *"dē Aegyptō trānstulistī, ejēcistī gentēs et plantāstī eam."*^B

Chapter 10

- third declension nouns: all genders

VOCABULARY

NOUNS

aqua, ae, f	water	(aquatic)
corpus, corporis, n.	body	(corporal)
caput, capitis, n.	head	(capital, chapter)
ferrum, ferrī, n.	iron; sword	(ferric)
iter, itineris, n.	journey	(itinerary, itinerate)
iuvenis, iuvenis, m./f.	youth, young man	(juvenile)
māter, mātris, f.	mother	(maternal, maternity)
pater, patris, m.	father	(paternal, paternity)
rēx, rēgis, m.	king	(regent)
rīpa, ae, f.	river bank, shore	(riparian)
rīvus, ī, m.	brook, small stream	(rival)
uxor, uxōris, f.	wife	(uxorious)
tyrannus, ī, m.	king, tyrant	(tyranny)

VERBS

dēleō, dēlēre, dēlēvī, dēlētum	to destroy	(delete)
nato, āre, āvī, ātum	to swim	(natatorium)
servō, āre, āvī, ātum	to guard, save	(preserve)
temptō, āre, āvī, ātum	to try, attempt	(tempt)
timeō, timēre, timuī	to be afraid, fear	(timid, timidity)

ADJECTIVES

timidus, a, um	afraid	(timid, timidity)

ADVERBS

etiam	also, even	

69

Exercise 1. Using the rules for syllabication and accent that you have learned, write out the syllables and accents for the vocabulary words above. Then practice pronouncing them aloud.

SECTION 29. THIRD DECLENSION: MASCULINE AND FEMININE

The majority of Latin nouns fall into the third declension. The nouns of the third declension can be a little deceptive. The nominative singular has a wide range of endings; for this reason grammar charts often use a symbol to represent this variable nominative ending. However, you can always recognize a third declension noun by the genitive singular that consistently ends in -is. So, once again it becomes increasingly important to memorize the genitive singular of each noun along with the nominative singular.

Exercise 2. Identify the stem and declension for each noun in the vocabulary list.

> Example: rēx, rēgis = rēg, third declension

The gender for most nouns in the first two declensions is fairly easy to discern. Most first declension nouns are feminine and end in -a. Most second declension nouns are masculine, ending in -us, or neuter, ending in -um. The third declension, however, has all three genders, and the nominative endings are not unique for each gender. So, the only way to be certain of a noun's gender is to memorize it. The masculine and feminine nouns share the exact same set of endings.

CASE	ENDINGS		MASCULINE		FEMININE	
	SING.	PLURAL	SING.	PLURAL	SING.	PLURAL
Nominative	*	-ēs	rēx	rēgēs	uxor	uxōrēs
Genitive	-is	-um	rēgis	rēgum	uxōris	uxōrum
Dative	-ī	-ibus	rēgī	rēgibus	uxōrī	uxōribus
Accusative	-em	-ēs	rēgem	rēgēs	uxōrem	uxōrēs
Ablative	-e	-ibus	rēge	rēgibus	uxōre	uxōribus

Exercise 3. Following the examples of *rēx* and *uxor*, decline the nouns *iuvenis* and *māter*.

SECTION 30. THIRD DECLENSION: NEUTER

The third declension contains many neuter nouns as well. For the most part, the neuter endings are the same as those for the masculine and feminine. However, the third declension still follows the same neuter rule that applies to second declension nouns (Section 19). **The neuter rule:** the neuter nominative and accusative endings are *always* the same, AND the nominative and accusative plural *always* end with a short **a.**

CASE	ENDINGS SING.	ENDINGS PLURAL	NEUTER SING.	NEUTER PLURAL
Nominative	*	-a	iter	itinera
Genitive	-is	-um	itineris	itinerum
Dative	-ī	-ibus	itinerī	itineribus
Accusative	*	-a	iter	itinera
Ablative	-e	-ibus	itinere	itineribus

TE **Exercise 4.** Following the example of *iter*, decline the noun *corpus, corporis*.

TE **Exercise 5.** Parse the following nouns identifying their case, number, and gender. Where the answer is ambiguous, provide all possible forms.

Example: urbe = ablative, singular, feminine

1. rēgis
2. mātrī
3. itinera
4. armīs
5. iuvenēs
6. patribus
7. corporum

TE **Exercise 6.** Parse and diagram the following sentences, then translate.

1. Tyrannus virōs rīvō prohibēre temptābat.

2. Cōpiae ferrō templum dēlēbunt.

3. Rēgem iuvenēs nōn timent.

4. Oppidum oppugnāre temptābant.

5. Pater dedit virō agrum.

Chapter Reading **TE**

HORATIUS AT THE BRIDGE

In bellō *cum Ētruscīs postquam* Rōmānī *expulērunt* tyrannum et sociōs, erat iuvenis validus *nōmine Horātius Cōcles*. Ētruscī erant *trāns Tiberim* rīvum et Rōmam oppugnāre temptābant. Horātius *illā diē pontem Sublicium dēfendēbat, pontem lignō aedificātum*. Multī Rōmānī timēbant, sed nōn Horātius. Rōmānī timidī *trāns* agrōs ad oppidum *fūgērunt*. **Hostēs currentēs dē monte Iāniculō** vīdit Horātius. Rōmānī etiam arma *dēiēcērunt* et ex agrīs *cucurrērunt*.

Horātius virōs *fugientēs* prohibēre temptābat. Deōs ōrāvit Horātius. Horātius dīxit, "Ferrō, *igne, aliō īnstrūmentō pontem dēlēte! Pontem* corpore *meō* servābō." Tum ambulāvit *sōlus* ad *pontem. Hostēs* **tantam audāciam nōn crēdidērunt!** *Duo* Rōmānī ad *pontem cucurrērunt*; sed, *brevī tempore*, Horātius *eōs dīmīsit*. Horātius tum *cum Ētruscīs sōlus* pugnāvit. Horātius *firmus contrā* multōs *hostēs* stetit. Postrēmō Rōmānī *pontem* dēlēvērunt. Horātius clāmāvit, "Pater Tiberīne, *ad tē* ōrō. Mē et arma mea in rīvum *tuum accipe!*" **In aquam sē iēcit** et tūtus ad rīpam *prope* Rōmam natāvit. Rōmānī habuērunt grātiam Horātiō erant: dedērunt *virō* agrum!

Hostēs currentēs dē monte Iāniculō = the enemy running down from the Janiculum Hill (hill near the Tiber River)
tantae audāciae nōn crēdidērunt! = they did not believe such bravery!
in aquam sē iēcit = he threw himself into the water

GLOSSARY

cum, prep. + abl.	with
Ētruscī, ōrum, m. pl.	the Etruscans
postquam	after
expellō, expellere, expulī, expulsum	to drive out, expel
nōmine	by the name of, called
Horātius Cōcles	Horatius Cocles, Roman hero
trāns, prep. + acc.	across
Tiberim	Tiber
illā diē	that day, on that day (ablative of time)
dēfendō, dēfendere, dēfendī, dēfensum	to defend
pōns, pontis, m.	bridge
Sublicius, ī, m.	A famous bridge built under the reign of King Numa Pompilius.
lignō aedificātum	built of wood (ablative of material)
trāns	across
ad, prep. + acc.	to, toward; at, near
fugiō, fugere, fūgī, fugitum	to flee
dēiciō, dēicere, dēiēcī, dēiectum	they threw down
currō, currere, cucurrī, cursum	to run
fugientēs, nom., pl., participle	running
ignis, ignis, m.	fire
alius, a, ud, adj.	other
īnstrūmentum, ī, n.	tool, instrument
dēlēte	destroy! (this is a plural command.)
meus, a, um, adj.	my
sōlus, a, um, adj.	alone
hostis, hostis, m.	enemy
tantae audāciae	such bravery
crēdō, crēdere, crēdidī, crēditum, + dat.	to believe
duo, dua, duo, numerical adj.	two
brevī tempore	in a short time
dīmittō, dīmittere, dīmīsī, dīmissum	to send away
eōs, acc., pl.	them
firmus, a, um, adj.	firm, solid
contrā, prep. + acc.	against
stetit	he stood
postrēmō, adv.	finally
tē, acc., sing.	you
accipe	receive! (this is a singular command.)
tuus, a, um, adj.	your
prope, prep. + acc.	near
grātus, a, um, adj.	grateful
vir	best translated here as "hero"

Notā Bene

1. Ablative of Time
This construction tells when something happened or within what time something happened. In the reading, what two Latin words tell within what time something happened?

2. Special Verbs that Govern the Dative
A few special verbs govern, or take, their objects in the dative. Such a verb in this reading is *crēdō* – believe. Generally, though there may be other Latin verbs not listed here, the Latin words with the meanings of the English words in the list below govern the dative.

please	threaten
displease	pardon
obey	spare
command	trust
serve	believe
resist	favor
envy	

3. The adjective *tūtus* means "safe"; however, it is often best to translate a Latin adjective used the way *tūtus* is here as an adverb.

Respondē Latīnē!

1. Quandō erat bellum inter (between) Ētruscōs et Rōmānōs?

2. Quid Ētruscī temptābant?

3. Quis dēfendēbat pontem lignō factam (made)?

4. Quis contrā hostēs Ētruscōs stetit firmus?

5. Quō sē iēcit Horātius?

quandō = when?, quid = what?, quis = who?, quō = to where?

Many of you—we hope all—will someday take an Advanced Placement test in Latin; and all of you we hope, will be taking the National Latin Exam on an upper level. The items below illustrate some of the types of items you will need to know about for those advanced tests.

1. "Ferrō, igne, aliō instrumentō," you will notice, has no conjunctions. This lack of connectors is called asyndeton. You will see it many times in Latin literature. What kind of sense do you think it gives to the sentence?

2. In the sentence beginning with *Horātius* in the second line of the passage, you may notice the unusual word order *pontem Sublicium, pontem ligneā aedificātum*. This phrase has the order of noun – adjective – noun – adjective (phrase). This ABAB pattern is synchysis, sometimes called interlocking word order. This device, since English is not an inflected language, is not one we often see in our own poetry.

Colloquāmur (Let's Talk)

Use the following questions and responses to review the nouns in the sentences above. Use some "eye" Latin to figure out what the responses mean.

interrogātiō:	**Cūius est numerī?**	What number is it?
respōnsum:	**Singulāriter est.**	
	Plūrāliter est.	
interrogātiō:	**Quō est cāsū?**	In what case is it?
respōnsum:	**Cāsū nōminātīvō est.**	
	Cāsū accūsātīvō est.	
	Cāsū datīvō est.	
	Cāsū ablātīvō est.	
interrogātiō:	**Cūius est generis?**	What gender is it?
respōnsum:	**Est virīlis.**	It is masculine.
	Est muliebris.	It is feminine.
	Est neutrālis.	It is neuter.

Chapter 10 Teacher's Pages

Exercise 1

a-qua, a-quae, f.
cor-pus, cor-po-ris, n.
ca-put, ca-pi-tis, n.
fer-rum, fer-rī, n.
i-ter, i-ti-ne-ris, n.
iu-ve-nis, iu-ve-nis, m./f.
mā-ter, mā-tris, f.
pa-ter, pa-tris, m.
rēx, rē-gis, m.
rī-pa, ae, f.

rī-vus, ī, m.
u-xor, u-xō-ris, f.
ty-ran-nus, ī, m.
dē-le-ō, dē-lē-re, dē-lē-vī, dē-lē-tum
na-to, ā-re, ā-vī, ā-tum
ser-vō, ā-re, ā-vī, ā-tum
temp-tō, ā-re, ā-vī, ā-tum
ti-me-ō, ti-mē-re, ti-mu-ī
ti-mi-dus, a, um
e-tiam

Exercise 2

aqua, aquae, f.   aqu, 1st Declension   pater, patris, m.   patr, 3rd Declension
corpus, corporis, n. corpor, 3rd Declension   rēx, rēgis, m.   rēg, 3rd Declension
caput, capitis, n.   capit, 3rd Declension   rīpa, ae, f.   rīp, 1st Declension
ferrum, ferrī, n.   ferr, 2nd Declension   rīvus, ī, m.   rīv, 2nd Declension
iter, itineris, n.   itiner, 3rd Declension   uxor, uxōris, f.   uxōr, 3rd Declension
iuvenis, iuvenis, m./f. iuven, 3rd Declension   tyrannus, ī, m.   tyrann, 2nd Declension
māter, mātris, f.   mātr, 3rd Declension

Exercise 3

CASE	SINGULAR	PLURAL	SINGULAR	PLURAL
Nominative	iuvenis	iuvenēs	māter	mātrēs
Genitive	iuvenis	iuvenum	mātris	mātrum
Dative	iuvenī	iuvenibus	mātrī	mātribus
Accusative	iuvenem	iuvenēs	mātrem	mātrēs
Ablative	iuvene	iuvenibus	mātre	mātribus

Exercise 4

CASE	SINGULAR	PLURAL
Nominative	corpus	corpora
Genitive	corporis	corporum
Dative	corporis	corporibus
Accusative	corpus	corpora
Ablative	corporis	corporibus

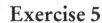

Exercise 5

1. rēgis   genitive, singular, masculine
2. mātrī   dative, singular, feminine
3. itinera   nominative/accusative, plural, neuter
4. armīs   dative/ablative, plural, neuter
5. iuvenēs   nominative/accusative, plural, masculine/feminine
6. patribus   dative/ablative, plural, masculine
7. corporum   genitive, plural, neuter

Exercise 6

        S   DO   AbS   Inf   V

1. Tyrannus virōs   rīvō   prohibēre temptābat.
      n/s/m   ac/p/m   ab/s/m   3/s/imp
   The tyrant was trying to keep the men from the river.

        S   AbMe   DO   V

2. Cōpiae   ferrō   templum   dēlēbunt.
      n/p/f   ab/s/n   ac/s/n   3/p/f
   The troops will destroy the temple with iron.

      DO   S   Adv   V

3. Rēgem   iuvenēs nōn   timent.
      ac/s/m   n/p/m   3/p/pr
   The youth do not fear the king.

       DO   Inf   S+V

4. Oppidum oppugnāre temptābant.
      ac/s/n   3/p/imp
   They were trying to attack the town.

       S   V   IO   DO

5. Pater   dedit   virō   agrum.
      n/s/m 3/s/per d/s/m ac/s/m
   The father gave a field to the man.

Translation

In the war with the Etruscans after the Romans drove away the tyrant and (his) allies, there was a brave youth named Horatius Cocles. The Etruscans were across the Tiber river and were trying to attack Rome. Horatius on that day was guarding the Sublicius Bridge, a bridge built of wood. Many Romans were afraid, but not Horatius. The fearful Romans fled across the fields to the town. Horatius saw the enemies running down from the Ianiculum Hill. The Romans also threw down their arms and ran from the fields.

Horatius was trying to hinder the fleeing men. Horatius prayed to the gods. Horatius said, "By iron, by fire, by other instrument, destroy the bridge! I will guard the bridge with my body." Then he walked alone to the bridge. The enemies did not believe such bravery! Two Romans ran to the bridge; but, in a short time, Horatius sent them away. Horatius then fought with the Etruscans alone. Horatius stood firm against many enemies. Finally the Romans destroyed the bridge. Horatius shouted, "Father Tiber, to you I pray. Receive me and my arms into your river!" He threw himself into the water and swam safe to the shore near Rome. The Romans were grateful to Horatius: they gave a field to the man/hero!

Respondē Latīnē!

1. Quandō erat bellum inter (between) Ētruscōs et Rōmānōs?
   Bellum erat postquam Rōmānī tyrannum expulērunt.

   When was the war between the Etruscans and Romans?
   The war was after the Romans expelled the tyrant.

2. Quid Ētruscī temptābant?
   Etruscī Rōmam oppugnāre temptābant.

   What were the Etruscans trying (to do)?
   The Etruscans were trying to attack the Romans.

3. Quis dēfendēbat pontem ligneā factam (made)?
   Horātius pontem Sublicium dēfendēbat.

   Who was guarding the bridge made of wood?
   Horatius was guarding the Sublicius Bridge.

4. Quis contrā hostēs Ētruscōs stetit firmus?
   Horātius contrā hostēs stetit firmus?

   Who stood firm against the Etruscan enemies?
   Horatius stood firm against the enemy.

5. Quō sē iēcit Horātius?
   Horātius in aquam/rivum sē iēcit.

   Where did Horatius throw himself?
   Horatius threw himself into the water/river.

Colloquāmur!

Interrogātiō:	Cūius est generis?	What gender is it?
Respōnsum:	Est virīlis.	It is masculine.
	Est muliebris.	It is feminine.
	Est neutrālis.	It is neuter.

Notes

Estō Perpetua!
May thou endure forever!
—Idaho state motto[A]

The dying apostrophe of Paolo Sarpi, church reformer
and author of the History of the Council of Trent,
in speaking of his beloved Venice.

[A]Emma Edwards Green, designer of The Great Seal of Idaho, is the only woman ever to design the Great Seal of a state. An art student and teacher, Mrs. Edwards entered a design contest for the seal in 1890 and won. The miner on the right represents the main source of revenue for the state. The woman, dressed as a Roman goddess, represents justice and liberty (note the scales and the liberty cap placed on her spear). The grain and cornucopiae at the bottom represent the bounty of the fields. The proud elk serves as a reminder of Idaho's game law, protecting elk and moose. The women's suffrage movement was in full swing during the late 1890's and Idaho was moving toward granting women the right to vote. The equal height and prominence of the man and woman on either side of the shield reflect the new equality recognized by the state.

Chapter 11

- third conjugation
  - present tense
- object prepositions
  - ablative
    - accompaniment
    - manner
    - place
    - separation
  - accusative
    - place

VOCABULARY

PART A[B]   [B]See p. 76 for this note.

NOUNS		
castra, castrōrum, n. pl.	camp	
mīles, mīlitis, m.	soldier	(military)
scrība, ae, m.	clerk; scribe	(scribe)
toga, togae, f.	toga	

VERBS		
currō, currere, cucurrī, cursum	to run	(current)
circumdō, circumdare, circumdedī, circumdatum	to surround	
dīcō, dīcere, dīxī, dictum	to speak, say, tell	(dictate)
gerō, gerere, gessī, gestum	to wear	
mittō, mittere, mīsī, missum	to send	(mission)
*petō, petere, petīvī / petiī, petītum	to aim at, attack, seek	(petulant)
pōnō, pōnere, posuī, positum	to put, place	(position)
probō, āre, āvī, ātum	to approve	(probation)
teneō, tenēre, tenuī, tentum	to hold	(tenacious)

cārus, a, um	dear, expensive, costly	
dexter, dextra, dextrum	right; f. noun right hand**	(dexterity)

PART B: PREPOSITIONS

ad (+ acc.) – to, toward, near, at

ā, ab (+ abl.) – from, away from

cum (+ abl.) – with

dē (+ abl.) – down from, about, concerning

ē, ex (+ abl.) – out of, from

in (+ acc.) – into; (+ abl.) in, on

per (+ acc.) – through

prō (+ abl.) – in front of, before

sub (+ acc.) – up to; (+ abl.) under

trāns (+ acc.) – across

> **B**Notice that this chapter has two vocabulary lists. The list is double because there is an unusually large amount of vocabulary needed for the lessons. We leave it to the teacher's discretion to determine which list should be required for memorization.

Notā Bene: Some verbs have an alternative spelling for the third principal part.
**The feminine form of this adjective can be used as a noun: dextra, -ae, or dextera, -ae, meaning "the right hand."

TE **Exercise 1.** Using the rules for syllabication and accent that you have learned, write out the syllables and accents for the vocabulary words above. Then practice pronouncing them aloud.

SECTION 31. Third Conjugation

Just as the third declension contains the majority of Latin nouns, so the third conjugation contains the largest group of Latin verbs. This group of verbs is distinguishable from the first two conjugations by its own unique infinitive, which ends in -ere. Notice that unlike the second conjugation (which ends in -ēre) this infinitive has a short **e**. The stem of these verbs is found in the same way as the first and second conjugation verbs.

2nd principal part – re = verb stem

1st conjugation	amā/re = amā
2nd conjugation	vidē/re = vidē
3rd conjugation	mitte/re = mitte

TE **Exercise 2.** Identify the stem and conjugation of each of the verbs in the vocabulary list of this chapter.

Example: currō, currere, cucurrī, cursum

curre, 3

SECTION 32. Present Tense

The third conjugation uses the same set of personal endings as the other groups of verbs. However, because its stem vowel is a short weak 'e' it weakens to an 'i' or 'u' before the personal endings.[c]

PERSON	SINGULAR	PLURAL
1	mittō	mittimus
2	mittis	mittitis
3	mittit	mittunt

[c]It is important to emphasize the difference between the "long strong" stem vowels of the first two conjugations in contrast to the "weak wimpy" stem vowel of the third conjugation. The weakness of this vowel will come into play many times hereafter.

Exercise 3. Following the example of *mittere*, conjugate the verbs *currere* and *petere* in the present tense. Include the English translations.[D]

Exercise 4. Parse each of the following verbs identifying their tense, person, and number. Then translate them into English.

LATIN	TENSE	PERSON	NUMBER	TRANSLATION
petis	Pres.	2	Sing.	you seek
līberābat				
curritis				
prohibēbis				
mittunt				
				we ran
				you (sing.) speak
				he places
				they approved

[D]Reminder: There is a conjugation worksheet available for this exercise. It would be beneficial to include the conjugation of some second conjugation verbs along with the third to help students become accustomed to the difference in the patterns.

SECTION 33. Prepositional Phrases

Latin uses prepositions much less than English does, for often the case endings indicate a preposition. The ablative of means (Section 28), for example, does not need a preposition. Latin, however, does have several prepositions and uses them quite frequently. The good news is that Latin prepositions are indeclinable; that is, they do not alter their endings in any way. However, each preposition requires a certain case for its object; so you must memorize the case each preposition "takes."

For example, the preposition *ad* must take an object in the accusative case.

> **ad oppidum**   to the town
> **ad rēgem**   to the king

If *oppidum* were placed in any case other than the accusative, the phrase would be grammatically incorrect. With some prepositions the result would be even more serious. Notice that *in* and *sub* can take either the ablative or accusative cases. The meaning, however, is very different depending upon which case you use.

> **Iēsus in aquā ambulat.**   Jesus walks on water.
> **Petrus in aquam ambulat.**   Peter walks into the water.

Exercise 5. Translate the following underlined prepositional phrases into Latin. Be careful to make sure that you are using the correct cases!

1. The Romans threw the tyrant <u>out of the town</u>.
2. I will cook dinner <u>with a friend.</u>
3. <u>With gratitude</u> the people worship God.
4. The boys are swimming <u>in the river</u>.
5. The army will keep the enemy <u>away from the king</u>.
6. The soldiers quickly march <u>toward the camp</u>.

As you can see, the types of phrases that use Latin prepositions can vary widely. These different uses are categorized as particular constructions. Here are some of the most common constructions that use Latin prepositions.[E]

1. **Ablative of accompaniment: cum + ablative**
   This construction indicates the person that someone is accompanying, or the person(s) *with* whom they are completing an action.

   > **Cum sociō** pugnō – I fight **with an ally.**
   > **Cum mātre** ambulās – You walk **with (your) mother.**

2. **Ablative of manner: cum + ablative**
   This construction describes the manner in which an action was done, or *how* an action was accomplished.

   > **Cum gaudiō** labōrat – He works **with joy.**

   When an adjective is used to modify the object of a preposition—and especially *cum*—it often precedes the preposition, creating a "sandwich."

   > magnā **cum** laude – with great praise [F]

3. **Ablative of separation: ā, ab + ablative**
   The ablative of separation is often used with the preposition *ā, ab* when used in reference to a person.

   Oppidum **ā malō rēge** servābitis. You will save the town **from the evil king.**

4. **Ablative of place where**
   Describes *where* something takes place.

   In viā ambulābāmus. We were walking **in the road.**
   Mīles **prō rēge** stat. The soldier stands **before the king.**

5. **Ablative of place from which**
   Shows motion away *from* an object.

   Populī **ab oppidō** festīnant. The people hurry **from the town**.

6. **Accusative of place to which**
   Shows motion *toward* an object.

   Mīles **ad ignem** ambulat. The soldier walks **toward the fire.**

Caveat Discipulus: Exceptions for Place Expressions!

As with many grammar rules in English, Latin too has exceptions to the rules. There are a few nouns that do not use the above prepositional phrases to express place. Instead they appear in the appropriate case as listed above without a preposition.

Ad oppidum ambulō.	I walk to the town.
Rōmam ambulō.	I walk to Rome.
Ab oppidō ambulō.	I walk from the town.
Rōmā ambulō.	I walk from Rome.

> [G]These nouns use the locative case for "place where." The locative will appear in *Latin Alive! Book 2*.

The names of cities, small islands in the Mediterranean, and the nouns *domus* (house/home) and *rūs* (country) do NOT use prepositions for expressions of place.[G]

Exercise 6. Identify each of the constructions underlined in Exercise 5.

Exercise 7. Parse and diagram the following sentences, then translate.

1. Mīlitēs cum scrībā, nōn cum rēge, dīxērunt.

2. Iuvenem ad rēgem portāvērunt.

3. Agricolae frūmentum in oppidum carrīs portābunt.

4. Esne vir validus?

5. Validī virī glōriam petunt.

Chapter Reading

GĀIUS MŪCIUS SCAEVOLA

CHARACTERS:

Lars Porsenna – an Etruscan king, an ally of Tarquinius Superbus, who attacked Rome in order to help Tarquinius reclaim the throne

Gāius Mūcius – a very brave citizen of Rome

Scrība – the king's scribe (secretary) who among other duties was in charge of distributing the soldiers' pay

Rēx *Ētruscōrum* erat Porsenna. Porsenna et mīlitēs *Ētruscī* urbem Rōmam circumdabant. Rōmānī multum frūmentum nōn habēbant; frūmentum, *igitur*, cārum erat. Iuvenis, *nōmine* Gāius Mucius, *rem dēplōrāvit* quod *ubī* rēgēs rēgnābant Rōmānōs *nēmō* circumdedērunt.

Gāius dīxit, "Dēsīderō ad castra *Ētruscōrum īre.*" Senātōrēs Rōmānī probāvērunt.

Gladium sub togā Gāius posuit. Ambulāvit ad castra. Ubī ad castra *pervēnit*, scrība mīlitibus *pecūniam* dabat. Mīlitēs cum scrībā, nōn rēge, dīcēbant. Scrība quoque togam **similem togae rēgis** gerēbat. Gāius *ambōs* virōs vīdit. Nōn dēsīderāvit **rogāre quem virum esset rēgem**. *Quod* nōn rogāvit, *forte* scrībam, nōn rēgem, necāvit.

Gāius per *turbam* cucurrit. Mīlitēs Gāium *cēpērunt* et iuvenem ad rēgem portāvērunt. *Stāns* prō rēge Gāius Mūcius clāmāvit, "*Cīvis* Rōmānus sum! Virī mē Gāium Mūcium *appellant*. Hostis *tuus* sum et, *ut* hostis, *tē* necāre dēsīderāvī. Dēsīderō *tē* necāre. *Trecentī* iuvenēs Rōmānī quoque tē necāre dēsīderant. *Semper necesse* erit timēre. *Ūnus* iuvenis *tē* necābit."

Rēx Porsenna *et* timidus *et* īrātus erat. **Rēx Gāium in ignem īnicī iussit.** Tum Gāius clāmāvit, "Spectās et vidēbis **quam vīle quī** glōriam petunt corpus habent." Dextram tum Gāius in *ignem* posuit. Dextram in igne tenēbat. Rēx ē *sellā salit* et "*abī*" dīcit, "es vir validus!" Rēx Gāium Mūcium līberāvit quod erat validus. *Posteā* Rōmānī Gāiō *agnōmen* "Scaevolam" dedērunt quod dextram *āmīserat.‡*

Notā Bene:
similem togae rēgis = similar to the king's toga
rogāre quem virum esset rēgem = to ask which man was the king.
Rēx Gāium in ignem īnicī iussit. = The king ordered Gaius to be thrown into the fire. (*inicī* is a present passive infinitive.)
quam vīle quī = how worthless those who . . .

‡*āmīserat* is the pluperfect tense and is best translated as "had lost." (*Scaevola* means "left-handed.")

GLOSSARY

Ētruscī, ōrum, adj. .... Etruscan
Ētruscōrum, gen. pl. .... of the Etruscans
igitur, adv. .... therefore
nōmine .... by the name of, called
rem, acc., sing. .... situation (in this sentence)
dēplōrō, āre .... to deplore
ubī, adv. .... when
nēmō .... nobody, no one
īre .... to go
gladius, ī, m. .... sword
pervēnit .... he arrived
pecūnia, ae, f. .... money
similis, adj. .... similar [to]
ambōs .... both
quod, conj. .... because
forte .... by chance
turba, ae, f. .... crowd
capiō, capere, cēpī, captum .... to capture
stāns .... standing
cīvis, cīvis, m. .... citizen
appellō, āre .... call [by name]
tuus, a, um, adj. .... your
ut .... as
ūnus .... one
tē, acc., sing. .... you
sōlus, a, um, adj. .... alone
cupiditās, cupiditātis, f. .... desire, wish
trecentī, numerical adj. .... three hundred
semper, adv. .... always
necesse .... necessary
et . . . et . . . . both . . . and . . .
īnicī .... to be thrown
habent .... best translated as "they consider"
ignis, ignis, m. .... fire
sella, ae, f. .... chair
saliō, salīre, saluī, salitum .... to jump
abī, command .... go [away]!
posteā, adv. .... afterwards
agnōmen .... a name added to the names one already has because of some deed he has accomplished

For Discussion:

How does war with Tarquinius Superbus and Lars Porsenna compare to the War of 1812? [H]

[H]The war of 1812 can be seen as an attempt by the British to retake the colonies.

Colloquāmur (Let's Talk)

Now that you have learned place expressions in Latin, let's learn some useful phrases for going places, and a few responses. Use your "eye" Latin to see if you can discern the meaning.[I]

Licetne mihi īre . . .   May I go . . .   (Literally: Is it permitted for me to go . . .)
Licetne nōbīs īre . . .   May we go . . .

ad officium?
ad lātrīnam?
ad fontem aquae?

ē lūdō?

[I]Encourage students to come up with some Latin phrases for other places more applicable to your surroundings.

Derivative Detective

Did any of the prepositions in the vocabulary list look familiar? They should, for many Latin prepositions appear as prefixes in English. Use your knowledge of Latin prepositions to decipher the meanings of the English words below.[J]

deport
export
import
transport
emit
transmit

submit
permission
transpose
deposit
imposition
exposition

[J]Students seem to struggle a bit with Latin compound verbs. It is helpful to prepare them for these verbs by studying the English counterparts with which they are already familiar.

Chapter 11 Teacher's Pages

Exercise 1

<u>cas</u>-tra, cas-<u>trō</u>-rum, n. pl.
<u>mī</u>-les, <u>mī</u>-li-tis, m.
scrī-ba, ae, m.
to-ga, <u>to</u>-gae, f.
<u>cur</u>-rō, <u>cur</u>-re-re, cu-cur-rī, <u>cur</u>-sum
cir-cum-dō, cir-<u>cum</u>-da-re, cir-<u>cum</u>-de-dī, cir-<u>cum</u>-da-tum
<u>dī</u>-cō, <u>dī</u>-ce-re, <u>dī</u>-xī, <u>dic</u>-tum
<u>ge</u>-rō, <u>ge</u>-re-re, <u>ges</u>-sī, <u>ges</u>-tum

<u>mit</u>-tō, <u>mit</u>-te-re, <u>mī</u>-sī, <u>mis</u>-sum
<u>pe</u>-tō, <u>pe</u>-te-re, pe-<u>tī</u>-vī / <u>pe</u>-ti-ī, pe-<u>tī</u>-tum
<u>pō</u>-nō, <u>pō</u>-ne-re, <u>po</u>-su-ī, <u>po</u>-si-tum
<u>pro</u>-bō, <u>ā</u>-re, <u>ā</u>-vī, <u>ā</u>-tum
te-ne-ō, te-<u>nē</u>-re, <u>te</u>-nu-ī, <u>ten</u>-tum
<u>cā</u>-rus, a, um
<u>dex</u>-ter, <u>dex</u>-tra, <u>dex</u>-trum

Exercise 2

currō, currere, cucurrī, cursum   curre, 3
circumdō, circumdāre, circumdedī, circumdatum   circumdā, 1
dīcō, dīcere, dīxī, dictum   dīce, 3
gerō, gerere, gessī, gestum   gere, 3
mittō, mittere, mīsī, missum   mitte, 3
petō, petere, petīvī / petiī, petītum   pete, 3
pōnō, pōnere, posuī, positum   pōne, 3
probō, probāre, probāvī, probātum   probā, 1
teneō, tenēre, tenuī, tentum   tenē, 2

Exercise 3

| | *currere* | | *petere* | |
PERSON	SINGULAR	PLURAL	SINGULAR	PLURAL
1	currō I run	currimus we run	petō I seek	petimus we seek
2	curris you run	curritis you (pl.) run	petis you seek	petitis you (pl.) seek
3	currit he/she/it runs	currunt they run	petit he/she/it seeks	petunt they seek

Exercise 4

LATIN	TENSE	PERSON	NUMBER	TRANSLATION
petis	Pres.	2	Sing.	you seek
līberābat	Imp.	3	Sing.	He was setting free
curritis	Pres.	2	Pl.	You run
prohibēbis	Fut.	2	Sing.	You will prevent
mittunt	Pres.	3	Pl.	They send
cucurrimus	Perf.	1	Pl.	we ran
dīcis	Pres.	2	Sing.	you (sing.) speak
pōnit	Pres.	3	Sing.	he places
probāvērunt	Perf.	3	Pl.	they approved

Exercise 5

1. The Romans threw the tyrant <u>out of the town</u>. ex oppidō
2. I will cook dinner <u>with a friend</u>. cum amīcō/amīcā
3. <u>With gratitude</u> the people worship God. cum grātiā
4. The boys are swimming <u>in the river</u>. in rīvō
5. The army will keep the enemy away <u>from the king</u>. ā rēge
6. The soldiers quickly march <u>toward the camp</u>. ad castra

Exercise 6

1. ablative of place from which
2. ablative of accompaniment
3. ablative of manner
4. accusative of place where
5. ablative of separation
6. accusative of place to which

Exercise 7

```
        S    P   OP  Adv  P  OP      V
1. Mīlitēs cum scrībā, nōn cum rēge,   dīxērunt.
   n/p/m      ab/s/m        ab/s/m  3/p/perf
```
The soldiers spoke with the scribe, not with the king.

```
        DO    P   OP     V
2. Iuvenem ad rēgem portāvērunt.
   ac/s/m,f  ac/s/m  3/p/perf
```
They carried the youth to the king.

```
        S         DO      P   OP  AbMe    V
3. Agricolae frūmentum in oppidum carrīs portābunt.
   n/p/m       ac/s/n      ac/s/n  ab/p/m  3/p/f
```
The farmers will carry the grain into town with (by means of) the wagons.

```
   LV   PrN  Adj
4. Esne  vir  validus?
   2/s/pr n/s/m  n/s/m
```
Are you a strong/brave man?

```
   Adj    S     DO     V
5. Validī  virī  glōriam  petunt.
   n/p/m  n/p/m  ac/s/f  3/p/pr
```
The brave/strong men seek glory.

As you review these exercises with your students, ask about the constructions that appear in each one. For example: What kind of ablative appears in sentence #1?

Translation

The king of the Etruscans was Porsenna. Porsenna and the Etruscan soldiers were surrounding Rome. The Romans were not having much grain; grain, therefore, was costly/expensive. A young man, named Gaius Mucius, deplored the situation because when the kings were ruling no one surrounded the Romans.

Gaius said, "I want to go to the camp of the Etruscans." The Roman Senators approved. Gaius placed a sword under (his) toga. He walked to camp. When he arrived at the camp, a scribe was giving money to the soldiers. The soldiers were speaking with the scribe, not with the king. The scribe was also wearing a toga similar to the king's toga. Gaius saw both men. He did not wish to ask which man was the king. Because he did not ask, by chance he killed the scribe, not the king.

Gaius ran through the crowd. The soldiers seized Gaius and carried the youth to the king. Standing before the king Gaius Mucius shouted, "I am a Roman citizen! Men call me Gaius Mucius. I am your enemy and, as an enemy, I wanted to kill you. I am not alone in the desire to kill you. Three hundred Roman youths also desire to kill you. It will always be necessary (for you) to fear. One youth will kill you."

King Porsenna was scared and angry. The king ordered Gaius to be thrown into the fire. Then Gaius shouted, "You watch and you will see how worthless those who seek glory hold (consider) their body." Then Gaius placed (his) right hand into the fire. He was holding (his) right hand in the fire. The king jumped out of his seat and said, "Go away; you are a brave man!" The king freed Gaius Mucius because he was brave. Afterwards the Romans gave the name Scaevola to Gaius because he had lost his right hand.

Colloquāmur!

Licetne mihi īre . . .	May I go . . . (Literally: Is it permitted for me to go . . .)
Licetne nōbīs īre . . .	May we go . . .
ad officium?	to work/duty
ad lātrīnam?	to the bathroom
ad fontem aquae?	to the water fountain
ē lūdō?	out of school

Notes

Ad astra per aspera.
To the stars through difficulties.
—Kansas state motto[A]

[A]Kansas adopted this seal on May 25, 1861, just a few months after becoming a state on January 29 of the same year. The sun rises on the right, representing the East. Over the horizon are 34 stars, representing Kansas' place as the 34th state to join the U.S. The steamboat travelling down the river represents the state's commerce. The cabin with the farmer plowing his field represents the hope of future commerce through agriculture. The wagon train headed west and the buffalo herd pursued by two American Indians are all representative of the westward expansion of the U.S.

Chapter 12

- genitive case
  - possession
  - origin
  - material
  - partitive

VOCABULARY

NOUNS		
dux, ducis, m.	leader	(conductor)
familia, ae, f.	family	(familial)
flūmen, flūminis, n.	river	(flume)
lēgātus, ī, m.	officer, lieutenant	(delegate)
obses, obsidis, m.	hostage	(obsess)
pāx, pācis, f.	peace	(pax, pacify)
perīculum, ī, n.	danger	(peril)
statua, ae, f.	statue	(statuesque)
virgō, virginis, f.	maiden	(Virginia)
VERBS		
legō, legere, lēgī, lēctum	to read; choose, gather	(legible)
prōpōnō, prōpōnere, prōposuī, prōpositum	to put before; to propose	(proposition)
revertō, revertere, revertī, reversum	to turn back, return	(reverse)
ADJECTIVES		
cēterī, cēterōrum, m. pl.	the rest	
līber, lībera, līberum	free	(liberty)
PREPOSITIONS		
circum (+ acc.)	around	
prope (+ acc.)	near	
CONJUNCTION		
quod	because	

TE **Exercise 1.** Using the rules for syllabication and accent that you have learned, write out the syllables and accents for the vocabulary words above. Then practice pronouncing them aloud.

SECTION 34. Genitive Case

As you have already learned, the genitive case (from Latin *genus*, family) is very important for it is the genitive singular that reveals the declension or noun family to which a noun belongs. However, it has several other uses which are also very valuable. The genitive is a fairly easy and reliable case to translate. In most cases it is the equivalent to the use of our English preposition "of." This preposition has many different uses in English—more than you may realize. So, let us take a look at the most common uses of the genitive case.

   a. **Possession** – expresses ownership or belonging
       arma **mīlitis** – the arms **of the soldier, the soldier's** arms

   b. **Origin** – expresses the place from which a person or group originates
       Cloelia **Rōmae** – Cloelia **of Rome**

   c. **Material** – expresses the material from which something is created
       gladius **ferrī** – a sword **of iron**

   d. **Partitive (Part of the Whole)** – expresses the whole or group of which a part is mentioned
       pars **placentae** – a piece **of cake**

TE **Exercise 2.** Underline the genitive construction that appears in each of the following sentences. Identify the type of construction and then translate the genitive phrase.

       Example: The soldiers <u>of the town</u> fought bravely.
                 origin, oppidī

   1. Inside the temple is a statue of bronze.

   2. The maiden's bravery was amazing.

   3. The king will free part of the hostages.

   4. The pride of the Romans was the Colosseum.

   5. Gāius Mūcium of Rome was later called Scaevola.

TE **Exercise 3.** Parse, diagram, and translate the following sentences.[B]

   1. Virgō trāns flūmen prope Rōmam natat.

   2. Ad castra mīlitum ambulāvit.

   3. Dux multōs iuvenēs lēgit.

   4. Multī patrēs fābulam dē Cloeliā puellīs narrāvērunt.

   5. Perīculum iuvenum erat magnum.

[B]Teachers may wish to have students identify the particular type of prepositional phrase (i.e. accusative of place to which, ablative of place from which, etc.) or the function of the genitive case (i.e. possession, partitive, etc.). You may want to ask in #3 how one can tell if the verb is present or perfect since both tenses appear to have the same ending. The answer is the stem *lēg* has a long ē, indicating that it must come from the third principal part.

Chapter Reading TE

CLOELIA, A BRAVE MAIDEN

Postquam Mūcius Rōmam revertit, rēx Porsenna etiam timidus erat. Pācem cum Rōmānīs prōposuit quod timidus erat. Rōmānīs *necesse* erat obsidēs dare *sī montem Iāniculum* līberum esse dēsīderāvērunt. *Itaque* pāx erat. *Ūna* ēx obsidibus, virgō *nōmine* Cloelia, *custōdēs ēlūsit. Illō tempore* Ētruscī et obsidēs in castrīs prope Tiberim flūmen erant. Cloelia erat dux: cēterās obsidēs ad flūmen dūxit. Sub *imbre tēlōrum* flūmen natābant. Tūtae ad familiās Rōmae revertērunt.

Ubī rēx Porsenna fābulam dē Cloeliā et cēterīs *audīvit,* īrātus erat. Lēgātōs Rōmam mīsit. Lēgātī dīxērunt, "*Necesse* est Rōmānīs Cloeliam Porsennae rēgī dare." Rēx cēterās virginēs *vīlēs* habuit. **Sī Cloelia ad castra Ētruscōrum nōn reverterit, pāx nōn iam erit. Sī reverterit, Cloeliam Rōmam tūtam rēx mittet.** *Et* Rōmānī *et* Ētruscī *cōnsentiēbant.* Cloelia quoque obsidēs esse līberōs—cum *permissiōne* rēgis— lēgit. Cloelia iuvenēs lēgit quod perīculum in castrīs *maximum* erat iuvenibus. *Posteā* Rōmānī Cloeliam *honōrāvērunt:* statuam Cloeliae in equō in *Viam Sacram* posuērunt.

Notā Bene:
Sī Cloelia ad castra^c Ētruscōrum nōn reverterit, pāx nōn iam erit. Sī reverterit, Cloeliam Rōmam tūtam rēx mittet. = If Cloelia does not return to the camp of the Etruscans, there will no longer be peace. If she does return, the king will send her safely [back] to Rome.
(These two sentences contain some complex verb tenses that you will learn later.)

GLOSSARY

postquam, adv.	after
Rōmam	to Rome
necesse	necessary
sī, conj.	if
mōns, montis, m.	hill
Iāniculum, ī, n.	Ianiculum (hill near the Tiber River)
itaque, adv.	thus, and so
ūna	one
nōmine	named
custōs, custōdis, m.	guard
ēlūdō, ēlūdere, ēlūsī, ēlūsum	to ward off, elude
illō tempore	at that time
imber, imbris, m.	rain, shower
tēlus, ī, m.	dart, spear
ubī, adv.	when
audiō, audīre, audīvī, audītum	to hear
vīlēs	unimportant
et . . . et	both . . . and . . . . (correlative conjunction)
cōnsentiēbant	they were agreeing
permissiō, permissiōnis, f.	permission
maximus, a, um, adj.	greatest
honōrō, āre	to honor
Via Sacra	The Sacred Road, a prominent road in Rome that led past many temples and into the Roman Forum.

^cThe neuter plural noun *castra* (introduced in chapter 11) appears often in this passage. Remind students that this noun is plural in form, but should be translated as singular "camp." Think of a single camp as a group of many individual tents.

This passage contains both forms of the dative that students have learned: indirect object and reference. A great review exercise is to ask students which use of the dative they are reading in a given sentence.

Respondē Latīnē!

 1. Quālis est rēx postquam Mūcius Rōmam revenit?

2. Ubī erat castra Ētruscōrum?

3. Quis Cloeliae permissiōnem dedit obsidēs legere?

4. Eratne Cloelia virgō valida?
   (Hint: See *Colloquāmur* in chapter 2 for an answer to this question.)

quālis = what kind of?, ubī = where?, quis = who?

ANSWER IN ENGLISH!^D

1. Under what conditions did the girls swim the Tiber?

2. What was the demand of the envoys Porsenna sent to the Romans?

^DThis is a good opportunity to discuss the use of figures of speech. Ask students to identify the figure of speech is the phrase *imbre tēlōrum*. Roman authors use metaphors such as this one a great deal. Why might this be more effective than simply saying "hundreds of spears?"

Culture Corner: Hostages in the Ancient World

The Romans had an expression for it: "*obsidēs inter sē dant*"—they exchange hostages. Today, terrorists and criminals take hostages and hold them under threat of death. Terrorists want to obtain the freedom of political prisoners. Criminals want ransom or security while escaping. Such was not the case in the ancient world. The ancients actually exchanged hostages rather than taking them. The exchange of hostages in the ancient world ensured that both parties would hold to some agreement. The exchange would also ensure that neither group would violate certain rules of behavior. This exchange was supposed to bring about peace and goodwill—at least temporarily—for the groups exchanging the hostages.

Colloquāmur (Let's Talk)

Use the following questions and responses to review the nouns in the sentences above. Use some "eye" Latin to figure out what the responses mean.

interrogātiō:	Cūius est numerī?	What number is it?
respōnsum:	Singulāriter est.	
	Plūrāliter est.	
interrogātiō:	Quō est cāsū?	In what case is it?
respōnsum:	Cāsū nōminātīvō est.	
	Cāsū accūsātīvō est.	
	Cāsū datīvō est.	
	Cāsū ablātīvō est.	
	Cāsū genitīvō est.	

Challenge Box

In an essay written in English, compare and contrast the stories of Gāius Mūcius Scaevola and Cloelia. Quote and translate as literally as possible at least one sentence from each story to prove one or more of your points. Put your Latin sentence into quotation marks (" ") and your translation in square brackets ([ ]). Use all the skills you have learned for writing an essay for your language arts or some other class.^E

^EThis essay is similar to one that might be posed on the AP exam. It is important that students learn how to use quotations directly from a given passage (translated as literally as possible) to support a thesis. You might begin this exercise with an oral discussion about possible similarities or differences amongst these heroes and then look together for quotations that would support those statements.

Exercise 1

dux, du-cis, m.
fa-mi-li-a, ae, f.
flū-men, flū-mi-nis, n.
lē-gā-tus, ī, m.
ob-ses, ob-si-dis, m.
pāx, pā-cis, f.
pe-rī-cu-lum, ī, n.
sta-tu-a, ae, f.
vir-gō, vir-gi-nis, f.

le-gō, le-ge-re, lē-gī, lēc-tum
prō-pō-nō, prō-pō-ne-re, prō-po-su-ī, prō-po-si-tum
re-ver-tō, re-ver-te-re, re-ver-tī, re-ver-sum
cē-te-rī, cē-te-rō-rum
lī-ber, lī-be-ra, lī-be-rum
cir-cum (+ acc.)
pro-pe (+ acc.)
quod

Exercise 2

1. Inside the temple is a statue <u>of bronze</u>.   material, aēneī
2. The <u>maiden's bravery</u> was amazing.   possession, virginis
3. The king will free part <u>of the hostages</u>.   partitive, obsidum
4. The pride <u>of the Romans</u> was the Colosseum.   possession, Rōmānōrum
5. Gāius Mūcium <u>of Rome</u> was later called Scaevola.   origin, Rōmae

Exercise 3

```
        S    P    OP    P    OP    V
```
1. Virgō trāns flūmen prope Rōmam natat.
   n/s/f   ac/s/n   ac/s/f 3/s/pr
   The maiden swims across the river near Rome.

```
     P  OP   PNA      V
```
2. Ad castra mīlitum ambulāvit.
      ac/p/n g/p/m 3/s/perf
   He/She walked to the camp of the soldiers.

```
      S    Adj      DO      V
```
3. Dux   multōs   iuvenēs   lēgit.
   n/s/m ac/p/m ac/p/m,f 3/s/perf
   The leader chose many of the youths.

```
      Adj      S      DO    P    OP    IO       V
```
4. Multī   patrēs fābulam dē Cloeliā puellīs narrāvērunt.
   n/p/m n/p/m   ac/s/f   ab/s/f d/p/f   3/p/perf
   Many fathers told the story about Cloelia to (their) girls.

```
         S       PNA    LV    PrA
```
5. Perīculum iuvenum   erat   magnum.
    n/s/n   g/p/m   3/s/imp n/s/n
   The danger of the youths was great.

It is very beneficial to have the students review and discuss their translations of these sentences as a class. This provides a wonderful opportunity to practice some oral skills with the Colloquāmur section below and those in previous chapters.

Translation

After Mucius returned to Rome, king Porsenna was still afraid. He proposed peace with the Romans because he was afraid. It was necessary for the Romans to give hostages if they desired the Ianiculum Hill to be free. Therefore there was peace. One of the hostages, a maiden named Cloelia, escaped the guards. At that time the Estruscans and the hostages were in a camp near the Tiber River. Cloelia was the leader: the remaining hostages she led to the river. Under a rain of spears they were swimming the river. They returned safe to the families of Rome.

When king Porsenna heard the story about Cloelia and the rest, he was angry. He sent delegates to Rome. The delegates said, "It is necessary for the Romans to give Cloelia to king Porsenna." The king held/considered the rest of the maidens worthless. If Cloelia will not have returned to the camp of the Etruscans, there will no longer be peace. If she will have returned, the king will send her safely [back] to Rome. Both the Romans and Etruscans were agreeing. Cloelia also chose hostages to be free – with the permission of the king. Cloelia chose youths because the danger in the camp was greatest for the youths. Afterwards the Romans honored Cloelia: they placed a statue of Cloelia on a horse onto the Via Sacra.

Respondē Latīnē!

1. Quālis est rēx postquam
Mūcius Rōmam revenit?
   Rēx Porsenna timidus erat.

   What kind (of man) is the king after
   Mucius returns to Rome?
   King Porsenna was [a] timid [man/ king].

2. Ubī erat castra Ētruscōrum?
   Castra Ētruscōrum prope Tiberim
   flūmen erant.

   Where was the camp of the Etruscans?
   The camp of the Etruscans was near
   the Tiber River.

3. Quis Cloeliae permissiōnem
dedit obsidēs legere?
   Rēx Porsenna Cloeliae permissiōnem dedit.

   Who gave permission to Cloelia
   to choose hostages?
   King Porsenna gave Cloelia permission.

4. Eratne Cloelia virgō valida?
   Sīc est! Clorlia erat virgō valida.

   Was Cloelia a strong/ able/ worthy young woman?
   Yes! [lit. "It is so!"] Cloelia was a strong young woman.

(Hint: See Colloquāmur in chapter 2 for an answer to this question.)

ANSWER IN ENGLISH!

1. Under what conditions did the girls swim the Tiber?
   Cloelia swam across the Tiber under a rain of spears.

2. What was the demand of the envoys Porsenna sent to the Romans?
   They demanded that Cloelia return to the camp of the Etruscans. If she did not, there would not be peace.

Deō grātiam habeāmus.
Let us be grateful to God.
—Kentucky state motto[A]
Adopted 2002

[A]On March 4, 2002, Mr. Tom Riner (House District 41, Jefferson) and Mr. Stan Lee (House District 45, Fayette) proposed House Bill No. 857, which requested that the House adopt this motto as the official Latin motto for Kentucky. The motto expresses the sentiment found in the Preamble to the Constitution of the Commonwealth of Kentucky, which reads "We, the people of the Commonwealth of Kentucky, grateful to Almighty God for the civil, political and religious liberties we enjoy, and invoking the continuance of these blessings, do ordain and establish this Constitution." On April 1, the Kentucky General Assembly adopted the motto and on April 11, Governor Paul E. Patton signed the legislation into law.

Chapter 13

- third conjugation
  - imperfect tense
  - future tense

VOCABULARY

NOUNS			
	marītus, ī, m.	husband	(marital)
	nūntius, ī, m.	messenger; message	(announcement)
	vīlla, vīllae, f.	farmhouse	(village)
	virtūs, virtūtis, f.	manhood, courage	(virtue)
VERBS			
ascendō, ascendere, ascendī, ascēnsum		to climb, to go up	(ascension)
claudō, claudere, clausī, clausum		to shut, close; close off	(closure)
ēvādō, ēvādere, ēvāsī, ēvāsum		to come out, escape	(evasion)
induō, induere, induī, indūtum		to put on	
respondeō, respondēre, respondī, respōnsum		to reply, respond	(responsive)
vincō, vincere, vīcī, victum		to conquer	(vanquish)
ADJECTIVES			
	nōtus, a, um	known	(notable)
	squālidus, a, um	dirty	(squalid)
ADVERBS			
	modo	only	
	posteā	afterwards	

TE **Exercise 1.** Using the rules for syllabication and accent that you have learned, write out the syllables and accents for the vocabulary words above. Then practice pronouncing them aloud.

As you learned in chapter 3, Latin uses tense markers to indicate the tense of a verb, or the time that the verb's action takes place. A tense marker is a letter or letters that signal a change in tense (Section 9). The third conjugation, however, uses a different set of tense markers for the imperfect and future tenses than the first and second conjugations.

Section 35. Imperfect Tense

The imperfect tense marker for the third conjugation is -ēba. This is very similar to the -ba used in the first two conjugations. Remember that the stem vowel for the third conjugation is a weak short *e*. The strong ē in the tense marker overpowers and absorbs this weak stem vowel, causing it to disappear.[B]

Imperfect Tense: I was sending, I used to send
stem: **mitte/re** + imperfect tense marker: **ēba** + personal endings

[B]Some texts teach that the tense marker remains -*ba*- for all conjugations. The -*ēba*- however, better explains the presence of the long ē in the imperfect tense for the third conjugation as well as the third -io and fourth conjugation verbs that you will see later.

Person	Singular	Plural
1	mittēbam	mittēbāmus
2	mittēbās	mittēbātis
3	mittēbat	mittēbant

Exercise 2. Following the example of *mittere*, conjugate *induere* in the imperfect tense.

Notice that the third conjugation looks just like the second conjugation in the imperfect tense. It is very important that you memorize the principal parts of each verb that you learn so that you can readily distinguish the two.

Exercise 3. Identify the conjugation for each of the following verbs.

1. ascendēbam
2. habēbāmus
3. ēvādēbātis
4. portābās
5. petēbant
6. quaerēbās
7. vidēbat

Section 36. Future Tense

The future tense marker is an -e in all forms except for the first person singular. The first person singular uses the ending -am instead.

Future Tense: I will send, I will be sending
stem: **mitte/re** + future tense marker: **e** + personal endings

Person	Singular	Plural
1	mitt**am**	mittēmus
2	mittēs	mittētis
3	mittet	mittent

Notā Bene:
The tense marker -e is long in the usual places: first person plural, and second person.

TE **Exercise 4.** Following the example of *mittere*, conjugate *vincere* in the future tense.[c]

TE **Exercise 5.** Parse each of the following verbs identifying their tense, person, and number. Then translate.

LATIN	PERSON	NUMBER	TENSE	TRANSLATION
mittēbam	1	Sing.	Imp.	I used to send
induētis				
vīdit				
claudēbant				
rogābō				
geram				
				He was returning
				You (s.) said
				We will conquer
				They escape
				I was wearing

[c]Reminder: You may wish to use the parsing worksheet included with this guide for this exercise.

TE **Exercise 6.** Change the following verbs to the future, keeping the same person and number.[D]

1. erat
2. arābat
3. vincunt
4. revertis
5. amābātis
6. dīcō
7. respondēs
8. gerimus
9. dōnō
10. induitis

[D]Teachers, remind students that they must first identify a verb's conjugation before they can correctly know which future tense chart they should use. This exercise contains verbs from every conjugation they have learned thus far.

Caveat Magister (Let the teacher beware): Students often will confuse the new future tense verbs with some noun cases that end in -*am*, -*em*, or -*ēs*.

TE **Exercise 7.** Parse, diagram, and translate the following sentences.

1. Hostis ducem Rōmānum circumdābat.

2. Cincinnatus in agrō cum lēgātīs dīcēbat.

3. Nōn gerēs squālidam togam.

4. Dux oppidum vincet cum mīlitibus Rōmānīs.

5. Rōma erit lībera.

CINCINNĀTUS

In bellō cum *Aequīs hostis* ducem Rōmānum, *nōmine* Minucius, circumdābat. Minucius et mīlitēs Rōmānī in monte *Algidō* erant. *Aequī* sub monte erant.

Erat vir *nōmine* Cincinnātus nōtus *virtūte*. *Certā diē* Cincinnātus agrum arābat. Uxor Cincinnātī lēgātōs Rōmānōs in viā prope vīllam vīdit. Ubī Rōmānī ad casam Cincinnātī uxōrisque *pervēnērunt*, lēgātī dīxērunt, "*Eritne* Cincinnātus dictātor Rōmae?"

Uxor "*Eum* rogābō" respondit. Ad agrum, igitur, *īvit* et nūntium Cincinnātō dedit. Cincinnātus labōrābat et vestis agricolae squālida erat. Dīxit marītus uxōrī, "*Fer mihi* togam bonam. Nōn geram squālidam vestem prō lēgātīs." Uxor togam bonam marītō portāvit. Togam induit Cincinnātus et tum cum lēgātīs *colloquēbātur*. Cincinnātus dictātōrem esse nōn *dēsīderāvit*, sed pātriam amābat. *Ita* Cincinnātus erit dictātor *paucōs diēs*, et Aequōs vincet *ūnā cum* mīlitibus Rōmānīs. Cincinnātus posteā ad agrum et *arātrum* revertet, laetus esse agricola et *cīvis* Rōmānus.

GLOSSARY

Aequī, ōrum, m.pl.	Aequi (an Italian tribe)
hostis, hostis, m.	enemy
nōmine	called
Algidus, ī, m.	Algidus (mountain in Latium)
virtūte	because of his virtue
certā diē	on a certain day
pervēnērunt	they arrived
eritne	*erit + ne*
dictātor, dictātōris, m.	dictator
eum, acc., sing., m.	him
īvit	he went
Fer mihi	bring me
colloquēbātur	he was talking
ita, conj.	thus, therefore
paucōs diēs	for a few days
ūnā cum + abl.	along with
arātrum, ī, n.	plough
cīvis, cīvis, m.	citizen

ANSWER IN ENGLISH!

1. Where had the enemy surrounded the Romans?

2. What were Cincinnatus' wishes about becoming dictator?

3. Why did Cincinnatus want to change clothes?

Exercise 8.

Change these plural nouns to the singular, keeping the same case.

Aequīs	mīlitēs	Rōmānī
lēgātōs	lēgātī	Aequōs

Historical Bridge

The events in the last three reading passages occurred around 508 BC. The story in this chapter occurred around 458 BC. So you can see that many years passed. The Romans finally were the victors in the war with the Etruscans. We may imagine that most Romans in the intervening years went about their daily routines of waking; eating breakfast, which they called ientāculum; working; playing; and visiting with their friends. Eventually, though, another war started, this time with the Aequi, a people living in central Italy.

For Discussion:

How was Cincinnātus like George Washington?[E]

[E]After the Revolution, Washington had returned to his farm, Mt. Vernon, where he hoped to spend the rest of his life farming and living with his wife. When the founding fathers asked him to become President of the United States under the new Constitution, he did not want the office, but he loved his country. After serving two terms as President, he returned to Mt. Vernon and resumed farming. Other world leaders such as King George III were amazed that a man who had held such power could lay it down so easily and with such contentment.

 **Exercise 9.**

Change these singular nouns to the plural, keeping the same case.

bellō	marītus	uxor
vīllam	vestem	toga

Culture Corner: Roman Dictators

The actions of the last kings of Rome prove that "power corrupts and absolute power corrupts absolutely." The Romans no longer trusted in kings. Instead, they created two consuls elected annually by the people. The consuls ruled jointly and each one held the power of veto over the other. Thus each man would keep the other from becoming too powerful. The Tarquins, however, were not to give up the power of the throne easily, and the next several years saw Rome at war to defend her new republic.

Soon the Romans felt there might still be times when the absolute authority of a single ruler might be necessary. So, in 501 BC, just nine years after the expulsion of Tarquinius Superbus, the Romans created the office called *dictātor*. Whenever Rome was in a state of emergency, the Senate (body of lawmakers) would pass a *senātūs cōnsultum*. The consuls would then nominate a dictator, who would have absolute power, but for a limited term of six months. The only dictatorships known to have extended beyond this term limit were those of Lūcius Cornēlius Sulla and Gāius Jūlius Caesar.

We derive our word "dictator" directly from the Latin office *dictātor*. Can you discern which Latin verb the Romans derived this title from? Why do you think this is appropriate?[F]

[F]They derived it from *dīcō*, meaning "say" or "tell." This derivation is appropriate because people have to do what a dictator says.

Colloquāmur (Let's Talk)

Use the following questions and responses to review the parsing exercise in this chapter. Use some "eye" Latin to figure out what the responses mean.

interrogātiō:	Cūius est numerī?	What number is it?
respōnsum:	Singulāriter est.	
	Plūrāliter est.	
interrogātiō:	Cūius est persōnae?	What person is it?
respōnsum:	Est prīmae persōnae.	
	Est secundae persōnae.	
	Est tertiae persōnae.	
interrogātiō:	Cūius est temporis?	What tense (time) is it?
respōnsum:	Est praesentis.	
	Est imperfectī.	
	Est futūrī.	
interrogātiō:	Cūius est coniugātiōnis?	What conjugation is it?
respōnsum:	Est prīmae coniugātiōnis.	
	Est secundae coniugātiōnis.	
	Est tertiae coniugātiōnis.	

Chapter 13 Teacher's Pages

Exercise 1

ma-rī-tus, ī, m.
nūn-ti-us, ī, m.
vīl-la, vīl-lae, f.
vir-tūs, vir-tū-tis, f.
as-cen-dō, as-cen-de-re, as-cen-dī, as-cēn-sum
clau-dō, clau-de-re, clau-sī, clau-sum
ē-vā-dō, ē-vā-de-re, ē-vā-dī, ē-vā-sum

in-du-ō, in-du-e-re, in-du-ī, in-dū-tum
rēs-pon-de-ō, rēs-pon-dē-re, rēs-pon-dī, rēs-pōn-sum
vin-cō, vin-ce-re, vī-cī, vic-tum
nō-tus, a, um
squā-li-dus, a, um
mo-do
po-ste-ā

Exercise 2

	IMPERFECT	
PERSON	SINGULAR	PLURAL
1	induēbam	induēbāmus
2	induēbās	induēbātis
3	induēbat	induēbant

Exercise 3

1. ascendēbam   3
2. habēbāmus   2
3. ēvādēbātis   3
4. portābās   1
5. petēbant   3
6. quaerēbās   3
7. vidēbat   2

Exercise 4

	FUTURE	
PERSON	SINGULAR	PLURAL
1	vincam	vincēmus
2	vincēs	vincētis
3	vincet	vincent

Exercise 5

Latin	Person	Number	Tense	Translation
mittēbam	1	Sing.	Imp.	I used to send
induētis	2	Pl.	Fut.	You will put on
vīdit	3	Sing.	Perf.	He saw
claudēbant	3	Pl.	Imp.	They were closing
rogābō	1	Sing.	Fut.	I will ask
geram	1	Sing.	Fut.	I will wear
revertēbat	3	Sing.	Imp.	He was returning
dīxisti	2	Sing.	Perf.	You(s.) said
vincēmus	1	Pl.	Fut.	We will conquer
ēvādunt	3	Pl.	Pres.	They escape
gerēbam	1	Sing.	Imp.	I was wearing

Exercise 6

1. erat   erit
2. arābat   arābit
3. vincunt   vincent
4. revertis   revertēs
5. amābātis   amābitis

6. dīcō   dīcam
7. respondēs respondēbis
8. gerimus   gerēmus
9. dōnō   donābō
10. induitis induētis

Exercise 7

```
        S    DO    Adj        V
1. Hostis ducem Rōmānum circumdābat.
   n/s/m  ac/s/m  ac/s/m   3/s/imp
   The enemy was surrounding the Roman leader.

         S      P OP  P  OP      V
2. Cincinnatus in agrō cum lēgātīs   dīcēbat.
   n/s/m      ab/s/m  ab/p/m 3/s/imp
   Cincinnatus was speaking in the field with the delegates.

   Adv  S+V    Adj      DO
3. Nōn gerēs squālidam togam.
       2/s/f   ac/s/f   ac/s/f
   You will not wear a dirty garment.

    S     DO    V    P    OP     Adj
4. Dux oppidum vincet cum mīlitibus Rōmānīs.
   n/s/m ac/s/n 3/s/f      ab/p/m  ab/p/m
   The leader will conquer the town with the Roman soldiers.

     S    LV   PrN
5. Rōma  erit  lībera.
   n/s/f 3/s/f n/s/f
   Rome will be free.
```

Translation

In the war with the Aequi, the enemy surrounded a Roman general by the name of Minucius. Minucius and the Roman soldiers were on Mount Algidus. The Aequi were under (at the foot of) the mountain.

There was a man by the name of Cincinnatus, noted for his courage. On a certain day, Cincinnatus was plowing his field. The wife of Cincinnatus saw ambassadors/delegates from the Romans on the road near the farmhouse. When the Romans arrived at the house of Cincinnatus and his wife, the ambassadors said, "Will Cincinnatus be dictator of Rome/at Rome?"

The wife responded, "I shall ask him." Therefore, she went to the field and gave the message to Cincinnatus. Cincinnatus was working, and the clothing of the farmer was dirty. The husband said to his wife, "Bring me my good toga. I shall not wear dirty clothes in front of the ambassadors." The wife carried the good toga to her husband. Cincinnatus put on the toga and then he spoke with the ambassadors. Cincinnatus did not want to be dictator, but he loved his country. Thus Cincinnatus will be dictator for a few days, and he will conquer the Aequi along with Roman soldiers. Cincinnatus afterwards will return to his field and to his plow, happy to be a farmer and a Roman citizen.

Answer in English!

1. Where had the enemy surrounded the Romans?
   The enemy had surrounded the Romans in a war with the Aequi.

2. What were Cincinnatus' wishes about becoming dictator?
   He did not want to be dictator.

3. Why did Cincinnatus want to change clothes?
   The clothes he had on were dirty.

Exercise 8

Aequīs ... Aequō	mīlitēs .... mīles, mīlitem	Rōmānī ......Rōmānus
lēgātōs.... lēgātum	lēgātī ...... lēgātus	Aequōs.......Aequum

Exercise 9

bellō .... bellīs	marītus... marītī	uxor............uxōrēs
vīllam ..... vīllīs	vestem.... vestēs	toga ....togae

Notes

ᴬSuggested Project: As a class, create a large map of the city of Rome. Plot on your map the places and events discussed in this unit. You can also trace the journey of Cornelius through the city as told in the "Tour of Rome" (pages 92–93).

Unit 3 Reading

Reading and Review for Chapters 10–13

TOUR OF ROME ᴬ
Karen Moore

Marcus Cornelius Natator and his wife, Aemilia, awoke sore and tired. For many days they had been making their way up the Appian Way, called *viārum rēgīna longārum* by the Romans, from Brundisium. In days long past the tribes of Italy had fought over the lands along this route. Now they were peaceably under Rome's control. The republic had grown much in size and power since the time of Cincinnatus and others who had fought to establish this new empire. Cornelius had proven himself a worthy magistrate in Brundisium and now he was offered a coveted seat in the Roman Senate. Today the couple would finally enter this city which was to be their new home.

Cornelius opened the curtains and peered out of the *raeda* (a four-wheeled carriage) in order to assess how far they had traveled over the course of the night. "Driver," he said, "when do you estimate our arrival in Rome?" "Look ahead, *vir optime*," was the reply. "The Servian Wall appears in the distance and the Caelian, first of Rome's seven hills, rises behind it." Cornelius made out the dark line of the wall in the distance. That ancient wall, built long ago under King Servius Tullius, had hindered many of Rome's enemies. Today it seemed to beckon them to enter within her protective arms.

A few hours later the caravan passed through the Servian Wall at the Porta Appia and all of Rome opened before them. The Palatine Hill loomed ahead, the Aventine stood on the left. These two hills had once been coveted by the brothers Romulus and Remus. Unable to decide which of them should be king, Remus took his followers to the Aventine and Romulus led others to the Palatine. A fit of jealousy anointed the crown of the Palatine with fraternal blood, and this peak became the seat of Rome's kings. As the carriage drew nearer the hills Cornelius could see the Circus Maximus which filled the valley between them. King Tarquinius Priscus had constructed this great racetrack. Then, the slopes of the Palatine and Aventine had served as stadium seating for the chariot races. Now, stone seats replaced the grassy ones, and beautiful homes of the rich and powerful occupied coveted space on the slopes of the Palatine. What Cornelius could not foresee was that in a few hundred years this same hill would give its name to the palatial palaces of king-like emperors that would adorn it. This site held little interest for Aemilia. Married women were not usually permitted to attend such spectacles as the Circus held. Instead she had her eyes fixed on the Caelian as the Via Appia wrapped around its base. This hill also held many homes for the Roman elite and it was on this hill that she would make her new home.

The caravan had now turned off the main road and climbed up through the residential areas of the Caelian. At last they arrived at their new house. Cornelius climbed out of the *raeda* and turned to assist his wife. It felt good to stretch their legs after the long journey. The couple strolled along the house grounds while the slaves unloaded their belongings, taking in the view of the city's landscape. In the valley below them they could see the Via Sacra leading men into the *Forum Rōmānum*. Across from them they could see the Esquiline Hill and beyond that the peak of the Quirinal, tallest of Rome's seven hills. The Viminal Hill, they knew, must lie somewhere between the two, but it was the smallest of the hills and could not be seen from where they stood. "Cornelius," asked Aemilia, "what lies on the Quirinal, the tallest of the hills?" "The Temple of Quirinus, my dear," he replied. "Quirinus was the god of the Sabines and that was their

hill long ago before their families joined with Romulus. Now Romulus-Quirinus is worshipped there; I believe it may be the city's most ancient monument." "And what," she asked, "lies beyond the Quirinal?" "The Servian Wall encompasses the city along its far side," said Cornelius, "and beyond that lies the Campus Martius, a training field for the Roman army. Rome's kings are buried there."

After a short time Aemilia's mind turned to setting up house. There was much work for her as the wife of a Roman senator and the mistress of his home. Cornelius, however, was restless in a quite different direction. He was anxious to see the Forum, the Senate, and the seat of government. He chose his most trusted advisor, an old and wise tutor, and the two set forth to conquer Rome. The pair made their way down to the Via Sacra and followed the sacred path past many of Rome's temples. At the base of the Palatine they saw Cloelia, virtuous heroine of old, seated upon her lofty stone horse. They continued on and soon reached the Forum. On either side tall Basilicas framed the square. These served as courts and business centers. They passed the round temple of Vesta, in which the Vestal Virgins tend the sacred flame. Fortuitous is the man whose path one of these blessed virgins cross. At last they came to the Curia Hostilia, the senate house so called after King Tullus Hostilius who had established the meeting place for the senators. The pair ventured inside and there came upon another senator, Caepio Senex, who had served Rome with great dignity for many years. "So, my young friend, you have finally made it to Rome?" he said. "Have you yet visited the Capitoline? You must pay your respects to Jupiter Optimus Maximus."

The three men made their way through the Forum and up the one hundred steps at the far end. They passed the temple to Juno Moneta on their right as they made their ascent. At the top of the mount stood the largest and greatest temple of Rome; inside, the immense solemn statue of Jupiter seemed to gaze out protectively over his city. The men made their sacrifices to the god and then walked around the temple. "This," said their guide, "is the Arx, the great Citadel of Rome. For centuries Romans have flocked to this mount when enemies threatened the city. This temple, this mount, was their fortress." Cornelius took in the scene before him. The steep cliffs of the Capitoline were reinforced with the unclimbable Servian Wall. The Tiber ran up alongside the wall at one place and then wandered out further to encircle the Campus Martius below them. To their backs, behind the wall and the great cliffs, the city lay snug and safe. "I can certainly see why the people would feel so protected here," said Cornelius. "It would prove incredibly difficult for any enemy to scale these walls, especially with such a formidable protector as the great army of Rome in front of them." "Difficult, yes," said Caepio, "but not unheard of." "Surely you know the story of the great general Manlius? He defended this very wall in front of you against the barbarians. It was not Rome's army alone, however, that prevented the citadel from being taken, but Juno's birds."

MANLIUS, THE GAULS, AND THE GEESE [B]

1.   *Ōlim* lēgātī ad Rōmānōs ex oppidō Clūsiō *appropinquāvērunt.* Sēnōnēs, populus
2. Gallicus, Clūsium oppugnābant. Tum Rōmānī monuērunt Sēnōnēs: "*Nōlīte*
3. *oppugnāre* amīcōs Rōmānōrum!" Ubī pugna *incēpit,* lēgātī Rōmānī, contrā *lēgem*
4. pātriārum, arma *cēpērunt* et populum *urbis* Clūsiī adiuvābant. Posteā Gallī
5. *compēnsātiōnem* ē Rōmānīs *postulāvērunt.* Rōmānī *recūsāvērunt.*
6. Gallī, igitur, Rōmam petīvērunt.
7.   Gallī prope flūmen nōmine Allia vīcērunt. Multī mīlitēs Rōmānī ad Vēiōs
8. *fūgērunt.* Multī aliī Rōmānī ad urbem Rōmam *fūgērunt.* Portās nōn etiam
9. *clausērunt,* sed cum uxōribus *līberīsque* ad *arcem fūgērunt. Ibi* manēbant.
10.   Gallī *aedificia* et casās *urbis cremābant.* Etiam *arcem* oppugnābant! Rōmānī
11. tamen in *arce* manēbant et *dēsuper* Gallōs oppugnābant. Pars Gallōrum in agrīs
12. frūmentum petīvērunt.
13.   **Dum haec geruntur** Rōmānī in *urbe* magnō in perīculō erant. *Nocte* Gallī
14. montem ascendērunt. Ascendērunt magnō cum *silentiō. Nē quidem*
15. *canēs lātrābant! Nōtitiam,* tamen, *ānserum* sacrōrum deae Iūnōnī nōn *ēvādērunt.*
16. *Somnus* Manlium, *clārum* ducem, tenēbat. Ānserēs Manlium *excitāvērunt. Ālās*
17. et *vōcēs ānserum notāvit* Manlius. Manlius ūnum ex Gallīs, **quī erat in summō**
18. **monte,** *dēiēcit.* Cēterī Rōmānī armīs *saxīsque ūnā cum* Manliō hostēs *fūgāvērunt.*
19. Gallī cucurrērunt dē monte **magnā cum celeritāte.** Rōmam *ānserēs* servāvērunt!

Notā Bene:

Dum haec geruntur = while these things are being done (Best translation:
                         "While these things were going on . . . .")
quī erat in summō monte = who was on the top of the mountain
magnā cum celeritāte = with great speed

GLOSSARY

ōlim	once upon a time
appropinquō, āre, āvi, ātum	approach
populus, ī, m.	people, population
Gallicus, a, um, adj.	Gallic, of Gaul (Gaul was a Roman province in what we today call France)
nōlīte oppugnāre	do not attack! (This is a negative command.)
incipiō, incipere, incēpī, inceptus	to begin
contrā, prep. + acc.	against
lēx, lēgis, f.	law
capiō, capere, cēpī, captus	to seize, capture
urbs, urbis, f	city
compēnsātiōnem	Use your "eye" Latin to figure this one out!
postulō, āre, āvī, ātum	to demand
recūsō, āre, āvī, ātum	to refuse
fugiō, fugere, fūgī, fugitum	to flee
līberī, liberōrum, m. pl.	[free born] children
ibi, adv.	there
cremō, āre, āvī, ātum	to burn
aedificium, ī, n.	This noun is related to the verb *aedificiō.* Can you decipher its meaning?
tamen, conj.	nevertheless
dēsuper, adv.	from above
nocte	at night (ablative of time)

mōns, montis, m.............................. hill
silentium, ī, n................................ silence
nē quidem.................................... not even
canis, canis, f............................... dog
lātrō, āre, āvī, ātum........................ bark, bay at, resound
nōtitia, ae, f................................. notice
ānser, ānseris, f. .... goose
somnium, ī, n............................... dream
clārus, a, um, adj.......................... famous
excitō, āre, āvī, ātum...................... arouse, awaken
vōx, vōcis, f................................. voice
āla, āe, f. .... wing
notō, āre, āvi, ātum .... to make known
dēiciō, dēicere, dēiēcī, dēiectum .... to throw down
saxum, ī, n. .... rock
ūnā cum, prep. + abl....................... along with
fūgāvērunt................................... put to flight, chased away

Question & Answer

1. The Sēnōnēs were ___.
    a. a group of Romans
    b. an Italian tribe
    c. allies of the Romans
    d. a Gallic tribe

2. According to lines 2 and 3, ___.
    a. the Romans feared the Sēnōnēs
    b. the Romans asked the Sēnōnēs to help them
    c. the Romans warned the Sēnōnēs not to do something
    d. the Romans attacked the Gauls without just cause

3   What group of words indicates the haste of the Romans upon reaching Rome?
    a. arma cēpērunt et populum urbis Clusiī adiuvant
    b. contrā lēgem patriārum
    c. portās nōn clausērunt
    d. Rōmānī in urbe magnō in perīculō erant

4. According to lines 10 and 11, what was the most significant danger to Rome?
    a. The Gauls were burning the city.
    b. Someone left the gates open.
    c. Too many Romans were crowded onto the citadel.
    d. The Gauls were attacking the Romans from a superior position.

5. Not even ___ aroused the Romans, according to lines 14 and 15.
    a. the rustling of the wings of birds
    b. the barking of the dogs
    c. the clash of armor
    d. the shouts of frightened women

6. What use of the genitive is in line 11?
   a. partitive
   b. possession
   c. material
   d. origin

7. What use of the ablative is in line 14?
   a. means
   b. manner
   c. accompaniment
   d. origin

8. According to this reading, why did some of the Gauls go into the countryside?
   a. to recruit more men
   b. to look for grain
   c. to buy more weapons
   d. to buy some geese for Juno

9. What character in the reading is a famous general?
   a. Manlius
   b. Clūsiō
   c. Veiōs
   d. Allia

10. What is true of *armīs* in line 18?
    a. It is ablative of means.
    b. It is a dative indirect object.
    c. It is a direct object of a verb that governs the dative.
    d. It is illustrative of ablative of manner.

TRANSLATION

Once upon a time, ambassadors from the town of Clusium approached the Romans. The Senones, a Gallic people, were attacking Clusium. Then the Romans warned the Senones: "Don't attack the friends of the Romans." When the fight began, the Roman ambassadors against the law of countries (i.e. international law), seized arms and helped the people of the city of Clusium. Afterwards, the Gauls demanded compensation from the Romans. The Romans refused. The Gauls, therefore, attacked Rome.

The Gauls were victorious [i.e., won a battle] near a river by the name of Allia. Many Roman soldiers fled to the Veii. Many other Romans fled to the city of Rome. They did not even close the gates but with their wives and children fled to the citadel. They were remaining/staying there.

The Gauls were burning the buildings and houses of the city. They even attacked the citadel! The Romans, however, stayed on the citadel and attacked the Gauls from above. Part of the Gauls sought grain in the fields.

While these things were going on, the Romans in the city were in great danger. By night/at night the Gauls ascended the mountain. They ascended with great silence. Not even the dogs barked! However, they did not escape the notice of the geese sacred to the goddess Juno. Sleep was holding Manlius, a famous general. The geese woke Manlius up. Manlius noticed the wings and voices of the geese. Manlius threw down [from the mountain] one of the Gauls who was on top of the mountain. The rest of the Romans with weapons and rocks, along with Manlius, put the enemy to flight. The Gauls ran down from the mountain with great speed. The geese saved Rome!

Dīrigō.
I guide.
—Maine state motto ^A

Chapter 14

- third declension i-stem: masculine, feminine, neuter

VOCABULARY

NOUNS		
*animal, animālis, n.	animal	(animal)
aurum, ī, n.	gold	(auric)
caelum, ī, n.	sky	(celestial)
collum, ī, n.	neck	(collar)
*fīnis, fīnis, m.	end, boundary	(finish, finite)
homō, hominis, m.	human, man	(homo sapiens)
*īnfāns, īnfantis, m./f.	baby	(infant)
*mare, maris, n.	sea	(marine)
*nāvis, nāvis, f.	ship	(naval)
nōmen, nōminis, n.	name, title	(nomination)
*nox, noctis, f.	night; darkness	(nocturnal)
*parēns, parentis, m/f.	parent	(parent)
*pars, partis, f.	part	(particle, partition)
*urbs, urbis, f.	city	(urbane, urban)

ADJECTIVES		
parvus, a, um	little, small	
praecipuus, a, um	special; principal	

VERBS		
appellō, āre, āvī, ātum	to speak to; call, name	(appellation)
dēdicō, āre, āvī, ātum	to consecrate, dedicate; declare	(dedicate)
iubeō, iubēre, iussī, iussum	to order, command	(jussive)

CONJUNCTION		
sī	if	

* i-stem nouns

Exercise 1. Using the rules for syllabication and accent that you have learned, write out the syllables and accents for the vocabulary words above. Then practice pronouncing them aloud.

Section 37. Third Declension i-stems: Masculine and Feminine

Within the third declension noun family is a subgroup of i-stem nouns. For the most part these nouns use all of the same endings as the regular third declension nouns that you learned in chapter 10. The i-stem nouns, however, add an extra **i** in a few places. For masculine and feminine nouns this difference is visible in only one place. Compare the following chart to that in chapter 10 (Section 29). Can you discern where the extra **i** appears?

CASE	ENDINGS		MASCULINE		FEMININE	
	sing.	plural	sing.	plural	sing.	plural
Nominative	*	-ēs	fīnis	fīnēs	urbs	urbēs
Genitive	-is	-ium	fīnis	fīnium	urbis	urbium
Dative	-ī	-ibus	fīnī	fīnibus	urbī	urbibus
Accusative	-em	-ēs	fīnem	fīnēs	urbem	urbēs
Ablative	-e	-ibus	fīne	fīnibus	urbe	urbibus

The only ending that is different for i-stem nouns is the genitive plural. All other cases are exactly the same as regular third declension nouns.

 Exercise 2. Following the examples of *fīnis* and *urbs*, decline the noun *pars*.[B]

Section 38. Third Declension i-stems: Neuter

For neuter i-stem nouns the **i** appears in a few more places. Compare the chart below with the chart for regular third declension neuter nouns in chapter 10 (Section 30). Identify the places where the **i** appears in the chart below.

CASE	ENDINGS		NEUTER	
	sing.	plural	sing.	plural
Nominative	*	-ia	mare	maria
Genitive	-is	-ium	maris	marium
Dative	-ī	-ibus	marī	maribus
Accusative	*	-ia	mare	maria
Ablative	-ī	-ibus	marī	maribus

Neuter i-stem nouns not only add an **i** in the genitive plural, but also in the ablative singular and the nominative and accusative plural.

 Exercise 3. Following the example of *mare*, decline the noun *animal*.

Section 39. Identifying i-stem nouns

You may have noticed that the differences for i-stem nouns do not affect the nominative or genitive singular, the two forms listed in your dictionary. So, how will you be able to know which nouns fall into this special subgroup? There are a few patterns that i-stems follow in their nominative and genitive singular.

If you memorize these, then you should have no problem recognizing i-stem nouns. Notice that the first two patterns apply to both the masculine and feminine nouns while the third pattern applies only to neuter nouns.

MASCULINE AND FEMININE:
Pattern #1

The nominative singular ends in -is or -es, AND the nominative and genitive singular are parasyllabic (have an equal number of syllables).
> e.g. **fīnis, fīnis**

Pattern #2

The nominative singular ends in -s or -x, AND the stem ends in a double consonant.
> e.g. **urbs, urbis**

NEUTER:
Pattern #3

Neuter nouns that end in -al, -ar, or -e.
> e.g. **mare, maris**

Exercise 4. Identify the regular third declension nouns from the i-stem nouns. If a noun is an i-stem, identify the pattern that it follows.[c]

> example: fīnis, fīnis   i-stem, #1

1. mare, maris, n.

2. māter, mātris, f.

3. ignis, ignis, m.

4. tempus, temporis, n.

5. nox, noctis, f.

6. lūx, lūcis, f.

7. exemplar, exemplāris, n.

8. cīvis, cīvis, m.

9. nūbēs, nūbis, f.

10. adulēscēns, adulēscentis, m/f.

[c]Teachers, this is an excellent exercise to repeat each time you have a new vocabulary list that contains third declension nouns. Repeating the exercise regularly will help imbed these rules.

Caveat Magister: There are a few third declension nouns which seem as though they should be i-stem nouns, but they are regular. While you may not want to ask students to memorize this list, you should make yourself aware of these exceptions in case you encounter them later on.

<u>always</u>
  iuvenis, iuvenis, m/f youth
  canis, canis, m/f dog
  pānis, pānis, m. bread
  senex, senis, m. old man
  struēs, struis, f. heap
  volūcris, volūcris, m/f a bird or
    flying insect

<u>usually</u>
  apis, apis, f. bee
  sēdēs, sēdis, f. seat
  vātes, vātis, m/f a soothsayer,
    prophet

<u>frequently</u>
  mēnsis, mēnsis, m. month

Exercise 5. Parse, diagram, and translate the following sentences.[D]

1. Iter animālium ad fīnem maris erat longum.

2. Casae cīvium nōn erant magnae.

3. Nāvem in marī vīdimus.

4. Parentēs aurum circum collum īnfantis posuērunt.

5. Parvae nūbēs sunt in caelō.

[D]Review these sentences aloud and ask students to identify the type of place expressions that appear in this exericise.

For example: ad fīnem – accusative
                  of place to which
          in marī – ablative of
                  place where

DIES LUSTRICUS

Ubi īnfāns **nātus est**, pater, sī īnfāns erat puella, iussit īnfantī *alimentum*. *Hōc modō* īnfantem pater *agnovit*. Sī īnfāns erat puer, īnfantem pater *sustulit* ad caelum. *Hōc modō* puerum *agnoscit*. **Octō aut novem diēs** hominēs īnfantem pūpam appellāvērunt.

Erat īnfantibus et familiīs *diēs* praecipuus. *Hic diēs* erat *diēs lustricus*. Hic diēs erat puellae **octāva diēs** vītae **nōna diēs** puerō.† *Hōc diē* īnfāns nōmen accēpit. Īnfāns quoque *crepundia* et *bullam* accēpit.

Crepundia erant *rēs quae crepitant*. Īnfantēs quoque *lūnulās* accēpērunt. Parentēs *crepundia* et *lūnulās* circum collum īnfantis posuērunt. *Lūnulae praecipuē* īnfantem *prōtēxērunt*. *Crepundia* īnfantem *dēlectāvērunt* ubi *crepitābant*. *Bulla* erat *similis* parvō *saccō*. *Bulla forsitan* aurī aut *alūtae* erat. Parentēs *bullam* circum collum īnfantis *rīte* posuērunt. Puellae *bullam* gerēbant *usque* ad noctem ante *nuptiās*, puerī togam *virīlem* induērunt.[E] Et puellae et puerī *bullam ad larēs* dēdicāvērunt ubi *bullam nōn iam* gerēbant. Puellae pūpās et *rēs puerīlēs dēposuērunt*. Puer partem *prīmae barbae* deīs *forsitan* dēdicāvit.

Ōlim nātī sunt Rōmae geminī. Geminī erant puella et puer. *Diē lūstricō* puella nōmen "Cornēlia" accēpit. *Diē lūstricō* puer nōmen "Marcus" *accēpit*. *Tōtum* nōmen Mārcī erat Marcus Cornēlius Natātor. Puella *sōlum* nōmen "Cornēlia" habuit. *Legētis plūrēs fābulās* dē Cornēliā et Mārcō.

---

nātus est = was born
octō aut novem diēs = for eight or nine days
(Accusative of Duration of Time)
octāva diēs... nōna diēs = eighth day... ninth day

† Hic diēs erat puellae octāva diēs vītae nōna diēs puerō. Notice the word order in this sentence. *Puellae* is dative, *octāva diēs* and *nōna diēs* are nominative, and *puerō* is dative. The use of these cases, then, sets up a pattern of ABBA. Such a pattern creates chiasmus. Notice also that *vītae* applies to the lives of both the boy and the girl.

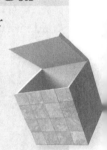

Challenge Box

What other sentence in the reading has an unusual pattern? What do we call the results of this pattern?[E]

[E] *Puella bullam gerēbant . . . .togam . . . induērunt.* (ABAB) Synchysis.

GLOSSARY

alimentum, alimentī, n.	nourishment
agnovit	recognized as his own
hōc modō	in this way
sustulit	he lifted
pūpus, pūpī, m.	doll (It appears that babies of both sexes were called pūpus until they had their names.)
diēs, diēī	day (This word may be either masculine or feminine.)
dies lustricus	The day of purification on which children received their names. (Can you think of a similar custom in the Judeo-Christian tradition?)
Hōc diē	on this day
hic	this
crepundia, ōrum, n. pl.	rattles, toys
bulla, ae, f.	bulla
rēs, reī, f.	thing
rēs quae crepitant	things that rattle
lūnula, ae, f.	little moon (These lunettes were thought to be especially protective against the evil eye.)
accipiō, accipere, accēpī, acceptum	to take, receive, accept
praecipuē	especially

prōtegō, prōtegere, prōtēxī, prōtectum ....to protect
dēlectō, āre, āvī, ātum ....to delight, amuse
crepitō, āre, āvī, ātum...................................to chatter, rattle
similis, nom., sing., adj. ....similar to, like (this adjective is often followed by a dative)
saccus, ī, m. ....bag
forsitan, adv. ....perhaps, maybe
alūta, ae, f..leather
rīte...according to ritual, ritualistically
nuptiae, nuptiārum, f. pl. ....marriage, wedding
virīlis..of manhood
larēs, m. pl. ....lares (household gods)
nōn iam...no longer
pūpa, ae, f. ....doll
aliī rēs puerīlēs..other childish things (From what word is *puerīlēs* derived? How are the meanings of these words related?)
dēposuērunt...This is a compound verb formed from *dē + pōnō, pōnere*. Can you discern its meaning?
prīmus, a, um, adj. ....first
barba, barbae, f. ....beard
ōlim nātī...once; once upon a time
tōtus, a, um, adj..whole
sōlus, a, um, adj..only, alone
legētis ....you will read
plūrēs ....more
fābula, ae, f. ....story

Culture Corner: The Larēs and Penātēs

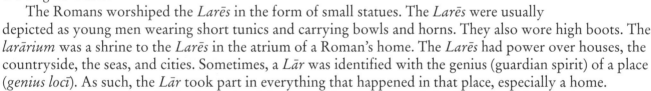

The original *Larēs* were the sons of Mercury and Lara, a Naiad. She was beautiful and talkative. Mercury fell in love with her, and she gave birth to two sons, who were the original *Larēs*.

The Romans worshiped the *Larēs* in the form of small statues. The *Larēs* were usually depicted as young men wearing short tunics and carrying bowls and horns. They also wore high boots. The *larārium* was a shrine to the *Larēs* in the atrium of a Roman's home. The *Larēs* had power over houses, the countryside, the seas, and cities. Sometimes, a *Lār* was identified with the genius (guardian spirit) of a place (*genius locī*). As such, the *Lār* took part in everything that happened in that place, especially a home.

The *Penātēs* were basically the gods of the pantry; however, Vergil, in the *Aeneid*, depicts the *penātēs* Aeneas rescues from Troy as national deities. Their name comes from Latin words signifying both "within" and "food."

Colloquāmur (Let's Talk)

Use the following questions and responses to review the nouns and adjectives in the sentences above. Use some "eye" Latin to figure out what the responses mean.

interrogātiō:	Cūius est numerī?	What number is it?
respōnsum:	Singulāriter est. Plūrāliter est.	
interrogātiō:	Quō est cāsū?	In what case is it?
respōnsum:	Cāsū nōminātīvō est. Cāsū accūsātīvō est. Cāsū datīvō est. Cāsū ablātīvō est.	
interrogātiō:	Cūius est generis?	What gender is it?
respōnsum:	Est virīlis. Est muliebris. Est neutrālis.	

Exercise 1

a-ni-mal, a-ni-mā-lis, n.
au-rum, ī, n.
cae-lum, ī, n.
col-lum, col-lī, n.
fī-nis, fī-nis, m.
ho-mō, ho-mi-nis, m.
īn-fāns, īn-fan-tis, m./f.
ma-re, ma-ris, n.
nā-vis, nā-vis, f.
nō-men, nō-mi-nis, n.

nox, noc-tis, f.
pa-rēns, pa-ren-tis, m/f.
pars, par-tis, f.
urbs, ur-bis, f.
par-vus, a, um
prae-ci-pu-us, a, um
ap-pel-lō, ā-re, ā-vī, ā-tum
dē-di-cō, ā-re, ā-vī, ā-tum
iu-be-ō, iu-bē-re, ius-sī, ius-sum
sī

Exercise 2

CASE	SINGULAR	PLURAL
Nominative	*pars*	*partēs*
Genitive	*partis*	*partium*
Dative	*partī*	*patiburs*
Accusative	*partem*	*partēs*
Ablative	*parte*	*partibus*

Exercise 3

CASE	SINGULAR	PLURAL
Nominative	*animal*	*animālia*
Genitive	*animālis*	*animālium*
Dative	*animālī*	*animālibus*
Accusative	*animal*	*animālia*
Ablative	*animālī*	*animālibus*

Exercise 4

1. mare, maris, n.   i-stem #3
2. māter, mātris, f.   regular
3. ignis, ignis, m.   i-stem #1
4. tempus, temporis, n.   regular
5. nox, noctis, f.   i-stem #2
6. lūx, lūcis, f.   regular
7. exemplar, exemplāris, n.   i-stem #3
8. cīvis, cīvis, m.   i-stem #1
9. nūbēs, nūbis, f.   i-stem #1
10. adulēscēns, adulēscentis, m/f.   i-stem #2

Exercise 5

```
        S    PNA   P   OP   PNA  LV   Adj
1. Iter animālium ad fīnem  maris  erat  longum.
   n/s/n   g/p/n      ac/s/m g/s/n 3/s/i nom/s/n
```
The journey of the animals to the boundary of the sea was long.

```
        S    PNA  Adv  LV    PrN
2. Casae cīvium nōn erant magnae.
   n/p/f  g/p/m      3/p/i  n/p/f
```
The houses of the citizens were not large/great.

```
      DO   P  OP    S+V
3. Nāvem in marī  vīdimus.
   ac/s/f  ab/s/n 1/p/perf
```
We saw the ship on the sea.

```
        S     DO    P    OP    PNA      V
4. Parentēs aurum circum collum īnfantis  posuērunt.
   n/p/m   ac/s/n       ac/s/n g/s/m,f   3/p/perf
```
The parents placed gold around the neck of the infant.

```
    Adj   S    LV  P OP
5. Parvae nūbēs  sunt in caelō.
   n/p/f  n/p/f 3/p/pr ab/s/n
```
The small clouds are in the sky.

Translation

When a baby was born, the father, if the baby was a girl, ordered food for the baby. In this way the father recognized the infant (as his own). If the baby was a boy, the father lifted the baby to the sky. In this manner the father recognized the boy (as his own). For eight or nine days men called the infant "doll."

There was a special day for babies and [their] families. This day was the *dies lustricus* (purification day). This day was for a girl the eighth day of life, for a boy the ninth day. On this day the infant received its name. The infant also received toys and the *bulla* (amulet).

The toys were things which rattle. The babies also received moon-shaped charms. The parents placed the rattles and the moon-shaped charms around the neck of the baby. The charms especially protected the baby. The rattles delighted the baby when they rattled. The bulla was like a small bag. Perhaps the bulla was of gold or soft leather. The parents placed the bulla around the baby's neck according to ritual. Girls wore the bulla up to the night before their weddings, boys up to/until [the time when] they put on the *toga virilis* (the white toga of manhood). Both boys and girls dedicated their bulla to the lares when they were no longer wearing the bulla. The girls put aside their dolls and childhood things. A boy, perhaps, dedicated a part of his first beard to the gods.

Once upon a time, twins were born at Rome. The twins were a girl and a boy. On the *dies lustricus*, the girl received the name [of] Cornelia. The boy received the name [of] Marcus. The whole name of Marcus was Marcus Cornelius Natator. The girl had only the name "Cornelia." You will read several stories about Cornelia and Marcus.

Scūtō bonae voluntātis tuae corōnāstī nōs.
With the shield of Your good will
You have encircled us.
—Maryland state motto[A]

This motto is adapted from Psalms 5:13 of the Latin Vulgate version of the Bible. *"Domine ut scūtō plācābilitātis corōnābis eum"*[B]

[B]Lord, you will crown him as with the shield of (your) placability.

[A]The design of this seal dates back to the days of the original British settlements in Maryland. There are actually two sides for the seal. The reverse side (shown here) is the most commonly seen. It depicts a farmer and a fisherman on either side of the state shield. Notice the British crown and armor placed above the shield. The obverse side (not shown) portrays Lord Baltimore as a mounted knight.

Chapter 15

- third declension adjectives
  - three termination
  - two termination
  - one termination

VOCABULARY

NOUNS		
annus, ī, m.	year	(annual)
ēducātiō, ēducātiōnis, f.	upbringing, rearing; education	(education)
lūdus, ī, m.	school, game	(ludicrous)
mēnsa, ae, f.	table	
VERBS		
doceō, docēre, docuī, doctum	to teach	(doctrine)
discō, discere, didicī	to learn	(discern)
scrībō, scrībere, scrīpsī, scrīptum	to write	(scribble)
ADJECTIVES		
ācer, ācris, ācre	sharp, eager; severe, fierce	(acrid, acrimony)
aptus, a, um	fitting, proper, apt, suitable	(aptitude)
brevis, breve	short, brief	(brevity)
celer, celeris, celere	swift, quick, rapid	(accelerate)
fortis, forte	strong, brave	(fortitude)
ingēns, ingentis	huge	
iuvenis, iuvenis	young, youthful	(juvenile)
omnis, omne	all, every	(omnibus, omnipresent)
pūblicus, a, um	public	(publicity)
senex, senis	old, aged; (as a noun) old man	(senate, senile)
gravis, grave	serious, important, weighty	(grave)

103

Exercise 1. Using the rules for syllabication and accent that you have learned, write out the syllables and accents for the vocabulary words above. Then practice pronouncing them aloud.

SECTION 40. Third Declension Adjectives

There are two categories of adjectives in Latin. The first are known as first and second declension adjectives because they use all the endings for both the first and second declension. The second category is known as third declension adjectives. The endings for this category are almost the same as the i-stem charts you just learned in chapter 14, with the exception that the ablative ends in -i rather than -e. Because the nominative singular varies so much in the third declension, this group of adjectives is broken down into three subgroups. As you study each of these subgroups notice that they differ only in the nominative singular.[c]

a. Three-termination adjectives

This group of adjectives has three forms (or terminations) for the nominative singular: one for each gender. Look to the second form to identify the stem.

celer, celeris, celere   stem = celer

[c]*Caveat Magister:* Students are sometimes overwhelmed by the variety of third declension patterns. Encourage them to look for similarities between other adjective and noun patterns.

This first pattern is similar to the first and second declension adjectives that students are already familiar with. The three forms presented represent the three genders.

SINGULAR

CASE	MASCULINE	FEMININE	NEUTER
Nom.	**celer**	**celeris**	**celere**
Gen.	celeris	celeris	celeris
Dat.	celerī	celerī	celerī
Acc.	celerem	celerem	celere
Abl.	celerī	celerī	celerī

PLURAL

CASE	MASCULINE	FEMININE	NEUTER
Nom.	celerēs	celerēs	celeria
Gen.	celerium	celerium	celerium
Dat.	celeribus	celeribus	celeribus
Acc.	celerēs	celerēs	celeria
Abl.	celeribus	celeribus	celeribus

Notā Bene: The masculine and feminine are identical except for the nominative singular.[D]

[D]Note also that all genders are the same in the genitive, dative, and ablative cases. Only the nominative and accusative differ.

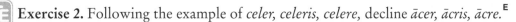 **Exercise 2.** Following the example of *celer, celeris, celere*, decline *ācer, ācris, ācre*.[E]

b. Two-termination adjectives
This group of adjectives has two forms (or terminations) for the nominative singular: one for the masculine and feminine, and a different form for the neuter. Look to the second form to identify the stem.[F]

omnis, omne   stem = omn

[E]*Caveat Magister*: Note that the 'e' drops out after the nominative, masculine, singular.

[F]This pattern is typical of third declension. Note how all third declension nouns that are masculine or feminine share the same forms too.

[G]Note again that all genders are the same in the genitive, dative, and ablative cases. Only the nominative and accusative differ.

SINGULAR

CASE	MASCULINE & FEMININE	NEUTER
Nom.	**omnis**	**omne**
Gen.	omnis	omnis
Dat.	omnī	omnī
Acc.	omnem	omne
Abl.	omnī	omnī

PLURAL[G]

CASE	MASCULINE & FEMININE	NEUTER
Nom.	omnēs	omnia
Gen.	omnium	omnium
Dat.	omnibus	omnibus
Acc.	omnēs	omnia
Abl.	omnibus	omnibus

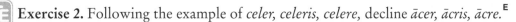 **Exercise 3.** Following the example of *omnis, omne*, decline *fortis, forte*.

c. One-termination adjectives
This group of adjectives has only one form (or termination) for the nominative singular. The dictionary provides the genitive singular of each adjective in order to help you identify the adjective's stem.

ingēns, ingentis   stem = ingent

SINGULAR

CASE	MASCULINE & FEMININE	NEUTER
Nom.	**ingēns**	**ingēns**
Gen.	ingentis	ingentis
Dat.	ingentī	ingentī
Acc.	ingentem	**ingēns**
Abl.	ingentī	ingentī

PLURAL

CASE	MASCULINE & FEMININE	NEUTER
Nom.	ingentēs	ingentia
Gen.	ingentium	ingentium
Dat.	ingentibus	ingentibus
Acc.	ingentēs	ingentia
Abl.	ingentibus	ingentibus

Caveat Discipulus: Notice that the neuter rule (Section 19) still applies for all third declension adjectives.

Exercise 4. Following the example of *ingēns, ingentis*, decline *senex, senis*.

Exercise 5. Make the following adjectives in parentheses agree with the noun they modify in case, number, and gender. Provide all possibilities.

> example: virī (omnis) omnēs, omnis

1. hastae (ācer)
2. sociōs (fortis)
3. rēgibus (senex)
4. animālī (celer)
5. mātrēs (bonus)
6. iter (brevis)
7. cēnā (ingēns)

Exercise 6. Parse, diagram, and translate the following sentences.

1. Puella celeris ad lūdum nōn ambulāvit, sed cucurrit.

2. Ēducātiō Cornēliae erat brevis.

3. Cornēlia erit uxor iuvenis.

4. Discunt puerī dē vītā pūblicā Rōmānōrum.

5. Habēbuntne Mārcus et Cornēlia ēducātiōnem gravem?

Chapter Reading TE

EDUCATION

Parentēs līberōs *primō* docēbant. *Usque ad septimum* annum vītae et puerōs
et puellās māter docēbat. Mārcus et Cornēlia, igitur, linguam Latīnam dīcere, legere, et scrībere ad mēnsam
sedentēs cum mātre, Aemiliā, discēbant. Pater Cornēlius quoque Mārcum *multa* docēbat dē vītā. Et māter et
pater līberōs docēbant dē *virtūte*.

Mārcus et Cornēlia, ubi *septem* annōs habuērunt, ad lūdum ambulāvērunt. *Grammaticus* in lūdō līberōs
legere, scrībere, et *arithmēticam* docēbat. Geminī lūdum amābant. *Paucīs annīs*, Cornēlia ad lūdum nōn iam
ambulāvit. In casā cum mātre manēbat et dē mātre discēbat. Mārcus, tamen, discēbat cum patre. Discēbat
Mārcus dē vītā pūblicā Rōmānōrum; ambulābat cum patre in *cūriam* ubi senātōrēs vidēbat et *audiēbat*.
Mārcus quoque dē *dialecticā* discēbat.

Cornēlia erit uxor iuvenis; ēducātiō igitur Cornēliae erit brevis. Mārcus, autem, *plūra* ēducātiōnis *accipiet*.
Mārcus ad Graeciam nāvigābit ubi discet *rhētoricam, artem dīcendī*. Et Mārcus et Cornēlia ēducātiōnem

gravem habēbunt, et ēducātiō *ambōrum* erit bona et apta.

Rōmānī semper līberōs multa docēbant et praecipuē dē *virtūte* et *bonitāte* docēbant. Marcus et Cornēlia quoque līberōs *suōs* docēbunt.

GLOSSARY

prīmō	at first
usque ad septimum	up until the seventh . . .
multa	many things (neuter plural)
sedentēs, nominative plural	sitting
virtūs, virtūtis, f.	courage, manliness, the qualities the Romans believed made a man (A woman had *muliēbritās*, the qualities that made her a good Roman matron.)
septem, indeclinable numerical adj.	seven
grammaticus, ī, m.	an elementary school teacher
arithmētica	Use your "eye" Latin to discern the meaning of this word.
paucīs annīs	in a few years (ablative of time within which)
cūria, ae, f.	the Senate House
audiō, audīre, audīvī, audītum	to hear
dialectica, ae, f.	logic
plūra	more
accipiō, accipere, accēpī, acceptum	to receive
rhētorica, ae, f.	rhetoric, art of oratory
artem dīcendī	the art of speaking
ambōrum	of both
bonitās, bonitātis, f.	goodness
suus, a, um, adj.	his own, their own

Respondē Latīnē!

 1. Quandō līberī dē parentibus discēbant?

2. Ubi sedēbant Mārcus et Cornēlia cum mātre?

3. Quis docēbat in lūdō?

4. Cūr est ēducātiō Cornēliae brevis?

5. Quis discet rhētoricam?

quandō = *when?*, quis = *who?*, ubi = *where?*, cūr = *why?*

ANSWER IN ENGLISH!

1. Where does the mother teach Cornelia?

2. Where will Marcus go to learn the art of speaking?

3. What feeling do both Marcus and Cornelia have about education?

4. How will the education of Marcus and Cornelia someday affect their own children?

You may also need to learn some classroom commands. In the chart below, singular commands are on the left and plural commands on the right.

Surge! – *Stand!*	Surgite! – *Stand!*
Sedē! – *Sit!*	Sedēte! – *Sit!*

Dispōne librōs! – *Put away your books!*
Taceās. – *[Please] be quiet.*
Scrībe in tabulā. – *Write on the board.*
Dā mihi chartam. – *Give me your paper.*

Dispōnite librōs! – *Put away your books!*
Taceātis. – *[Please] be quiet.*
Scrībite in tabulā. – *Write on the board.*
Date mihi chartās. – *Give me your papers.*

Colloquāmur (Let's Talk)[H]

[H]In addition to the oral activity below, you can also use the Colloquāmur from chapter 14 (page 102) to parse adjectives.

Adjectives are words that we use to describe people, places, and other nouns. Use the conversational prompts below to practice describing things around your classroom or school. Then take a nature walk around your home or campus and see how many things you can describe to your friends.[I]

interrogātiō:	rēspōnsum:
Quālis discipulus/discipula est?	Est celer.
Quālis sella est?	Est parva.
Quālēs sellae sunt?	Sunt ingentēs.

quālis, quāle, interrogative – what sort of, what kind of?

CLASSROOM
sella, ae, f. .... chair
mēnsa, ae, f. .... table
liber, librī, m. .... book
magister/magistra m./f. ... teacher
toga, ae, f. .... toga (shirt)
vestis, vestis, f. .... clothing
stylus, ī, m. .... pen
fenestra, ae, f. .... window
iānua, ae, f. .... door

OUTDOORS
arbor, arboris, f. .... tree
baculum, ī, n. .... stick
flōs, flōris, m. .... flower
herba, ae, f. .... grass
saxum, ī, n. .... rock
nūbēs, nūbis, f. .... cloud
animal, animālis, n. .... animal
īnsectum, ī, n. .... insect
aedificium, ī, n. .... building

COLORS
ruber, rubra, rubrum ...... red
pūniceus, a, um .... pink
flāvus, a, um .... yellow
viridis, viride .... green
caeruleus, a, um .... blue
violus, a, um .... violet
purpureus, a, um .... purple
fuscus, a, um .... brown
albus, alba, album .... white
āter, ātra, ātrum .... black

Things in School

If you take the Exploratory Latin Exam or some other national test regarding Latin, you will more than likely need to know the Latin names for the people and things that surround you in your classroom.

sella .... *student's chair or seat*
cathēdra .... *teacher's chair*
cēra .... *wax tablet*
stylus .... *stylus (pointed on one end, blunt on the other writing instrument)* {Why do you think it was blunt on one end?}
crēta .... *chalk*
tabula picta .... *painted board (It used to be black, then green; now it is probably white.)*
liber .... *book*
volūminis ...... *scroll, volume*
charta .... *paper*
tabellae .... *notebook*
iānua .... *door*
fenestra .... *window*
parietis .... *wall*
discipulus ...... *boy student*
discipula .... *girl student*
magister *or* magistra .... *teacher*

[I]Teachers, encourage students to review adjectives and nouns from other vocabulary lists and even look up a few new ones in a Latin-English/English-Latin dictionary.

Exercise 1

an-nus, ī, m.
ē-du-cā-ti-ō, ē-du-cā-ti-ōn-is, f.
lū-dus, ī, m.
mēn-sa, mēn-sae, f.
do-ce-ō, do-cē-re, do-cu-ī, doc-tum
dis-cō, dis-ce-re, di-di-cī
scrī-bō, scrī-be-re, scrip-sī, scrip-tum
ā-cer, ā-cris, ā-cre
ap-tus, a, um

bre-vis, bre-ve
ce-ler, ce-ler-is, ce-le-re
for-tis, for-te
in-gēns, in-gen-tis
iu-ve-nis, iu-ve-nis
om-nis, om-ne
pū-bli-cus, a, um
se-nex, se-nis
gra-vis, gra-ve

Exercise 2

CASE	SINGULAR			PLURAL		
	MASCULINE	FEMININE	NEUTER	MASCULINE	FEMININE	NEUTER
Nominative	ācer	ācris	ācre	ācrēs	ācrēs	ācria
Genitive	ācris	ācris	ācris	ācrium	ācrium	ācrium
Dative	ācrī	ācrī	ācrī	ācribus	ācribus	ācribus
Accusative	ācrem	ācrem	ācre	ācrēs	ācrēs	ācria
Ablative	ācrī	ācrī	ācrī	ācribus	ācribus	ācribus

Exercise 3

CASE	SINGULAR		PLURAL	
	MASCULINE & FEMININE	NEUTER	MASCULINE & FEMININE	NEUTER
Nominative	fortis	forte	fortēs	fortia
Genitive	fortis	fortis	fortium	fortium
Dative	fortī	fortī	fortibus	fortibus
Accusative	fortem	forte	fortēs	fortia
Ablative	fortī	fortī	fortibus	fortibus

Exercise 4

CASE	SINGULAR		PLURAL	
	MASCULINE & FEMININE	NEUTER	MASCULINE & FEMININE	NEUTER
Nominative	senex	senex	senēs	senia
Genitive	senis	senis	senium	senium
Dative	senī	senī	senibus	senibus
Accusative	senem	senex	senēs	senia
Ablative	senī	senī	senibus	senibus

Exercise 5

1. hastae (ācer)	ācrēs, ācris, ācrī		5. mātrēs (bonus)	bonae, bonās
2. sociōs (fortis)	fortēs		6. iter (brevis)	breve
3. rēgibus (senex)	senibus		7. cēnā (ingēns)	ingentī
4. animālī (celer)	celerī			

Exercise 6

```
         S      Adj  P  OP  Adv    V      C    V
```
1. Puella celeris ad lūdum nōn ambulāvit, sed cucurrit.
   n/s/f n/s/f   ac/s/m   3/s/perf   3/s/perf
   The swift girl did not walk to school, but ran.

```
        S        PNA     LV    PrN
```
2. Ēducātiō Cornēliae erat brevis.
   n/s/f   g/s/f   3/s/imp n/s/f
   The education of Cornelia (Cornelia's education) was brief.

```
        S      LV   PrN    Adj
```
3. Cornēlia erit uxor iuvenis.
   n/s/f   3/s/f n/s/f n/s/f
   Cornelia will be a young wife.

```
         V      S     P   OP    Adj       PNA
```
4. Discunt puerī dē vītā pūblicā Rōmānōrum.
   3/p/pr   n/p/m   ab/s/f ab/s/f   g/p/m
   The boys learn about the public life of the Romans.

```
          V        S    C   S      DO        Adj
```
5. Habēbuntne Mārcus et Cornēlia ēducātiōnem gravem?
   3/p/f   n/s/m   n/s/f   ac/s/f   ac/s/f
   Will Marcus and Cornelia have a serious education/upbringing?

Translation

At first the parents taught the children. Up until the seventh year of life, the mother taught both the boys and the girls. Marcus and Cornelia, therefore, learned to speak, to read, and to write the Latin language sitting at the table with [their] mother, Aemilia. Father Cornelius also taught Marcus many things about life. Both the mother and the father taught the children about courage/virtue.

Marcus and Cornelia, when they were seven [when they had seven years], walked [went] to school. An elementary school teacher taught the children in the school reading, writing and arithmetic. The twins liked school. Within a few years, Cornelia no longer went to school. She remained in the house with her mother and learned from her mother. Marcus, however, learned with his father. Marcus learned about the public life of the Romans; he used to walk with his father into the senate house where he saw and listened to/heard the senators. Marcus also learned about logic.

Cornelia will be a young wife; therefore, the education of Cornelia will be brief. Marcus, however, will receive more (of) education. Marcus will sail to Greece, where he will learn rhetoric, the art of speaking. Both Marcus and Cornelia will have a serious education, and the education of both will be good and proper.

The Romans always taught their children many things, and they especially taught about courage and goodness. Marcus and Cornelia will also teach their own children.

Respondē Latīnē!

1. Quandō līberī dē parentibus discēbant?

   When were children learning from their parents (i.e. at home)?

   usque ad septimum annum vītae

   up to the seventh year of life

2. Ubi sedēbant Marcus et Cornēlia cum mātre?

   Where were Marcus and Cornelia sitting with their mother?

   ad mēnsam

   at the table

3. Quis docēbat in lūdō?

   Who was teaching in the school?

   grammaticus

   the [grammar-school] teacher

4. Cūr est ēducātiō Cornēliae brevis?

   Why is education of/for Cornelia short?

   quod erit uxor iuvenis

   because she will be a young wife

5. Quis discet rhētoricam?

   Who will learn rhetoric?

   Mārcus

   Marcus

ANSWER IN ENGLISH!

1. Where does the mother teach Cornelia?

   at home

2. Where will Marcus go to learn the art of speaking?

   in Greece

3. What feeling do both Marcus and Cornelia have about education?

   They like it.

4. How will the education of Marcus and Cornelia someday affect their own children?

   They will teach their own children.

Notes

Ēnse petit placidam sub lībertāte quiētem.
By the sword he seeks quiet peace under liberty.
—Massachusetts state motto[A]

This motto quotes Algernon Sydney (1622-1683), an English political writer who worked with William Penn for religious freedom in both England and Pennsylvania.

Manus haec inimīca tyrannīs ēnse petit placidam sub lībertāte quiētam.
—*Discourses Upon Government*

[A]Governor John Hancock adopted this seal on December 13, 1780. The Indian in the center of the shield is of the Algonquin nation. He grasps a bow in his right hand and an arrow pointed downwards in his left as a symbol of peace. The star on the shield represents Massachusetts's place as one of the original thirteen colonies (remember each colony was represented by a single star on the original American flag). Massachusetts was in fact the sixth state to officially join the U.S. Above the crest in gold is a strong right arm grasping a broadsword. The arm represents the state's motto written on the blue ribbon in gold. Notice also that the shield is surrounded by another

Chapter 16

- third conjugation, -io verbs
- imperative mood
- vocative case
  - direct address

VOCABULARY

Latin phrase, "SIGILLUM REIPUBLICAE MASSACHUSETTENSIS" – The Seal of the State of Massachusetts. You will learn the etymology of the word *reī pūblicae* in chapter 29.

The full quote from Algernon Sydney translates, "This hand unfriendly to tyrants seeks quiet peace by the sword under liberty."

camera, ae, f.	room	
flōs, flōris, m.	flower, blossom	(floral)
ignis, ignis, m.	fire	(igneous)
lectus, ī, m.	couch, bed; bier	
nux, nucis, f.	nut; nut tree	

VERBS		
accipiō, accipere, accēpī, acceptum	to receive	(accept)
capiō, capere, cēpī, captum	to take, seize; capture	(capture)
cōnspiciō, cōnspicere, cōnspexī, cōnspectum	to catch sight of	(conspicuous)
cōnsūmō, cōnsūmere, cōnsūmpsī, cōnsūmptum	to consume, eat	(consume)
iaciō, iacere, iēcī, iactum	to throw	(eject)
incipiō, incipere, incēpī, inceptum	to begin	(inception)
faciō, facere, fēcī, factum	to do, make	(fact)
ōrnō, āre, āvī, ātum	to decorate, adorn	(ornate)
surgō, surgere, surrēxī, surrēctum	to rise, arise	(resurrection)
vīvō, vīvere, vīxī, vīctum	to live	(vivacious)

ADJECTIVES		
fēlīx, fēlīcis	happy	(felicity)
flammeus, a, um	fiery; flame covered; as a neuter noun – bridal veil	(flammable)

Exercise 1. Using the rules for syllabication and accent that you have learned, write out the syllables and accents for the vocabulary words above. Then practice pronouncing them aloud.

SECTION 41. Third Conjugation -io

Just as the third declension nouns have a subset of i-stem nouns, so the third conjugation has a subset of -io verbs. This subgroup of the third conjugation has earned this designation because the first person singular ends in -io. The infinitive and verb stem, however, are the same as any other third conjugation verb.[B]

2nd principal part – re = verb stem

1st conjugation	amā/re = amā
2nd conjugation	vidē/re = vidē
3rd conjugation	mitte/re = mitte
3rd conjugation -io	cape/re = cape

[B] I often use the example of a child dressing up in a costume. A seven year old can dress up in a spiderman costume and run through the house as though swinging from buildings. That does not, however, change the fact that on the inside underneath the mask he is still, in reality, just a little seven-year-old boy. Likewise, third -io verbs can "dress up" to look like another verb group (they are similar to the fourth conjugation that you will see in chapter 27), but the infinitive reveals that they are, in reality, still third conjugation verbs.

Exercise 2. Identify the stem and conjugation of each of the verbs in the vocabulary list of this chapter. Circle each third conjugation -io verb.

a. Present Tense for Third Conjugation -io

The third conjugation -io verbs also have a short **e** in the infinitive, just as the regular third conjugation verbs. This weak vowel changes to an **i** once the personal endings are added. Notice that the extra **i** for the -io group appears only in the first person singular and third person plural.

capiō, capere   stem = cape

PERSON	SINGULAR	PLURAL
1	capiō	capimus
2	capis	capitis
3	capit	capiunt

Since an **i** already precedes the ending in the other forms another **i** is not needed. It would not make sense linguistically, as it is harder to pronounce and to understand.

Exercise 3. Following the example of *capiō, capere*, conjugate the present tense of *faciō, facere*.[C]

b. Imperfect and Future Tenses for Third Conjugation -io

The imperfect and future tenses are nearly identical to those you have already learned for third conjugation. The only difference is an extra **i** that appears before the tense marker. Compare the following charts with those in chapter 13, sections 35 and 36.

[C] You may wish to include some regular third conjugation verbs in this exercise as well to help demonstrate the different patterns.

IMPERFECT

PERSON	SINGULAR	PLURAL
1	capiēbam	capiēbāmus
2	capiēbās	capiēbātis
3	capiēbat	capiēbant

FUTURE

Person	Singular	Plural
1	capiam	capiēmus
2	capiēs	capiētis
3	capiet	capient

ᴰYou may wish to include some regular third conjugation verbs (cōnsūmō, surgō, vīvō) in this exercise as well to help demonstrate the different patterns.

Exercise 4. Following the example of *capiō, capere*, conjugate *incipiō, incipere* in the imperfect and future tenses.ᴰ

Exercise 5. Parse each of the following verbs identifying their tense, person, and number. Then translate.

Latin	Person	Number	Tense	Translation
mittēbam	1	Sing.	Imp.	I used to send
incipiēbāmus				
faciunt				
cōnspiciētis				
capis				
				He will seize
				We were beginning
				You (sing.) catch sight of
				They were making
				I send

Section 42. The Imperative Mood

The **mood** of a verb indicates the attitude of the subject towards the action that takes place. Up until now you have seen only the indicative mood. The **indicative mood** (from Latin *indicāre*, to give information) simply indicates what is taking place. Latin uses this mood for declarative and interrogative sentences. Another mood is the **imperative** (from Latin *imperāre,* to command). This mood is used to express commands. Imperative verbs in Latin appear almost exclusively in the second person, since you generally are giving a command directly to the person to whom you are speaking. This mood is probably the easiest to form. The singular imperative is simply the stem of a verb. To make the imperative plural just add -te.

	Singular	Plural
1st conjugation	amā	amāte
2nd conjugation	vidē	vidēte
3rd conjugation	mitte	mittite
3rd conjugation -io	cape	capite

Notā Bene: The stem vowel for the third conjugation weakens to an **i** when the plural ending is added.

111

Caveat Discipulus: The verbs *dīcō, dīcere* (to say); *dūcō, dūcere* (to lead); *faciō, facere* (to do); and *ferō, ferre* (to bring) have an irregular form in the singular imperative. The plural form is regular.

dīc	dīcite
dūc	dūcite
fac	facite
fer	ferte

You will learn more about the verb *ferre* in a later chapter. For now memorize this little saying to help you remember this unusual set of imperatives.[E]

[E]Chapter 18 will teach the irregular verb *ferre*.

dīc, dūc, fac, and *fer* should have an 'e,' but the 'e' ain't there!

Exercise 6. Form the singular and plural imperative for each of the following verbs.

Example: cantāre: cantā cantāte

1. incipere
2. quaerere
3. cantāre
4. facere
5. saltāre
6. currere
7. ambulāre
8. vīvere

SECTION 43. The Vocative Case

In addition to the five main cases that you have been studying, there are two more cases that occur less frequently: locative and vocative. For now we will learn only the vocative, and save the locative for another place and time. The vocative case (from Latin *vocāre*, to call) is the case of direct address. We use this case when talking directly to someone or something. This case frequently appears with the imperative mood.

Students, read your books. **Discipulī, librōs legite.**
Poet, sing a song. **Poēta, carmen cantā.**

You may have noticed that the vocative case looks like the nominative. In fact, most declensions use the same forms for both the nominative and vocative cases. The only exceptions are for second declension nouns ending in -us or -ius. Study the examples below.[F]

[F]If the students chose Roman names for themselves in chapter 1, you might use those names to practice the vocative case. This exercise would provide a good opportunity for some more oral practice.

DECLENSION	NOMINATIVE	VOCATIVE
1st declension	puella, puellae	puella, puellae
2nd declension	puer, puerī	puer, puerī
	discipulus, discipulī	**discipule**, discipulī
	fīlius, fīliī	**fīlī**, fīliī
3rd declension	rēx, rēgēs	rēx, rēgēs

Notice the exceptions in bold type. If the nominative ends in -us, then the vocative ends in -e. When the nominative of a proper noun ends in -ius, then the vocative ends in a solitary -ī. The noun *fīlius* also follows this rule; however, other common nouns ending in -ius merely change the -us to an -e. Otherwise, the vocative endings mirror the nominative.

Exercise 7. Parse, diagram, and translate the following sentences.[G]

1. Cornēlia ē lectō surrēxit et in cameram cum mātre ambulāvit.

2. In caput Cornēliae fēminae flammeum posuērunt.

3. Puellae flōrēs in capitibus gerēbant.

4. Ancillae, parāte cēnam in camerā.

5. Nucēs in viam iaciēmus.

[G]Notice that imperatives still have person, number, and tense! Make sure that students recognize that *in + acc.=* "into," NOT "in." This is another great opportunity to reinforce the lesson on place expressions by identifying what type of expressions are in this exercise.

Chapter Reading

CORNELIA'S WEDDING DAY

Certā diē multō māne Cornēlia ē lectō surrēxit et cameram cum mātre, Aemiliā, *intrāvit.* In camerā cum Cornēliā et mātre erat *prōnuba.* Aemilia et *prōnuba* Cornēliam induere tunicam rēctam iuvērunt. Tunica rēcta erat tunica *texta sine sūtūrā.* Circum *medium corpus* Cornēliae erat *zōna facta nōdō Hērculāneō. Capillī* Cornēliae *in sex partēs hastā dīvīsaī sunt.* Tum in caput Cornēliae fēminae flammeum *imposuērunt.* Flammeum erat *vēlum colōre simile* flammīs. Flōrēs in capite quoque gerēbat.

Tōta caerimōnia erat in casā Cornēliī, patris Cornēliae. Ancillae casam flōribus, *foliīs,* et *ligāmentīs lānae* ornāverant. *Post adventum spōnsī,* nōmine Lūcius Iūlius Scriptor, *haruspex exta* spectāvit. *Ōmina* bona fuērunt! Tum Cornēlia et Lūcius, *quī* quoque flōrēs in capite gerēbat, in *ātrium* ambulāvērunt. *Prōnuba* dextrās Cornēliae Lūciīque *iūnxit.* Cornēlia tum dīxit, "*Quandō* tū Gāius, ego Gāia." *Pontificēs* deinde *farreum lībum* deīs dēdicāvērunt. Omnēs "*Fēlīciter!*" clāmāvērunt.

Post *caerimōniam* est ingēns cēna. Novus *nūptus* et nova *nūpta mustāceum* cōnsūmunt. Post cēnam est *pompa* ad casam novī *nūptī.* In viīs multī *pompam* spectant et verba fēlīcia sīcut "Vīvite bene!" et "Bonam fortūnam!" clāmant. Lūcius nucēs in viam iacit. Cornēlia rogat, "Lūcī, *cūr* nucēs iacis?" Et Lūcius, "Nucēs," dīcit, "sunt signa *fertilitātis,* Cornēlia." Ad casam Lūcius novam *nūptam* trāns *līmen* portat. In *ātriō* novae casae Cornēlia aquam et ignem ā Lūciō accipit. *Iānuās ligāmentīs lānae* ornat Cornēlia. Lūcius Cornēliaque fēlīcēs sunt! Cornēlius Aemiliaque etiam fēlīcēs sunt!

Dum Mārcus mīlitābat cum Scīpiōne in Āfricā, Cornēlia nūpsit.

While Marcus was serving as a soldier with Scipio in Africa, Cornelia married.

The Tunica Rēcta and the Nōdus Hērculāneus

The bride wore a garment the Romans called **tunica rēcta**. There are two ideas about the name. One is that the tunic was straight from top to bottom and woven in one piece; therefore, there were no seams. The other is that the tunic was called that because it was woven on an old-fashioned loom, a loom that would have, presumably, stood straight and upright.

The **nōdus Hērculāneus** was the type of knot with which the bride's belt was tied. It was probably called that because Hercules was the guardian of married life. Only the husband would be privileged to untie the knot.

certā diē ....on a certain day
multō māne ....early in the morning
intrō, āre, āvī, ātum.....................................to enter
suus, a, um, adj...his, her, its own
prōnuba, ae, f. ....matron of honor (The *prōnuba* had to be a woman married to her first husband.)
textus, a, um, adj..woven
sine, prep. + abl..without
sūtūra, ae, f...seam
medium corpus ....the waist
zōna, ae, f. ....belt
facta ....tied
nōdus, ī, m..knot
capillī, capillōrum, m. pl..............................hair
in sex partēs hastā dīvīsī sunt ....divided by a miniature spear into six parts
dīvīsī sunt ....is divided
impōnō, impōnere, imposuī, impositum .....This is a compound verb formed from *in* + *pōnere*. Can you decipher its meaning?
vēlum, ī, m. ....veil
color, colōris, m...color
similis, nom., sing., adj. ....similar to, like (this adjective is often followed by a dative)
tōtus, a, um, adj..whole, entire
caerimōnia, ae, f..ceremony
folium, foliī, m. ....leaf
ligāmentum, ī, n..band, binding
lāna, ae, f...wool
post adventum ....after the arrival
spōnsus, ī, m..the (prospective) bridegroom
haruspex, haruspicis, m.................................diviner (from entrails)
exta, extōrum, n. pl..entrails
ōmen, ōminis, n..omen
quī, nom., sing. ....who
ātrium, ī, n...atrium (large front hall and reception area of the house)
iungō, iungere, iūnxī, iūnctum.....................to join together, unite
quandō, adv. ....when
pontifex, pontificis, m. ....high priest
farreum lībum..a cake made of spelt, a kind of grain
Fēlīciter!...This literally means "happily". However, we need to interpret it as something that originated as "May you live happily!"
novus nūptus ....the (newly married) bridegroom. What do you think *nūpta* means?
mustāceum, ī, n..wedding cake
pompa, ae, f..parade, procession
cūr ....why
līmen, līminis, n. ....threshold
iānua, ae, f...door
fertilitās, fertilitātis, f..................................fertility

Challenge Box

Write a paragraph discussing the symbolism of the nuts, water, fire, wool, the knot, and the threshold in the story. Be sure to tell how at least one of these symbols is still associated with weddings.[H]

[H]The nuts symbolize life and fertility. The water and fire are the necessary things of the home. The knot may be a religious symbol of unity and remind the Romans of Hercules. The carrying of the bride over the threshold ensures that she won't stumble, since stumbling would be a bad omen. The wool symbolizes the domestic role of the wife. Today we throw rice or birdseed at weddings as the newlywed couple departs. The groom carries the bride over the threshold.

Respondē Latīnē!

1. Quō Cornēlia multō māne īvit?

2. Quid ēgērunt māter et prōnuba Cornēliae?

3. Quantās in partēs erant capillī spōnsae dīvīsī?

4. Quis est color flammeī?

5. Quis iūnctiōne dextrārum perfūncta est (*performed*)?

> quō = *where?*, quantās = *how many?*,
> quid = *what?*, quis = *who?*

> *Perfūncta est* is from *perfungor*, a compound of *fungor*. *Fungor* is one of a special group of verbs and their compounds governing the ablative.

ANSWER IN ENGLISH!

1. How was the bride's father's house decorated?

2. What type of augury did the haruspex perform?

3. During the procession, what did Lucius throw into the streets?

4. In the atrium of her new home, what did Cornelia receive?

5. With what did Cornelia decorate the doors of her new home?

Grammar Exercise

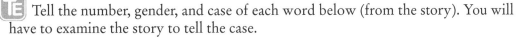

Tell the number, gender, and case of each word below (from the story). You will have to examine the story to tell the case.

1. diē
2. lectō
3. sūtūrā
4. partēs
5. pontificēs
6. ōmina
7. deīs
8. pompa
9. līmen
10. casae

Latin in Science

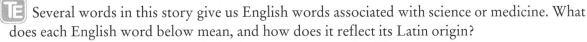

Several words in this story give us English words associated with science or medicine. What does each English word below mean, and how does it reflect its Latin origin?

suture (noun)
suture (verb)
capillary
ligament

fertility
lanolin
subliminal

Colloquāmur

Use the imperative mood and the vocative case to play "Magistra dīcit!" Here are a few phrases to get started. Once you've got the hang of it, make up more commands on your own. (Hint: use some of the imperatives in exercise 6.)

Discipulī, surgite!

Puerī, sedēte!
Puellae, ambulāte circum mēnsās!
. . . cantāte
. . . vertite
. . . verberāte caput
. . . tollite pedem
. . . tollite manum

Culture Corner

WHERE ROMANS LIVED

Most people in ancient Rome lived in *īnsulae*. These *īnsulae* were like modern apartment buildings. They were up to six stories tall, and the apartments on the upper floors were the cheapest ones. (Today in large cities such as New York the apartments on the highest floors are the most expensive.)

People like the family of Marcus and Cornelia would have lived in a *domus*. A *domus* was a private house, usually in the city. (A *vīlla* was a country house.) Many families rented out rooms on the street sides of the house to merchants. These were the *tabernae*, or shops. One entered the *domus* through the door in the *vestibulum*, or entryway. The main room of the house was the *ātrium*. Notice how, in the floor plan below, the *ātrium* is truly the center of the house.

There was an opening in the ceiling in the middle of the *ātrium*. This opening was the *compluvium*. It let in light. Rain would fall through the *compluvium* and into the *impluvium*, a pool in the floor. The *cubicula* (bedrooms) were off the *ātrium*. The *ālae* (wings) were spaces behind the *ātrium* which had no specific use. The *trīclīnium* was the dining room. It had this name because three couches surrounded the dining table, upon which men would recline while eating. The *tablīnum* was the master's study. The *culīna* was the kitchen. The colonnaded garden at the rear of the house was called the *peristylium*. The house in the plan below has more bedrooms around the *peristylium*; however, this feature was not true of all houses. In Rome, as in our communities today, people's houses reflected their economic capabilities as well as their tastes and desires. The *exedra* in this plan was another room not in all houses. It was a room for conversation. It might be like a second living area in a modern home, since the *ātrium* was the main living room or reception room of the *domus*.

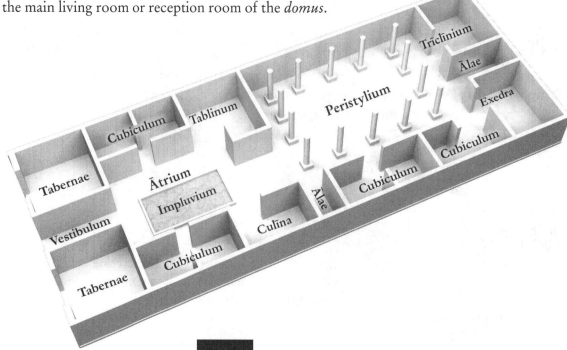

Chapter 16 Teacher's Pages

Exercise 1

ca-me-ra, ae, f.
flōs, flō-ris, m.
ig-nis, ig-nis, f.
lec-tus, ī, m.
nux, nu-cis, f.
ac-ci-pi-ō, ac-ci-pe-re, ac-cē-pī, ac-cep-tum
ca-pi-ō, ca-pe-re, cē-pī, cap-tum
cons-pi-ci-ō, cons-pi-ce-re, cōn-spe-xī, cons-pec-tum
cōn-sū-mō, cōn-sū-me-re, cōn-sūm-psī, cōn-sūmp-tum

ia-ci-ō, ia-ce-re, iē-cī, iac-tum
in-ci-pi-ō, in-ci-pe-re, in-cē-pī, in-cep-tum
fa-ci-ō, fa-ce-re, fē-cī, fac-tum
ōr-nō, ā-re, ā-vī, ā-tum
sur-gō, sur-ge-re, sur-rē-xī, sur-rec-tum
vī-vō, vī-ve-re, vī-xī, vīc-tum
fē-līx, fē-lī-cis
flam-me-us, a, um

Exercise 2

accipiō, accipere, accēpī, acceptum   accipe, 3rd io

capiō, capere, cēpī, captum   cape, 3rd io

cōnspiciō, cōnspicere, cōnspexī, cōnspectum   cōnspice, 3rd io

cōnsūmō, cōnsūmere, cōmsūmpsī, cōnsūmptum   cōnsūme, 3rd

iaciō, iacere, iēcī, iactum   iace, 3rd io

incipiō, incipere, incēpī, inceptum   incipe, 3rd io

faciō, facere, fēcī, factum   face, 3rd io

ōrnō, ōrnāre, ornāvī, ōrnātum   ōrnā, 1st

surgō, surgere, surrēxī, surrēctum   surge, 3rd

vīvō, vīvere, vīxī, vīctum   vīve, 3rd

Exercise 3

	PRESENT	
PERSON	SINGULAR	PLURAL
1	faciō	facimus
2	facis	facitis
3	facit	faciunt

Exercise 4

	IMPERFECT		FUTURE	
PERSON	SINGULAR	PLURAL	SINGULAR	PLURAL
1	incipiēbam	incipiēbamus	incipiam	incipiēmus
2	incipiēbas	incipiēbatis	incipiēs	incipiētis
3	incipiēbat	incipiēbam	incipiet	incipient

Exercise 5

LATIN	PERSON	NUMBER	TENSE	TRANSLATION
mittēbam	**1**	**Sing.**	**Imp.**	**I used to send**
incipiēbāmus	1	Pl.	Imp.	We were beginning
faciunt	3	Pl.	Pres.	They make/do
cōnspiciētis	2	Pl.	Fut.	You will catch sight of
capis	2	Sing.	Pres.	You seize
capiet	3	Sing.	Fut.	**He will seize**
incipiēbāmus	1	Pl.	Imp.	**We were beginning**
cōnspicis	2	Sing.	Pres.	**You (sing.) catch sight of**
faciēbant	3	Pl.	Imp.	**They were making**
mittō	1	Sing.	Pres.	**I send**

Exercise 6

1. incipere   incipe   incipite
2. quaerere   quaere   quaerite
3. cantāre   cantā   cantāte
4. facere   fac   facite
5. saltāre   saltā   saltāte
6. currere   curre   currite
7. ambulāre   ambulā   ambulāte
8. vīvere   vīve   vīvite

Exercise 7

Translations in ( ) are implied/understood in the Latin sentence. Translations in [ ] are acceptable alternatives.

```
      S  P OP       V  C P  OP    P  OP    V
```
1. Cornēlia ē lectō   surrēxit et in cameram cum mātre ambulāvit.
   n/s/f ab/s/m 3/s/perf   ac/s/f   ab/s/f 3/s/perf
   Cornelia rose from (her) bed and walked into the room with (her) mother.

```
      P  OP     PNA    S     DO       V
```
2. In caput Cornēliae fēminae flammeum posuērunt.
   ac/s/n g/s/f   n/p/f   ac/s/n   3/p/perf
   The women placed a bridal veil on the head of Cornelia [on Cornelia's head].

```
      S    DO  P  OP      V
```
3. Puellae flōrēs in capitibus gerēbant.
   n/p/f ac/p/m   ab/p/n   3/p/imp
   The girls were wearing flowers on their heads.

```
      DA      V     DO  P  OP
```
4. Ancillae, parāte   cēnam in camerā.
   v/p/f 2/p/pres ac/s/f   ab/s/f
   Maidservants, prepare dinner in the room.

```
      DO  P  OP    SV
```
5. Nucēs in viam iaciēmus.
   ac/p/f   ac/s/f 1/p/f
   We will throw nuts into the road.

Translation

On a certain day, early in the morning, Cornelia arose from [her] bed and entered a room with her mother, Aemilia. In the room with Cornelia and [her] mother was the matron of honor. Aemilia and the matron of honor helped Cornelia to put on the *tunica recta*. The *tunica recta* was a tunic woven without a seam. Around the middle of Cornelia's body there was a belt made with the knot of Hercules. Cornelia's hair was divided into six parts with a spear. Then the women put the *flammeum* onto Cornelia's head. The *flammeum* was a veil similar to flames in color. She was also wearing flowers on [her] head.

The whole ceremony was in the house of Cornelius, Cornelia's father. The maids had decorated the house with flowers, leaves, and wool bands. After the arrival of the bridegroom, by name Lucius Julius Scriptor, the haruspex looked at the entrails. The omens were good. Then Cornelia and Lucius, who was also wearing flowers on [his] head, walked into the atrium. The matron of honor joined the hands of Cornelia and Lucius. Cornelia then said, "When you are Gaius, I [am] Gaia." The priests then dedicated a spelt cake to the gods. All shouted "May you live happily!"

After the ceremony there is a huge dinner. The new groom and the new bride consume the wedding cake. After dinner there is a procession to the house of the newly married couple. In the streets many watch the procession and shout happy words such as "live well!" and "Good luck!" Lucius throws nuts into the street. Cornelia asks, "Lucius, why are you throwing nuts?" And Lucius says, "Nuts are a symbol of fertility, Cornelia." At the house Lucius carries the new bride across the threshold. In the atrium of the new house, Cornelia receives water and fire from Lucius. Cornelia decorates the doors with bands of wool. Lucius and Cornelia are happy. Cornelius and Aemilia are also happy!

Respondē Latīnē!

1. Quō Cornēlia multō māne īvit?
   Multō māne Cornēlia cameram intrāvit.

   Where did Cornelia go early in the morning?
   Early in the morning, Cornelia entered a room.

2. Quid ēgērunt māter et prōnuba Cornēliae?

   Aemilia et prōnuba Cornēliam induere tunicam rēctam iūvērunt.

   What did (her) mother and the matron of honor do for Cornelia?
   Aemilia and the matron of honor helped Cornelia to put on the *tunica recta*.

3. Quantās in partēs erant capillī spōnsae dīvīsī?
   Capillī Cornēliae in sex partēs hastā dīvīsī sunt.

   Into how many parts was Cornelia's hair divided?
   The hair of Cornelia was divided into six parts.

4. Quid est color flammeī?
   Flammeum erat vēlum colōre simile flammīs.

   What is the color of the flammeum (bridal veil)?
   The flammeum was a veil similar in color to flames.

5. Quis iūnctiōne dextrārum perfūncta est (performed)?
   Prōnuba dextrās Cornēliae Lūciīque iūnxit.

   Who performed the joining of the right hands?
   The matron of honor joined the hands of Cornelia and Lucius.

ANSWER IN ENGLISH!

1. How was the bride's father's house decorated?
   The maids had decorated the house with flowers, leaves, and wool bands.

2. What type of augury did the haruspex perform?
   The haruspex looked at the entrails.

3. During the procession, what did Lucius throw into the streets?
   Lucius throws nuts into the street.

4. In the atrium of her new home, what did Cornelia receive?
   In the atrium of the new house, Cornelia receives water and fire from Lucius.

5. With what did Cornelia decorate the doors of her new home?
   Cornelia decorates the doors with bands of wool.

Grammar Exercise

1. diē	S/F/Ab	6. ōmina	P/N/Nom
2. lectō	S/M/Ab	7. deīs	P/M/Dat
3. sūtūrā	S/F/Ab	8. pompa	S/F/Nom
4. partēs	P/F/Ac	9. līmen	S/N/Ac
5. pontificēs	P/M/Nom	10. casae	S/F/Gen

Latin in Science

suture (noun) stitching (particularly in a medical context) [from *suō*, "I sew/ tie together"]

suture (verb) to stitch (particularly in a medical context) [from *suō*, "I sew/ tie together"]

capillary tiny blood vessels. [from *capillī*, "hair"]

ligament a band of strong tissue that holds bones together. [from *ligāre* to "bind"]

fertility the condition of being able to reproduce. [from *fertilis*, "fruitfull/ fertile, which comes from *ferō*, "I carry/bear"]

lanolin a greasy yellow substance akin to the wax that comes from woolly creatures, used primarily as a lubricant. [from *lāna*, "wool"]

subliminal below the threshold of conscious perception. [from *sub*, "under" + *līmen, līminis*, "threshold"]

Notes

Sī quaeris paenīnsulam amoenam, circumspice.
If you seek a delightful peninsula, look around.
—Michigan state motto[A]

Perhaps inspired by the inscription on the tomb of Sir Christopher Wren in St. Paul's Cathedral, London, "**Sī Monumentum Requīris Circumspice**" (If you seek [his] monument look around). Wren was the chief architect of St. Paul's when it was rebuilt (AD 1698-1710)

[A]Lewis Cass, Michigan's second governor, presented the idea for this seal (inspired by that of the Hudson Bay Fur Company) to the Constitutional Convention of Michigan. The Convention accepted the seal on June 2, 1835. In the center of the shield, a man stands with his rifle on the edge of a peninsula, no doubt overlooking one of the Great Lakes. The rifle and the peninsula are reflective of the two Latin phrases also appearing on the shield. An elk and a moose hold the shield in place while an eagle hovers above with the U.S. motto.

Two other Latin phrases appear on this state seal.
Tuēbor! I will defend
Ē Plūribus Ūnum What does this one mean?

Chapter 17

- dative case
  - special intransitive verbs
  - dative with adjectives
  - dative of possession

VOCABULARY

NOUNS		
honor, honōris, m.	honor	(honorable)
officium, ī, n.	office, duty	(officiate)
tempus, temporis, n.	time	(temporal)
VERBS		
administrō, āre, āvī, ātum	to manage	(administer)
faveō, favēre, fāvī, fautum (+ dat.)	to favor, to support	
noceō, nocēre, nocuī, nocitum (+ dat.)	to harm, to be harmful to	(innocuous)
pāreō, pārēre, pāruī, pāritum (+ dat.)	to obey, to be obedient to	
placeō, placēre, placuī, placitum (+ dat.)	to please, to be pleasing to	(placate)
stō, stāre, stetī, statum	to stand	(statue, statute)
studeō, studēre, studuī (+ dat.)	to study, to direct one's zeal to	(studious)
ADJECTIVES		
amīcus, a, um	friendly (to)	(amicable)
cārus, a, um	dear (to)	(caress)
dissimilis, dissimile	unlike	(dissimilar)
fidēlis, fidēle	faithful, loyal (to)	(fidelity)
inimīcus, a, um	unfriendly (to)	(inamicable)
pār, paris	equal (to)	(partial)
similis, simile	like, similar (to)	(similarity)
ADVERBS		
bene	well	
iterum	again	

117

TE **Exercise 1.** Using the rules for syllabication and accent that you have learned, write out the syllables and accents for the vocabulary words above. Then practice pronouncing them aloud.

SECTION 44. Special Intransitive

In chapter 5 you learned the difference between transitive and intransitive verbs (Section 14). The transitive verb must take a direct object, which appears in the accusative case.

Rēgīna puellam accūsat.	The queen accuses the girl.

The intransitive verb, however, does not take a direct object.

Nautae nāvigant.	The sailors sail.
Helena est rēgīna.	Helen is a queen.
In lūdō discimus.	We learn in school.

As you can see, you have already learned several different types of intransitive sentences that use intransitive verbs. Now let us add another to our repertoire. The **special intransitive** is a verb that takes a dative object. These verbs <u>do not</u> take a direct object in the accusative case.

Puella **mātrī** placet.	The girl is pleasing **to her mother.**
	The girl pleases **her mother.**
Deō pārēbimus.	We will be obedient **to God.**
	We will obey **God.**

Notice that you may sometimes use the familiar preposition '**to**' with the dative case when it appears with a special intransitive verb.

TE **Exercise 2.** Following the example sentences above, translate the following special intransitives in two different ways. [B]

> [B]Students do not necessarily need to parse and diagram these. It is good at this point to move into sight reading, particularly with short sentences such as these.

1. Omnibus officiīs pūblicīs studēbās.

2. Discipulī magistrō placēbant.

3. Hostis oppidō nocet.

4. Bonī puerī mātrī pārēre dēbent.

5. Placuit officium Mārcī Rōmae.

SECTION 45. Dative with Adjectives

In addition to this special group of verbs, there is also a special group of adjectives that often appear with the dative case. Now these adjectives do not *have* to use a dative, but often they do in order to communicate quality, relation, or even an attitude towards an object. Notice that you can still translate the dative using the familiar prepositions '**to**' or '**for**,' and that this translation fits comfortably with our own English style of speaking.

Puerī **puellīs** sunt **amīcī.**	The boys are **friendly to the girls.**
Bellum **aptum** nōn est **līberīs.**	War is not **suitable for children.**
Saxum **similem testūdinī** formam habet.	The rock has a shape **like a turtle.**[C]

> [C]For this example you could also say, "The rock has a shape similar to a turtle."

Exercise 3. In the following sentences, circle the adjectives that take the dative and underline their dative partners. Then, translate.[D]

1. Aptum est līberīs studēre.
2. Īnfantēs sunt cārī parentibus.
3. Hostis est Rōmae inimīcus.
4. Uxor cāra marītō erit semper fidēlis.

[D]If you wish further practice on the dative with special verbs and adjectives, consider asking students to compose their own sentences. Allow them plenty of room for creativity as long as they abide by the rules of grammar. You can then review the creative writing as a class.

SECTION 46. Dative of Possession

The linking verb *sum, esse* also appears quite often with the dative case in another construction called the dative of possession. The **dative of possession** uses the dative case + a form of *esse* in order to communicate ownership. In this construction translate the verb *esse* not as *to be*, but as <u>to belong to</u>.

Cōnsulī est officium.	The office **belongs to the consul.**
	The consul has the office.
Discipulīs erant librī.	The books **belonged to the students.**
	The students had books.

You may also translate this construction in a seemingly backwards manner. The dative can be translated as the subject and *esse* as the English verb *to have*. This sometimes makes for a more natural English interpretation of the phrase. You can think of this method of translating as an example of "the last shall be first, and the first shall be last." The object in an English translation (here the dative of possession) will become the subject, and the subject will become the object.[E]

DP LV SN	SN V DO
Cōnsulī est officium.	**The consul has** the office.

Translation can often be a tricky business for one language will never translate smoothly to another 100% of the time. As a translator, your most important task is to communicate the meaning and intent of the author as clearly as possible.

Exercise 4. In each sentence underline and translate the dative of possession construction only.

1. Mārcō erant multī librī.

2. Lūdus erit multīs līberīs.

3. Magnus honor Mārcō erat.

4. Uxōrī nōmen est Marcia.[F]

[E]Teachers, I highly recommend that you ask students to translate the dative of possession in both of the ways described above. This can prove a bit tricky for some students, so you will want to review this as a class.
[F]Students saw this phrase in the Colloquāmur segment for chapter 1 (page 9)!

Exercise 5. Parse, diagram, and translate the following sentences. Watch out for the new datives!

1. Rōmae semper erant magnī ducēs.

2. Officium viās et lūdōs pūblicōs cūrābat.

3. Lēgātus iterum bene fēcit in officiō.

4. Aptum est līberīs studēre magnīs ducibus.

5. Magnus honor Mārcō erat.

6. Lingua Latīna similis est linguae Graecae.

MĀRCUS AND THE CURSUS HONŌRUM

Posteā cum Scīpiōne *mīlitāvit* et **in mātrimōnium dūxit** fēminam nōmine
Marcia, etiam placuit Mārcō Rōmae *servīre*; *itaque intrāvit cursum honōrum. Cursus honōrum* erat *seriēs* in
quā Rōmānī officia tenēbant. *Prīmō necesse est* Mārcō esse *quaestor. Quaestor* erat vir *quī* multa fēcit. Inter
officia *quaestōrum* erat *thēsaurum cūrāre.* Rōmānī virīs *quī* habēbant *trīgintā* annōs *ut quaestōres* favēbant.
Simulatque Mārcus *satis* annōrum habēbat, *quaestor* erat.

Quod *quaestor* bonus erat, magnus honor Mārcō erat; ubi, igitur, Mārcus *trīgintā septem* annōs habuit,
Rōmānī eum *aedīlem* lēgērunt. *Aedīlēs* viās, lūdōs pūblicōs, *macella* cūrābant. Mārcus iterum bene fēcit in
officiō.

Deinde Mārcus, *cui* nunc sunt *trēs* līberī et nunc *quadrāgintā* annōs habet, *factus est praetor. Praetōrēs*
erant virī *quī cōnsulēs* administrāre *iūstitiam adiuvābant.* **Praetōrēs quoque mīlitibus praeerant.** *Praetōribus*
erant multa officia! *Ut* semper, Mārcus officia *praetōris* bene fēcit.

Tribus annīs Mārcus *cōnsul* erit. Rōmae semper erant duo *cōnsulēs.* Virī erant *maximī* ducēs cīvitātis
Rōmānae. Mārcus mox *cursum honōrum complēbit.*

Notā Bene:
in mātrimōnium dūxit = he married
Praetōrēs quoque mīlitibus praeerant. = The praetors were also in charge of/commanded the soldiers/
army. Notice how *praeerant* (from *praesum*) governs the dative case.

GLOSSARY

mīlitō, āre, āvī, ātum	to serve, be a soldier
serviō, servīre, servīvī, + dat.	to serve
itaque, adv.	thus
intrō, āre, āvī, ātum	to enter
cursus honōrum	course of honors
seriēs	<u>Use your eye Latin to determine the meaning of *seriēs*.</u>
in quā	in which
prīmō	first
necesse est	it is necessary (followed by complementary infinitive)
quaestor, quaestōris, m	quaestor
quī, nominative, singular	who
thēsaurum cūrāre	to look after the storehouse
trīgintā, indeclinable numerical adj.	thirty (XXX)
ut	as
simulatque	as soon as
satis, satis, adj. (+ genitive)	enough
trīgintā septem	thirty-seven (XXXVII)
aedīle	aedile
macellum, ī, n.	market
faciō, facere, fēcī, factum	do (Here, perhaps the best interpretation is *perform*.)
cui, dative, sing.	who/whom (hint: this pronoun is part of a dative of possession)
trēs, numerical adj.	three (III)
quadrāgintā, indeclinable numerical adj.	forty (XL)
factus est	he became
praetor, praetōris, m	praetor
cōnsul, cōnsulis, m.	consul (highest office in Roman Republic)
iūstitia, ae, f.	justice

adiuvō, āre, adiūvī, adiūtum ....help, assist (cf. *iuvāre*, chapter 7)
tribus annīs..in three years (ablative of time)
maximus, a, um, adj. ....greatest, chief, main, principal
compleō, complēre, complēvī, complētum ....to complete, finish

Derivative Detective

 Give the Latin root and its meaning for each of the English words below.
HINT: Look at the vocabulary for the chapter AND for the chapter reading.

placate

service

thesaurus

favorite

justice

reiterate

adjutant

contemporary

Respondē Latīnē!

 1. Quid est nōmen uxōrī Mārcī? ^G

2. Quantōs annōs necesse est habēre quaestōrī?

3. Quantōs annōs necesse est habēre cōnsulī?

4. Quandō erit Mārcus cōnsul?

quid = *what?*, quantōs = *how many?*, quandō = *when?*

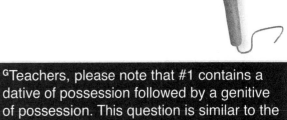
^GTeachers, please note that #1 contains a dative of possession followed by a genitive of possession. This question is similar to the Culture Corner exercise in chapter 1 where students learn to introduce themselves.

ANSWER IN ENGLISH!

1. Upon what course must Marcus embark in order to serve Rome after he has already served in the army?

2. What was the minimum age for the aedileship?

GRAMMAR EXERCISE

Find all the verbs in the reading that govern the dative and write them down in Latin along with their objects.

Culture Corner:

CURSUS HONŌRUM

Beginning in the sixth century BC, Rome was a Republic ruled by elected officials, also called magistrates. Roman citizens held office in a certain order. They called this order the *cursus honōrum* (course of honor). Roman law dictated limitations for each office, such as age, term limitations, re-election, and assigned duties or powers. The chart below lists the offices and their functions in order. Men, such as our friend Marcus, who desired to hold public office would have already served in the army for ten years.

- quaestor – managed the expenditure of state funds and assisted the praetors in preventing and investigating crimes

- praetor – served as a judge in peacetime, led an army in wartime

- censor – served with a co-censor (One of the censors would take a census and value property; the other would watch over the activities and character of candidates for office, guard the honor of women, and oversee education. They also tried to prevent extravagance.)

- consul – served, with another man, as chief executive of the government. (He was analogous to our president.) Each consul carried a veto power not only over the senate but over the other consul as well. Both consuls must agree in order for legislation to pass. In this way, no single man could hold supreme power in a manner similar to a king.

Men held these offices for one year except for the censors. They served for five years. A man must wait a year after serving in one office before running for the next office in the course for seeking re-election to the same office.

Outside the formal *cursus honōrum* were two other very important offices. Each of these could also be held for only a year. Often these served as a starting point for those who desired political office, thus skipping the office of quaestor.

- aedile – provided and oversaw, among other things, public works and games. He tried to become popular with the people by providing elaborate and costly games for their entertainment.

- tribune – protected the people against oppression and the creation of unfair laws. These men also had the power of veto over any laws proposed by the senate or even the consuls.

Romans did not have distinct political parties, such as the United States does today. Instead they had two classes of citizens determined by family or birth: plebeians and patricians. At first the plebeians, the lower class, were not represented well by the officials and could not seek the highest offices. The patricians, therefore, were able to create laws that were helpful for them, but harmful to the plebeians. The plebeians created the office of tribune as their representative to protect them from unfair laws. Only a plebeian could be a tribune. Eventually, the classes became fairly equal with one another. And some plebeian men held the office of consul.

Colloquāmur

SPECTĀTIŌ NŪBIUM • CLOUD WATCHING

Have you ever lain in the grass watching shapes of clouds as they drift across a blue sky? Now you can use this same activity to practice the dative case with adjectives. Here are a few examples and a few descriptive nouns to get you started. Use a Latin dictionary to come up with even more.

Nūbēs est montī similis.
Nūbēs est serpentī similis.
Nūbēs est vehiculō similis.

nāvis, nāvis..................ship
castellum, castellī........castle, fort
canis, canis..................dog
ursus, ursī...................bear
nix, nivis.....................snow
mōnstrum, ī...............monster

Latin in Science

Here is something else to think about *nūbēs spectāns.* The types of clouds, as with many other things in our universe, have scientific names in Latin. Below is a list of the various types of clouds as meteorologists know them. Use a Latin dictionary for a bit of detective work to find out what kinds of clouds these are.

Nimbus
Cumulus
Stratus
Cirrus

Chapter 17 Teacher's Pages

Exercise 1

ho-nor, ho-nō-ris, m.
of-fi-ci-um, ī, n.
tem-pus, tem-po-ris, n.
ad-mi-nis-trō, ā-re, ā-vī, ā-tum,
fa-ve-ō, fa-vē-re, fā-vī, fau-tum
no-ce-ō, no-cē-re, nocu-ī
pa-re-ō, pa-rē-re, pa-ru-ī
pla-ce-ō, pla-cē-re, pla-cu-ī
stō, stā-re, ste-tī, sta-tum,
stu-de-ō, stu-dē-re, stu-du-ī

a-mī-cus, a, um
cā-rus, a, um
dis-si-mi-lis, dis-si-mi-le
fi-dē-lis, fi-dē-le
i-ni-mī-cus, a, um
pār, pa-ris
si-mi-lis, si-mi-le
be-ne
i-te-rum

Exercise 2

1. Omnibus officiīs pūblicīs studēbās.
   You were studying all the public offices. You were directing your zeal to all the public offices.

2. Discipulī magistrō placēbant.
   The students were pleasing the teacher. The students were pleasing to the teacher.

3. Hostis oppidō nocet.
   The enemy harms the town. The enemy is harmful to the town.

4. Bonī puerī mātrī pārēre dēbent.
   The good boys ought to obey (their) mother. The good boys ought to be obedient to (their) mother.

5. Placuit officium Mārcī Rōmae.
   The duty of Marcus/Marcus' duty/office pleased Rome.
   The duty of Marcus/Marcus' duty/office has been pleasing to Rome.

Exercise 3

1. Aptum est līberīs studēre.
   It is fitting for students to study.

2. Īnfantēs sunt cārī parentibus.
   Children are dear to their parents.

3. Hostis est Rōmae inimīcus.
   The enemy is unfriendly to Rome.

4. Uxor cāra marītō erit semper fidēlis.
   The faithful wife will always be dear to her husband.

Exercise 4

1. Mārcō erant multī librī.
   Many books were belonging to Marcus. Marcus had many books.

2. Lūdus erit multīs līberīs.
   The school will belong to many students. Many students will have a/the school.

4. Magnus honor Marcō erat.
   Great honor was for/belonged to Marcus. Marcus had great honor.

5. Uxōrī nōmen est Marcia.
   The name belonging to the wife is Marcia. The name for the wife is Marcia.
   The wife's name is Marcia.

Exercise 5

```
      DP    Adv   LV    Adj    S
```
1. Rōmae semper erant magnī ducēs.
   d/s/f   3/p/imp n/p/m n/p/m
   Great leaders always belonged to Rome. Rome always had great leaders.

```
       S    DO  C  DO    Adj      V
```
2. Officium viās et lūdōs pūblicōs cūrābat.
   n/s/n   ac/p/f ac/p/m ac/p/m 3/s/imp
   The office was taking care of/caring for the roads and public schools.

```
        S    Adv  Adv   V   P   OP
```
3. Lēgātus iterum bene fēcit in officiō.
   n/s/m   3/s/perf ab/s/n
   The officer again did well in office.

```
     Adj    LV   Dadj   V    Adj   DO
```
4. Aptum   est   līberīs studēre magnīs ducibus.
   n/s/n 3/s/p d/p/m   inf. d/p/m d/p/m
   It is fitting for students to study great leaders.

```
     Adj    S    DP    LV
```
5. Magnus honor Mārcō   erat.
   n/s/m n/s/m d/s/m 3/s/imp
   Marcus had great honor.

```
       S   Adj   Adj  LV  Dadj    Adj
```
6. Lingua Latīna similis est   linguae Graecae.
   n/s/f n/s/f n/s/f 3/s/pr d/s/f   d/s/f
   The Latin language is similar to the Greek language.

Translation

Afterwards when he served in the military with Scipio and married a woman by the name of Marcia, it still pleased Marcus to serve Rome; and so he entered the *cursus honorum*. The *cursus honorum* was the series in which Romans held office. First, it is necessary for Marcus to be a quaestor. A quaestor was a man who did many things. Among the duties of quaestors was to take care of the treasury. The Romans favored men who were [at least] thirty years old as quaestors. As soon as Marcus had enough years (i.e. was old enough), he was a quaestor.

Because he was a good quaestor, Marcus had great honor/there was great honor to/for Marcus; therefore, when he was thirty-seven, the Romans elected him aedile. The aediles used to care for/were caring for roads, public games, [and] markets. Marcus again did well in office/in his duties.

Then Marcus, who now had three children and who now has forty years (i.e. was forty years old), was made/became praetor. Praetors were men who helped the consuls administer justice. Praetors were also in charge of soldiers. Praetors had many duties! As always, Marcus did the job of praetor well.

Within three years, Marcus will be consul. There were always two consuls at Rome. The men were the greatest leaders of the Roman state. Marcus will soon complete the *cursus honorum*.

Derivative Detective

placate (placeō): to pacify

service (serviō): an act of help

thēsaurus (thesaurum): dictionary of synonyms

favorite (faveō): thing regarded w/ special preference

justice (iūstitia): the quality of being just

reiterate (iterum): to say repeatedly

adjutant (adiuvō): a staff officer

contemporary (tempus): belonging to the same time

octave (octāvus): a tone on the eighth degree (Ordinal numbers will be covered in chapter 22.)

Respondē Latīnē!

1. Quid est nōmen uxōrī Marcī?   What is the name of Marcus' wife?
   Marcia

2. Quantōs annōs necesse est habēre quaestōrī?   How many years is it necessary for a quaestor to have?
   trīgintā

3. Quantōs annōs necesse est habēre cōnsulī?   How many years is it necessary for a consul to have?
   quadrāgintā

4. Quandō erit Marcus cōnsul?   When will Marcus be consul?
   tribus annīs

ANSWER IN ENGLISH!

1. Upon what course must Marcus embark in order to serve Rome after he has already served in the army?
   the cursus honorum/ the course of honors

2. What was the minimum age for the aedileship?
   thirty-seven

GRAMMAR EXERCISE

Verb	Object
placuit	Mārcō
servīo	Rōmae
favēbant	virīs
praeerant	mīlitibus

Latin in Science

Nimbus: rain clouds (Latin: rain cloud)

Cumulus: clouds that appear like mounds or towers with flat bases and puffy tops (Latin: pile, mound)

Stratus: low altitude clouds appearing as a great big blanket (Latin: blanket)

Cirrus: high altitude cloud appearing with this wisps or narrow bands (Latin: curl)

Notes

Unit 4 Reading

Reading and Review for Chapters 14–17

A FAMILY LEGACY
Karen Moore

It had been more than thirty years since the Cornelii family first moved to the city of Rome. Aemilia sat in the peristylium gazing out at the stars twinkling in the dark night sky. It was hard to believe that it was so long ago that Vesper* had smiled on her wedding night. Fortune had granted her a good life with Cornelius. As the *paterfamiliās* he had absolute control over their children, grandchildren, and even Aemilia herself. Yet, he had proven a kind father, not a hard tyrant. Some of her friends had not been so lucky.

The two of them had made a good team. She managed the house and their country estate and helped run his business at home. An educated woman herself, Aemilia had tended to the early education of both her son and daughter. Although women did not possess careers of their own, it was they who were responsible for raising their sons. Girls must obtain a good education, knowledge of Rome's history, and an understanding of her moral ideals, for one day they would be the mothers who would shape the future men of Rome.

Aemilia's devotion to home allowed Cornelius to spend a great deal of time in the Forum and with influential men so that he might establish his career not only as a senator but also in his private trade business. The salary of a senator was quite small. One needed both reputation and money to succeed in this city. Cornelius and Aemilia often hosted lavish banquets for fellow senators and other notable men. Aemilia would sit by her husband and listen to the discussions of politics and events. A cunning and intelligent woman, she used this information and whatever influence she acquired to further her son's career. Marcus had benefited greatly from his parents' devotion to their family. He had quickly moved through the *cursus honōrum* and it seemed the consulship was a near certainty for him. There could be no greater honor for a Roman father than to see his son obtain this office.

Aemilia wondered whether Cornelius would see Marcus as consul. The Fates,* three goddesses who determined the length of a mortal's life, had granted Cornelius an exceptionally long life. In recent weeks, however, he had grown very weak. It looked as though Atropos would soon cut his thread. Aemilia walked slowly into the atrium and stared at the sacred altar of the *mānēs*, the ancestral spirits. The waxen masks bore the images of Cornelius' ancestors. It has been Cornelius' duty to lead his family in the traditions and rituals which honor the spirits of the dead. Soon his image would join theirs and that duty would fall to Marcus as the new *paterfamiliās*.

But what would become of Cornelius? The priests taught that Mercury would lead his soul to Dis, the land of the dead. There Charon would ferry his soul across the river Styx. On the opposing shore sat the judges of the dead who would question him about his life. Had he conducted himself honorably on earth?

Had he upheld his duty to the gods, to his family, and to Rome? Those deemed worthy would pass on to the Plain of Asphodel or perhaps even to the Elysian Fields, had they offered something exceptionally noble or heroic in their life. Those who had been cruel or unjust were sentenced to do penance in Tartarus, the punishment and time made to fit the offenses committed. Cornelius had been an honorable and pious man. Surely his soul would pass on to Asphodel. First, however, the judges would require him to drink from the River Lethe so that he might forget his past life; he would forget Aemilia. That thought stung a bit. It was fruitless, however, to question the will of the gods. What was important now was to ensure that his memory live on. His memory would live on in the waxen images of the family altar; it would live on in the memory of his family and friends; it would live on in the deeds of his son. As long as some part of Rome remembered Marcus Cornelius Natator as an honorable man who had conducted himself with piety and dignity a piece of him would gain immortality.

Vesper – The evening star, the planet Venus. Romans and Greeks closely associated this star with weddings.

Fates – Three sisters who determine the length of a man's life. Clotho spins the thread of life, Lachesis guides it, and Atropos cuts it.

STEPS FOR A READING COMPREHENSION EXERCISE

1. Read the title.
2. Read the story all the way through.
3. Read the questions so that you know what to look for in the reading.
4. Read the selection again and begin to answer the questions.

On an Advanced Placement Latin Exam you will want to read the questions and then the reading selection.

THE DEATH AND FUNERAL OF THE FATHER OF MARCUS AND CORNELIA

1.   **Miserum dictū**, pater Mārcī et Cornēliae, vir *grandaevus*, mortuus est. Mārcus prope
2.   lectum patris stābat cum Cornēliā et mātre. Mārcus *sē inclīnāvit suprā* patrem et
3.   patris nōmen clāmāvit. Pater nōn respondit. Mārcus tum "*Conclāmātum*" dīxit "*est.*"
4.   Pater *enim* vīxit. Mārcus *oculōs* patris clausit. Corpus patris *togātum* tum in *ātriō*
5.   posuērunt servī. Flōrēs circum corpus posuērunt.
6.   *Paucīs diēbus* patrī *fūnus* erat. Erat *processiō*. In *processiōne* erant familia, *vīcīnī*,
7.   amīcī, et *mūsicī.* Mārcus et amīcī patris corpus in *humerīs* portāvērunt. *Ante*
8.   *processiōnem* ambulāvērunt hominēs *quī* patrem mortuum *laudāvērunt. Imāginēs*
9.   *cēreās remōtās* ab *ātriō* actōrēs gerēbant. *Actōrēs* quoque *vestēs antīquōs* gerēbant.
10. *Vidēbantur māiōrēs* vīvere et ambulāre in viā et virum mortuum ad *īnferōs* dūcere.
11. Virī *facēs ferentēs* erant *ultimī* hominēs in *processiōne. Processiō* stetit in *forō*
12. *Rōmānō* et Mārcus *laudātiōnem aliter ōrātiōnem* habuit. Mārcus omnia bona dē
13. patre dīxit.
14. *Processiō* tum *processit extrā* urbem ad Viam *Appiam.* Prope Viam *Appiam* erat
15. *sepulcrum* patris. Ad *sepulcrum* erat *rogus. Aliquis condīmenta* et *odōrem* et dōna in
16. corpus iēcit. Tum corpus *cremāvērunt.* Ignem *exstīnxērunt vīnō* et aquā. Omnēs
17. "*Valē!*" clāmāvērunt. *Aliquis* omnēs aquā *sparsit.* Omnēs *praeter* familiam
18. *abīvērunt.* Familia *suem sacrificāvit. Sacrificium locum* sacrum facit. Omnis
19. familia *silicernium* cōnsūmpsit. Tum familia *domum* revertit. *Domī, Laribus*
20. *oblātum offerēbant. Fūneris* fīnis erat.

_____

Miserum dictū = sad to say

grandaevus, a, um, adj. .... old, aged
sē inclīnāvit .... leaned (himself)
suprā, prep. + acc.................................... over
conclāmātum est .... it [his name] has been called
enim, adv. .... indeed, truly
vīxit.. he has lived, meaning has lived but does not live now;
i.e. he has died

oculus, ī, m.. eye
togātum .... clad in a toga
ātrium, ī, n.. atrium
paucīs diēbus .... in a few days (ablative of time)
fūnus, fūneris, n. .... funeral
prōcessiō, prōcessiōnis, f. .... procession
vīcīnus, ī, m.. neighbor
mūsicus, ī, m.. musician
humerus, ī, m. .... shoulder
ante, prep. + acc...................................... before, in front of
quī, nominative, pl. .... who
laudō, āre, āvī, ātum .... to praise
imāginēs cēreās... wax images; *i.e.*, masks
remōtās (modifying *cērās*) .... removed, having been removed
actor, actōris, m. .... use your "eye" Latin to discern the meaning of this word.
vestis, vestis, f. .... clothing
antīquus, a, um, adj................................ ancient, old
vidēbantur.. they seemed
māiōrēs .... ancestors
īnferōs .... the underworld
fax, facis, f. .... torch
ferentēs .... carrying, bearing
ultimus, a, um, adj. .... last
stetit .... stopped
forō Rōmānō .... Roman forum
laudātiō, laudātiōnis, f. .... speech of praise, eulogy
aliter... otherwise, in other words
ōrātiōnem habuit....................................... he delivered a speech
prōcēdō, prōcēdere, prōcessī, prōcessum ...... to proceed
extrā, prep. + abl. .... outside of
Via Appia.. Appian Way, famous Roman road
sepulcrum, ī, n... sepulcher, tomb
rogus, ī, m.. funeral pyre
aliquis .... someone, somebody
condīmentum, ī, n.................................... spices
odor, odōris, m. .... perfume
cremō, āre, āvī, ātum .... to burn, cremate
exstīnxērunt... they extinguished
vīnum, ī, n.. wine
Valē!.. Farewell!
spargō, spargere, sparsī, sparsum .... sprinkle
praeter, prep. + acc.................................. except
abeō, abīre, abīvī, abitum......................... to go away
sūs, suis, m. .... swine, a pig
sacrificō, āre, āvī, ātum .... to sacrifice

LA!

For Discussion:

How does the Greco-Roman view of the afterlife affect how Romans live their lives?

How do the Greco-Roman beliefs in this story compare to Judeo-Christian beliefs about death and the life that awaits us after death? In what ways are they similar? In what ways are they different?

sacrificium, ī, n... sacrifice
locus, ī, m.. place
silicernium .... special foods eaten at a funeral
domus, domūs, f.. home
domī... at home (locative case)
oblātum .... an offering
offerō, offerre, obtulī, oblātum...................... to offer, to make an offering

Question & Answer

1. What does the use of *grandaevus* in line 1 instead of *senex* do to the tone of the selection?
   a. It adds a touch of frivolity to an otherwise unbearable topic.
   b. It adds a feeling of dignity and grandeur.
   c. It emphasizes that the narration is from Marcus's point of view.
   d. It creates a neutral feeling in the reader.

2. What is the tense of *vīxit* in line 4?
   a. present
   b. imperfect
   c. future
   d. perfect

3. What factor in the reading is common to both weddings and funerals?
   a. closing the eyes
   b. crying "Conclāmātum est."
   c. flowers
   d. wax masks

4. Which of the following sentences containing a genitive can have two interpretations focusing on the genitive?
   a. Mārcus oculōs patris clausit.
   b. Mārcus et amīcī patris corpus in humerīs portāvērunt.
   c. Mārcus prope lectum patris stābat cum Cornēliā et mātre suā.
   d. Corpus patris togātum tum in ātriō posuērunt servī.

5. The wax images have been in the ___.
   a. bedroom
   b. sepulcher
   c. atrium
   d. master's study

127

6. According to line 11, the torch bearers ___.
   - (a.) were last in the funeral procession
   - b. were in front of the musicians
   - c. did not march in the procession but played from the roadside
   - d. wore clothes from an earlier time

7. The subject of *vidēbantur* in line 10 is ___.
   - a. corpus
   - b. dūcere
   - (c.) māiōrēs
   - d. antīquōs

8. Lines 15 and 16 tell us that ___.
   - a. the body was buried
   - (b.) the body was burned
   - c. the family had special permission to bury the body within the city walls
   - d. there was trouble getting the fire started

9. A synonym for *suem* in line 18 is ___.
   - a. canem
   - b. patrem
   - (c.) porcum
   - d. fēlem

10. The sacrifice ___, according to line 18.
   - a. makes the family feel better
   - b. ensures a safe passage for the father's soul to the underworld
   - (c.) makes the place holy
   - d. concerns food

11. Where does the family make an offering to the Lares?
   - a. near the tomb
   - (b.) at home
   - c. on the Appian Way
   - d. outside the city

12. Considering all of the reading, which of the following is the best alternative title for the selection?
   - a. A Terribly Sad Time
   - b. A Family's Sorrow
   - (c.) Some Funeral Customs of the Romans
   - d. Marcus Is Now the *Paterfamiliās*

13. What is the tense of *facit* in line 18?
    - (a.) present
    - b. imperfect
    - c. future
    - d. perfect

14. Generally, the reading implies that ___.
    - a. the Romans had no belief in an afterlife
    - b. the Romans must have been mostly irreligious
    - (c.) the Romans must have been basically religious and had some belief in the afterlife
    - d. these burial customs were only ostentatious formalities

15. *Laribus* in line 19 recalls ___.
    - (a.) *imāginēs*, line 8
    - b. *lectum*, line 2
    - c. *odor*, line 15
    - d. *vīnō*, line 16

Suggested Project: This unit has described several events that occurred within the Roman home. Chapter 16 provided a great description of the different types of Roman housing. Assign students the task of designing their own model of a Roman home.

TRANSLATION

Sad to say, the father of Marcus and Cornelia, an old man, is dead. Marcus was standing near the father's bed with [his] mother and Cornelia. Marcus leaned over his father and called his father's name. The father did not respond. Marcus then said, "It [his father's name] has been called." Indeed, he has lived (has died). Marcus closed [his] father's eyes. Then the servants placed the father's toga-clad body in the atrium. They put flowers around the body.

Within a few days, there was a funeral for the father. There was a procession. In the procession were the family, neighbors, friends, and musicians. Marcus and the friends of his father carried the body on [their] shoulders OR Marcus and the friends carried the body of the father on their shoulders. Before the procession walked men who praised the dead father. Actors wore wax images removed from the atrium. Actors also wore old clothing. The ancestors seemed to live and to walk in the street and to lead the dead man to the underworld. Men carrying torches were the last people in the procession. The procession stopped in the Roman forum, and Marcus delivered a eulogy/speech of praise; that is, an oration. Marcus said good things about his father.

The procession then proceeded outside the city to the Appian Way. The father's tomb was near the Appian Way. At the tomb there was a funeral pyre. Someone threw spices and perfume and gifts onto the body. Then they burned the body. They extinguished the fire with wine and water. All shouted, "Farewell!" Someone sprinkled everybody with water. Everyone except the family went away. The family sacrificed a pig. The sacrifice makes the place sacred. All the family ate the special food prepared for the funeral. Then the family returned home. At home, they made an offering to the Lares. The funeral was finished.

Virtūte et armīs
By virtue and arms
—Mississippi state motto[A]

Chapter 18

- irregular verbs and their compounds
  - *īre*
  - *ferre*
  - *posse*
- complementary infinitives

[A]Mississippi adopted this coat of arms in 1894. The state abandoned their first coat of arms when they seceded from the Union. The eagle in the middle of the blue shield holds a bundle of arrows as a symbol of war in his left talon. He holds a palm branch, symbol of peace, in his right. Notice that his head is turned toward the palm branch showing a preference for peace. Beneath the blue shield are branches of the cotton plant.

VOCABULARY

NOUNS		
captīvus, ī, m.	captive, prisoner of war	(captivity)
proelium, ī, n.	battle	
senātor, senātōris, m.	senator, member of the Roman senate	(senator)
verbum, ī, n.	word	(verbose)
VERBS		
āmittō, āmittere, āmīsī, āmissum	to let go, lose	(amiss)
dēbeō, dēbēre, dēbuī, dēbitum	ought, must	(debt)
eō, īre, iī/īvī, itum	to go	(exit)
ferō, ferre, tulī, lātum	to bring, carry	(ferry, transfer)
maneō, manēre, mānsī, mānsum	to stay, remain	(mansion)
possum, posse, potuī	to be able, can	(possible)
prōcēdō, prōcēdere, prōcessī, prōcessum	to advance, proceed	(process)
superō, āre, āvī, ātum	to surpass, outdo; overcome	
reddō, reddere, reddidī, redditum	to give back, return	
ADJECTIVES		
potēns, potentis	able, capable; powerful	(potent)
vīcīnus, a, um	neighboring, nearby; (as a noun) neighbor	(vicinity)
PREPOSITION		
apud, prep. + acc.	among	

Exercise 1. Using the rules for syllabication and accent that you have learned, write out the syllables and accents for the vocabulary words above. Then practice pronouncing them aloud.

SECTION 47. Irregular verbs

The English language is full of irregular verbs—verbs that do not follow the normal pattern for principal parts. In fact, they do not typically follow any recognizable pattern at all. For generations students have simply had to memorize all the irregular English verbs and their principal parts.

Regular:	to love	(he) loves	loved	loved
Irregular:	to be	(he) is	was	been
	to go	(he) goes	went	gone
	to bring	(he) brings	brought	brought

Latin also has its share of irregular verbs. The most common of these is the verb *esse*, which you learned in chapter 7 (Section 23). The irregular verbs all use the same personal endings that you have learned. Their stems, however, are a little bit different. The verb *eō, īre* for example has a stem that consists of only a single letter. The personal endings, however, are the same as those for the first and second conjugations.

eō, **īre**, iī/īvī, itum, to go   stem: **ī/ re**

SINGULAR

PERSON	PRESENT	IMPERFECT	FUTURE
1	eō	ībam	ībō
2	īs	ībās	ībis
3	it	ībat	ībit

PLURAL

PERSON	PRESENT	IMPERFECT	FUTURE
1	īmus	ībāmus	ībimus
2	ītis	ībātis	ībitis
3	eunt	ībant	ībunt

The stem of the verb *ferō, ferre* is also irregular in that *fer* does not end in a vowel as do most verbs. The personal endings, however, are the same as those of the third conjugation.

ferō, **ferre**, tulī, lātum, to bring, carry   stem: **fer / re**

SINGULAR

PERSON	PRESENT	IMPERFECT	FUTURE
1	ferō	ferēbam	feram
2	fers	ferēbās	ferēs
3	fert	ferēbat	feret

131

PLURAL

PERSON	PRESENT	IMPERFECT	FUTURE
1	ferimus	ferēbāmus	ferēmus
2	fertis	ferēbātis	ferētis
3	ferunt	ferēbant	ferent

We form the perfect tense of all irregular verbs according to the same formula you learned in chapter 8 (Section 27). Find the stem from the third principal part and then add the special set of perfect endings.[B]

3rd principal part – ī = perfect stem
amō, amāre, **amāv/ī** = amāv
ferō, ferre, **tulī** = tul
eō, īre, **iī** = i (or īv)

PERSON	SINGULAR	PLURAL
1	-ī	-imus
2	-istī	-istis
3	-it	-ērunt

[B]Although the text has already provided the forms for the imperfect and future tenses of these verbs, teachers may wish to use the conjugation worksheets to have students practice writing out these forms again. Such practice really helps students to memorize these forms.

Exercise 2. Conjugate the verbs *īre* and *ferre* in the perfect tense.

Exercise 3. Parse each of the following verbs identifying the person, number, and tense. Then translate.

1. eunt
2. ībātis
3. fertis
4. ībimus
5. ferent

6. tulistī
7. it
8. ferēbās
9. iimus
10. tulērunt

Exercise 4. Make the following verbs perfect tense without changing the person and number. Example: capit = cēpit

1. facimus
2. ferō
3. prōcēdunt
4. superat
5. petis

6. est
7. capiō
8. facitis
9. mittunt
10. possumus

Section 48. Compound verbs

Latin often forms compound verbs by adding prepositions as prefixes to verbs. It should be of interest to note that English often uses these same Latin prepositions to form its own compound verbs.

For example: *ex (out of) + it (he goes) = exit (he goes out)*

 Exercise 5. For each compound verb identify the prefix and root word along with their meanings. Example: adsum ad (near) sum (I am)

1. trānsīmus
2. aderās
3. prōferent
4. exībis
5. trānstulit
6. aberitis
7. prōvidēbō
8. reddō
9. īnferēbant
10. commovēbāmus

Section 49. Compound verb: posse

The English language also combines two words to form compound words instead of using a prefix. The word "lighthouse," for example, combines the words "light" and "house." Each of these words expresses an idea on its own, but when the two come together they express a new idea. Latin also uses this same principle. The most common compound verb in the Latin language could be the irregular verb possum, posse. This verb combines the irregular verb sum, esse (to be) with the adjective potēns (able). Can you guess what it means? (Hint: look at the vocabulary list for this chapter.) Study the tenses of the verb posse in the following chart.[c]

possum, posse, potuī – to be able, can

SINGULAR

PERSON	PRESENT	IMPERFECT	FUTURE
1	possum	poteram	poterō
2	potes	poterās	poteris
3	potest	poterat	poterit

PLURAL

PERSON	PRESENT	IMPERFECT	FUTURE
1	possumus	poterāmus	poterimus
2	potestis	poterātis	poteritis
3	possunt	poterant	poterunt

[c]In chapter 7 (Section 23) we demonstrated how the combination of the nasal sounds 'm/n' with 's' cause the stem of the verb *esse* to change to *su*. A similar linguistic phenomenon occurs here with *posse*. Linguistics classifies the sound 's' as a sibilant, a sound made by forcing air through the narrow passage towards the edge of the teeth. Linguistics classifies 't' as a dental, a sound made by the tongue pressing against the teeth. When the dental and sibilant come together (i.e. t + s) one often drops out or changes. It would be very difficult to properly pronounce a word such as *potsum* without losing the 't' sound.

Notice that the conjugation of *possum* is simply the conjugation of *sum* with the addition of the prefix *pot-*. The *t* changes to an *s* only when it appears before another *s* (i.e. possum, possumus, possunt).

Like the other irregular verbs you have learned in this chapter, *sum* and *possum* conjugate in the perfect tense according to the same formula that you have already learned for regular verbs (Section 27).

 Exercise 6. Conjugate the irregular verb *sum* and its compound *possum* in the perfect tense.

Section 50. Complementary Infinitives

You have already learned that the second principal part is known as the infinitive, and may be translated with the English preposition "to." Often both Latin and English use this infinitive to complete the action or meaning of the main verb. A **complementary infinitive** is an infinitive that completes the main verb of a sentence or phrase. In the case of the verb *possum*, which often takes a complementary infinitive, you might think of it this way: if you are able, you are able to do something. A complementary infinitive expresses what you are able to do.

ambulāre possum	I am able **to walk**
pugnāre optat	he chooses **to fight**

 Exercise 7. Identify the main verb and the complementary infinitive in each sentence. Translate these verb phrases only.

Example: Puer ad lūdum <u>īre parat</u>. he prepares to go

1. Ad proelium revertere dēbeō.
2. Potestisne accipere captīvōs in castra?
3. In Āfricā manēre nōn dēsīderāvit.
4. Fortēs virī ferre aquam ad nāvem poterant.
5. Īre trāns flūmen dēbēmus.

 Exercise 8. Parse, diagram, and translate the following sentences.

1. Multōs necāvērunt mīlitēs Rōmānī.
2. Auxilium ā vīcīnīs accipere potuimus.
3. Verbum meum dedī sociīs.
4. Urbēs cēpit fortis dux Rōmānus.
5. Dux in proeliō nāvēs āmīsit.
6. Multōs captīvōs in castra ferēbant.

Chapter Reading

REGULUS

CHARACTERS:

> M. Atilius Regulus – Consul of Rome, 250 BC
> Hamilcar Barca – Carthaginian General in First Punic War
> Hannibal Barca – Son of Hamilcar, Carthaginian General in Second Punic War, one of the greatest military leaders in history
> L. Manlius Vulso – Consul of Rome, 250 BC

Prīmō in bellō cum *Poenīs*, **M. Atīlius Rēgulus** erat fortis dux Rōmānus. Rōmānī in proeliō *nāvālī* *Poenōs* vīncērunt. *Poenus* dux Hamilcar Barca, pater Hannibālis, in proeliō LXIV nāvēs āmīsit. Rōmānī in Āfricam prōcessērunt. Urbs *Poenōrum sē trādidit* Rōmānīs. Rēgulus et *alter* dux, **L. Manlius Vulso**, Carthāginem prōcessērunt. Vulso **victor** Rōmam revertit. Rēgulus in Āfricā mānsit. Cum mīlitibus *suīs* Rēgulus ducēs *Poenōs trīnōs* pugnāvit. Multōs mīlitēs necāvērunt Rōmānī. Multōs captīvōs, XVIII ingentēs *elephantōs*, XXIV urbēs cēpit Rēgulus. *Poenī victī* pācem ā *fortī* Rōmānō duce petīvērunt. Rēgulus *recūsāvit.* *Poenī* tum auxilium ā vīcīnīs accēpērunt. *Xanthippī*, auxiliō, vīcīnī et ducis, *Poenī* Rēgulum superāvērunt. Fortis Rēgulus nunc erat captīvus. *Poenī* Rēgulum ad *carcerem* tulērunt.

Poenī deinde Rēgulum *Rōmam* mīsērunt. Dīxērunt Rēgulō, "Rēgule, pete pācem *Poenīs* ā Rōmānīs et reverte Carthāginem." Rēgulus *cōnsēnsit.* *Poenī* quoque dēsīderāvērunt captīvōs **dare et accipere**. Rēgulus Rōmam *iter fēcit.* **Rōmae** Rēgulus senātōribus dīxit, "*Nōlīte* pācem *Poenīs* dare. *Nōlīte* captīvōs dare et accipere." Senātōrēs *cōnsēnsērunt.* Senātōrēs Rēgulō dīxērunt, "*Nōlī* Carthāginem revertere! **Rōmae** manē!"

Sed Rēgulus, vir magnō honōre et magnā virtūte, senātōribus dīxit, "Verbum meum dedī *Poenīs*; **necesse est mihi**, igitur, Carthāginem revertere. Dēbeō *redīre*."

Ubi Rēgulus Carthāginem revertit, *Poenī* eum necāvērunt. Rēgulus apud Rōmānōs erat *hērōs* et *martyr*.

Notā Bene:
M. Atīlius Rēgulus = Mārcus Atīlius Rēgulus
L. Manlius Vulso = Lūcius Manlius Vulso
Since the Romans had fewer than twenty **praenōmina** for males, they abbreviated **praenōmina**. When you see the abbreviations, you must always read aloud in Latin or translate the name, not the abbreviation; for example, M. is always Marcus and L. is always Lucius.
victor = as a victor (victor is an appositive of Vulso.)
dare et accipere = to give and receive; i.e., to exchange
Rōmae = at Rome
necesse est mihi = it is necessary for me

GLOSSARY

prīmus, a, um, adj.	first
Poenī, Poenōrum	the Carthaginians (who were originally from Phoenicia)
nāvālis, nāvāle, adj.	naval
sē trādidit	surrendered
alter, altera, alterum, adj.	other (of two)
suus, a, um, adj.	his/her own
trīnī, adj.	in threes, three each
elephantus, ī, m.	use your "eye" Latin to discern the meaning of this word.
Rōmam	to Rome
victī	conquered
recūsō, āre, āvī, ātum	to refuse, decline
Xanthippus, ī, m.	Xanthippus, a mercenary general from Sparta
carcer, carceris, m.	prison, jail
cōnsentiō, cōnsentīre, cōnsēnsī, cōnsēnsum	to agree
iter fēcit	made a journey, traveled
nōlī, nōlīte	"don't!" (negative command)
hērōs, hērōis, m.	hero, demi-god
martyr	martyr. (This is a Greek word adopted into Latin and English. A martyr is someone who dies for a cause.)
redeō, redīre, rediī/redīvī, reditum.	to go back, return

Respondē Latīnē!ᴰ

1. Quālis dux erat Rōmānus Rēgulus?

2. Quot nāvēs āmīsērunt Poenī in proeliō nāvālī?

3. Quot ducēs Poenōs pugnāvit Rēgulus?

4. Quae animālia Rēgulus et Rōmānī mīlitēs cēpērunt?

5. Quālis vir erat Rēgulus honōre et virtūte?

quālis = *what kind of?*, quot = *how many?*, quae = *which?*

ᴰAt this point in their studies encourage students to answer in complete Latin sentences if they have not already been doing so. The answers can often be taken straight from the reading. Students can also repeat the question to form a more complete answer.

ANSWER IN ENGLISH!

1. What two Roman generals are characters in the story?

2. Which of the two returned to Rome first?

3. Why would Rēgulus not stay in Rome?

4. Where did Rēgulus meet his death?

5. After his death, how did the Romans regard Rēgulus?

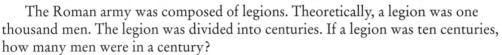

Culture Corner

The Roman army was composed of legions. Theoretically, a legion was one thousand men. The legion was divided into centuries. If a legion was ten centuries, how many men were in a century?

In actuality, for example in Gaius Julius Caesar's army, a legion was six hundred soldiers. In Caesar's army, then, how many men were in a century? (No matter how many men were in the century, their leader was called a *centurion*. Tradition holds that it was a centurion, Longinus, who pierced the side of Christ during his crucifixion.) Sometimes a legion may have been more than a thousand. We are told that 15,000 Romans died at the hands of the traitor Arminius at the Battle of Teutoburg Forest in Germany. We also hear this number referred to as three legions. If that large number is correct, how many men were in a legion in Augustus' army at Teutoburg? How many would have been in a century? Augustus often said, "Give me back my legions." He never recovered spiritually and morally from that great loss.

Negative Imperatives

Sometimes we want to tell someone not to do something. In Latin, in order to issue a negative command, we use the irregular verb *nōlō, nōlle* in the imperative. If we are giving a negative command to one person, we naturally use the singular imperative *nōlī*; if we are giving a negative command to more that one person, we naturally use the plural imperative *nōlīte*. We follow both these imperatives with a complementary infinitive that tells what it is that we do not want the person to do.

Cassī, nōlī currere! Cassius, don't run! (Literally, "Cassius, be unwilling to run.")

Discipulī, nōlīte currere! Students, don't run!

Colloquāmur

Make the following commands.

Tell Marcus to run.
Tell Lucius not to run.
Tell Claudia to sit.
Tell Claudia and Publius not to sit.
Tell Marcus to stand.

Now make up some of your own commands and use them to play "magister dīcit."

Derivative Detective

LATIN PREFIXES IN ENGLISH WORDS

We borrowed most of our English prefixes directly from the Latin language. Identify the prefix in each of the following English words. What is the meaning of this prefix in Latin? How does it influence the meaning of the English root word?[E]

posthumous   transport
postindustrial   transfer
postpone   transit
postwar   expire
preamble   export
preoccupy   extract
premonition   emit
inerrant   admit
infallible   absence
descend
deduce

[E]Most of the root words in this exercise are derived from Latin as well. Ask students to identify the origin of the root word as well as the prefix. This will be great practice for them as students sometimes have difficulty identifying the root word in both Latin words and English derivatives, particularly when the root is irregular. A good English dictionary will prove helpful in this exercise.

Chapter 18 Teacher's Pages

Exercise 1

cap-tī-vus, ī, m.
proe-li-um, ī, n.
se-nā-tor, se-nā-tō-ris, m.
ver-bum, ī, n.
ā-mit-tō, ā-mit-te-re, ā-mī-sī, ā-mis-sum
dē-be-ō, dē-bē-re, dē-bu-ī, dē-bi-tum
e-ō, ī-re, i-ī/ī-vī, ī-tum
fe-rō, fer-re, tu-lī, lā-tum

ma-ne-ō, ma-nē-re, mān-sī, mān-sum
pos-sum, pos-se, po-tu-ī
prō-ce-dō, prō-ce-de-re, prō-ces-sī, prō-ces-sum
su-pe-rō, ā-re, ā-vī, ā-tum
red-dō, red-de-re, red-di-dī, red-di-tum
po-tēns, po-ten-tis
vī-cī-nus, a, um
a-pud

Exercise 2

PERSON	*īre*		*ferre*	
	SINGULAR	PLURAL	SINGULAR	PLURAL
1	*īvī or iī*	*īvimus or iimus*	*tulī*	*tulimus*
2	*īvistī or iistī*	*īvistis or iistis*	*tulistī*	*tulistis*
3	*īvit or iit*	*īvērunt or iērunt*	*tulit*	*tulērunt*

Exercise 3

1. eunt — 3, pl, pres. – they go
2. ībātis — 2, pl, imp. – you were going
3. fertis — 2, pl, pres. – you carry
4. ībimus — 1, pl, fut. – we will go
5. ferent — 3, pl, fut. – they will carry
6. tulistī — 2, sing, perf. – you carried
7. it — 3, sing, pres. – he goes
8. ferēbās — 2, sing, imp. – you were carrying
9. iimus — 1, pl, perf. – we went
10. tulērunt — 3, pl., perf. – they carried

Exercise 4

1. facimus — fēcimus
2. ferō — tulī
3. prōcēdunt — prōcessērunt
4. superat — superāvit
5. petis — petīvistī
6. est — fuit
7. capiō — cēpī
8. facitis — fēcistis
9. mittunt — mīsērunt
10. possumus — potuimus

Exercise 5

1. trānsīmus — trāns (across) īmus (we go)
2. aderās — ad (near) erās (you were)
3. prōferent — prō (before) ferent (they will bring)
4. exībis — ex (out of) ībis (you will go)
5. trānstulit — trāns (across) tulit (he carried)
6. aberitis — ab (away) eritis (you will be)
7. prōvidēbō — prō (before) vidēbō (I will see)
8. reddō — re (back) ddō (I give)
9. īnferēbant — in (in) ferēbant (they were carrying)
10. commovēbāmus — com (with/together) movēbāmus (we were moving)

Exercise 6

PERSON	sum		possum	
	SINGULAR	PLURAL	SINGULAR	PLURAL
1	fuī	fuimus	potuī	potuimus
2	fuistī	fuistis	potuistī	potuistis
3	fuit	fuērunt	potuit	potuērunt

Exercise 7

1. Ad proelium <u>revertere dēbeō</u>.   I ought to return
2. <u>Potestisne accipere</u> captīvōs in castra?   are you able to accept
3. In Āfricā <u>manēre</u> nōn dēsīderāvit.   he desired to remain
4. Fortēs virī <u>ferre</u> aquam ad nāvem <u>poterant</u>.   they were able to carry
5. <u>Īre</u> trāns flūmen <u>dēbēmus</u>.   we ought to go

Exercise 8

```
     Adj       V          S       Adj
```
1. Multōs necāvērunt mīlitēs Rōmānī.
```
   ac/p/m   3/p/perf   n/p/m   n/p/m
```
The Roman soldiers killed many.
We know that *mīlitēs* is likely the subject because of its placement just before the nominative adjective *Rōmānī*.

```
     DO     P    OP      Inf      S+V
```
2. Auxilium ā vīcīnīs accipere potuimus.
```
   ac/s/n      ab/p/m            1/p/perf
```
We were able to receive help from (our) neighbors.

```
     DO    Adj     S+V       IO
```
3. Verbum meum dedī sociīs.
```
   ac/s/n  ac/s/n  1/s/perf  d/p/m
```
I gave my word to the allies.

```
     DO     V    Adj     S      Adj
```
4. Urbēs cēpit fortis dux Rōmānus.
```
   ac/p/f  3/s/perf  n/s/m  n/s/m  n/s/m
```
The strong Roman leader/general seized the cities.

```
    SN  P   OP    DO      V
```
5. Dux in proeliō nāvēs amīsit.
```
   n/s/m  ab/s/n  ac/p/f  3/s/perf
```
The leader/general lost ships in the battle.

```
     Adj      DO    P    OP      V
```
6. Multōs captīvōs in castra ferēbant.
```
   ac/p/m   ac/p/m     ac/p/n  3/p/imp
```
They were bringing many captives into camp.

Translation

In the first war with the Carthaginians, M. Attilius Regulus was a brave Roman leader. The Romans conquered the Carthaginians in a naval battle. The Carthaginian leader Hamilcar Barca, father of Hannibal, lost 64 ships in the battle. The Romans proceeded into Africa. The city of the Carthaginians surrendered to the Romans. Regulus and another leader, L. Manlius Vulso, proceeded to Carthage. Vulso returned to Rome as a victor. Regulus remained in Africa. Regulus fought the Carthaginian leaders three times with his own soldiers. The Romans killed many soldiers. Regulus seized many captives, 18 huge elephants, 24 cities. The conquered Carthaginians sought peace from the brave Roman leader. Regulus refused. The Carthaginians then received aid from neighboring (cities). With the aid of Xanthippus, a neighboring leader, the Carthaginians overcame Regulus. The brave Regulus was now a prisoner of war. The Carthaginians brought Regulus to prison.

Then the Carthaginians sent Regulus to Rome. They said to Regulus, "Regulus, seek peace for Carthaginians from the Romans and return to Carthage." Regulus agreed. The Carthaginians also desired to exchange (lit. to give and receive) prisoners of war. Regulus made the journey to Rome. Regulus said to the senators of Rome, "Do not give peace to the Carthaginians! Do not exchange prisoners of war!" The senators agreed. The senators said to Regulus, "Do not return to Carthage! Remain in Rome!" But Regulus, a man with great honor and great virtue, said to the senators, "I gave my word to the Carthaginians; it is necessary, therefore, for me to return. I must go back."

When Regulus returned to Carthage, the Carthaginians killed him. Among the Romans Regulus was a hero and martyr.

Respondē Latīnē!

1. Quālis dux erat Rōmānus Rēgulus?
   Rēgulus erat fortis dux Rōmānus.

   What kind of Roman leader was Regulus?
   Regulus was a brave/ strong Roman leader.

2. Quot nāvēs āmīsērunt Poenī in proeliō nāvālī?
   LXIV nāvēs āmīsērunt.

   How many ships did the Carthaginians lose in the naval battle?
   They lost 64 ships.

3. Quot ducēs Poenōs pugnāvit Rēgulus?
   Rēgulus ducēs Poenōs trīnōs pugnāvit.

   How many Carthaginian leaders did Regulus fight?
   Regulus fought three Carthiginian leaders.

4. Quae animālia Rēgulus et Rōmānī mīlitēs cēpērunt?
   Elephantōs cēpērunt.

   Which animals did Regulus and the Roman soldiers capture?
   They captured elephants.

5. Quālis vir erat Rēgulus honōre et virtūte?
   Rēgulus erat vir magnō honōre et magnā virtūte.

   What kind of man was Regulus in honor and virtue?
   Regulus was a man of great honor and great virtue.

ANSWER IN ENGLISH!

1. What two Roman generals are characters in the story?
   M. Attilius Regulus and L. Manlius Vulso were generals and consuls.

2. Which of the two returned to Rome first?
   Vulso returned to Rome first.

3. Why would Rēgulus not stay in Rome?
   Regulus would not remain in Rome because he had given his word to the Carthaginians that he would return.

4. Where did Rēgulus meet his death?
   Regulus met his death (was killed/died) in Carthage.

5. After his death, how did the Romans regard Rēgulus?
   The Romans regarded Regulus as a hero and martyr.

Colloquāmur!

Tell Marcus to run.	Mārce, curre!
Tell Lucius not to run.	Lūcī, nōlī currere!
Tell Claudia to sit.	Claudia, sedē!
Tell Claudia and Publius not to sit.	Claudia et Publī, nōlīte sedēre!
Tell Marcus to stand.	Mārce, stā! *or* Marce, surge!

Derivative Detective

posthumous	Happening after a person's death (from the Late Latin *posthumus*, a variant spelling of *postumus*, the superlative of *posterus*, "following;" altered in Late Latin according to some sources by association with *hūmare*, "to bury." This is perhaps a trick question as the "post-" here is, strictly speaking, perhaps not a prefix, having been a built-in part of its earliest Latin root.)
postindustrial	Relating to a period in a nation's history when the importance of manufacturing ["industry"] has declined relative to that of information and services in its economy. (from the Latin *post* "after" + *industria* "diligence, activity, industry" = "after industry")
postpone	To delay or put off (from the Latin *post* "after" + *pōnere* "to place" = "to place after")
postwar	After the war (the Latin prefix/ preposition *post* "after" is here added to the Germanic root word "war" to indicate something occurring after the war in question.)
preamble	A short, generally explanatory, introduction to a larger work, especially to a formal document (from the Latin *prae* "before" + *ambulāre* "to walk" = "to walk before," a figurative description of what a preamble is supposed to accomplish in reference to a larger work.)
preoccupy	1. To completely occupy the thoughts. 2. To take possession of beforehand (from Latin *prae* "before" + *ob* "completely" + *capere* "to seize/ take possession of" = "to take possession of completely and/or beforehand.")
premonition	A forewarning, usually of a coming danger (from the Latin *prae* "before" + *monēre* "to warn" = "to warn beforehand.")
inerrant	Without mistakes [errors] (from the Latin *in* "not" + *errāre* "to make a mistake/ err" = "to not err.")
infallible	Incapable of error (from the Latin *in* "not" + *fallibilis* "prone to error or deceit" = "not prone to error or deceit" from *fallere* "to deceive.")
descend	To go down (from the Latin *dē* "down" + *scandere* "to climb" = "to climb down.")
deduce	To reach a conclusion by applying rules of logic to a given set of premises (from the Latin *de* "from or concerning" + *dūcere* "to lead" = "to lead from or concerning.")
transport	To carry across (from the Latin *trans* "across" + *portāre* "to carry" = "to carry across.")
transfer	To carry across (from the Latin *trans* "across" + *ferō, ferre* "to carry" = "to carry across.")
transit	To go across (from the Latin *trans* "across" + *eō, īre* "to go" + "to go across.")
expire	To breathe out or to die (from the Latin *ex* "out" + *spīrāre* "to breathe" = "to breathe out" or "out of breaths.")
export	To carry away or to sell goods in a foreign country (from the Latin *ex* "out" + *portāre* = "to carry out.")
extract	To draw out (from the Latin *ex* "out" + *trahere* "to draw" = "to draw out.")
emit	To send out (from the Latin *ē/ex* "out" + *mittere* "to send" = "to send out.")
admit	To allow to enter or to concede (from the Latin *ad* "to/ toward" + *mittere* "to send" = "to send toward.")
absence	To be away (from the Latin *absēns* "to be away," the present active participle of *absum* "I am away" from: *ab* "away" + *sum* "I am" = "I am away.")

Salūs populī suprēma lēx estō.
The welfare of the people shall be the supreme law.
—Missouri state motto[A]

This motto was taken from Cicero's Oration, *Dē Lēgibus*, Book III, Part III, Sub. VIII.

[A]Judge and congressman Robert William Wells designed this seal, adopted on January 11, 1822. The center shield depicts an eagle, representing the nation, on the right and a bear and crescent moon, representing the state of Missouri, on the left. Around the shield supported by two grizzly bears are the words "United We Stand, Divided We Fall." The Latin motto appears beneath the bears with a series of Roman numerals revealing the year Missouri became a state (MDCCCXX = 1820). There are 23 small stars at the top representing each of the 23 states to precede Missouri. The larger star represents Missouri herself, the 24th state to join the Union.

Chapter 19

- personal pronouns
  - ego
  - tū
  - is, ea, id

VOCABULARY

NOUNS		
amor, amōris, m.	love	(amorous)
cōnsilium, cōnsiliī, n.	plan	
corium, coriī, n.	skin, hide	(excoriate)
fātum, ī, n.	fate	(fatal)
frāter, frātris, m.	brother	(fraternal)
līnum, ī, n.	line, rope; thread	(linear)
prīnceps, prīncipis, m.	prince, leader	(principate)
soror, sorōris, f.	sister	(sorority)

PRONOUNS		
ego	I	
is, ea, id	he, she, it	
nōs, nostrī/nostrum	we	
tū	you	

VERBS		
adamō, āre, āvī, ātum	to fall in love with	
circumscrībō, -scrībere, -scrīpsī, -scrīptum	to draw a line around	(circumscribe)
condō, condere, condidī, conditum	to found, establish	
crēdō, crēdere, crēdidī, crēditum (+ dat. of person, + acc. of thing)	to believe, trust	(creed)
effugiō, effugere, effūgī	to run away, escape	
relinquō, relinquere, relīquī, relictum	to leave behind	(relinquish)

ADJECTIVES			
	crūdēlis, crūdēle	hard-hearted, cruel	(crudelity)
	miser, misera, miserum	unhappy, wretched, miserable	(miser)
PREPOSITIONS			
	contrā, prep. + acc.	against	(contrary)
	post, prep. + acc.	after	

Exercise 1. Using the rules for syllabication and accent that you have learned, write out the syllables and accents for the vocabulary words above. Then practice pronouncing them aloud.

Section 51. Personal Pronouns

While English uses nouns (from Latin *nōmen*, name) to name something or someone, it uses pronouns (from Latin *prō nōmen*, on behalf of a name) to take the place of a noun. **Personal pronouns** are those pronouns that specifically refer to a person or thing from the speaker's point of view. These are the same pronouns that we see represented in the personal endings of verbs (I, we, you, they, etc.). Since the personal endings of finite verbs identify the subject, Romans used the nominative case with pronouns only to indicate special emphasis.

These pronouns do not fit neatly into any one of the noun declensions. Instead, they follow their own pattern.

SINGULAR

CASE	1ST PERSON	2ND PERSON
Nom.	ego	tū
Gen.	meī	tuī
Dat.	mihi	tibi
Acc.	mē	tē
Abl.	mē	tē

PLURAL

CASE	1ST PERSON	2ND PERSON
Nom.	nōs	vōs
Gen.	nostrī, nostrum	vestrī, vestrum
Dat.	nōbīs	vōbīs
Acc.	nōs	vōs
Abl.	nōbīs	vōbīs

Like nouns, pronouns have case and number. Unlike nouns, the first and second person pronouns do not have gender. The gender for these pronouns in Latin, just as in English, is ambiguous. It is left for the reader to discern based on the context of the sentence.

Notā Bene:
The preposition *cum* sometimes appears as a suffix for pronouns in the ablative case.
    mēcum = cum mē
    nōbīscum = cum nōbīs

Can you discern the gender of the pronouns in each of these sentences?

I am a girl.	Ego sum puella.
I love you.	Tē amō.
Come with us.	Venīte nōbīscum.

Caveat Discipulus: These pronouns do NOT show possession (e.g. my ball). Latin uses a special possessive adjective for that purpose, which we will learn later on. Pronouns can use the genitive case, however, for other purposes such as the partitive genitive (Section 34) or the objective genitive, which we will discuss in another chapter.[B]

[B]The objective genitive appears in *Latin Alive! Book 2.*

Exercise 2. Identify the case and number of the pronouns as they appear in the sentences.

1. The force will be with you.
2. Give it to me.
3. A part of me goes with you (pl).
4. You are not the boss!
5. Will mother carry us to bed?

1. Tū es sōrōr.
2. Nōmen mihi est Anna.
3. Vōbīs nōn crēdidit.
4. Ambulābisne mēcum ad lūdum?
5. Nōs parentēs amant.

Section 52. Third Person Pronouns

The third person pronouns in both English and Latin have gender. The singular forms have a few new endings, but the plural follow the same pattern as that of first and second declension nouns. Notice that these pronouns, like all nouns and adjectives, also follow the neuter rule (Section 19).

SINGULAR

Case	Masculine	Feminine	Neuter
Nom.	is	ea	id
Gen.	ēius	ēius	ēius
Dat.	eī	eī	eī
Acc.	eum	eam	id
Abl.	eō	eā	eō

PLURAL

Case	Masculine	Feminine	Neuter
Nom.	eī	eae	ea
Gen.	eōrum	eārum	eōrum
Dat.	eīs	eīs	eīs
Acc.	eōs	eās	ea
Abl.	eīs	eīs	eīs

Notā Bene: Third person pronouns may use the genitive case to show possession, but only if the pronoun showing possession does *NOT* refer to the subject.

Vir gladium ēius tenet.

Correct:
The man holds his (someone else's) sword.
Incorrect:
The man holds his (own) sword.[c]

[c]The possessive adjective *suus* would be used in this case: *Vir gladium suum tenet.* Possessive adjectives will be taught in chapter 24.

TE **Exercise 3.** Identify the case, and number of the pronouns as they appear in the sentences. Translate the pronouns only.

1. Is fuit magister multōrum discipulōrum.

2. Vīdimus eōs in viā prope templum.

3. Date nōbīs librōs.

4. Mēnsa est in ēius casā.

5. Ingēns cēna eī placēbit.

TE **Exercise 4.** Parse, diagram, and translate the following sentences.

1. Frāter ēius erat vir crūdēlis.

2. Prīnceps eī terram multam dedit.

3. Fātum ducis erat ad Ītaliam nāvigāre et urbem condere.

4. Tū cum sociīs magnam urbem fēcistī.

5. Nōs relinquere temptāvit.

Dido's "Prophecy" of Hannibal

In Book IV of the *Aeneid*, Vergil told of the love of Aeneas and Dido, a love doomed because Aeneas' fate compelled him to go to Italy, not to stay with Dido in Carthage. Dido, the founder of Carthage, had been the queen of Phoenicia; for this reason the Romans called the Carthaginians, their bitterest enemy, the Poeni. When Aeneas left Carthage to pursue his fate, Dido was furious. She cursed the Trojans and their descendants, saying:

Then you, Carthaginians, and all your tribe and descendants to come, exercise your hatred; send these duties to my ashes: there will be no love, no agreement between our peoples. Let some avenger arise from my bones who will pursue the Trojans and forever and always use [Punic] strength against them throughout time.
Aeneid, Book IV, ll. 622–627, Trans. Gaylan DuBose

One can imagine a Roman hearing these lines saying to himself, "Hannibal!"

An Interesting Side Note

Perhaps when you were a child, your mother or father told you the bugbear or the boogie man would get you if you misbehaved. After the Second Punic War, Roman parents said "Hannibal ad portās" (Hannibal is at the gates) to their children to remind them to be good.

DIDO

CHARACTERS:

Dido/Elissa – founder and Queen of Carthage
Sychaeus – murdered husband of Dido
Pygmalion – Dido's treacherous brother
Iarbas – African prince
Aeneas – Prince of Troy, leader of Trojan remnant
Venus – goddess of love, mother of Aeneas
Cupid – archer god of love, son of Venus
Ascanius – son of Aeneas

Dīdō erat rēgīna pulchra. *Alterum* nōmen rēgīnae Elissa erat. Erat uxor Sychaeī, rēgis Phoenīciae. Frāter ēius Pygmaliōn erat, vir crūdēlis. Pygmaliōn marītum **Dīdūs** obtruncāvit. Dīdō pātriam *suam* effūgit. Tulit **opēs Poenōs** et *tandem* in Āfricam *pervēnit*. Iarbās, Āfricānus dux, iuvenem rēgīnam adamāvit et eī terram dedit. Terra **quam** Dīdō circumscrībere potuit coriō *taurī* **futūra erat** urbs *nova*. *Callida* Elissa corium in līna *secuit* et *ea coniūnxit*. Sīc multam terram circumscrībere potuit *longō* līnō. Dīdō magnam urbem Carthāginem fēcit. **Dux fēmina factī.**

Paucōs post annōs Aenēās, dux Trōiānus et fīlius Veneris deae, ad urbem *vēnit*. Venus, dea amōris, *alterō* cum fīliō Cupīdō, rēgīnam Carthāginis **Aenēān** adamāre dēsīderāvit. **Rēs ita est.** Iarbās, fīlius *Iovis Āfricānī*, et aliī prīncipēs *Āfricānī* nunc iuvenem rēgīnam *ōdērunt*. Aenēās, tamen, fātum habuit. Fātum ducis Trōiānī erat ad Ītaliam cum fīliō Ascaniō et aliīs Trōiānīs nāvigāre et urbem condere. Itaque Africam *clam* relinquere temptāvit. Rēgīna cōnsilia *agnōscit*. Fātum Aenēae nōn crēdidit. Erat **īrātissima**! Aenēān *vituperābat*. Dīxit fēmina misera deīs, "Ferte *ultōrem ossibus* meīs! *Sit* omnibus cum Poenīs inimīcus Trōiānīs nunc et semper." Postquam Aenēās ab Āfricā **nāvigāverat**, *sē interfēcit*. Multōs post annōs Hannibal erat magnus dux *quī* contrā Rōmānōs bellum gerēbat.

Dīdūs – an unusual genitive: of Dido
opēs Poenōs = Phoenician resources, *i.e.*, the treasure
quam = which
futūra erat = was going to be
Dux fēmina factī = A woman was the leader of the deed.
(This is directly from Vergil's *Aeneid*, Book I, l. 364. Notice that the verb is omitted. Roman writers often did not express forms of *sum* but rather understood that the reader would understand what the verb was and supply the thoughts. Very often modern textbooks will have notes such as "*sc.* erat". The *sc.* means "supply." This omission of the verb is known as ellipsis. You will also frequently notice ellipsis in mottoes.)
Aenēān – Greek accusative
Rēs ita est. – The affair turned out like that; *i.e.*, she did fall in love with him. (The affair is thus.)
īrātissima = very angry (superlative degree)
sit = let there be
nāvigāverat = had sailed
ille – When *ille* follows a noun, we may interpret it as "that famous."

GLOSSARY

alter, altera, alterum, adj.	the other (of two)
obtruncō, obtruncāre, obtruncāvī, obtruncātum	to cut down, slaughter
suus, a, um	his/her own
tandem, adv.	finally
perveniō, pervenīre, pervēnī, perventum	to come to, arrive, reach

taurus, ī, m.	bull
novus, a, um, adj.	new
callidus, a, um, adj.	clever, crafty
secō, secāre, secuī, sectum	to cut
coniungō, coniungere, coniūnxī, coniūnctum	to join together; yoke
sīc, adv.	in this way
longus, a, um, adj.	use your "eye" Latin to discern the meaning of this adjective.
veniō, venīre, vēnī, ventum	to come
Iovis, genitive sing. of *Iuppiter*	
Āfricānus, a, um, adj.	use your "eye" Latin to discern the meaning of this adjective.
ōdērunt	they hated
clam, adv.	secretly
agnōscō, agnōscere, agnōvī, agnitum	to know, understand
vituperō, āre, āvī, ātum	to blame
ultor, ultōris, m.	avenger, punisher
os, ossis, n.	bone; (figurative) very soul
sē interfēcit	she killed herself
quī, nominative, sing.	who

Respondē Latīnē!

 1. Quae sunt nōmina rēgīnae?

2. Quālis frāter erat Pygmaliōn?

3. Quis est Iarbās?

4. Quam urbem Dīdō fēcit?

5. Quis est Aenēās?

quid = *what?*, quālis = *what kind of?*, quis = *who?*, quam = *which?*

ANSWER IN ENGLISH!

1. Why did Dido flee Phoenicia?

2. How did Dido obtain land from Iarbas?

3. Why did Aeneas leave Dido?

4. What did Dido prophesy regarding their descendants?

5. How did Dido perish?

Colloquāmur

Use the following questions and responses to review the pronouns in the sentences above. Use some "eye" Latin to figure out what the responses mean.

interrogātiō:	**Cūius est numerī?**	What number is it?
respōnsum:	**Singulāriter est.**	
	Plūrāliter est.	
interrogātiō:	**Quō est cāsū?**	In what case is it?
respōnsum:	**Cāsū nōminātīvō est.**	
	Cāsū accūsātīvō est.	
	Cāsū datīvō est.	
	Cāsū ablātīvō est.	

Culture Corner: The Aeneid

The *Iliad* and the *Odyssey* are epic poems, composed by the blind bard Homer, which recall the great deeds and legends of Ancient Greece. Though mostly fictional, these poems contain much history for the tribes of Greece as well. They recall ancient kingdoms, their nobility, and a common struggle against a very real place called Troy. Back then children did not have history texts or even story books to learn about their heritage. Instead these stories were told through an oral tradition. Often these stories became embellished like your grandfather's fishing stories, but that was all a part of the entertainment. These epic poems united the sometimes warring tribes with a sense of common history.

When Caesar Augustus came to power he reunited a Rome that was at war with itself and ushered in the *Pāx Romāna*. He recognized a need for unity amongst Romans of all political factions and so encouraged a great poet by the name of Publius Vergilius Maro to write an epic history for Rome. Vergil, as we call him today, followed Homer's example of weaving fact and fiction together to create a masterful epic. The *Aeneid* follows a journey (as does the *Odyssey*) in search of a homeland. Prince Aeneas of Troy, called by destiny, must find Italy and found the Roman race. Along the way he has many adventures, but his time with Dido, queen of Carthage, dominates nearly a third of the epic poem. Aeneas and Dido may be fictional characters, but they represent very real people and places.

Vergil knew that the three Punic Wars had been the greatest external threat to Rome's sovereignty. Carthage, and Hannibal in particular, had been Rome's greatest enemy. It was only fitting that Vergil weave the history of these two great enemies into his epic story for Rome. The conflict between these two nations begins with the opening lines of the *Aeneid* where Juno is fuming at the fate of her favored city of Carthage; for it has long been foretold that the city of Rome, founded by the descendants of Aeneas, will one day destroy this great city and eventually rule the world. When Aeneas and Dido meet and obviously share a mutual admiration for one another, Juno conspires with Venus to unite the two leaders in bonds of love. Unfortunately, destiny proves stronger than love and drives Aeneas from Dido's arms. Love turns to hate and the epic struggle between the two great nations is set in motion.

Exercise 1

a-mor, a-mō-ris, m.
co-ri-um, co-ri-ī, n.
fā-tum, -ī, n.
frā-ter, frā-tris, m.
lī-num, -ī, n.
so-ror, so-rō-ris, f.
e-go
is, e-a, id
tū

a-da-mō, ā-re, ā-vī, ā-tum
cir-cum-scrī-bō, -scrī-be-re, -scrīp-sī, -scrīp-tum
con-dō, con-de-re, con-di-dī, con-di-tum
crē-dō, crē-de-re, crē-di-dī, crē-di-tum
ef-fu-gi-ō, ef-fu-ge-re, ef-fū-gīprīn-ceps, prīn-ci-pis, m.
re-lin-quō, re-lin-que-re, re-lī-quī, re-lic-tum
mi-ser, mi-se-ra, mi-se-rum
con-trā
post

Exercise 2

1. The force will be with you.   ablative, sing.
2. Give it to me.   dative, sing.
3. A part of me goes with you (pl).   me – genitive, sing.; you – ablative, pl.
4. You are not the boss!   nominative, sing.
5. Will mother carry us to bed?   accusative, pl.

1. Tū es sōrōr.   nominative, sing.
2. Nōmen mihi est Anna.   dative, sing.
3. Vōbīs nōn crēdidit.   dative, pl. (crēdō takes a dative object)
4. Ambulābisne mēcum ad lūdum?   ablative, sing.
5. Nōs parentēs amant.   accusative, pl.

Exercise 3

1. Is fuit magister multōrum discipulōrum.   nom., sing. = he
2. Vīdimus eōs in viā prope templum.   acc., pl. = them
3. Date nōbīs librōs.   dat., pl. = us, to us
4. Mēnsa est in ēius casā.   gen., sing. = his/her
5. Ingēns cēna eī placēbit.   dat., sing. = him/her

Exercise 4

```
        S     PNA    LV    PrN    Adj
1. Frāter  ēius   erat   vir  crūdēlis.
   m/n/s  g/s/m,f 3/s/i m/s/n m/s/n
   His/her brother was a cruel man.
```

```
        S     IO     DO     Adj     V
2. Prīnceps  eī   terram  multam  dedit.
   n/s/m  d/s/m,f ac/s/f  ac/s/f 3/s/perf
   The prince/leader gave him/her much land.
```

```
        S    PNA    LV   P    OP    Inf    C  DO    Inf
3. Fātum  ducis  erat  ad  Ītaliam nāvigāre et urbem condere.
   n/s/n  g/s/m 3/s/i      ac/s/f            ac/s/f
   The fate of the leader was to sail to Italy and to found a city.
```

```
         S    P    OP     Adj    DO      V
```
4. Tū cum sociīs magnam urbem fēcistī.
```
    n/s  ab/pl/m  ac/s/f  ac/s/f  2/s/perf
```
   You made a great city with (your) allies.

```
   DO     Inf          V
```
5. Nōs relinquere temptāvit.
```
   ac/p            3/s/perf
```
   He tried to leave us.

Translation

Dido was a beautiful queen. Another name for the queen was Elissa. She was the wife of Sychaeus, king of Phoenicia. Her brother was Pygmalion, a cruel man. Pygmalion slaughtered the husband of Dido. Dido fled from her own country. She carried Phoenician wealth and finally arrived in Africa. Iarbas, an African leader, fell in love with the young queen and gave her land. The land which Dido was able to draw a line around with the hide of a bull was going to be the new city. Clever Elissa cut the hide into lines and joined them together. In this way she was able to draw a line around much land with a long line. Dido made Carthage a great city. A woman was the leader of the deed.

After a few years Aeneas, a Trojan leader and son of the goddess Venus, came to the city. Venus, goddess of love, with her other son Cupid, desired the queen of Carthage to fall in love with Aeneas. The affair was thus. Iarbas, son of African Jove, and the other African princes now hated the young queen. Fate, nevertheless, held Aeneas. The fate of the Trojan leader was to sail to Italy with his son Ascanius and other Trojans and to build a city. Thus he tried to secretly leave Africa behind. The queen recognized the plans. She did not believe the fate of Aeneas. She was very angry! She was blaming Aeneas. The sad woman said to the gods, "Bring an avenger from my bones! May he with all Carthaginians now and always be an enemy to the Trojans." After Aeneas had sailed from Africa, she killed herself. After many years Hannibal was a great leader who began waging war against the Romans.

Respondē Latīnē!

1. Quae sunt nōmina rēgīnae?
   Dīdō et Elissa sunt nōmina rēgīnae.

   What are the names of the queen?
   Dido and Elissa are the names of the queen.

2. Quālis frāter erat Pygmaliōn?
   Pygmaliōn erat frāter crūdēlis.

   What kind of brother was Pygmalion?
   Pygmalion was a cruel brother.

3. Quis est Iarbās?
   Iarbās est Āfricānus dux.

   Who is Iarbas?
   Iarbas is an African leader.

4. Quam urbem Dīdō fēcit?
   Dīdō urbem Carthāginem fēcit.

   What city did Dido make?
   Dido made the city of Carthage.

5. Quis est Aenēās?
   Aenēās est dux Trōiānus et fīlius Veneris deae.

   Who is Aeneas?
   Aeneas is a Trojan leader and the son of Venus.

ANSWER IN ENGLISH!

1. Why did Dido flee Phoenicia?
   Her brother murdered her husband the king.

2. How did Dido obtain land from Iarbas?
   Aeneas left Dido because fate destined him to found a city in Italy.

3. Why did Aeneas leave Dido?
   She obtained land.

4. What did Dido prophesy regarding their descendants?
   Dido prophesied that an avenger would rise from her descendants and that the descendants of Carthage and Troy would always be enemies.

5. How did Dido perish?
   Dido killed herself.

Crēscit Eundō
It Grows as It Goes
—New Mexico state motto[A]

From Lucretius' Dē Rērum Nātūrā, Book VI, Line 341.

Chapter 20

- demonstrative pronouns/adjectives
  - hic
  - ille
  - is
- intensive pronoun
  - ipse

VOCABULARY

NOUNS		
iniūria, ae, f.	wrong, injury; insult	(injurious)
*hostis, hostis, m.	enemy	(hostile)
legiō, legiōnis, f.	legion (up to 6000 men); (pl.) troops, army	(legionnaire)
*mōns, montis, m.	mountain	(montane)
odium, odiī, n.	hatred	(odious)
victōria, ae, f.	victory	(victorious)

VERBS		
dēmōnstrō, dēmōnstrāre, dēmōnstrāvī, dēmōnstrātum	to point out, show	(demonstrate)
exspectō, āre, āvī, ātum	to wait for; to see, expect	(expect)
iūrō, āre, āvī, ātum	to swear, take an oath	(jurat)

PRONOUNS/ADJECTIVES		
hic, haec, hoc	this, these	
ille, illa, illud	that, those	
ipse, ipsa, ipsum	himself, herself	
iste, ista, istud	that (of yours/near you)	
parātus, a, um	prepared	(preparatory)

ADVERBS		
semper	always	
sīc	thus, so, in this way	

*i-stem nouns[B]   [B]Review the i-stem rules taught in chapter 14. Why are these nouns classified as i-stems?

TE **Exercise 1.** Using the rules for syllabication and accent that you have learned, write out the syllables and accents for the vocabulary words above. Then practice pronouncing them aloud.

SECTION 53. Demonstratives

Demonstratives (from the Latin *dēmōnstrāre*, to point out) place special emphasis on, or "point out," a certain person or object. They can appear either as an adjective modifying a noun (e.g. *hic vir*, this man). Or, they may act as a pronoun that completely replaces the noun they are meant to describe. When a noun follows one of these words, e.g. *hic*, it means "this"; when no noun follows it, it means "he." In either event, demonstratives must agree in case, gender, and number with the nouns that they are pointing out. In the plural forms they primarily use the familiar first and second declension endings, but the singular forms follow a slightly different pattern.

a. hic
The pronoun *hic* means "this" in the singular or "these" in the plural and usually refers to something or someone near the speaker.

Hoc mālum optō.	I choose **this apple.**
Hunc sciō.	I know **this man.**

SINGULAR

CASE	MASCULINE	FEMININE	NEUTER
Nominative	hic	haec	hoc
Genitive	hūius	hūius	hūius
Dative	huic	huic	huic
Accusative	hunc	hanc	hoc
Ablative	hōc	hāc	hōc

PLURAL

CASE	MASCULINE	FEMININE	NEUTER
Nominative	hī	hae	haec
Genitive	hōrum	hārum	hōrum
Dative	hīs	hīs	hīs
Accusative	hōs	hās	haec
Ablative	hīs	hīs	hīs

Notā Bene:
The accusative singular uses an 'n' in place of the common 'm.'[c]
The neuter nominative and accusative are the same.
The plural forms are the common first and second declension endings, with the exception of the neuter nominative and accusative.

TE **Exercise 2.** Choose the correct form of the pronoun *hic* that will agree with the following nouns. Include all possibilities.

Example: puellae – hūius, huic, hae

1. proeliō
2. animal
3. verba
4. duce

[c]The change of the 'm' to an 'n' is not uncommon with Latin. These nasal sounds often seem to fluctuate. You will see the same change in the intensive pronouns that will be taught in Book 2.

5. mīlitēs
6. victōriae
7. montium
8. patris

b. ille and iste

The pronoun *ille* means "that" in the singular or "those" in the plural and usually refers to something or someone at a distance from the speaker (*ille, ille,* that far away). The demonstrative *iste* also means "that," but refers to an object that is near the person to whom the speaker is referring.

Vīdistīne **illam pugnam**?	Did you see **that battle?**
Stolam **istam** amō!	I love **that dress of yours!**

In Latin literature *iste* tends to take on a derogatory meaning. You can imagine the speaker with his nose turned up in the air as he refers to *iste vir,* who is clearly beneath him.

Populus iste nōs vincere numquam poterit!
That people will never be able to conquer us!

SINGULAR

CASE	MASCULINE	FEMININE	NEUTER
Nominative	ille	illa	illud
Genitive	illīus	illīus	illīus
Dative	illī	illī	illī
Accusative	illum	illam	illud
Ablative	illō	illā	illō

PLURAL

CASE	MASCULINE	FEMININE	NEUTER
Nominative	illī	illae	illa
Genitive	illōrum	illārum	illōrum
Dative	illīs	illīs	illīs
Accusative	illōs	illās	illa
Ablative	illīs	illīs	illīs

Notā Bene:
- *Iste* follows the same pattern as *ille*. Simply replace *ill-* with *ist-*.
- The genitive singular has a form similar to that for *hic, haec, hoc,* but note the long ī.
- The dative singular is the same as third declension.
- The remainder of the endings follow the pattern of first and second declension nouns, with the exception of the neuter nominative and accusative singular.
- The neuter rule still applies!

c. is, ea, id

In the preceding chapter you learned *is, ea, id* as a personal pronoun translated as "he, she, it." It is also commonly used as a demonstrative meaning "that."

Exercise 3. Choose the correct form of the demonstrative in parentheses to replace the underlined noun in each sentence.^D ᴰSee p. 148 for this note.

Example: I will fight with the <u>sword</u>. (ille)   illō

1. I will give the doll to <u>her</u>. (is)
2. I will drink the <u>water</u>. (ille)
3. We saw that despicable <u>brother</u> of yours. (iste)
4. We wondered when the <u>boy</u> would arrive. (ille)
5. You have the <u>girl's</u> doll. (ille)
6. We saw the <u>man</u> as he left the building. (is)
7. Mother and I wanted to go with <u>Father</u>. (ille)

ᴰFor additional practice ask students to repeat this same exercise using *hic*. You can also ask them to repeat Exercise 2 using *ille* and *iste*.

SECTION 54. Intensive Pronoun: ipse, ipsa, ipsum

Intensive pronouns bring special emphasis on the nouns they modify. They are a bit peculiar in that they can emphasize a noun or pronoun in any person (i.e. first, second, or third person). Thus, there are a variety of translations for *ipse*: the very ____, the actual ____; (first person) myself/ourselves; (second person) yourself/yourselves; (third person) himself/herself/itself/themselves. You will need to watch the context clues of the sentence or passage in order to discern which of these numerous translations is the best choice.

Hannibal **ipse** Pūnicās cōpiās dūxit. ....Hannibal **himself** led the Carthaginian troops.
Ipse Hannibalem vīdī. ....I **myself** saw Hannibal.
Pater **ipsum** scūtum Hannibalis habet. ....My father has **the very** shield of Hannibal.

 Exercise 4. Following the example of *ille*, decline the pronouns *iste* and *ipse*.ᴱ

ᴱThe declension worksheets will work well for this exercise, too. Students will need three charts per pronoun for the three genders.

Exercise 5. Parse, diagram, and translate the following sentences.

1. Ego ipse tē vīdī!

2. Caesar ipse id dīxit!

3. Ambulābimus cum Caesare ipsō.

4. Iste hostis numquam nōs superābit.

5. Soror rēgīnae ipsī dīxit.

6. Erat gladius Hannibalis ipsīus.

Chapter Reading

HANNIBAL
CHARACTERS:
Hamilcar Barca – Carthaginian general, father of Hannibal
Hannibal – Carthaginian general during Second Punic War
Publius Scipio – Roman general
Tiberius Sempronius Longus – Roman general

Hamilcar Barca, magnus dux *Poenus*, erat pater Hannibalis. Ubi Hannibal erat puer, pater dīxit eī, "Semper habē odium Rōmae. Iūrā Rōmam dēlēre." Hannibal *sīc* iūrāvit. Hannibal semper **in memoriā tenēbat** verba patris.

Hannibal, vir, magnus dux *Poenus* **est**. *Secundō* in Bellō *Pūnicō*, bellō cum Rōmānīs, Hannibal Poenōs dūxit. Dēsīderāvit Rōmānōs vincere dum Rōmānī nōn erant parātī et bellum nōn exspectābant. *Montēs Alpēs trānsīvit* cum elephantīs et multīs mīlitibus. *Pervēnit* ad urbem *Augustam Taurīnōrum*. Deinde **P. Scīpiōnem** vīcit in proeliō prope *Tīcīnum*. Post victōriam prope *Tīcīnum* Hannibal victōriam habuit prope *Trebiam*, flūmen in *Galliā Cisalpīnā*. Rōmānī ducēs in illō proeliō erant P. Scīpiō et **Ti. Semprōnius Longus**. Post illum proelium Hannibal *Ētrūriam* oppugnāvit. In *Ētrūriā* multa iniūria *in Ētruscōs* fēcit Hannibal. Hannibal etiam *Flāminium* et mīlitēs *Flāminiī* vīcit. Proelium cum *Flāminiō* erat ad *lacum Trasumēnum*. *Duōs* legiōnēs Rōmānōs Hannibal dēlēvit. Tum *Poenī* sub duce Hannibale *hiemābant*.

in memoriā tenēbat = he remembered (literally: he was holding in [his] memory)
est (historical present) = was
P. Scīpiōnem: The abbreviation P. stands for Publius. Read aloud and translate P. as Publius.
Ti. Semprōnius Longus: The abbreviations Ti. stands for Titus. Read aloud and translate Ti. as Titus.

GLOSSARY

Poenus, a, um, adj. .... Carthaginian
sīc .... thus
secundus, a, um, adj. .... second
Pūnicus, a, um, adj. .... Punic, Carthaginian
Montēs Alpēs .... the Alps
trānsīvit, pervēnit .... These are compound verbs. Can you discern the meanings?
                                        Hint: *trāns + īvit   per + vēnit*
Augusta Taurīnōrum .... modern day Turin
Tīcīnum .... modern day Pavia
Trebia .... a river in Cisalpine Gaul
Gallia Cisalpīna .... Gaul on the Italian side of the Alps, called Cisalpine Gaul.
Ētrūria .... modern day Tuscany
in Ētrūscōs .... against the Etruscans (in this context *in* = against)
Flāminius .... a Roman general
lacus Trasumēnus .... Lake Trasimene (modern day *Lago di Perugia* = Lake Perugia)
duōs .... two
hiemābant .... went into winter quarters

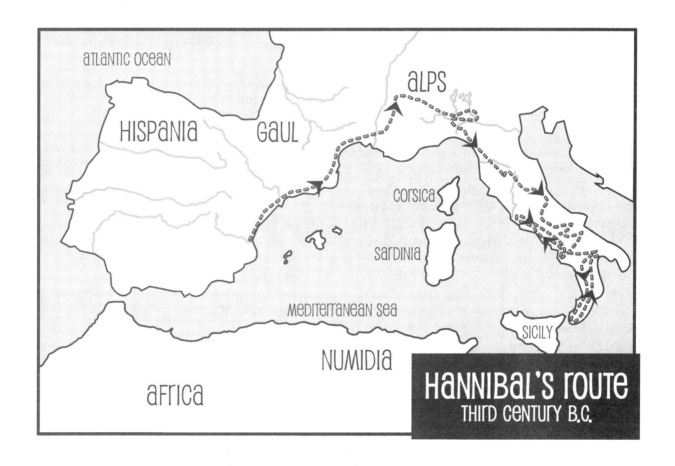

Respondē Latīnē!

1. Quis est pater Hannibalis?

2. Quid Hannibal semper in memoriā tenēbat?

3. Quibuscum Poenī pugnāvērunt Secundō in Bellō Pūnicō?

4. Quālibus cum animālibus transīvit Alpēs Hannibal?

5. Quis erat dux Rōmānus in proeliō prope Tīcīnum?

quis = who?, quid = what?,
quibuscum = with whom?, quālibus = what kind of?

ANSWER IN ENGLISH!

1. What were the feelings of Hannibal's father toward Rome and the Romans?

2. Under what conditions did Hannibal want to defeat the Romans at the beginning of the Second Punic War?

3. What did Hannibal do to the Etruscans?

4. What happened to the Romans at Lake Trasimene?

5. What did the Carthaginians do after the Battle of Lake Trasimene?

[F]"BC" stands for *Before Christ*, and is the English equivalent to the Latin term "AC," *Ante Chrīstum*.

Culture Corner: Fabius and Scipio, Roman Generals

In the year 217 BC.[F] Hannibal posed such a threat to Rome that the consuls elected Quintus Fabius Maximus Verrucosus* as dictator (see Culture Corner on Roman dictators in chapter 13). Fabius had already served two terms as consul and was a well-respected leader. He recognized, however, that to fight open battles against Hannibal and his troops had proven futile. He also realized that although Hannibal had a strong army at present, he was far from his home base and supply sources back in Carthage. Fabius determined therefore to avoid open battle against Hannibal and instead engage in small hit and run tactics. At first the Romans were frustrated with Fabius's constant flight before their enemy and called him Fabius Cunctator, the Delayer. Eventually, however, they began to realize that Fabius' tactic was wearing down Hannibal's troops and supplies by forcing the Carthaginians to chase Fabius all over Italy. Rome recovered from Hannibal's devastation and began to take the offensive.

In 205 BC one of the consuls, Publius Cornelius Scipio, led other Roman legions in an invasion of Africa. Scipio would prove to be one of the finest generals in military history. Many called him the "Roman Hannibal." Carthage called upon Hannibal to return and protect the city, a call he could not refuse. Just three years later these two great generals would meet face to face at the Battle of Zama for one of history's greatest showdowns.

*Fabius received the name Verrucosus because of a wart (verrūca) on his lip.

For Discussion:

George Washington used this gradual and cautious policy in war, known as Fabianism, in the Revolutionary War against the British army. Recall your past lessons on American and Roman history and discuss how these two situations were similar.[G]

[G]Washington also would not face the British in open battle, but favored raids and retreat. He too was at first criticized, but later praised for these tactics.

Derivative Detective

 English uses many ancient Latin phrases that include demonstratives. Many appear in legal documents and the courtroom. Translate the following phrases as literally as possible. Then look them up in an English dictionary to find out how we use them.
(Hint: Many dictionaries have sections in the back for abbreviations and foreign phrases.)

id est (i.e.)
ad hoc
in hāc parte
hoc age
propter hoc, ergō hoc
in hōc signō vincēs

Military Mottoes

 Throughout this text we have introduced you to the Latin mottoes adopted by many of our nation's states. Did you know that many of the divisions in our armed forces have also adopted Latin mottoes to represent their units and rally their forces? See how many of these you recognize. You may need a Latin-English dictionary.[H]

Caveat Discipulus: Because English does not use long marks, these mottoes almost always appear without any macra. You must use some of your Latin detective skills to determine the proper form in order to translate properly.

Semper Fidelis ........................U.S. Marine Corps

Paratus et Fidelis ....4th Cavalry

Semper Paratus ....12th Cavalry Regiment, U.S. Coast Guard, several infantry units

Fidus Ultra Finem.................2nd Air Defense Military Regiment

Non Cedo, Ferio....................3rd Air Defense Military Regiment

Semper Ultimo ....16th Engineer Battalion

Semper Tentare.......................321st Engineer Battalion

Videmus Omnia ....55th Wing, Airforce

Ex Hoc Signo Victoria...........14th Field Artillery Regiment

In Omnia Paratus...................18th Infantry Regiment, 4th Marine Logistics Groups

In Cruce Mea Fides................30th Medical Brigade

Pro Deo, Patria, Vicino..........104th Medical Battalion

Volens et Potens ....101st Airborne Division (this one is a challenge!)

[H]Most divisions of the military have Latin mottoes. You might consider assigning students the task of finding out the mottoes for the divisions in your region.

Chapter 20 Teacher's Pages

Exercise 1

in-iū-ri-a, ae, f.
hos-tis, hos-tis, m.
le-gi-ō, le-gi-ōn-is, m.
mōns, mon-tis, m.
o-di-um, o-di-ī, n.
vic-tō-ri-a, ae, f.
dē-mōns-trō, dē-mōns-trā-re,
   dē-mōns-trā-vī, dē-mōns-trā-tum
ex-spec-tō, ā-re, ā-vī, ā-tum

iū-rō, ā-re, ā-vī, ā-tum
hic, haec, hoc
il-le, il-la, il-lud
ip-se, ip-sa, ip-sum
is-te, is-ta, is-tud
pa-rā-tus, a, um
sem-per
sīc

Exercise 2

1. proeliō hōc, huic
2. animal hoc
3. verba haec

4. duce hōc
5. mīlitēs hī, hōs
6. victōriae hae, huius, huic

7. montium hōrum
8. patris hūius

Exercise 3

1. I will give the doll to her. (is)   eī
2. I will drink the water. (ille)   illam
3. We saw that despicable brother of yours. (iste)   istum
4. We wondered when the boy would arrive. (ille)   ille
5. You have the girl's doll. (ille)   illīus
6. We saw the man as he left the building. (is)   eum
7. Mother and I wanted to go with Father. (ille)   illō

Exercise 4

CASE	SINGULAR			PLURAL		
	MASCULINE	FEMININE	NEUTER	MASCULINE	FEMININE	NEUTER
Nominative	iste	ista	istud	istī	istae	ista
Genitive	istīus	istīus	istīus	istōrum	istārum	istōrum
Dative	istī	istī	istī	istīs	istīs	istīs
Accusative	istum	istam	istud	istōs	istās	ista
Ablative	istō	istā	istō	istīs	istīs	istīs

CASE	SINGULAR			PLURAL		
	MASCULINE	FEMININE	NEUTER	MASCULINE	FEMININE	NEUTER
Nominative	ispe	ipsa	ipsum	ipsī	ipsae	ipsa
Genitive	ipsīus	ipsīus	ipsīus	ipsōrum	ipsārum	ipsōrum
Dative	ipsī	ipsī	ipsī	ipsīs	ipsīs	ipsīs
Accusative	ipsum	ipsam	ipsum	ipsōs	ipsās	ipsa
Ablative	ipsō	ipsā	ipsō	ipsīs	ipsīs	ipsīs

Exercise 5

```
          S     Adj    DO     V
1. Ego  ipse    tē    vīdī!
   n/s  n/s/m  ac/s  1/s/perf
   I myself saw you!
```

```
           S      Adj    DO      V
2. Caesar ipse     id    dīxit!
   n/s/m  n/s/m  ac/s/n  3/s/perf
   Caesar himself said it!
```

```
             S+V        P     OP      Adj
3. Ambulābimus cum  Caesare  ipsō.
      1/p/f            ab/s/m  ab/s/m
   We will walk with Caesar himself.
```

```
   Adj      S       Adv     DO      V
4. Iste   hostis numquam  nōs   superābit.
   n/s/m  n/s/m            ac/p   3/s/f
   That enemy will never overcome us.
```

```
       S      IO     IO      V
5. Soror rēgīnae  ipsī   dīxit.
   n/s/f  d/s/f   d/s/f  3/s/perf
   (My) sister spoke to the queen herself.
```

```
      LV    PrN       PNA       Adj
6. Erat gladius  Hannibalis  ipsīus.
   3/s/i  n/s/m    g/s/m      g/s/m
   This was the sword of Hannibal himself.
```

Translation

Hamilcar Barca, a great Carthaginian leader, was the father of Hannibal. When Hannibal was a boy, (his) father said to him, "Always hold hatred for Rome. Swear to destroy Rome." Hannibal swore thus (in this way). Hannibal always held in his memory (always remembered) his father's words.

Hannibal, the man, is a great Carthaginian leader. In the Second Punic War, war with the Romans, Hannibal led the Carthaginians. He desired to conquer the Romans while the Romans were not prepared and were not expecting war. He crossed the Alps with elephants and many soldiers. He arrived at the city Augusta Taurinorum. Then he conquered P. Scipio in a battle near Ticinum. After the victory near Ticinum Hannibal had a victory near Trebia, a river in Cisalpine Gaul. The Roman leaders in that battle were P. Scipio and Ti. Sempronius Longus. After that battle Hannibal attacked Etruria. In Etruria Hannibal made many injuries against the Etruscans. Hannibal also won Flaminius and the soldiers of Flaminius. The battle with Flaminius was near Lake Trasimene. Hannibal destroyed two Roman legions. Then the Carthaginians went into winter quarters under their leader Hannibal.

Respondē Latīnē!

1. Quis est pater Hannibalis?
   Hamilcar Barca est pater Hannibalis.

   Who is the father of Hannibal?
   Hamilcar Barca is the father of Hannibal.

2. Quid Hannibal semper in memoriā tenēbat?
   Hannibal semper in memoriā tenēbat verba patris.

   What was Hannibal always remembering?
   Hannibal was always remembering the words of his father.

3. Quibuscum Poenī pugnāvērunt Secundō in Bellō Pūnicō?
   Poenī pugnāvērunt cum Rōmānīs.

   With whom did the Carthaginians fight in the Second Punic War?
   The Carthaginians fought with the Romans.

4. Quālibus cum animālibus trānsīvit Alpēs Hannibal?
Alpēs trānsīvit cum elephantīs.

With what animals did Hannibal cross the Alps?
He crossed the Alps with elephants.

5. Quis erat dux Rōmānus in proeliō prope Tīcīnum?
P. Scīpiōnem erat dux Rōmānus in proeliō prope Tīcīnum.

Who was the Roman leader in the battle near Ticinum?
P. Scipio was the Roman leader in the battle near Ticinum.

ANSWER IN ENGLISH!

1. What were the feelings of Hannibal's father toward Rome and the Romans?
Hannibal's father hated Rome.

2. Under what conditions did Hannibal want to defeat the Romans at the beginning of the Second Punic War?
He wanted to defeat them unprepared and not expecting battle

3. What did Hannibal do to the Etruscans?
He injured many Etruscans.

4. What happened to the Romans at Lake Trasimene?
Hannibal destroyed two Roman legions near Lake Trasimene.

5. What did the Carthaginians do after the Battle of Lake Trasimene?
They went into winter quarters. Made camp for the winter.

Derivative Detective

id est (i.e.)	that is
ad hoc	to this
in hāc parte	in this part
hoc age	do this
propter hoc, ergō hoc	because of this, therefore this
in hōc signō vincēs	in this sign you will conquer (words spoken in a vision seen by Constantine)

Military Mottoes

Semper Fidelis	Always Faithful
Paratus et Fidelis	Prepared and Faithful
Semper Paratus	Always Prepared
Fidus Ultra Finem	Faithful Beyond the End
Non Cedo, Ferio	I do not yield, I strike
Semper Ultimo	Always to the Top
Semper Tentare	Always Testing / Always Trying
Videmus Omnia	We See All Things
Ex Hoc Signo Victoria	Victory by This Sign
In Omnia Paratus	Prepared in All Things
In Cruce Mea Fides	In the Cross My Faith
Pro Deo, Patria, Vicino	For God, My Country, and My Neighbor
Volens et Potens	Willing and Able (These two Latin verbs are present participles. Latin participles will be taught in Book 2.)

Notes

Excelsior!
Ever Higher!
—New York state motto[A]

The Great Seal of New York, established in 1777, bears the state coat of arms surrounded by the official words The Great Seal of the State of New York. Many other states also include their coat of arms within the state seal. In the center is a beautiful landscape which portrays the sun rising behined a mountain with two ships sailing in the foreground. On either side of the crest stand Liberty and Justice. Justice appears blindfolded and holds the scales of justice. Liberty holds a pole with the Phrygian cap (see chapter 7). Above the crest an American eagle perches upon a globe showing the North Atlantic Ocean.

Chapter 21

- The naughty nine (special adjectives)
  - ŪNUS NAUTA
- Irregular Verbs: volō and nōlō

VOCABULARY

NOUNS			
fortūna, ae, f.	fortune, luck	(fortunate)	
ratiō, ratiōnis, f.	reason	(ration, rational)	
VERBS			
dēcipiō, dēcipere, dēcēpī, dēceptum	to deceive	(deception)	
intellegō, intellegere, intellēxī, intellēctum	to understand	(intelligence)	
metuō, metuere, metuī, metūtum	to fear		
nōlō, nōlle, nōluī	to not wish, to be unwilling		
volō, velle, voluī	to wish, want, be willing	(volition, volunteer)	
ADJECTIVES			
alius, alia, aliud	other, another	(alias, alibi)	
alter, altera, alterum alter . . . alter	the other (of two) one . . . the other	(alternative, alternate)	
neuter, neutra, neutrum	neither	(neuter, neutral)	
nūllus, nūlla, nūllum	no, none, not any	(nullify, annul)	
sōlus, sōla, sōlum	alone, only	(solo, solitude)	
tōtus, tōta, tōtum	whole, entire	(total)	
ūllus, ūlla, ūllum	any		
ūnus, ūna, ūnum	one	(unify, union)	
uter, utra, utrum	either, which (of two)		
CONJUNCTION			
igitur	therefore		

PREPOSITION			
ob, prep. + acc.	in front of; on account of, for	(obvious)	
ADVERBS			
numquam	never		
sīcut	just as		

Exercise 1. Using the rules for syllabication and accent that you have learned, write out the syllables and accents for the vocabulary words above. Then practice pronouncing them aloud.

SECTION 55. Special Adjectives with -īus

In this chapter we introduce a group of adjectives that have come to be known as "the naughty nine." These nine adjectives look deceptively like normal first and second declension adjectives, but looks can be deceiving. While these adjectives follow the "normal" first and second declension pattern in most cases, they are a bit "naughty" when it comes to the genitive and dative singular.

SINGULAR

CASE	MASCULINE	FEMININE	NEUTER
Nom.	ūllus	ūlla	ūllum
Gen.	**ūllīus**	**ūllīus**	**ūllīus**
Dat.	**ūllī**	**ūllī**	**ūllī**
Acc.	ūllum	ūllam	ūllum
Abl.	ūllō	ūllā	ūllō

PLURAL

CASE	MASCULINE	FEMININE	NEUTER
Nom.	ūllī	ūllae	ūlla
Gen.	ūllōrum	ūllārum	ūllōrum
Dat.	ūllīs	ūllīs	ūllīs
Acc.	ūllōs	ūllās	ūlla
Abl.	ūllīs	ūllīs	ūllīs

Do these endings for the genitive and dative singular look familiar? They should! These are the same endings that *ille* uses, which you learned in the previous chapter. So, it should help you to remember that the naughty nine behave like the first and second declension in most places, but like *ille* in the genitive and dative singular.

You should be aware that the adjective *alius* is extra naughty in the singular forms.

CASE	MASCULINE	FEMININE	NEUTER
Nom.	alius	alia	**aliud**
Gen.	alīus *alterīus	alīus alterīus	alīus alterīus
Dat.	aliī	aliī	aliī
Acc.	alium	aliam	**aliud**
Abl.	aliō	aliā	aliō

For starters, this adjective has a less common form for the neuter nominative and accusative. Second, the genitive form *alterīus*, taken from another naughty adjective *alter*, is a common "alternative" to the regular form *alīus*. The plural forms of *alius*, like the rest of the naughty nine, behave like any other good first and second declension adjective should, except for the noun *ūnus (one)*, which of course does not have a plural form.

It is easy to remember the members of "the naughty nine" gang with the acronym ŪNUS NAUTA:

Ūnus Nūllus Ūllus Sōlus
Neuter Alter Uter Tōtus Alius

TE **Exercise 2.** Make each of these naughty adjectives agree with the assigned noun in case, number, and gender. Include all possibilities.

1. (alter) ego
2. (sōlus) Deō
3. (ūnus) bellum
4. (neuter) fortūnae
5. (nūllus) ratiōnis
6. (uter) virōs
7. (ūllus) arma
8. (tōtus) urbem
9. (alius) mīlitibus

TE **Exercise 3.** Parse, diagram, and translate the following sentences.

1. Alter dux senex erat, alter iuvenis erat.

2. Nunc ratiō mē dūcet, nōn fortūna.

3. Nōtus es ob virtūtem.

4. Nunc arma capimus ob perīculum sociōrum.

5. Hīs verbīs et aliīs magnus vir dīxit.

SECTION 56. Volō and Nōlō

In chapter 18 we introduced three very common irregular verbs, including *ferō, ferre*. You may recall that this verb was irregular because of its stem and the manner in which it conjugates in the present tense. All other tenses, however, seemed to conjugate quite normally. Such is the case with our next pair of irregular verbs, commonly used to express wanting. The verb *volō, velle, voluī* has an infinitive unlike any other verb we have seen. Stranger yet, the infinitive does not seem to produce the present stem as is customary for verbs. Nonetheless, the personal endings do remain the same as all other verbs.

PERSON	SINGULAR	PLURAL
1	volō	volumus
2	vīs	vultis
3	vult	volunt

The negative counterpart to *volō*, is simply the negative *nōn + volō*, resulting in the contracted forms *nōlō, nōlle, nōluī*. Notice that the contracted form neither appears in the second person, nor in the third person singular. Once again, however, the personal endings are regular.

PERSON	SINGULAR	PLURAL
1	nōlō	nōlumus
2	nōn vīs	nōn vultis
3	nōn vult	nōlunt

You will be happy to know that the irregularities that appear for *volō* and *nōlō* in the present tense do not continue throughout the remaining tenses. Like *ferō, ferre* these verbs follow the same patterns as regular third conjugation verbs.

	IMPERFECT	
PERSON	VOLŌ	NŌLŌ
1	volēbam	nōlēbam
2	volēbās	nōlēbās
3	volēbat	nōlēbat

	FUTURE	
PERSON	VOLŌ	NŌLŌ
1	volam	nōlam
2	volēs	nōlēs
3	volet	nōlet

	IMPERFECT	
PERSON	VOLŌ	NŌLŌ
1	volēbāmus	nōlēbāmus
2	volēbātis	nōlēbātis
3	volēbant	nōlēbant

	FUTURE	
PERSON	VOLŌ	NŌLŌ
1	volēmus	nōlēmus
2	volētis	nōlētis
3	volent	nōlent

The perfect tense is quite normal, consisting of the perfect stem (3rd principal part) and the typical endings of the perfect tense which were taught in chapter 8.

Exercise 4. Conjugate the verbs *volō* and *nōlō* in the perfect tense. Translate each form into English. **B**

Exercise 5. Parse, diagram, and translate the following sentences.

1. Sī deī volunt, ego pācem dabō.

2. Hannibal fortūnam petere nōluit.

3. Rōmānī proeliō ūllī studēbant.

4. Hamilcar fīlium iūrāre contrā Rōmānōs volēbat.

5. Hannibal cum elephantīs per montēs īre voluit.

6. Vīsne sōlam fortūnam bonam?

> **B**You may want to have students practice conjugating these verbs in the present, future, and imperfect tenses as well. For additional practice mix up the forms in the parsing worksheet included with this guide and ask students to practice identifying the tense, person, and number of these irregular verbs.

SECTION 57. Negative Commands

As you learned in chapter 16, Latin expresses commands by using the imperative mood (Section 42). Do you remember how to form positive commands? Simply remove the -re ending from the infinitive when issuing a command to one person. When addressing more than one, add -te.

	SINGULAR	PLURAL
1st conjugation	amā	amāte
2nd conjugation	vidē	vidēte
3rd conjugation	mitte	mittite
3rd conjugation -io	cape	capite

The negative command (commanding someone NOT to do something) is nearly as easy. Simply use the infinitive of the verb plus the imperative form of *nōlle*. You are literally saying, "do not even wish to do this!" Or, as your mom might say, "don't even think about it!"

| nōlī vidēre | nōlīte vidēre | don't look |
| nōlī capere | nōlīte capere | don't seize |

Exercise 6. Make the following commands negative, then translate.

Example: amā   nōlī amāre = don't love

1. dēcipite
2. habē
3. dēlēte
4. dūc
5. parā
6. metue
7. date
8. ferte

Chapter Reading ⒯Ⓔ

THE SUMMIT MEETING AT ZAMA

CHARACTERS:

Zama – City in Carthage
Hannibal – Carthaginian general
Scipio – Roman general
Trasumen and Canna – famous battles of the Second Punic War
Syphax – King of Numidia, ally of Carthage

Ante proelium *Zamae*, ultimum proelium *Secundō* in Bellō *Pūnicō*, Hannibal cum Scīpiōne *Zamae* *convēnit*. Senex Hannibal, Scipiō iuvenis erat.* Hannibal "Scīpiō," *inquit*, "nunc senex sum, et *lassus*. Et bonam et *malam* fortūnam habuī. Nunc ratiōnem, nōn fortūnam *sequor*. Sed tū es iuvenis, et modo bonam fortūnam habuistī. *Itaque* metuō **tibi nōn opus esse quiētīs cōnsiliīs**. Vir *quem* fortūna numquam dēcēpit *incerta* fortūnae nōn timet. Tū nunc es sīcut ego fuī ad proelia *Trasumēnī* et *Cannae*. Et nōtus es ob virtūtem et *pietātem* quod *mortēs* patris et *pātruī* **ultus es**. *Recēpistī* prōvinciam *āmissam*. Rōmānī tē *cōnsulem* creāvērunt. *Trānsīvistī* in Āfricam *postquam duōs exercitūs Poenōs* dēlēvistī. **Bīna castra** in Āfricā prope Carthāginem ignī dēlēvistī. Rēgem potentem Syphācem cēpistī. Sed *opīniō* mihi est: **maximae cuique fortūnae minimē crēdendum est**. Sī deī volunt, ego pācem dabō. Sed deī pācem nōlunt, **ita adnītar nē quem pācis per mē partae paeniteat**."

Ad haec Scīpiō "Hannibal, *sciō tē ad mē vēnisse ut pācem peterēs*. *Condiciōnēs* pācis intellegō. Sed *condiciōnēs* pācis in meīs nōn tuīs *manibus* sunt. *Neque* **patrēs** nostrī *neque* nōs dē *Siciliā* aut dē *Hispāniā* bellum gessimus. Sed nunc arma capimus ob perīculum sociōrum *Māmertīnōrum* et *excidium Saguntī*. Bellum, igitur, parā *quoniam* **pācem patī nōn potuistis**!"

Hīs verbīs et aliīs *dēsīderāta* pācī Hannibalis Scīpiō *rēiēcit*, et proelium Zamae **secūtum est**.

_____

tibi nōn opus esse quiētīs consiliīs = that you have no need for quiet discussions
ultus es = you have avenged
bīna castra = two camps (literally, "camp – two at a time)
maximae cuique fortūnae minimē crēdendum est = the greater a man's good fortune, the less ought he to count upon it.
ita adnītar nē quem pācis per mē partae paeniteat = so I shall do my utmost to prevent any one from regretting the peace I gained [for Carthage]
ad mē vēnisse ut pācem peterēs = that you have come to me to seek peace
patrēs = ancestors
pācem patī nōn potuistis = you have not been able to allow peace
secūtum est = followed

*Notice the word order. (Senex Hannibal, Scīpiō iuvenis erat.) The word order here, excluding *erat*, sets up the pattern ABBA. This pattern is called chiasmus. Notice how close together the word order puts Hannibal and Scipio.

GLOSSARY
ante, adv. .... before
Zamae.. at Zama (This is an example of the locative case, used to show place where for the names of cities).

secundus, a, um, adj.	second
Pūnicus, a, um, adj.	Punic, Carthaginian
conveniō, convenīre, convēnī, conventum	come together, meet
Zamae	at Zama
inquit	says
lassus, a, um, adj.	tired
malus, a, um, adj.	bad
sequor	I follow
itaque, adv.	thus
quem, acc., sing.,	whom
incerta	uncertainties
Trasumēnī et Cannae	at Trasimenus and Cannae
pietās, pietātis, f.	piety, duty
mors, mortis, f.	death
pātruus, pātruī, m.	uncle (father's brother: *avunculus* = uncle on mother's side)
recipiō, recipere, recēpī, receptum	to retake; (mil) occupy
prōvincia, ae, f.	province, territory
āmissam	lost (from *āmittere*)
cōnsul, cōnsulis, m.	consul
trānsīvistī	compound verb: *trāns + īvistī*
postquam, adv.	after (cf. *antequam*)
duōs, acc. pl. m.	two
exercitus, exercitūs, m.	army
Poenus, a, um, adj.	Carthaginian
opīniō, opīniōnis, f.	opinion
sciō, scīre, scīvī, scītum	to know
condiciō, condiciōnis, f.	terms
manus, manūs, f.	hand
neque . . . neque	neither . . . . nor (correlative conjunction)
Sicilia, ae, f.	Sicily
Hispānia, ae, f.	Spain
excidium, excidiī, n.	destruction
Māmertīnī, ōrum, m. pl.	Mamertines (mercenary troops who occupied Messana)
Saguntum, ī, n.	(town in E. Spain)
quoniam, conj.	since, seeing that
dēsīderāta	desires, literally desired things
rēiciō, rēicere, rēiēcī, rēiectum	to reject, refuse

Respondē Latīnē!

 1. Ubi erat ultimum proelium Secundī Bellī Punicī?

2. Quālem fortūnam habuit Scīpiō, secundum (*according to*) Hannibalem?

3. Quem Rōmānī cōnsulem creāvērunt?

4. Quis castra in Āfricā dēlēvit?

5. Quem rēgem Scīpiō cēpit?

ubi = where?, quālem = what kind of?, quem = whom?, quis = who?

Challenge Box

Do you ever favor following luck rather than reason? Why or why not? Write a good English paragraph explaining your choice.

1. What will Hannibal follow now that he is old?

2. What does a man whom fortune has not deceived not yet fear?

3. According to Scipio, who has the right to choose war or peace?

4. Why does Scipio say the Romans will make war now?

5. What does Scipio reject?

Grammar Exercise

 Change the following singular nouns to the plural, keeping the same case.

1. proelium
2. fortūnam
3. iuvenis
4. mortem
5. prōvinciam

6. rēgem
7. opīniō
8. rēgis
9. patrī
10. bellō

Derivative Detective

 In the last chapter we looked at Latin demonstratives that are alive and well in English. Many of the special adjectives in this chapter also live on in our legal lingo. Translate the following phrases as literally as possible. Then look them up in an English dictionary to find out how we use them today.

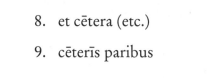

(Hint: Many dictionaries have sections in the back for abbreviations and foreign phrases.)

1. in tōtō

2. et aliī (et al.)

3. alter ego

4. alter īdem

5. nūlla bona

6. nōlō contendere

7. nōlle prōsequī

8. et cētera (etc.)

9. cēterīs paribus

Culture Corner

THE ROMAN ARMY DURING THE REPUBLIC

One of the things that made Rome so strong, even during the Republic—the time of the Punic Wars—was the army. All Roman citizens were required to serve in the army. In fact, it was the army, when assembled, that was actually the real law-making body of the Romans. Roman citizens were divided into centuries. The first eighteen centuries gave Rome her cavalry. The so-called "first class" formed the infantry. Our Marcus would have been in the infantry in Scipio's army.

As an infantryman under Scipio and as a member of the first class, Marcus would have been armed with two spears, a dagger, and a sword. He would have worn a bronze helmet, a cuirass, and greaves. A shield would have protected him also. Members of the second class would not have had the cuirass. Soldiers from the third and fourth classes would not have had any armor. Members of the fifth class had only slingshots.

During the time Marcus was serving in the army, a legion was 4200 infantrymen, 300 cavalrymen, and various other groups. Each legion was divided into centuries, groups of one hundred men. A centurion commanded a century. Every legion had its *vexillum*. The *vexillum* was the colored flag of which the legion was so very proud. The honor of the soldiers was concentrated on preservation of the flag: it must never be captured. Officers might throw the *vexillum* into the enemy ranks to inspire the men to fight harder, since they had to capture the flag from the enemy.

Exercise 1

for-tū-na, ae, f.
ra-ti-ō, ra-ti-ōn-is, f.
dē-ci-pi-ō, dē-ci-pe-re, dē-cē-pī, dē-cep-tum
in-tel-le-gō, in-tel-le-ge-re, in-tel-lē-xī, in-tel-lec-tum
me-tu-ō, me-tu-e-re, me-tu-ī, me-tū-tum
nō-lō, nōl-le, nō-lu-ī
vo-lō, vel-le, vo-lu-ī
a-li-us, a-li-a, a-li-ud
al-ter, al-te-ra, al-te-rum, al-ter . . . al-ter
neu-ter, neu-tra, neu-trum

nūl-lus, nūl-la, nūl-lum
sō-lus, sō-la, sō-lum
tō-tus, tō-ta, tō-tum
ūl-lus, ūl-la, ūl-lum
ū-nus, ū-na, ū-num
u-ter, u-tra, u-trum
i-gi-tur
ob
num-quam
sī-cut

Exercise 2

1. (alter) ego	alter, altera
2. (sōlus) Deō	sōlī, sōlō
3. (ūnus) bellum	ūnum
4. (neuter) fortūnae	neutrae, neutrīus, neutrī
5. (nūllus) ratiōnis	nūllīus
6. (uter) virōs	utrōs
7. (ūllus) arma	ūlla
8. (tōtus) urbem	tōtam
9. (alius) mīlitibus	aliīs

Exercise 3

```
    Adj    S    PrN    LV    Adj    PrN    LV
1. Alter  dux  senex  erat,  alter  iuvenis  erat.
   n/s/m  n/s/m  n/s/m  3/s/i  n/s/m  n/s/m  3/s/i
```
One leader was old, the other was young.

```
    Adv   S    DO    V    Adv    S
2. Nunc ratiō  mē  dūcet, nōn  fortūna.
        n/s/f  ac/s  3/s/f       n/s/f
```
Now reason will lead me, not fortune.

```
    PrN    LV   P    OP
3. Nōtus  es   ob  virtūtem.
   n/s/m  2/s/p    ac/s/f
```
You are known because of courage/virtue.

```
    Adv   DO     S+V      P    OP       PNA
4. Nunc arma  capimus  ob  perīculum  sociōrum.
        ac/p/n  1/p/pr       ac/s/n    g/p/m
```
Now we seize arms because of the danger of the allies.

```
    Adj      AbMe  C  AbMe   Adj     S      V
5. Hīs     verbīs et aliīs  magnus  vir   dīxit.
   ab/p/n  ab/p/n    ab/p/n  n/s/m  n/s/m  3/s/per
```
With these words and others the great man spoke.

Exercise 4

PERSON	SINGULAR	PLURAL
1st	*voluī* I wanted	*voluimus* we wanted
2nd	*voluistī* you wanted	*voluistis* you (pl.) wanted
3rd	*voluit* he/she/it wanted	*voluērunt* they wanted

PERSON	SINGULAR	PLURAL
1st	*nōluī* I did not want	*nōluimus* we did not want
2nd	*nōluistī* you did not want	*nōluistis* you (pl.) did not want
3rd	*nōluit* he/she/it did not want	*nōluērunt* they did not want

Exercise 5

```
   C    S     V     S    DO    V
1. Sī   deī  volunt, ego pācem dabō.
   N/P/M 3/P/Pr N/S Ac/S/F 1/S/F
```
If the gods are willing, I will give peace.

```
        S       DO    Inf   V
2. Hannibal fortūnam petere nōluit.
   N/S/M  Ac/S/F        3/S/Perf
```
Hannibal did not want to seek fortune.

```
       S      DO    Inf    V
3. Rōmānī proeliō ūllī studēbant.
   N/P/M  D/S/N  D/S/N  3/P/I
```
The Romans were eager for any battle.

```
       S     DO    Inf   P     OP     V
4. Hamilcar fīlium iūrāre contrā Rōmānōs volēbat.
   N/S/M  Ac/S/M         Ac/P/M      3/S/I
```
Hamilcar was wanting his son to swear an oath against the Romans.

```
        S    P     OP    P    OP   Inf  V
5. Hannibal cum elephantīs per montēs īre voluit.
   N/S/M    Ab/P/M      Ac/P/M    3/S/Perf
```
Hannibal wanted to go through the mountains with the elephants.

```
   SV    Adj    DO     Adj
6. Vīsne sōlam fortūnam bonam?
   2/S/P Ac/S/F Ac/S/F Ac/s/f
```
Do you want good fortune only?

Exercise 6

1. dēcipite — nōlīte dēcipere — don't deceive
2. habē — nōlī habēre — don't hold, have, consider
3. dēlēte — nōlīte dēlēre — don't destroy
4. dūc — nōlī dūcere — don't lead
5. parā — nōlī parāre — don't prepare

6. metue	nōlī metuere	don't fear
7. date	nōlīte dare	don't give
8. ferte	nōlīte ferre	don't carry, bring

Translation

Before the battle of Zama, the last battle in the Second Punic War, Hannibal met with Scipio at Zama. Hannibal was an old man, Scipio was young (a young man). Hannibal said, "Scipio, I am now an old man, and tired. And I have had both good and bad fortune. Now I follow reason, not fortune. But you are a young man, and you have had only good fortune. Therefore I fear that you have no need for quiet discussions. A man whom fortune has never deceived does not fear the uncertainties of fortune. You are now just as I was at the battles of Trasumen and Canna. And you are known for virtue and piety because you avenged the deaths of your father and uncle. You have taken back the lost province. The Romans have elected you consul. You crossed into Africa after you destroyed two Carthaginian armies. You destroyed two camps with fire in Africa near Carthage. You seized the powerful king Syphax. But it is my opinion: the greater a man's good fortune the less he ought to count upon it. If the gods are willing, I will give peace. But if the gods are unwilling, so I shall do my utmost to prevent anyone from regretting the peace I gained [for Carthage]."

To these (words) Scipio (said) "Hannibal, I know you that you have come to me to seek peace. I understand the conditions of peace. But the conditions of peace are in my hands, not in your hands. Neither our ancestors nor we have waged war concerning Sicily or concerning Spain. But now we seize (take up) arms on account of the danger of the Mamertine allies and the destruction of Saguntum. Prepare war, therefore, since you have not been able to allow peace!"

With these words and others Scipio rejected Hannibal's desires for peace, and the battle at Zama followed.

Respondē Latīnē!

1. Ubi erat ultimum proelium
   Secundī Bellī Punicī?
   Proelium Zamae erat ultimum proelium.

   Where was the last battle of the
   Second Punic War?
   Zama was the last battle.

2. Quālem fortūnam habuit Scīpiō,
   secundum according to Hannibalem?
   Scīpiō modo bonam fortūnam habuit.

   What kind of fortune did Scipio have,
   according to Hannibal?
   Scipio had only good fortune.

3. Quem Rōmānī cōnsulem creāvērunt?
   Rōmānī cōnsulem Scīpiōnem creāvērunt.

   Whom did the Romans elect consul?
   The Romans elected Scipio consul.

4. Quis castra in Āfricā dēlēvit?
   Scipiō castra in Āfricā dēlēvit.

   Who destroyed camps in Africa?
   Scipio destroyed the camps in Africa.

5. Quem rēgem Scīpiō cēpit?
   Rēgem potentem Syphācem cēpit.

   Which king did Scipio seize?
   Scipio seized the able/capable/powerful king Syphax.

ANSWER IN ENGLISH!

1. What will Hannibal follow now that he is old?
   Hannibal will follow reason, not fortune.

2. What does a man whom fortune has not deceived not yet fear?
   He does not fear the uncertainties of fortune.

3. According to Scipio, who has the right to choose war or peace?
   The Romans have the right to choose war or peace.

4. Why does Scipio say the Romans will make war now?
   They will make war because of the Mamertines and the destruction of Saguntum.

5. What does Scipio reject?
   Scipio rejects Hannibal's desires for peace.

Grammer Exercise

1. proelium   proelia
2. fortūnam   fortūnās
3. iuvenis   iuvenēs
4. mortem   mortēs
5. prōvinciam   prōvinciās
6. rēgem   rēgēs
7. opīniō   opīniōnēs
8. rēgis   rēgum
9. patrī   patribus
10. bellō   bellīs

Derivative Detective

1. in tōtō   in whole, on the whole
2. et aliī (et al.)   and others (also et alia – and other things)
3. alter ego   another self
4. alter idem   a second self, another self (cf. alter ego)
5. nūlla bona   nothing good
6. nōlō contendere   I do not wish to contend, no contest
7. nōlle prosequī   to be unwilling to pursue
8. et cētera (etc.)   and the rest (always refers to things not people)
9. cēterīs paribus   with other things [being] the same/equal

Unit 5 Reading

CARTHAGO DELENDA EST
Christopher Schlect

In February of 1985, the mayor of Rome, Ugo Vetere, marveled at the surviving traces of destruction that Rome had wrought upon Carthage 2,130 years earlier. On that day he and the mayor of Carthage signed a peace treaty, a diplomatic technicality that formally ended the ancient conflict that once raged between their two cities. Rome fought three wars against Carthage from 264 to 146 BC, during which time she became the mightiest power in the known world. In the modern-day treaty ceremony, the two mayors stood amazed at the blackened remains of Carthage that survive today as a testimony to the bitterness of this conflict, and to the harshness with which Rome sometimes treated her conquered enemies.

The beginnings of Carthage date from earlier than Rome's founding. The Romans called the Carthaginians "Poeni" because originally they were Phoenician colonists. These Poeni took not only their name from the Phoenecians, but also their seafaring skills. Carthaginian traders sailed throughout the Mediterranean and they were protected by their city's great navy.

Rome was just a land power in 264 BC At that time she controlled the entire Italian peninsula. Surrounding the peninsula were vast Mediterranean waters that lay outside Rome's control, as the historian Polybius observed: "Not only had they no decked ships, but no warships at all, not so much as a single galley" (I.20). The First Punic War began when Carthage pressed its influence into northeast Sicily, and the Romans felt threatened and declared war. Using a captured Carthaginian ship as a model, the boatless Romans imitated its design to create their first ships. The war dragged on for many years, depleting resources on both sides and deepening their hatred for one another. Finally, the exhausted Carthaginians surrendered in 241 BC and let Rome take Sicily. Sicily became the first non-Italian territory that Rome controlled. The task of governing this great island was Rome's first step toward organizing its holdings into provinces. Three years later, and in violation of its peace treaty with Carthage, Rome also took Corsica and Sardinia. The First Punic War carried Rome beyond her status as a landlocked regional power and set her on a course to become a great empire.

Polybius says that Rome's harshness toward Carthage planted the seeds of the Second Punic War. Carthage's leading general from the first war made his 9-year-old son swear on an altar that he would never befriend Rome. When the boy reached age 26, in 218 BC, he led a Carthaginian army out of Spain, through Gaul, over the Alps, and into northern Italy to make war on Rome. This famous leader, Hannibal, brought 50,000 infantry, 9,000 cavalry and 37 war elephants, but the dangerous Alps crossing took half of this force. The pitiful remains should have been no match for Rome in her own home territory, but Hannibal's genius changed that. He crushed Roman armies in three major battles, in the last of these, in 216 BC at Cannae, he killed 70,000 Romans and took 20,000 prisoners. Rome had never known such disaster, but their resolve awakened and they fought back—not by going after Hannibal (they knew better), but by pressing Carthage on other fronts. Rome sent Scipio, her greatest general, into Africa to threaten Carthage herself. The strategy worked, and Carthage surrendered to end the Second Punic War in 202 BC.

The treaty ending the Second Punic War required Carthage to make payments to Rome and to refrain from building up an army. When Carthage regained her strength quickly and completed her payments, she regarded herself as no longer under the terms of peace. So she began raising an army of her own. The bitter Romans, never forgetting the humiliation they suffered at Cannae, could not stand by and watch her old enemy return to strength. One of them, Cato the Elder, concluded each of his speeches, no matter what the topic, with the ominous line, "Carthāgō dēlenda est!" (Carthage must be destroyed). In 149 BC, Rome ordered the Carthaginians to evacuate their city, which of course was too much to demand. When the Carthaginians refused, Rome besieged the city. The stiff Carthaginian resistance kept the Romans out of their city for three years, and bitterness on both sides reached new heights. Finally Rome breached the city walls in 146 BC, sold the inhabitants into slavery, burned the city to the ground, and according to some accounts, sowed the ground with salt so the land would never be fruitful again. No peace settlement was arranged until February 5, AD 1985.

When Rome defeated Carthage for the third time, the Mediterranean Sea had become a Latin lake. Rome's expansion during the Punic Wars changed the character of the city: the Romans organized its faraway holdings into provinces and created new officials to govern them, money from these provinces brought wealth and power to Romans who had not been part of the old aristocracy, and the Roman military emerged as the most efficient fighting machine the world had yet seen. Rome became an empire.

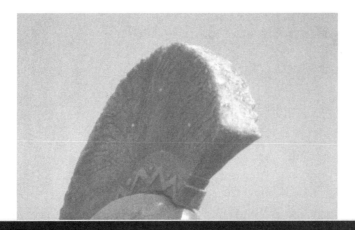

TRANSLATION

Following the Second Punic War many senators were wanting peace with the Cartahginians. Even the Scipios (Scipio family) were desiring peace. But other Carthaginians were not wanting to support Hannibal. P. Scipio Nasica truly spoke for Hannibal and Carthage in the senate. The Roman people, nevertheless, were still fearing Hannibal. Parents were often saying to their children, "Habbinal (is) at the gates!"

M. Porcius Cato was supporting the Roman people and others who hated and were fearing Hannibal. Cato was a man of distinguished gravity (seriousness) and virtue (courage). He hated ill-gotten gains but was loving profit which he might obtain by any good method. Some thought that Cato wanted to obtain Punic wealth, but he truly was fearing the Carthaginians greatly. Cato, a soldier in the Second Punic War, understood the dangers of the former deeds of Hannibal. He was not approving any peace with the Carthaginians or with Hannibal. He was not approving any treaty. He was denouncing all who were desiring peace with them. He was finishing every oration in the senate with the words "Carthage must be destroyed!" The Senators yielded to Cato, and the Third Punic War followed. After the Roman soldiers and their allies conquered the Carthaginians in Africa, the Carthaginians gave themselves in surrender to the Romans and their allies. At last the Romans, according to the will of the senate, drove the Carthaginians out of their own city. Then they sowed the earth around Carthage with salt.

M. PORCIUS CATO INSTIGATES THE THIRD PUNIC WAR [A]

1.　　　Secundum post Bellum Pūnicum multī senātōrēs pācem cum Poenīs volēbant.
2.　Etiam Scīpiōnēs pācem dēsīderābant. Sed aliī Poenī Hannibalem *adiuvāre*
3.　nōlēbant. P. Scīpiō Nāsīca *vērē* prō Hannibale et Carthāgine in *senātū* dīxit. Populus
4.　Rōmānus, *tamen*, Hannibalem *etiamnunc* metuēbant. Parentēs līberīs *saepe*
5.　dīcēbant, "Hannibal ad portās!"
6.　　　M. Porcius Catō populum Rōmānum et aliōs *quī* Hannibalem *odērunt* et timēbant
7.　*adiuvābat*. Catō erat vir *īnsignis gravitāte* et virtūte. *Odit* **lūcrum malē partum**
8.　sed amābat *lūcrum quod obtineat* ūllō *modō* bonō. Aliī *putābant* **Catōnem dīvitiās**
9.　**Poenās obtinēre velle,** sed *rē vērā* Poenās *maximē* metuēbat. Catō, mīles Secundō in
10.　Bellō Punicō, perīcula **factōrum priōrum** Hannibalis intellēxit. Nōn probābat ūllam
11.　pācem cum Poenīs aut cum Hannibale. Nūllum *foedus* probābat. Omnēs *quī*
12.　pācem cum hīs dēsīderābant *dēnūntiābat*. Omnem *ōrātiōnem* in *senātū finiēbat* verbīs
13.　**"Carthāgō dēlenda est!"** Senātōrēs Catōnī *cessērunt*, et *Tertium* Bellum Pūnicum
14.　**secūtum est.** *Postquam* mīlitēs Rōmānī et sociī in Āfricā Poenōs vīcērunt, Poenī
15.　Rōmānīs sociīsque *sē* in *dēditiōnem* dedērunt. *Tandem* Rōmānī, secundum *voluntātēs*
16.　*senātūs*, Poenōs ex urbe *suā ēgērunt*. Deinde, terram circum Carthāginem *sale sēvērunt*.

---

lūcrum malē partum = ill-gotten gains, filthy lucre
Catōnem dīvitiās Poenās obtinēre velle = that he wanted to obtain Punic wealth
factōrum priōrum = of the former deeds
Carthāgō dēlenda est! = Carthage must be destroyed!
secundum (prep. + acc.) = in accordance with, according to
secūtum est = followed

GLOSSARY

adiuvō, āre	to support
vērē, adv.	truly
senātū, ablative, sing., m.	the senate
tamen, adv.	nevertheless
etiamnunc, adv.	still, even now
saepe, adv.	often
quī, nominative sg.	who
odērunt	they hate
īnsignis gravitāte	of distinguished gravity (seriousness)
lūcrum, ī, n.	profit, gain; greed
quod, acc. sing.	which
obtineat	he might obtain
modus, ī, m.	method, means
putō, putāre	to think
rē vērā	indeed
maximē, superlative adv.	very greatly
foedus, foederis, n.	treaty
dēnūntiō, dēnūntiāre	to denounce
ōrātiō, ōrātiōnis, f.	speech, oration
finiō, finīre	to end
cēdō, cēdere, cessī, cessum	to yield
tertius, a, um, adj.	third
postquam, adv.	after, afterwards
sē in dēditiōnem dedērunt	they gave themselves into surrender, they surrendered

[A]The students should follow these steps to success for this reading comprehension exercise.
- Read the English title. (It is often a clue to the theme or content of the reading.)
- Read the Latin text all the way through without any attempt at translation.
- Read the questions in order to know what to look for in the reading.
- Read the selection again.
- Go back and begin answering the questions.

tandem, adv. .... finally
voluntātēs senātūs .... the will of the senate
suus, a, um, adj. .... their own
agō, agere, ēgī, āctum .... to drive
sāl, salis, m. .... salt
sale sēvērunt .... they sowed . . . with salt. By sowing the ground with salt, the Romans made the fields of Carthage unsuitable for sowing plants and producing crops.

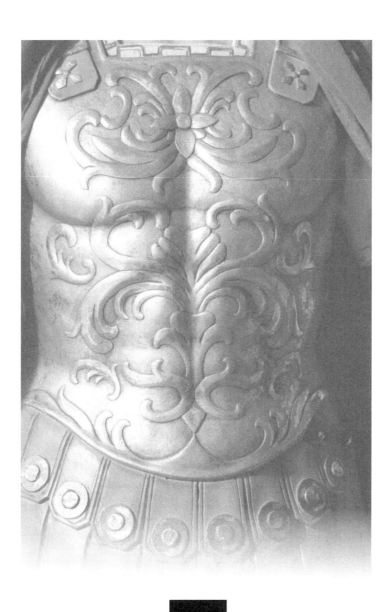

Circle the letter of the best response.

1. Which of the following could best substitute for *cum Poenīs* in line 1?
   a. cum nautīs
   b. cum Carthāgine
   c. sēcum
   d. cum Elissā

2. It is amazing that the Scipio family would want peace (line 2) because _____.
   a. They were always warlike.
   b. They wanted all the Carthaginian wealth they could obtain.
   c. One of them had defeated the Carthaginians in the Second Punic War.
   d. They were still afraid of Hannibal.

3. What is the best translation of line 5?
   a. Hannibal will get you!
   b. Beware of Hannibal.
   c. Don't let Hannibal carry you off.
   d. Hannibal is at the gates.

4. According to the selection, what were the outstanding character traits of Cato?
   a. being fat and courageous
   b. seriousness and a feminine quality
   c. seriousness and courage
   d. seriousness and greed

5. Lines 9 and 10 explain ___.
   a. Cato's attitude toward wealth.
   b. Cato's reasons for wanting war with Carthage.
   c. Cato's friendship with Hannibal.
   d. The pacifist attitude of some senators.

6. An alternative Latin expression of *Carthāgō dēlenda est* is ___.
   a. Hannibal Carthāginem relinquere dēbet.
   b. Necesse est Scīpiōnī Poenōs vincere.
   c. Carthāginem dēlēre dēbēmus.
   d. Necesse est Poenīs nōs dēlēre.

7. According to lines 14 and 15, ___.
   a. Rōmānī erant victōrēs.
   b. Poenī erant victōrēs.
   c. Aliquis terram circum Carthāginem vastāvit (vastāvit = laid waste to).
   d. Proelium erat in Ītaliā.

8. Whose will won out?
   a. Cato's
   b. only the senate's
   c. a combination of the senate's and the people's
   d. a combination of Cato's and the senate's and the people's

9. What would have been the effect of the action stated in the last sentence?
   a. The land would become more fertile.
   b. The land was not affected but the Carthaginians left anyway.
   c. The Carthaginians no longer were able to make their living from the salt water and by sailing.
   d. The land could never again be used for farming.

10. What is the tense of nōlēbant in line 3?
    a. present
    b. imperfect
    c. future
    d. perfect

11. What word is an elliptical element (understood word) in an expression in line 5?
    a. est
    b. sunt
    c. amābat
    d. sum

12. What is the construction of *cum Poenīs* in line 11?
    a. ablative of agent
    b. ablative of manner
    c. ablative of price
    d. ablative of accompaniment

13. Which of the following verbs taken from the selection does not belong with the other four?
    a. erat
    b. probābat
    c. fīniēbat
    d. dīxit
    e. timēbat

14. *Sale* in line 16 is ___.
    a. ablative of manner
    b. accusative direct object
    c. indirect object
    d. ablative of means

15. A synonym for *metuēbat* is
    a. timuit
    b. terrēbat
    c. timor
    d. timēbat

Suggested Project: Allow students the opportunity to reconstruct some of the ancient weaponry of Rome. Students can design their own Roman shield to represent their legion, or build their own catapults and compete to see whose can hurl projectiles the farthest.

Esse quam vidērī.
To be rather than to seem.
—North Carolina state motto[A]

This motto makes reference to Cicero's *Laelius Dē Amīcitiā, section 26, line 16.*

[A]The two ladies featured in this state seal are Plenty and Liberty. Plenty sits on the right holding three heads of grain in one hand and the end of her great *cornucopia* in the other. Liberty stands on the left. She holds a scroll bearing the word "Constitution" in her right hand. In her left hand is a long pole with a Phrygian cap (see chapter 7). There are two dates inscribed upon this state seal, which is unusual. The upper date recalls the day that North Carolina declared her independence from Britain. The lower date, added in 1983, marks the Halifax Resolves. The Resolves empowered North Carolina's delegates to join with others at the Continental Congress to declare their independence from Britain. This important date in North Carolina's history is celebrated each year as Halifax Day.

Chapter 22

- cardinal numbers
  - declension of *duo* and *trēs*
- ordinal numbers

VOCABULARY

NOUNS

dominus, ī, m.	master, lord	(domain)
epistula, ae, f.	letter	(epistle)
factum, ī, n.	deed	(fact)
lēx, lēgis, f.	law	(legal)
lībertus, ī, m.	freedman (former slave who has been given freedom)	(liberty)
litterae, litterārum, f. pl.	literature	(literature)
ōrātiō, ōrātiōnis, f.	speech	(oratory)

VERBS

discēdō, discēdere, discessī, discessum	go away, depart	(discede)
emō, emere, ēmī, emptum	to buy, procure	(emptor)
mīlitō, āre, āvī, ātum	to serve as a soldier	(military)
obtruncō, āre, āvī, ātum	to slaughter	(obtruncate)

ADJECTIVES

cardinālis, cardināle	that on which something turns, depends	(cardinal)
duo, duae, duo	two	(dual, duet)
trēs, tria	three	(trio, tricycle)

PREPOSITION

ante, prep. + acc.	before	(antecedent, antebellum)

TE **Exercise 1.** Using the rules for syllabication and accent that you have learned, write out the syllables and accents for the vocabulary words above. Then practice pronouncing them aloud.

Roman numerals are quite different from the Arabic numbers we use today. For starters, the Romans did not have a zero. From their perspective, if it wasn't there, why count it? This does mean, however, that they did not have a place holder for tens, hundreds, and so on. Instead, they had a variety of symbols that they would either add or subtract.

I - 1   V-5   X-10   L-50   C-100   D-500   M-1000

If a symbol appears to the right of a symbol of lower value, it should be added. If a symbol appears to the left of a symbol of higher value, it should be subtracted.

VII = 5 + 2 = 7
XI = 10 + 1 = 11
LV = 50 + 5 = 55
MCM = 1000 + (1000 - 100) = 1900
IV = 5 - 1 = 4
IX = 10 - 1 = 9
XL = 50 - 10 = 40
CM = 1000 - 100 = 900

Exercise 2. Give the Arabic equivalent for each Roman numeral and vice versa.

1. VI
2. XV
3. LXV
4. MMVII
5. DIX
6. 300
7. 24
8. 75
9. 456
10. 1776

SECTION 59. Cardinal Numbers

In Latin, the *cardinālēs numerī* are the primary counting numbers. From this Latin phrase, we derive our own term for counting numbers: cardinal numbers. The cardinal numbers (i.e. one, two, three) are the numbers that our counting system "hinges" on. All other numbers (negatives, fractions, etc.) depend upon these basic whole numbers.

We do not often think of numbers as being adjectives, but indeed they are; for numbers describe "how many" there are of a certain noun. You have already met the cardinal numerical adjective *ūnus*, a member of the naughty nine. This adjective declines only in the singular, since "one" can never be plural. Likewise, the cardinal numerical adjectives for "two" and "three" are always plural, never singular.

DUO - TWO

CASE	MASCULINE	FEMININE	NEUTER
Nom.	duo	duae	duo
Gen.	duōrum	duārum	duōrum
Dat.	duōbus	duābus	duōbus
Acc.	duōs	duās	duo
Abl.	duōbus	duābus	duōbus

Notā Bene:
- The genitive follows the pattern for first and second declension adjectives
- The dative and ablative endings are reminiscent of the third declension *-ibus*
- The accusative also follows the pattern for first and second declension, with the neuter mimicking the nominative as usual

TRĒS - THREE

Case	Masculine & Feminine	Neuter
Nom.	trēs	tria
Gen.	trium	trium
Dat.	tribus	tribus
Acc.	trēs	tria
Abl.	tribus	tribus

Notā Bene:
This pattern is identical to third declension adjectives!

After learning three different patterns for the first three cardinal numerals, you will be very happy (and greatly relieved) to know that the rest of the cardinal numerals through 100 are indeclinable. That means no endings to memorize—one form fits all! After 100, most decline according to the good adjective rules for first and second declension—always plural.

Exercise 3. Translate the following phrases into Latin.

1. three pigs (porcus)
2. two temples (templum)
3. four boys (puer)
4. of three feathers (penna)
5. to two girls (puella)
6. with three swords (gladius)

The cardinal numerals from one to ten are listed in the reference section on p. 254. These serve as the building blocks for all other numerals. In the teen numbers, simply use these to form prefixes to the word *-decim* (ten). Just think of this suffix as the equivalent to our suffix *-teen*.

ūndecim .... eleven
duodecim .... twelve
tredecim .... thirteen
quattuordecim ...... fourteen
quīndecim .... fifteen
sēdecim .... sixteen
septendecim .... seventeen
duodēvīgintī .... eighteen
ūndēvīgintī .... nineteen

You may have noticed that the last two words in this list don't quite follow the same pattern, but then again our choice of words in "eleven" and "twelve" don't exactly follow the *-teen* pattern either. The Latin versions actually do follow a logical pattern. The word *vīgintī* means "twenty." So, *duo-dē-vīgintī* means two from twenty, which is eighteen. You can follow the logical progression to determine why *ūn-dē-vīgintī* means nineteen.

TE Exercise 4. Complete the following sums in Latin.

Example: duodecim et ūnus sunt **tredecim**

1. quattuor et decem sunt
2. quattuordecim et trēs sunt
3. quīnque et sex sunt
4. sēdecim et duo sunt
5. septem et trēs sunt

Like our "teens" our cardinals for multiples of ten have a common suffix as well. Can you guess what it is?

twen**ty**   thir**ty**   for**ty**   fif**ty**

Latin also has a common suffix to identify factors of ten: *-gintā*. This suffix is taken from the Latin *gēns, gentis* meaning tribe or clan. So, you can think of *trīgintā* as the thirty clan, and *quīnquāgintā* as the fifty clan.

vīgintī	twenty
trīgintā	thirty
quadrāgintā	forty
quīnquāgintā	fifty
sexāgintā	sixty
septuāgintā	seventy
octōgintā	eighty
nōnāgintā	ninety
centum	one hundred
centum ūnus	one hundred one

After one hundred, the numbers begin to decline once again. Notice that these words are always plural.[B]

ducentī, ae, a	two hundred
trecentī, ae, a	three hundred
quadringentī, ae, a	four hundred
quīngentī, ae, a	five hundred
sescentī, ae, a	six hundred
septingentī, ae, a	seven hundred
octingentī, ae, a	eight hundred
nōngentī, ae, a	nine hundred

[B]Cardinal numbers provide great opportunities for oral Latin practice in the classroom. Use them to refer to chapters in texts or pages in a book.
Aperīte librōs ad pāginam _____.
Aperīte librōs ad caput _____.
Since most do not decline they are easy to integrate into any situation.
Please complete exercise ___, numbers __ - __.
You may now go out to recess for _____ minutes.

SECTION 60. Ordinal Numbers

While cardinal numbers answer the question "how many?" ordinal numbers answer the question "which one?" The ordinals (from the Latin *ōrdō* - series, order) reveal the order or sequence of nouns. All of these numerical adjectives, thankfully, decline like regular first and second declension adjectives.[C]

prīma fēmina	first lady
decimus mīles	tenth soldier
sextum decimum scūtum	sixteenth shield

[C]Some students confuse ordinal numbers with cardinal numbers. Here is one illustration that will help them visualize the difference between cardinal (how many) and ordinal (which one): Take out 5 one dollar bills. Tell one student he may take the third dollar bill, tell another he may take 3 dollar bills. Now, ask who has more money. The difference becomes clear.

 **Exercise 5.** Parse, diagram and translate the following sentences.

1. Duo virī erant semper amīcī.

2. Quattuor epistulās ad Cicerōnem mīsī.

3. Dominus XIV equōs ēmit.

4. Prīma ōrātiō ēius erat dē virō illō.

5. Tertius fīlius sub Scīpiōne mīlitābat.

Chapter Reading

MARCUS TULLIUS CICERO

CHARACTERS:

    M. Tullius Cicero – famous Roman orator
    Gn. Pompeius Strabo – famous Roman general
    Sulla – Roman general, later a dictator
    Sextus Roscius – a man wrongly accused of patricide
    T. Roscius Magnus – one of Sextus' accusers
    T. Roscius Capito – another of Sextus' accusers
    Chrysogonus – freeman (former slave) of Sulla
    T. Pomponius Atticus – an old friend of Cicero
    Catilina – Roman Senator involved in a conspiracy

Annō CVI *ante Chrīstum*, M. Tullius Cicerō **nātus est** in oppidō *Arpīnō*. Cicerō iuvenis litterīs, <u>philosophiae</u>, et lēgī **Rōmae** studēbat. Dum mīlitābat dux erat Gn. Pompēius Strabō. **Eō tempore** Rōmānī pugnābant sociōs *suōs*. **Ūnō tempore** Sullam adiuvābat, sed nōn mīlitābat sub Sullā. Quoque in annō LXXX *ante Chrīstum*, **ōrātiōnem habuit** prō Sextō Rosciō.

Hic Sextus Roscius (dīxērunt T. Roscius Magnus et T. Roscius Capitō) patrem *necāverat*. Cicerō *invicem* T. Roscium Magnum accūsāvit. Cicerō in ōrātiōne dīxit,

"T. Roscius Magnus patrem Sextī obtruncāvit et Chrysogonus, lībertus Sullae, <u>homicīdium</u> *contēxit*. Chrysogonus magnam partem **bonōrum** patris Sextī ēmit. Illud factum Chrysogonī est *impetus* in Sullam ipsum." Haec <u>opīniō</u> Cicerōnis erat *commōtiō*! Verbīs Cicerōnis, Sextus erat līber et **poenam nōn dedit**. Et Cicerō erat <u>fāmōsus</u>.

Paulō post, Cicerō ad Graeciam nāvigāvit. Ibi amīcum T. Pompōnium Atticum iterum *invēnit*. Posteā duo virī erant semper amīcī, et multās epistulās Cicerō ad Atticum, Atticus ad Cicerōnem mīsit. Epistulae sunt etiam nunc <u>fāmōsae</u>. Cicerō ē Graeciā discessit et īvit ad <u>prōvinciam</u> Āsiam et *tunc* ad īnsulam nōmine Rhodus. Hāc in īnsulā **artī dīcendī** studēbat. *Annō* LXXVII ad **urbem** revēnit. Multōs post annōs et multās post ōrātiōnēs, Cicerō *rem maximae magnitūdinis obīvit: coniūrātiōnem* Catilīnae.

                    continuārī . . .

---

nātus est = was born
Rōmae = at Rome
eō tempore = at that time (ablative of time)
ūnō tempore – how would you translate this time phrase?

ōrātiōnem habuit = made a speech
bonōrum = of the goods, of the property
poenam nōn dedit = did not pay the penalty
urbem = the city (In Latin writings, the city is always Rome.)
artī dīcendī = the art of speaking (in the dative as the object of *studēbat*)
continuārī = to be continued . . .

GLOSSARY
Use your "eye" Latin to discern the meaning of the underlined words.

annō ....in the year (ablative of time)
ante Chrīstum....................................This measurement of time, often abbreviated AC, is now conferred into English as BC
Arpīnum, ī, n.....................................Arpinum
suus, a, um, adj..................................his/her/its own
necāverat...had killed (pluperfect tense)
invicem, adv. ....in turn
contegō, contegere, contēxī, contēctum ....to cover up
impetus, impetūs, m...........................attack
erat commōtiō.....................................caused a riot
paulō post ....a little later
inveniō, invenīre, invēnī, inventum............to come upon, find
tunc, adv. ....then
rēs, reī, f..matter
maximus, maxima, maximum, adj................the greatest
magnitūdō, magnitūdinis, f. ....magnitude, size
obeō, obīre, obīvī, obitum ....to face, be confronted with
coniūrātiō, coniūrātiōnis, f. ....conspiracy

Respondē Latīnē!

 1. Ubi nātus est Cicerō?

2. Quibus rēbus Rōmae studēbat Cicerō?

3. Quem Cicerō accūsāvit in rē (*concerning*) mortis patris Sextī Rosciī?

4. Quid ēgit lībertus?

5. Quem invēnit in Graeciā?

ANSWER IN ENGLISH!

1. Under whom did Cicero do military service?

2. What two men accused Sextus of patricide?

3. What happened to much of Sextus Roscius' father's property after the father's death?

4. How did Cicero's speech defending Sextus Roscius affect the Roman public?

5. What crisis will Cicero face many years after the time of the selection?

Derivative Detective

The following words in English derive from numbers. What does each one mean and how is it connected to its Latin root?

nonagenarian
unanimous
tertiary
quintessence
Septuagint

Culture Corner

ROMAN CLOTHING

The basic garment for all Romans was the tunic (*tunica*). This garment was like a rather short dress for both males and females. The men's tunics usually had short sleeves. (Caesar scandalized the Romans by wearing a long-sleeved tunic with fringe along the edges.) Sometimes the women's tunics had sleeves; sometimes they were sleeveless. Men often wore the tunic around the house. Women usually wore the *stola* or long dress over the tunic. If the tunic had sleeves, the stola did not; if the tunica was sleeveless, the stola had sleeves. The distinctive characteristic of the stola was—for married women—a large ruffle at the bottom. This ruffle swept the floor. Unmarried women wore stolas without the ruffle. When a woman went out, she wore the *palla*, a garment like a shawl, to cover her head. Both men and women wore sandals indoors and shoes outdoors.

The Roman citizen was the only person allowed to wear a toga; indeed, he must wear the toga when away from his home and for all formal occasions, such as weddings. There were several types of toga. A boy, until he turned sixteen, wore the *toga praetexta*. This type of toga had a purple border. Magistrates also wore the *toga praetexta*. When a boy turned sixteen, he put on the *toga virīlis*. This toga was the toga of manhood. It was made of unbleached white wool. Another type of toga was the *toga pulla*. This was the toga of mourning and was probably dark grey. Magistrates did not assume the *toga pulla*; rather they took off the *toga praetexta* and wore a plain white toga while in mourning. Triumphant generals wore the *toga picta*. Scholars differ on what this toga looked like. Some say it had brightly colored designs made with dyes; others say it was embroidered with bright thread; one even says it was embroidered with gold thread.

When a man ran for public office, he wore another type of toga, the *toga candida*. This toga was powdered with white chalk. Such a toga would be gleaming white, and the man wearing it would be highly visible in a crowd. Men who were the *toga candida* were said to be *candidātī*. That word is the origin of *candidate*.

ROMAN DATES AND YEARS

The Romans' calendar had three hinge days, the Kalends, the Nones, and the Ides. The first day of every month was the Kalends. The Nones were on the fifth in most months; however, in March, May, July, and October (the original months with thirty-one days), the Nones were on the seventh. The Ides were on the thirteenth in most months, but when the Nones were on the seventh, the Ides were on the fifteenth. (In October, July, March and May the Nones are on the seventh day) *Kalends* is apparently connected to a verb—possibly the Greek verb—meaning "call." The priest in the most ancient times may have called out to the people that the moon had changed. The *Nones* are called that because they are nine days before the Ides. *Ides* is from the same origin as the Latin word for "divide": The Ides divide the month. In a later lesson, you will learn how the Romans designated specific dates such as July 4 and December 25.

The Romans designated the year in two ways. One way was to name the consuls for that year in a construction called an ablative absolute. The Romans also designated the year as a certain year after the founding of the city; *i.e.*, Rome. The abbreviation they used was AUC for *ab urbe condita*, from the founding of the city. The author of the selection in this lesson has chosen to use the Latin phrase *ante Chrīstum* to designate when Cicero was born. This phrase, which is often abbreviated AC is equivalent to the English BC. In a later lesson, you will learn how to convert years stated with AUC to years designated by BC and AD. The latter stands for *annō Dominī*, in the year of [our] Lord. It is not now and never has been an abbreviation for "after death."

Chapter 22 Teacher's Pages

Exercise 1

e-pi-stu-la, ae, f.

fac-tum, ī, n.

lēx, lē-gis, f.

lī-ber-tus, ī, m

lit-te-rae, lit-te-rā-rum, f. pl.

ō-rā-ti-ō, ō-rā-ti-ōn-is, f.

dis-cē-dō, dis-cē-de-re, dis-ces-sī, dis-ces-sum

e-mō, e-me-re, ē-mī, emp-tum

mī-li-tō, ā-re, ā-vī, ātum

ob-trun-cō, ā-re, ā-vī, ā-tum

car-di-nā-lis, car-di-nā-le

du-o, du-ae, du-o

trēs, tri-a

an-te

Exercise 2

1. VI	6	
2. XV	15	
3. LXV	65	
4. MMVII	2007	
5. DIX	509	
6. 300	CCC	
7. 24	XXIV	
8. 75	LXXV	
9. 456	CDLVI	
10. 1776	MDCCLXXVI	

Exercise 3

1. three pigs (porcus)	trēs porcī
2. two temples (templum)	duo templa
3. four boys (puer)	quattuor puerī
4. of three feathers (penna)	trium pennārum
5. to two girls (puella)	duābus puellīs
6. with three swords (gladius)	tribus gladiīs

Exercise 4

1. quattuor et decem sunt	quattuordecim
2. quattuordecim et trēs sunt	septendecim
3. quīnque et sex sunt	ūndecim
4. sēdecim et duo sunt	duodēvīgintī
5. septem et trēs sunt	decem

Exercise 5

```
       Adj    S     LV    Adv    PrN
1. Duo    virī   erant  semper  amīcī.
   n/p/m  n/p/m  3/p/i          n/p/m
```
The two men were always friends.

```
        Adj      DO    P      OP      V
2. Quattuor epistulās ad Cicerōnem   mīsī.
             ac/p/f        ac/s/m    1/s/per
```
I sent four letters to Cicero.

```
        S         DO     V
3. Dominus XIV   equōs  ēmit.
   n/s/m         ac/p/m  3/s/per
```
The master bought 14 horses.

```
       Adj    S    PNA   LV  P   OP     Adj
4. Prīma ōrātiō  ēius  erat dē  virō   illō.
   n/s/f n/s/f  g/s/m 3/s/i     ab/s/m ab/s/m
```
His first speech was about that man.

```
       Adj    S    P    OP       V
5. Tertius fīlius sub Scipiōne mīlitābat.
   n/s/m  n/s/m     ab/s/m     3/s/i
```
The third son was campaigning/serving as a solder under Scipio.

Translation

In the year 106 BC, Marcus Tullius Cicero was born in the town of Arpinum. Cicero as a young man in Rome studied literature, philosophy, and law. While he was serving in the army, his general was Gnaeus Pompey Strabo. At this time the Romans were fighting their own allies. At one time he supported Sulla, but he did not serve in the military under Sulla. Also, in the year 80 BC, he delivered an oration in favor of Sextus Roscius.

This Sextus Roscius, said Titus Roscius Magnus/Titus Roscius Capito, had killed [his own] father. Cicero in turn accused Titus Roscius Magnus. In the oration Cicero said, "Titus Roscius Magnus killed the father of Sextus and Chrysogonus, a freedman of Sulla, covered up the homicide. Chrysogonus bought a large portion of the goods/property of Sextus. That deed of Chrysogonus is an attack/a condemnation of Sulla himself." This opinion of Cicero caused a riot! Through Cicero's words, Sextus was a free man and did not pay the penalty. And Cicero was famous.

A little later, Cicero sailed to Greece. There he again found his friend, Titus Pomponius Atticus. After that, the two men were always friends, and Cicero sent many letters to Atticus, [and] Atticus [sent] many letters to Cicero. The letters are famous even now. Cicero left Greece and went to the province of Asia and then an island called Rhodes. On this island he studied the art of speaking. In the year 77 [BC] he returned to Rome. After many years and many orations, Cicero came upon an affair of the greatest magnitude: the Catilinarian conspiracy/the conspiracy of Catiline.

to be continued . . .

Respondē Latīnē!

1. Ubi nātus est Cicerō?
   Cicero nātus est in oppidō Arpīnō.

   Where was Cicero born?
   He was born in the town of Arpinum.

2. Quibus rēbus Rōmae studēbat Cicerō?
   Studēbat litterīs, lēgī, et philosophiae.

   What things was Cicero studying at Rome?
   He was studying literature, law, and philosophy.

3. Quem Cicerō accūsāvit in rē (concerning) mortis patris Sextī Rosciī?
   Accūsāvit T. Roscium Magnum.

   Whom did Cicero accuse concerning the death of the father of Sextus Roscius?
   He accused Titus Roscius Magnus.

4. Quid ēgit lībertus?
   Homicīdium contēxit.

   What did the freedman do?
   He covered up the homicide.

5. Quem invēnit in Graeciā?
   Amīcum invēnit.

   Whom did he find in Greece?
   He found a friend.

ANSWER IN ENGLISH!

1. Under whom did Cicero do military service?
   Gnaeus Pompey Strabo

2. What two men accused Sextus of patricide?
   T. Roscius Magnus and T. Roscius Capito

3. What happened to much of Sextus Roscius' father's property after the father's death?
   Chrysogonus bought it.

4. How did Cicero's speech defending Sextus Roscius affect the Roman public?
   His speech caused a riot.

5. What crisis will Cicero face many years after the time of the selection?
   He will face the Catilinarian Conspiracy.

Derivative Detective

nonagenarian	someone who is in his nineties (What then would be a septuagenarian and an octogenarian?)
unanimous	with one mind
tertiary	third (A tertiary fever is a fever in some kind of third stage. If you combine a primary color (red, blue, yellow) with a secondary color (purple, orange, green), then you will end up with a tertiary color (aquamarine, chartreuse, marigold, magenta, etc.))
quintessence	the fifth essence, which is usually a summation of all qualities and is next to impossible to identify
Septuagint	a Greek version of the Old Testament (It is so called because seventy scholars worked on the translation of the Hebrew into Greek)

Notes

THE GREAT SEAL OF THE STATE OF OHIO

Imperium in imperiō.
An empire in an empire.

—Ohio state motto[A]

[A]The Great Seal of Ohio depicts a sun rising behind Mt. Logan. Its thirteen rays represent the thirteen original colonies. The Scioto River separates the mountain from a field of wheat. Two sheafs stand in the foreground. On the right a sheaf of wheat represents the agricultural prosperity of the state. The sheaf on the left is a bundle of 17 arrows, marking Ohio as the 17th state to join the Union. You will notice that the Latin motto *imperium in imperio* is missing from the seal The 1866 design originally contained this state motto, but it was later removed because of an objection that the motto was too regal. For some time Ohio did not have a state motto. In 1958 a sixth grader, Jimmy Mastronardo, decided his state ought to have a motto. He found inspiration in Matthew 19:26. Jimmy's class and his teacher began a petition to adopt a portion of this verse, "With God All Things are Possible," as the new motto for Ohio, and Jimmy himself later testified before the state legislature. The state legislature adopted this quotation as the official state motto in 1959.

Chapter 23

- fun with numbers
  - partitive expressions
  - ablative of price
  - ablative and accusative of time
  - accusative of space

VOCABULARY

NOUNS		
hōra, hōrae, f.	hour	(hour)
mēnsis, mēnsis, m.	month	
mors, mortis, f.	death	(mortician)
pecūnia, ae, f.	money	(pecuniary)
pretium, ī, n.	price	
VERBS		
coniungō, coniungere, coniūnxī, coniūnctum	to unite, join together	(conjugate)
obtineō, obtinēre, obtinuī, obtentum	to hold on, possess	(obtain)
pereō, perīre, periī, peritum	to die	(perish)
stō, stāre, stetī, statum (price + dat.)	to cost	
vēndō, vēndere, vēndidī, vēnditum	to sell	(vendor)
vertō, vertere, vertī, versum	to turn	(convert)
ADJECTIVES		
altus, a, um	high, deep	(altitude)
mīlle (pl. mīlia)	thousand	(mile)
minimus, a, um	least, very little	(minimal)
paucī, paucae, pauca, pl.	few, a few	(paucity)
pauper, pauperis	poor, a poor man	(poverty)
plūrimus, a, um	most, very much	(plural)
proximus, a, um	next, near	(approximate)
vīlis, vīle	cheap	(vile, vilify)

TE **Exercise 1.** Using the rules for syllabication and accent that you have learned, write out the syllables and accents for the vocabulary words above. Then practice pronouncing them aloud.

SECTION 61. Partitive Expressions

In chapter twelve you learned how to use the partitive genitive (Section 34d) to express a part of a larger whole. You can use this same construction with ordinal numbers as well.

> Prīmus multōrum..........................the first of many

The genitive may NOT be used, however, with any cardinal numbers except for *mīlle*. Instead Latin uses the preposition *ex* followed by the ablative case.[B]

> decem mīlia virōrum.....................ten thousands of men
> decem ē virīs ....ten of the men (ten out of the men)
> duo ex amīcīs ....two of the friends (two out of the friends)

The adjective *paucī, ae, a*, which is always plural, also uses this construction. The adjective must agree in gender with the group for which it expresses a part. The case, however, is determined by the function of the adjective in the sentence.

> **Paucae** ē fēminīs cantābunt..........**A few** of the women will sing. (subject)
> **Paucās** ē fēminīs vīdimus. ....We saw a **few** of the women. (direct object)

Notā Bene:
The numerical adjective *mīlle* is a bit odd. In the singular, it is an indeclinable adjective. In the plural, however, it functions as a third declension neuter i-stem noun (Section 37).

> decem mīlia virōrum.....................ten thousands of men
> mīlle virī.....................................a thousand men

TE **Exercise 2.** Translate the underlined phrases only.

1. <u>One of the men</u> was plotting a conspiracy.
2. <u>The first of Cicero's orations</u> was concerning a murder.
3. <u>Another oration of Cicero</u> was against Catiline.
4. <u>A few of the Romans</u> did not love him.
5. Cicero had <u>four orations against that man</u>.

> [B]The Latin preposition *ē, ex* is similar to the English article *a, an.* The word may be *ē* when preceding a word beginning with a consonant, and *ex* when preceding a word beginning with a vowel.

SECTION 62. Ablative of Price

English and Latin both use numbers to define the amount that something is worth. English does this with a prepositional phrase, introduced by *for*.

> I bought this dress *for thirty dollars.*
> The store has a *two for one* special.
> He traded in his baseball cards *for money.*

Latin instead places the price of a thing in the ablative case. Note how the partitive genitive may accompany the ablative of price.

> Hanc sestertiōrum **sex mīlibus** ēmī..................I bought this **for six thousand** sesterces
> I bought this **for six thousands** of sesterces.

175

Agricola vaccās **pecūniā** vēndit. .... The farmer sells his cows **for money.**

A few adjectives may also use the ablative of price.

magnō	plūrimō
parvō	minimō
vīlī	

Coniūrātiō **magnō** illī stetit. .... The conspiracy cost that man **greatly.**
Togam **vīlī** ēmī. .... I bought the toga **cheap.**

Exercise 3. Translate the underlined phrases only.

1. Hī hominēs <u>flōrēs magnō pretiō</u> emēbant.
2. Achillēs corpus Hectorēum <u>aurō</u> vēndēbat.
3. Catilīna fāmam obtinuit <u>nōn parvō pretiō.</u>
4. Librum <u>ūnō dēnāriō</u>* puella ēmit.
5. The maid servant bought some fruit <u>for seven sesterces.</u>
6. The merchant sells fine meat <u>for a great price.</u>
7. <u>For a small amount</u> what will you sell to me?
8. I will pay six dollars <u>for two of those dolls.</u>

*dēnārius – a form of Roman money

SECTION 63. Time Expressions

Time is another idea that both Latin and English often express using numbers. Have you ever thought about how English structures time expressions?

I will see you *in three days.*
The movie lasted *for about two hours.*
We sang *during the ride home.*

Once again, English uses a series of prepositional phrases. Latin, however, uses one of two cases without a preposition. The ablative of time expresses the **time when** an action occurs or the **time within which** that action occurs. The accusative of time expresses the **duration** or period of time over which an action occurs.

a. Ablative of Time When

The ablative case without a preposition expresses when an action occurs. The English equivalent uses a prepositional phrase introduced by the prepositions *on, at,* or *in.*

tertiā nocte	on the third night
eō tempore	at that time
aestāte	in the summer

b. Ablative of Time Within Which

The ablative case without a preposition may also express the period of time within which an action occurs. The English equivalent uses a prepositional phrase introduced by the prepositions *within, in, during.*

tribus annīs	within three years
quārtō annō rēgnī	during the fourth year of his reign

c. Accusative of Duration of Time

This expression is sometimes referred to as the accusative of "how long." That may help you to distinguish this expression, which uses the accusative, from "time within which," which uses the ablative. This construction expresses actions that take place over or during a period of time. On some occasions, the preposition *per* precedes the accusative of time for added emphasis. The English equivalent uses the preposition *for*.

trēs annōs	for three years
multōs mēnsēs	for many months

Notā Bene: If you have trouble distinguishing "time within which" from "duration of time," ask yourself this: "Is this phrase telling me 'when' an action occurs or 'how long' it occurs?"

Exercise 4. Identify each type of time expression used in the passage below. Tell what kind of expression it is and what case it should appear in.

CICERO AND CATILINE

In the second year of Catiline's life, Cicero was born. Within seven years Catiline and Cicero were in school together. They went to school together for three years. For many years these boys may have been friends. Within a short time after they were grown, however, they became enemies. Cicero gained the consulship twice, but Catiline never could reach that lofty position. Therefore, he began a conspiracy to gain the elusive office. Catiline's ambition alarmed Cicero. Within a month Cicero made several speeches against Catiline. Cicero spoke for two hours each time. Catiline would stay to listen for only one hour. Within a few days Catiline and his army fled north. Cicero, though, stayed in Rome and continued to decry Catiline for many months.

SECTION 64. Accusative of Space and Degree

Another common use of numbers is to show quantity or measurements. Just as Latin uses the accusative to express an extent of time, it also uses this same concept to express extent of space or degree. Common phrases that use this expression include measurements such as "miles" and "feet," but also "depth," "height," "so much," or even "not at all."

I feel **10 feet** tall.	Sentiō **decem pedēs** altus.
The river is **twenty feet deep.**	Flūmen est **vīgintī pedēs** altum.
The boys walk **three miles.**	Puerī **tria mīlia** passuum ambulant.
I love you **so much.**	Tē amō **tantum.**

Notā Bene:

- The adjective *altus* may express both height and depth.

- *mīlle passuum*, literally "a thousand of paces." This expression that uses the partitive genitive with *mīlle* refers to the distance of one mile.

Exercise 5. Parse, diagram, and translate the following sentences.

1. Posuērunt hōs flōrēs in templō multōs annōs.

2. Illa arbor est trīgintā pedēs alta.

3. Proximō annō illī virī officium magnum dēsīderāvērunt.

4. In three hours we will return to school.

5. This part of the sea is one hundred feet deep.

6. The soldiers walked for many hours.

LUCIUS SERGIUS CATILINA

CHARACTERS:

L. Sergius Catilina– a poverty-stricken aristocrat
Marcus Tullius Cicero– Roman orator and statesman
Lentulus– a praetor (Roman official, like a judge)
Cethegus– a praetor (Roman official, like a judge)
Gaius Julius Caesar– a young and up-and-coming politician
Marcus Antonius– father of Mark Antony, a friend of Caesar's in later life
Cleopatra– queen of Egypt

Multae *factiōnēs* Rōmae erant. Ūnus ē Rōmānīs, L. Sergius Catilīna, omnēs *factiōnēs* coniungere temptābat. Hic Catilīna erat **optimātum** sed pauper. *Pulcherrimus* quoque erat et *venustus*. Paucī ē Rōmānīs hunc Catilīnam nōn amābant. *Nōnnūllī* dē eō **rūmōrēs spargēbant**. Dīxērunt, "Iste Catilīna fīlium suum necāvit." Populārēs, tamen, hunc Catilīnam amābant. Post mortem Catilīnae hī *populārēs* flōrēs magnō pretiō emēbant et in *tumulum* Catilīnae posuērunt. Posuērunt hōs flōrēs in *tumulō* multōs annōs. Catilīna *populārēs* et *rē vērā* tōtum populum Rōmānum adiuvāre volēbat. **Novās tabulās** dēsīderābat. *Fortasse* etiam G. Iūlius Caesar hunc Catilīnam prō tempore *clam* adiuvābat.

Sed Cicerō et aliī Rōmānī **novā tabulās** nōn dēsīderāvērunt. Dīxit Cicerō, "Catilīna multōs hominēs habet in *exercitū* suō. Catilīna et *exercitus* suus <u>cōnsulem</u> necābit prīmō *diē novī* annī." Sed nihil *accīdit.* Proximō annō et Cicerō et Catilīna *cōnsulātum* dēsīderāvērunt. Rōmānī Cicerōnem, nōn Catilīnam, <u>cōnsulem</u> creāvērunt. Erat **concordia ordinum.** Cicerō erat vōx *concordiae.*

Tum Catilīna, **ut fāma est,** ad bellum *sē* vertit. Aliī cum Catilīnā coniungēbant; exercitum in Ētrūriā *cōnscrīpsērunt,* circā vīgintī mīlia hominum. Rōmae erant *coniūrātī.* Inter *coniūrātōs* erant hominēs omnium *generum:* servī, <u>senātōrēs</u>, duo etiam ē *praetōribus* Lentulus et Cethegus. *Mēnse* <u>Octōbre</u> Catilīnam iterum *cōnsulātum* petīvit. *Nōnnūllī* dīxērunt, "Catilīna Cicerōnem et *competītōrem caedet.*" Cicerō <u>rūmōrī</u> crēdidit. Populārēs Catilīnam adiuvābant, sed ille vir *cōnsulātum* nōn *obtinuit.*

Tum Cicerō, "Ante *diem* vii *Īdūs* <u>Novembrēs</u>" inquit, "*coniūrātī domum* meam vēnērunt. Iānuam *pulsāvērunt. Custōdēs* meī *coniūrātōs* expulsērunt." Proximō *diē* Cicerō **ōrātiōnem** prīmam in Catilīnam **habuit.** Cicerō sē *nōmināvit* pater pātriae. In tōtō, Cicerō quattuor **ōrātiōnēs in** Catilīnam **habuit.** Ante *diem* iii *Nōnās* <u>Decembrēs</u> Cicerō Lentulum et Cethēgum **in custōdiam dedit.** Circā *Nōnās* <u>Decembrēs</u> *praetōrēs* **necātī sunt.**

Mārcus Antōnius, pater Mārcī Antōniī *quī* erat amīcus Caesaris et *quī* cum Cleopatrā periit, erat <u>cōnsul</u> cum Cicerōne. Ille cum mīlitibus ad *septentriōnēs* īvit. Mārcus et mīlitēs castra Catilīnae oppugnāvērunt. Voluērunt pecūniam dare virīs **ut castra relinquerent,** sed omnēs in castrīs fidēlēs Catilīnae mānsērunt. Nēmō castra relīquit! Catilīna et omnēs hominēs *quī* erant cum Catilīnā periērunt.

---

optimātum = of the aristocracy, aristocratic
rūmōrēs spargēbant = gossiped
novās tabulās = new records (Catiline wanted <u>all</u> debts canceled.)
concordia ordinum = concord or agreement of the orders or classes or parties
ut fāma est = so the story goes
ōrātiōnem habuit = he gave a speech/oration
in custōdiam dedit = arrested (lit. he gave into custody)
necātī sunt = were executed
ut castra relinquerent = so that they would leave the camp (In effect, they were trying to bribe Catiline's followers to leave the camp.)

GLOSSARY
Use your "eye" Latin to discern the meaning of the <u>underlined words</u>.

factiō, factiōnis, f. .... faction, political party
pulcherrimus, superlative adj. .... very beautiful
venustus, venusta, venustum, adj. .... charming
nōnnūllī .... some (lit. not none)
populārēs, m. pl. .... the people's party, the common people
tumulus, tumulī, m. .... tomb
rē vērā .... indeed
fortasse, adv. .... perhaps
clam, adv. .... secretly
exercitus, exercitūs, m. .... army
diēs, diēī, m. .... day
novus, a, um .... new
accidō, accidere, accīdī .... to happen
cōnsulātus, cōnsulātūs, m. .... consulship
concordia, ae, f. .... friendship, accord
sē, acc. pronoun .... himself
cōnscrībō, cōnscrībere, cōnscrīpsī, cōnscrīptum ...... to enlist in the army
coniūrātī, coniūrātōrum, m. pl. .... conspirators
genus, generis, n. .... class
praetor, praetōris, m. .... praetor (official)
mēnsis, mēnsis, m. .... month
competītor, competītōris, m. .... rival candidate
caedet .... will murder
obtineō, obtinēre, obtinuī, obtentum .... to gain, win; to possess
Īdūs .... Ides (date on the Roman Calendar)
domus, domūs, f. .... home
pulsō, āre, āvī, ātum .... to strike, beat
custōs, custōdis, m. .... guard
nōminō, āre, āvī, ātum .... to name, appoint
Nonās .... Nones (date on the Roman Calendar)
quī, nominative .... who
circā, prep. + acc. .... around, about
septentriōnēs .... north

Respondē Latīnē!

 1. Quis omnēs factiōnēs coniungere temptābat?

2. Quī Catilīnam amāvērunt?

3. Quandō cōnsulem necābit Catilīna?

4. Quī erant praetōrēs?

5. Quis cum Cleopatrā mortuus est (died)?

ANSWER IN ENGLISH!

1. What adjective in the story is connected to the name of the Roman goddess of love and beauty?

2. What desire of Catiline's would especially endear him to the common people but not to the aristocracy?

3. What happened in October?

4. Who claimed that he was the father of his country?

Derivative Detective

MONTHS OF THE YEAR [c]

[c]There is an additional lesson on the history of the Roman Calendar (and how it has affected our own) in an appendix to this text. This lesson is accompanied by a Roman Calendar project.

You should have noticed several familiar words in the chapter reading—particularly the names of a few months (i.e., Octōbrēs, Novembrēs, and Decembrēs). Our modern calendar still uses the same names for the months as did the ancient Roman calendar. Some of these months are named for Roman deities, others for their sequence in the original calendar attributed to Rōmulus. The first Roman calendar had only ten months and a "winter gap." You may recall from chapter seven that King Numa Pompilius created a twelve-month calendar, dividing this gap into two months (Iānuārius and Februārius). See if you can discern the origins for the twelve months.

ROMAN MONTH	LATIN ORIGIN	MODERN MONTH
Iānuārius		January
Februārius	Purification festival	
Mārtius		
Āprīlis	goddess Aphrilis (Aphrodite, goddess of love)	
Māius		
Iūnius		
Iūlius (originally Quīnctīlis)		
Augustus (originally Sextīlis)		
September		
Octōber		
November		
December		

Culture Corner

The Roman calendar had three hinge days. This first hinge day of the month was the Kalends (*Kalendae*), always the first day of the month. The other hinge days were the Nones (*Nōnae*) and the Ides (*Īdūs*). The Nones were on the fifth of the month except in March, May, July, and October. In those months, the Nones were on the seventh day of the month. The Ides were on the thirteenth of the month except in March, May, July, and October, when they were on the fifteenth. (Those were the four original thirty-one-day-long months.) The Nones are called that because they were nine days before the Ides. The word *Īdūs* (Ides) is from the same root as *divide*: the Ides divided the month roughly in two.

The Romans dated everything in the month as either on or before one of the hinge days. When the date was on an actual hinge day, the Romans used the ablative case to name the date; e.g., December 1 would be stated *Kalendīs Decembribus*. All other days were so many days before the next hinge day, and the Romans used the accusative to specify those dates; e.g., December 2 would be *ante diem iv Nōnās Decembrēs* (four days before the Nones of December). December 6 would be *ante diem viii Īdūs Decembrēs* (eight days before the Ides of December). Notice that the Romans counted both the actual day and the hinge day when naming the day. The day before a hinge date was in the accusative with *prīdiē*. December 31 would be *prīdiē Kalendās Iānuāriās*.

In naming the dates, *ante diem*, though two words, counts as one preposition governing the accusative. Notice that the name of the month becomes an adjective (feminine plural) to agree with the name of the hinge day. *Prīdiē* is also considered a preposition. When the date is a hinge day, the Romans used the ablative of time with the name of the month as an adjective to modify the name of the hinge day. There was never "two days" before the hinge date, only "the day before."

Calendar Calculations

Give the dates below in the way a Roman would have given them. Remember to be extra careful with March, May, July, and October.

September 15
October 4
December 25
May 1
July 4
April 3
March 15
July 31

Chapter 23 Teacher's Pages

Exercise 1

hō-ra, hō-rae, f.
mēn-sis, mēn-sis, f.
mors, mor-tis, f.
pe-cū-ni-a, ae, f.
pre-ti-um, ī, n.
co-ni-un-gō, co-ni-un-ge-re,
  co-ni-un-xī, co-ni-unc-tum
ob-ti-ne-ō, ob-ti-nē-re,
  ob-ti-nu-ī, ob-ten-tum
pe-re-ō, pe-rī-re, pe-ri-ī, pe-ri-tum
stō, stā-re, ste-tī, sta-tum

vēn-dō, vēn-de-re, vēn-di-dī, vēn-di-tum
ver-tō, ver-te-re, ver-tī, ver-sum
al-tus, a, um
mīl-le (pl. mīlia)
mi-ni-mus, a, um
pau-cī, pau-cae, pau-ca, pl.
pau-per, pau-pe-ris
plūrimus, a, um
pro-xi-mus, a, um
vī-le

Exercise 2

1. <u>One of the men</u> was plotting a conspiracy.   ūnus ē virīs

2. <u>The first of Cicero's orations</u> was concerning a murder. prīmus ōrātiōnium Cicerōnis

3. <u>Another oration of Cicero</u> was against Catiline. alia ōrātiō Cicerōnis

4. <u>A few of the Romans</u> did not love him. paucī ē Rōmānīs

5. Cicero had <u>four orations against that man</u>. quattuor ōrātiōnēs contrā virum illum/istum

Exercise 3

1. Hī hominēs <u>flōrēs magnō pretiō</u> emēbant. they were buying flowers for a great price

2. Achillēs corpus Hectorēum <u>aurō</u> vēndēbat. he was selling for gold

3. Catilīna fāmam obtinuit <u>nōn parvō pretiō</u>. for not a small price (i.e. for a great price)

4. Librum <u>ūnō dēnāriō</u>* puella ēmit. for one denarius

5. The maid servant bought some fruit <u>for seven sesterces</u>. septem sesterciīs

6. The merchant sells fine meat <u>for a great price</u>. magnō pretiō

7. <u>For a small amount</u> what will you sell to me? parvō pretiō

8. I will pay six dollars <u>for two of those dolls</u>. duābus ē pūpīs illīs

Exercise 4

[1]<u>In the second year</u> of Catiline's life, Cicero was born. [3]<u>Within seven years</u> Catiline and Cicero were in school together. They went to school together [2]<u>for three years</u>. [2]<u>For many years</u> these boys may have been friends. [3]<u>Within a short time</u> after they were grown, however, they became enemies. Cicero gained the consulship twice, but Catiline never could reach that lofty position. Therefore, he began a conspiracy to gain the elusive office. Catiline's ambition alarmed Cicero. [3]<u>Within a month</u> Cicero made several speeches against Catiline. Cicero spoke [2]<u>for two hours</u> each time. Catiline would stay to listen [2]<u>for only one hour</u>. [3]<u>Within a few days</u> Catiline and his army fled north. Cicero, though, stayed in Rome and continued to decry Catiline [2]<u>for many months</u>.

   1 = time when (abl.)
   2 = duration of time (acc.)
   3 = time within which (abl.)

Exercise 5

```
        SV      Adj        DO   P   OP      Adj      AcT
1. Posuērunt  hōs    flōrēs  in  templō  multōs  annōs.
   3/p/perf  ac/p/m  ac/p/m     abl/s/n  ac/p/m  ac/p/m
   They placed these flowers in the temple for many years.
```

```
   Adj      S    LV    Adj     AcSp   Adj
2. Illa    arbor  est  trīgintā  pedēs  alta.
   n/s/f   n/s/f  3/s/p          ac/p/m  n/f/s
   That tree is thirty feet high/tall.
```

```
     Adj      AbT    Adj   S     DO       Adj         V
3. Proximō  annō   illī  virī  officium  magnum  dēsīderāvērunt.
   ab/s/m   ab/s/m  n/p/m  n/p/m  ac/s/n   ac/s/n      3/p/perf
   The next year those men desired great office.
```

```
     AcT         S  HV  V   P   OP
4. In three hours we  will  return to school.
   Tribus  horīs  revertēmus  ad  lūdum.
   ab/p/f  ab/p/f   1/p/f       ac/s/m
```

```
     Adj  S   PG       LV   Adj     AcSp
5. This part of the sea is one hundred feet deep.
   Haec  pars  maris  est  centum  pedēs  alta.
   n/s/f  n/s/f  g/s/n  3/s/p        ac/p/m  ac/s/f
```

```
        S      V        AcT
6. The soldiers walked for many hours.
   Mīlitēs  ambulāvērunt  multās  horās.
   n/p/m     3/p/perf     ac/p/f  ac/p/f
```

Translation

There were many political parties in Rome. One of the Romans, Lucius Sergius Catilina, tried to unite all these factions. This Catiline was an aristocrat but a poor man. He was also very handsome and charming. A few of the Romans did not like this Catiline. Some gossiped about him. They said, "That Catiline killed his own son." The Populares [party of the common people], however, loved Catiline. After the death of Catiline, these Populares bought flowers at a great price and placed them on his tomb. They placed these flowers on his tomb for many years. Catiline wanted to help the common people and indeed the total population of Rome. He wanted new tablets [i.e., he wanted all debts canceled]. Perhaps even Gaius Julius Caesar secretly supported this Catiline for a time.

But Cicero and other Romans did not want new tablets. Cicero said, "Catiline has many men in his army. Catiline and his army will kill the consul on the first day of the new year." But nothing happened. In the next year, both Cicero and Catiline wanted the consulship. The Romans elected Cicero, not Catiline, consul. There was concord of the orders. And Cicero was the voice of the concord.

Then Catiline, so they say/as the report is, turned himself to war. Some were joining with Catiline; they drafted in Tuscany an army of about twenty thousand men. There were conspirators in Rome. Among the conspirators were men of all kinds: slaves; senators; even two praetors, Lentulus and Cathegus. In the month of October, Catiline again sought the consulship. Some said, "Catiline will kill Cicero and his opponent." Cicero believed the rumor. The common people supported Catiline, but he/ that man did not win the consulship.

Then Cicero said, "On November 7, conspirators came to my house. They knocked on the door. My guards drove the conspirators away." On the next day Cicero delivered the first oration against Catiline. Cicero called himself the father of his country. In all, Cicero delivered four speeches against Catiline. On December 3 Cicero arrested Lentulus and Cathegus. Around December 5 the praetors were executed.

Mark Antony, the father of Mark Antony who was a friend of Caesar and who died with Cleopatra, was consul with Cicero. He went north with his soldiers. Marcus and (his) soldiers attacked Catiline's camp. They wanted to bribe the soldiers to desert [Catiline and the camp], but all the men in the camp remained faithful to Catiline. Nobody left the camp! Catiline and all the men who were with Catiline died.

Respondē Latīnē!

1. Quis omnēs factiōnēs coniungere temptābat?
[Lūcius Sergius] Catilīna omnēs factiōnēs coniungere temptābat.

Who was trying to join together all the factions/parties?
Catoline [or Lucius Sergius Catolina] was trying to join together all the factions

2. Quī Catilīnam amāvērunt?
Populārēs Catilīnam amāvērunt.

Who loved Cataline?
The Populares [party of the people] loved Catoline.

3. Quandō cōnsulem necābit Catilīna?
Cōnsulem necābit prīmō diē novī annī.

When will Cataline kill the consul?
He will kill the consul on the first day of the new year.

4. Quī erant praetōrēs?
Lentulus et Cethegus erant praetōrēs.

Who were the praetors?
Lentulus and Cethegus were praetors.

5. Quis cum Cleopatrā mortuus est (died)?
Mārcus Antōnius cum Cleopatrā periit.

Who was with Cleopatra when she died?
Mark Antony died with Cleopatra.

ANSWER IN ENGLISH!

1. What adjective in the story is connected to the name of the Roman goddess of love and beauty?
venustus

2. What desire of Catiline's would especially endear him to the common people but not to the aristocracy?
his desire to cancel all debts

3. What happened in October?
Catiline sought the consulship.

4. Who claimed that he was the father of his country?
Cicero

Derivative Detective

ROMAN MONTH	LATIN ORIGIN	MODERN MONTH
Iānuārius	god Ianus	January
Februārius	Purification festival	February
Mārtius	Mars, Roman god of war and legendary father of Romulus	March
Aprīlis	goddess Aphrilis (Aphrodite, goddess of love)	April
Māius	Maia, mother of Mercury star in constellation Pleiades	May
Iūnius	goddess Juno , queen of gods, goddess of marriage	June
Iūlius (originally Quīnctīlis)	Julius Caesar (fifth)	July
Augustus (originally Sextīlis)	Augustus Caesar (sixth)	August
September	Seventh	September

October	Eighth	October
November	Ninth	November
December	Tenth	December

Calendar Calculations

September 15	ante diem xvii Kalendās Octōbrēs (seventeen days before the Kalends of October)
October 4	ante diem iv Nōnās Octōbrēs (four days before the Nones of October)
December 25	ante diem viii Kalendās Iānuāriās (eight days before the Kalends of January)
May 1	Kalendīs Māiīs (the Kalends of May)
July 4	ante diem iv Nōnās Iūliās (four days before the Nones of July)
April 3	ante diem iii Aprīlēs (three days before the Nones of April)
March 15	Īdibus Martiīs (the Ides of March)
July 31	prīdiē Kalendās Augustās (the day before the Kalends of August)

Notes

Labor omnia vincit.
Work conquers all.
—Oklahoma state motto[A]

This phrase is an adaptation from Vergil's *Georgics*, Book I, Line 145.

Chapter 24

- reflexive pronouns
  - *mē, tē, sē*
- reflexive possessive adjectives
  - *meus, tuus, suus*

[A]This great seal features one large star representing the state of Oklahoma and the five Civilized Indian Nations that called her home. In the top point a warrior with his bow and shield represents the Chickasaw Nation. To the right a warrior representing the Choctaw Nation holds a bow, three arrows, and a tomahawk. The lower right point depicts a warrior in a canoe who represents the Seminoles. The lower left portrays a member of the Creek Nation holding a sheaf of wheat and a plow. The final point contains the seal of the Cherokee Nation, a seven-pointed star surrounded by a wreath of oak leaves. In the center a Native shakes hands with a white man. An olive branch surrounds the two men, symbolizing the intertwining of cultures and the hope for peace. Above them appears the Latin motto. The 45 smaller stars represent the states that preceded Oklahoma.

VOCABULARY

NOUNS		
factiō, factiōnis, f.	political party, faction	(faction)
inimīcus, inimīcī, m.	personal enemy	(enmity)
iūs, iūris, n.	law	(jurisprudence)
ōs, ōris, n.	mouth	(oral)
praemium, ī, n.	reward; booty, loot	(premium)
vigil, vigilis, m.	watchman; (m.pl.) a fire brigade, firemen	(vigilant)
VERBS		
exstinguō, exstinguere, exstīnxī, exstīnctum	to put out, extinguish	(extinct)
interficiō, interficere, interfēcī, interfectum	to kill	
postulō, āre, āvī, ātum	to demand	(postulate)
reflectō, reflectere, reflexī, reflexum	to bend back	(reflect)
ADJECTIVES		
dīves, dīvitis	rich	(dives)
meus, a, um	my, mine	
mītis, mīte	gentle	
noster, a, um	our	
senior, seniōris	older, elder	(seniority)
suus, a, um	his, her, its, their	(suicide)
tuus, a, um	your, yours	
vester, a, um	your (plural)	

Exercise 1. Using the rules for syllabication and accent that you have learned, write out the syllables and accents for the vocabulary words above. Then practice pronouncing them aloud.

SECTION 65. Reflexive Pronouns

In chapter 19 we introduced personal pronouns (Sections 51 and 52). These refer to a person or thing from the speaker's point of view, a person or thing that is different from the speaker or the subject. **Reflexive pronouns** (from the Latin *reflectere*, to bend back) always direct the reader to the subject. Read over the following examples and determine how English differentiates between personal and reflexive pronouns.

Personal Pronoun	Reflexive Pronoun
You love *me*.	I love *myself*.
The teacher teaches *us*.	We teach *ourselves*.
She baked cookies *for her* (a friend).	She baked cookies *for herself*.

Not only does English add the suffix -*self*, but it also often changes the spelling of the pronoun: *me = my; us = our*. Latin is much simpler, particularly when it comes to the first and second person. Study the reflexive pronouns below. What does this chart remind you of?

SINGULAR

CASE	1ST PERSON	2ND PERSON	3RD PERSON
Gen.	meī	tuī	suī
Dat.	mihi	tibi	sibi
Acc.	mē	tē	sē
Abl.	mē	tē	sē

PLURAL

CASE	1ST PERSON	2ND PERSON	3RD PERSON
Gen.	nostrī	vestrī	suī
Dat.	nōbīs	vōbīs	sibi
Acc.	nōs	vōs	sē*
Abl.	nōbīs	vōbīs	sē*

*sēsē sometimes appears instead for emphasis, but the meaning remains the same.

This chart should remind you of the chart you studied for personal pronouns in chapter 19 (Section 51). Latin uses the same forms for first and second person reflexive pronouns as it does for personal pronouns. The only difference is the absence of the nominative case. Since reflexive pronouns are always directing attention towards the subject, they never serve as the subject of the sentence. Therefore, the nominative case is not needed.

As for the third person, it is necessary for Latin to use a different pronoun here in order to distinguish from other places where the subject is speaking about itself or using a personal pronoun to speak about someone else. You may also have noticed that the forms for both the singular and plural forms for the third person are the same, and that these pronouns do not have genders. You will need to depend on the context of the sentence to know the best way to translate the third person. This is usually easy to do, however, since the subject will be there to guide you.

Marcus sees *him*. .... Marcus videt *eum*.
Marcus sees *himself*. .... Marcus videt *sē*.
Julia sees *her*. .... Jūlia videt *eam*.
Julia sees *herself*. .... Jūlia videt *sē*.
They see *them*. .... Vident *eōs*.
They see *themselves*. .... Vident *sē*.

Exercise 2. Determine whether each of the following sentences is using a personal pronoun or a reflexive pronoun. Translate the pronouns only.

Example: Portia saw <u>herself.</u>   herself: reflexive, sē

1. You love to learn about the Romans.
2. I am writing a book.
3. Don't kid yourself!
4. Father saw them in the street.
5. Marcus and Cornelia looked at themselves.
6. Livia did not look at him.
7. As soon as Sextus saw those girls, <u>he</u> liked them.

SECTION 66. Possessive Adjectives

Remember way back in chapter 19 when we warned that the genitive case of the first and second personal pronouns could *not* ever show possession (Section 51)? The reason for this is that there is a special reflexive possessive adjective for just that very purpose. The good news is that these are the familiar first and second declension adjectives. You do not need to use the genitive at all in this case. Just simply have the possessive adjectives agree with the object of possession in case, number, and gender.

meus, mea, meum= my, mine
tuus, tua, tuum= your, yours
*suus, sua, suum= his own, her own, its own; their
noster, nostra, nostrum= our
vester, vestra, vestrum= your (plural)

Meus pater est altus................................ My father is tall.
Tuus pater est fortis................................ Your father is strong.
Mārcus suum patrem amāvit. .... Marcus loved his own father.
Mea māter est pulchra............................ My mother is beautiful.
Tua māter est bona. .... Your mother is good.
Is suam mātrem vīdit.............................. He saw his own mother.
Sacerdōs suum templum intrābit. .... The priest will enter his own temple.

*Use *suus* when the subject is showing the possession. Use *ēius* (Section 52) when the one possessing is someone other than the subject.

This is **his** (someone else's) horse. .... Hic est **ēius** equus.
This is **his own** horse. .... Hic est **suus** equus.

 Exercise 3. Translate the underlined phrases only. [B]

Example: I love <u>my mother</u>. meam mātrem

1. Marcus saw <u>his own horse</u>.
2. Portia told Marcia that she had seen <u>her flowers</u> in the garden.
3. This is <u>my reward</u>.
4. Where is <u>your house</u>?
5. The cook put food into <u>his own mouth</u>.

> [B]For additional practice ask students to compose their own Latin sentences using reflexive pronouns and possessive adjectives. Then, have the class translate the new sentences together.

Exercise 4. Parse, diagram, and translate the following sentences.

1. Nōbīs pecūniam suam dedit.

2. Tibi praemium obtinēbis.

3. Malī virī pecūniam nostram postulāvērunt.

4. Exstinguētisne vōs flammās in casā meā?

5. Pater ēius fuit clārus, nōn meus pater.

6. Multam pecūniam sibi dēsīderāvit habēre.

7. Multa aedificia et multās casās sibi obtinēbant.

8. Habēs tuōs amīcōs et familiam.

Chapter Reading

MARCUS LICINIUS CRASSUS

CHARACTERS:
M. Licinius Crassus – a very wealthy and ambitious man
Crassus senior – Crassus the Elder, Crassus' father
Sulla – Roman general, later a dictator

M. Licinius Crassus erat nōtus vir *maximīs* dīvitiīs. Pater ēius fuit <u>ōrātor</u> *clārus*, <u>cōnsul</u>, *cēnsor*. Pugnāvit Crassus senior prō Sullā, et sē interfēcit **nē ad Marium cēderet**. Sulla ipse, igitur, Crassō *iuniōrī* praemium dedit: Crassus ēmit *bona* inimīcōrum Sullae parvō pretiō. M. Licinius Crassus iuvenis litterīs et <u>philosophiae</u> studuit. Quoque iūrī studuit. Pecūniae tamen erat amor *maximus* Crassō.

Crassus multam pecūniam sibi dēsīderāvit habēre; is vir, igitur, vigilēs *īnstituit. Numquam anteā* in historiā Rōmae fuērunt vigilēs! Hī vigilēs ad *incendia* properāvērunt et praemia postulāvērunt. Sī hominēs praemia dare nōluērunt, vigilēs nōn temptābant flammās exstinguere. **Aliter** aedificia, *quae* in flammīs erant, parvō pretiō ēmērunt et *modo tum* flammās exstīnxērunt. Ita Crassus multa aedificia et multās casās sibi obtinēbat. Is deinde multam pecūniam obtinēbat ab **mercibus habitātiōnum**. Crassus dīxit, "Nūllus homō dīves est *quī* nōn *exercitum* suum *sustinēre* potest." *Quamquam* Crassus erat Rōmānus *dītissimus*, nōn laetus erat. Volēbat *magistrātus* esse.

Crassus erat vir mītis *benīgnusque*. Habēbat multōs amīcōs. Vīvēbat *simpliciter. Ambābus* factiōnibus pecūniam et *sapientiam* suam **dedit.** Hōc modō *ambitiōnem* suam *cōnfēcit*: AUC DCLXXXIV† -- Spartacum iam *vīcerat*—Rōmānī eum <u>cōnsulem</u> creāvērunt et iterum AUC DCXCIX‡. Erat quoque *gubernātor* Syriae. Iūvit cōnscrībere *exercitum* **in** *Parthiam*. Hostis eum superāvit *Carrhae* et eum interfēcit. Crassō dīxērunt, "Tū aurum *ēsuris*; nunc tuum aurum *ede!*" *Aliquī* hostium caput Crassī *praecīdērunt* et **aurum liquefactum** in ōs *fūdērunt.*

---

nē ad Marium cēderet = so that he would not [have to] yield to Marius
aliter = in another way, alternatively
mercibus habitātiōnum = rent, rent paid for a dwelling
dedit = lent
in = against
aurum liquefactum = molten gold

†70 BC
‡55 BC

GLOSSARY

Use your "eye" Latin to discern the meaning of the underlined words.

maximīs dīvitiīs .... of greatest wealth (ablative of respect)
clārus, clāra, clārum, adj. .... clear, bright, famous
cēnsor, cēnsōris, m. .... censor (Roman office)
iūnior, iūniōris, adj. .... junior, younger
bona, bonōrum, n. pl. .... goods, property
īnstituō, īnstituere, īnstituī, īnstitūtum .... to set up, establish
numquam .... never
anteā .... before
incendium, incendiī, n. .... fire
properō, āre, āvī, ātum .... to hurry, hasten
quae, n. pl. .... which
modo tum .... only then
quī, nom. .... who
exercitus, exercitūs, m. .... army
sustineō, sustinēre, sustinuī, sustentum .... to hold up, support
quamquam, adv. .... although
dītissimus, superlative adj. .... richest
magistrātus, magistrātūs, m. .... magistrate, public official
benīgnus, benīgna, benīgnum, adj. .... kind
simpliciter, adv. .... simply
ambō, ambae, ambō, adj. .... both
sapientia, ae, f. .... wisdom
ambitiō, ambitiōnis, f. .... ambition
cōnficiō, cōnficere, cōnfēcī, cōnfectum .... to complete, accomplish
vīcerat .... he had defeated
gubernātor, gubernātōris, m. .... governor
Parthia, ae, f. .... Parthia
Carrhae .... at Carrhae (town in Parthia)
ēsuriō, ēsurīre, ēsurītum .... to hunger for
edō, edere, ēdī, ēsum .... to eat
aliquī, aliqua, aliquod, adj. .... some
praecīdō, praecīdere, praecīdī, praecīsum .... cut off
fundō, fundere, fūdī, fūsum .... to pour

Respondē Latīnē!

 1. Cūr pater Crassī sē interfēcit?

2. Quibus studēbat Crassus iuvenis?

3. Quis prīmus vigilēs Rōmae īnstituit?

4. Quālis vir erat Crassus?

5. Cūius prōvinciae erat Crassus gubernātor?

ANSWER IN ENGLISH!
1. What was the greatest love of Crassus from his young manhood onward?
2. What innovation did Crassus institute at Rome?
3. What was Crassus' opinion of what characterized a truly rich man?
4. Whom had Crassus defeated before he became consul for the first time?
5. What happened to Crassus at Carrhae?

Culture Corner

ROMAN MONEY

The Romans did not use paper money as we do today. Instead, they used a series of coins made from a variety of metals.

as – This was the base unit for the money scale, much like our penny or one-cent piece. Originally it was made from a pound of copper *(aes)*. Over time the size diminished to 1/24 of a pound.

> sēstertius = 2.5 asses, made of silver *(argentum)*
> quīnārius = 5 asses, made of silver
> dēnārius = 10 asses, made of silver
> aureus = 25 denarii, made of gold *(aurum)*

The *sēstertius* (translated sesterces), also called the *nummus*, was used in calculating sums of money. When discussing amounts of money in units of ones, tens, and hundreds you may simply use the appropriate cardinal.

> quīnque sēstertiī = 5 sesterces
> decem sēstertiī = 10 sesterces
> trecentī sēstertiī = 300 sesterces

When discussing amounts in units of thousands, use the partitive genitive or the word *sēstertia*.

> duo mīlia sēstertium or duo sēstertia = 2,000 sesterces

When discussing amounts over one million sesterces, use the genitive plural for *sēstertium* (understood here to mean 100,000) with the numerical adverb.

> deciēs sēstertium = 1,000,000 (10 x 100,000) sesterces
> vīciēs sēstertium = 2,000,000 (20 x 100,000) sesterces.

Colloquāmur

Now that you have learned the basic units of Roman coins and how to express their amounts, set up a Roman shop in your class and practice bargaining with your local vendor. Here are a few phrases to get you started.

Quid est (genitive noun) **pretium?** ....What is the price of _____?
Tibi vēndam (ablative amount). ....I will sell it to you for _____.

Est cāra!..That is expensive!
Est vīlis!..That is cheap!
Est pactum!...It's a deal!

Chapter 24 Teacher's Pages

Exercise 1

fac-ti-ō, fac-ti-ōn-is, f.

i-ni-mī-cus, i-ni-mī-cī, m.
iūs, iū-ris, n.
ōs, ō-ris, n.
prae-mi-um, ī, n.
vi-gil, vi-gi-lis, m.
ex-stin-gu-ō, ex-stin-gu-e-re, ex-stīn-xī, ex-stin-ctum
in-ter-fi-ci-ō, in-ter-fi-ce-re, in-ter-fē-cī, in-ter-fec-tum

pos-tul-ō, pos-tu-lā-re,
   pos-tu-lā-vī, pos-tu-lā-tum
re-flec-tō, re-flec-te-re, refle-xī, re-flex-um
dī-ves, dī-vi-tis
me-us, a, um
mī-tis, mī-tis
sē-ni-or, se-ni-ō-ris
su-us, a, um
tu-us, a, um

Exercise 2

1. You love to learn about the Romans.   you: personal, tū, vōs

2. I am writing a book.   I: personal, ego

3. Don't kid yourself!   yourself: reflexive, tē

4. Father saw them in the street.   them: personal, eōs, eās, ea

5. Marcus and Cornelia looked at themselves.   themselves: reflexive, sē, sēsē

6. Livia did not look at him.   him: personal, eum

7. As soon as Sextus saw those girls, he liked them.   he: personal, is; them: personal, eās

Exercise 3

1. Marcus saw his own horse.   suum equum

2. Portia told Marcia that she had seen her flowers in the garden.   ēius flōrēs

3. This is my reward.   meum praemium

4. Where is your house?   tua casa

5. The cook put food into his own mouth.   suum ōs

Exercise 4

```
   IO    DO    Adj    V
1. Nōbīs pecūniam suam    dedit.
   d/p    ac/s/f  ac/s/f  3/s/per
   He gave his own money to us.

   DR    DO       V
2. Tibi praemium obtinēbis.
   d/s   ac/s/n    2/s/f
   You will obtain the reward for yourself.

   Adj    S    DO        Adj       V
3. Malī   virī pecūniam nostram   postulāvērunt.
   n/p/m  n/p/m ac/s/f   ac/s/f    3/p/perf
   Bad men demanded our money.
```

a

```
             V        S     DO   P   OP    Adj
4. Exstinguētisne vōs flammās in casā   meā?
      2/p/f      n/p  ac/p/f    ab/s/f ab/s/f
   Will you put out the flames on my house?

       S    PNA    LV    PrN  Adv  Adj   PrN
5. Pater  ēius   fuit  clārus, nōn  meus  pater.
   n/s/m  g/s/m 3/s/pf  n/s/m       n/s/m n/s/m
   His father was famous, not my father.

        Adj     DO    DR     V      Inf
6. Multam pecūniam sibi dēsīderāvit habēre.
    ac/s/f  ac/s/f  d/s  3/s/perf
   He desired to have much money for himself.

        Adj     DO   C  Adj   DO   DR     V
7. Multa aedificia et multās casās  sibi  obtinēbant.
   ac/p/n  ac/p/n    ac/p/f ac/p/f d/p  3/p/i
   They were obtaining many buildings and many houses for themselves.

      S+V   Adj      DO   C   DO
8. Habēs  tuōs    amīcōs et  familiam.
   2/s/pr ac/p/m  ac/p/m      ac/s/f
   You have your friends and family.
```

Translation

Marcus Licinius Crassus was a man noted for very great riches. His father was a famous orator, consul, [and] censor. The older Crassus fought for Sulla, and committed suicide rather than yield to Marius. Sulla himself, therefore, gave a reward to the younger Crassus. Crassus bought the goods of the enemies of Sulla for a small price. Marcus Licinius Crassus as a young man studied literature and philosophy. He also studied law. Money, however, was the greatest love of Crassus.

Crassus desired to have much money for himself; that man, therefore, established fire brigades/groups of firemen. Never before in the history of Rome were there/have there been fire-fighting companies! These firemen rushed to fires and demanded rewards [for putting out the fires]. If the people did not wish to give rewards/pay, the firemen did not try to extinguish the flames. Alternatively, they bought the buildings that were in flames for a small price and only then extinguished the flames. Thus Crassus obtained many buildings and many houses for himself. He then obtained much money from the rents. Crassus said, "No man is rich who cannot sustain his own army." Although Crassus was the richest Roman, he was not happy. He wanted to be an elected official.

Crassus was a gentle and kind man. He had many friends. He lived simply. He gave his money and his wisdom to both factions. In this way he fulfilled his ambition. In 70 BC—he had already defeated Spartacus – the Romans elected him consul again in 55 BC. He was also the governor of Syria. He helped to recruit an army against Parthia. The enemy overcame him at Charrae and killed him. They said to Crassus, "You are hungry for gold; now eat your gold." Some of the enemy cut off his head, and they poured molten gold into his mouth.

Respondē Latīnē!

1. Cūr pater Crassī sē interfēcit?
   Sē interfēcit nē ad Marium cēderet.

   Why did Crassus' father kill himself?
   He killed himself so as not to yield to Marius.

2. Quibus studēbat Crassus iuvenis?
   Crassus iuvenis litterīs et philosophiae studēbat.

   What was the young Crassus studying?
   The young Crassus was studying literature and philosophy.

3. Quis prīmus vigilēs Rōmae īnstituit?
   Crassus vigilēs īnstituit.

   Who established the first fire brigade for Rome?
   Crassus established the fire brigade.

4. Quālis vir erat Crassus?   What kind of man was
   Crassus?
   Crassus erat vir mītis benīgnusque.   Crassus was a gentle and
   kind man.
   Crassus dīves erat et pecūniam amāvit.   Crassus loved riches and
   money.

5. Cūius prōvinciae erat Crassus gubernātor?   Crassus was governor of
   which province?
   Erat gubernātor Syriae.   He was governor of Syria.

ANSWER IN ENGLISH!

1. What was the greatest love of Crassus from his young manhood onward?
   Money

2. What innovation did Crassus institute at Rome?
   Fire Brigade

3. What was Crassus' opinion of what characterized a truly rich man?
   No man is rich who cannot sustain his own army.

4. Whom had Crassus defeated before he became consul for the first time?
   Spartacus

5. What happened to Crassus at Carrhae?
   The Parthians killed him (cut off his head) and then poured liquid gold
   down his throat.

Notes

_____

_____

_____

_____

_____

_____

_____

_____

_____

_____

_____

_____

Notes

AThe center of the seal is a shield rich with symbols of Oregon. Two ships appear near the Oregon shore. The first, a British man-of-war, sails away as a symbol of an end to British influence in the region. The second, an American merchant ship, sails toward the shore as a symbol of American independence and strong commerce. On the right stand the beautiful trees of Oregon's forests with the mountains behind them. In the center are oxen and a wagon, reminiscent of the first settlers and the old Oregon Trail. The elk, pick ax, wheat and plow all represent the various resources of the land. Beneath the crest are 33 stars representing the number of states in 1859. Over all this an American eagle stretches her wings.

Ālīs volat prōpriīs.
She flies with her own wings.
—Oregon state mottoA

The official state seal no longer bears the Latin motto. However, the Oregon Territorial Seal of 1854 does. Judge Jesse Quintin Thornton composed the state motto "She Flies With Her Own Wings" in English. The Territorial Legislature translated the motto into Latin later for the state seal. In 1957, the motto was changed to "The Union." In 1987, however, the motto was again changed to the English translation of the first motto, "She Flies with Her Own Wings."

Teachers: You may wish to assign students the task of tracking down the territorial seal and comparing it to the state seal.

Chapter 25

- relative pronouns
- interrogative pronouns

VOCABULARY

VERBS

agnōscō, agnōscere, agnōvī, agnitum	to know, understand, identify	
antecēdō, antecēdere, antecessī, antecessum	to precede, to surpass	(antecedent)
referō, referre, rettulī, relātum	to bring back, carry back; report	(relate, relative)

PRONOUNS

aliquis, aliquidB	somebody, something	BThis pronoun will decline like *quis, quid* in the following lesson.
quī, quae, quod, rel. pron.	who, which	
quis, quid, interrog. pron.	who, what	

ADJECTIVES

plēnus, a, um	full	(plenty)
ultimus, a, um	last	(ultimatum)

CONJUNCTION

postquam	after	

ADVERBS

umquam	ever, at any time	
tam	so	

Exercise 1. Using the rules for syllabication and accent that you have learned, write out the syllables and accents for the vocabulary words above. Then practice pronouncing them aloud.

Section 67. Relative Pronouns

The relative pronouns (from the Latin *referre, rettulī, relātum* to carry back) in English are *who, which,* and *that.* These pronouns introduce a subordinate clause that tells more about a previous noun in the main clause known as the antecedent (from the Latin *antecēdere,* to precede). A relative pronoun *must* have an antecedent. The antecedent must come before or precede the relative pronoun just as the Latin verb *antecēdere* implies. Can you identify the relative pronoun and its antecedent in the following sentence?

Spartacus was a gladiator who led many slaves in a revolt against Rome.

The relative pronoun is "who." This pronoun refers to the gladiator. The antecedent, therefore, is "gladiator." Try another one.

Spartacus fought against the Roman army that was led by Crassus.

The relative pronoun in this sentence is "that." The antecedent is "army."

Exercise 2. Make a list of the relative pronouns and their antecedents, which appear in the famous Gettysburg Address. (Some words have been italicized for the Derivative Detective segment at the end of this chapter.)

Hint: Remember that a relative pronoun MUST refer to an antecedent. If you cannot find the antecedent, then it is another kind of pronoun.

President Lincoln delivered the Gettysburg Address on November 19, 1863 on the battlefield near Gettysburg, Pennsylvania.

"*Four* score and *seven* years ago our fathers brought forth, on this *continent,* a new *nation, conceived in liberty,* and *dedicated* to the *proposition* that all men are *created equal.* Now we are engaged in a great *civil* war, *testing* whether that *nation,* or any *nation* so *conceived,* and so *dedicated,* can *long endure.* We are met on a great battle-field of that war. We have come to *dedicate* a *portion* of that field, as a *final resting-place* for those who here gave their lives, that that *nation* might live. It is altogether fitting and *proper* that we should do this. But, in a *larger sense,* we cannot *dedicate,* we cannot *consecrate*—we cannot hallow—this ground. The brave men, living and dead, who struggled here, have consecrated it far above our *poor power* to *add* or *detract.* The world will little *note,* nor *long remember* what we say here, but it can never forget what they did here. It is for us the living, rather, to be *dedicated* here to the *unfinished* work which they who fought here have thus far so *nobly* advanced. It is rather for us to be here *dedicated* to the great task *remaining* before us—that from these honored dead we take *increased devotion* to that *cause* for which they here gave the last full *measure* of *devotion*—that we here highly *resolve* that these dead shall not have died in vain—that this *nation,* under God, shall have a new birth of freedom, and that *government* of the *people,* by the *people,* for the *people,* shall not *perish* from the earth."

What do you think would be the English form(s) for each of the following cases?

Nominative .... **Who**
Genitive .... whose
Dative .... to/for whom
Accusative .... whom
Ablative .... by/with/from whom

How do you know the antecedent for each relative pronoun? Does the number match? Does the case match?

The forms for Latin relative pronouns are a bit more numerous. Fortunately, many of the endings should look familiar.

189

Chapter 25

SINGULAR

Case	Masculine	Feminine	Neuter
Nominative	quī	quae	quod
Genitive	cūius	cūius	cūius
Dative	cui	cui	cui
Accusative	quem	quam	quod
Ablative	quō	quā	quō

PLURAL

Case	Masculine	Feminine	Neuter
Nominative	quī	quae	quae
Genitive	quōrum	quārum	quōrum
Dative	quibus	quibus	quibus
Accusative	quōs	quās	quae
Ablative	quibus	quibus	quibus

Notā Bene:
- The endings for the genitive and dative singular follow the pattern of *ille*.
- The ablative singular and most of the plural forms follow the pattern for first and second declension nouns.
- The dative and ablative plural are similar to third declension.
- The neuter nominative and accusative cases are the same—as always.

In Latin, relative pronouns serve the same purpose as they do in English. They introduce a relative clause while referring to an antecedent. Because these pronouns are referring to and in a sense describing a noun, they function similar to an adjective. You may recall that in Latin an adjective must agree with the noun it modifies in case, number, and gender. **A relative pronoun must also agree with its antecedent (the noun it refers to) in number and gender, but *not* in case.** Look back at the previous English paragraph. Did the relative pronouns always serve the same function as their antecedent? If the antecedent was a subject, was the relative pronoun also a subject? If the antecedent was showing possession, was the relative pronoun doing so as well? So also in Latin a relative pronoun will not always serve the same function as the antecedent to which it refers. Therefore, a relative pronoun may not have the same case as its antecedent.

Exercise 3. Circle the relative clause in each of the following sentences. Then identify the appropriate case, number, and gender for the relative pronoun. Translate the subordinate clause only.

> Example: Spartacus was a slave (who led an army against Rome.)
> *nominative, singular, masculine*
> *quī exercitum contrā Rōmam dūxit.*

1. It was Spartacus whom the Romans feared.

2. Crassus, who was a great general, went to fight the slaves.

3. The slaves, who were strong, did not fear Crassus.

4. Crassus saw the man with whom Spartacus was speaking.

5. Caesar, who stayed in the city, did not fight Spartacus and his slave band.

SECTION 68. Interrogative Pronouns

How do these interrogative pronouns differ from the relative ones you just learned?

SINGULAR

CASE	MASCULINE & FEMININE	NEUTER
Nominative	quis	quid
Genitive	cūius	cūius
Dative	cui	cui
Accusative	quem	quid
Ablative	quō	quō

PLURAL

CASE	MASCULINE	FEMININE	NEUTER
Nominative	quī	quae	quae
Genitive	quōrum	quārum	quōrum
Dative	quibus	quibus	quibus
Accusative	quōs	quās	quae
Ablative	quibus	quibus	quibus

Notā Bene:
- The singular forms combine the masculine and feminine genders.
- The nominative singular is the only form that differs from the relative pronoun.
- The plural forms are identical to the relative pronoun.
- The preposition *cum* also attaches itself as an enclitic (*quōcum*) with the ablative to mean "with whom."

As you can see, the interrogative pronouns are very similar to their relative counterparts. Indeed there is really only one case that is different. The main difference is in how these two pronouns are used. The relative pronoun introduces a relative clause. The interrogative pronoun (from the Latin *rogāre*, to ask) introduces a question. The interrogative pronouns in English are *who, whose, whom, which,* and *what.*

Exercise 4. Parse, diagram, and translate the following sentences.

1. Quī sunt illī hominēs in viā?

2. Quōrum librī sunt in mēnsā?

3. Quis erat vir in ātriō?

4. Cui flōrēs dedistī?

5. Quibuscum ambulābās?

6. Quae erant puellae tēcum?

7. Quārum pūpae sunt?

8. Quōcum dīxistis?

9. Quis est in casā cum familiā?

10. Quem vīdistī ad lūdōs?

SPARTACUS

CHARACTERS:

Lentulus Batiātus – Gladiator Trainer
Spartacus – Gladiator General
Marcus Licinius Crassus – Roman general
Pompeius – Roman general who assisted Crassus in this campaign

Erat *Capuae lanista* nōmine Lentulus Batiātus. Ūnus ē gladiātōribus Lentulī erat Spartacus, quī erat *Thrācius*. Aliquī dīcunt **Spartacum fuisse mīlitem quī exercitum relīquisset fuisse**. Spartacus *ūnā cum* multīs aliīs in lūdō Lentulī vītam gladiātōris nōn amābat, quod gladiātōrēs servī erant. Spartacus igitur gladiātōrēs Lentulī dūxit in *sēditiōnem*.

Annō LXXIII ante Chrīstum Spartacus et ducentī aliī gladiātōrēs ē lūdō Lentulī effugere temptābant. Spartacus et septuāgintā et octō erant fēlīcēs. Hī virī arma cēpērunt et ad montem Vesuvium īvērunt. Oppida prope Vesuvium oppugnābant et in hīs oppidīs cibum invēnērunt. Cibum ē cīvibus oppidōrum capiēbant. Multī dē Spartacō dīxērunt, "Spartacus erat vir magnā virtūte, magnō *spīritū*, magnā fortitūdine. Erat quoque mītis."

Hic vir tam mītis et tam fortis **hortātus est** omnēs servōs *Ītalōs* esse līberōs. Eōs servōs omnēs ad arma advocāvit. Mox septuāgintā mīlia hominum habēbat. Hī erant virī quī līberī esse volēbant. Servī sub Spartacō arma sua faciēbant. Discēbant pugnāre. Hī servī erant *fortissimī: plūrēs* annōs *nēmō* eōs superāre poterat. Dīvitēs Ītaliae *plēnī* timōris erant ob victōriās Spartacī servōrumque ēius. Servī Ītaliae ob **eandem causam** plēnī *speī* erant. Ūsque centum et vīgintī mīlia servōrum sē coniūnxērunt Spartacō, sed Spartacus eōs nōn accēpit quod nōn potuit eōs cūrāre aut eīs cibum prōvidēre. Spartacus et *exercitus* suus ad Alpēs iter fēcērunt. Voluit virōs suōs trānsīre Alpēs et **exauctōrāre et vītam līberam ibi agere.**

Virī, tamen, negāvērunt. Spartacō nōn iam pārēbant. Oppida prope Alpēs oppugnāre *incēpērunt*. Plūrēs *exercitūs* Rōmānī Spartacum et virōs oppugnābant. Spartacus *exercitum* Crassī superāvit. Tum ad urbem iter vertit. Quis superāre Spartacum potest? *Nēmō* Spartacum superāre posse *vidēbātur*. Mārcus Licīnius mīlitēsque tandem Spartacum et *exercitum* servōrum superāvērunt. Pompēius Crassum adiuvābat. Spartacus ipse **vulnerātus est** in ultimō proeliō bellī et **mortuus est pugnāns** in *genibus* suīs postquam duōs centuriōnēs interfēcit. Corpus Spartacī *nēmō* umquam potuit agnōscere, sed Crassus **multōs** in Viā Appiā **crucī adfīxit.**

Spartacum fuisse mīlitem quī exercitum relīquisset fuisse. = that Spartacus had been a soldier who had deserted
hortātus est = encouraged
eandem causam = the same cause
exauctōrāre et vītam līberam ibi agere. = to leave [the army] and live a free life
vulnerātus est = was wounded
mortuus est pugnāns = he died fighting
multōs . . . crucī adfīxit. = he crucified many

Crucifixion was a means of execution reserved for the worst criminals. The victims were either nailed or tied down to a wooden cross. The hanging weight of their body caused them to slowly suffocate in a very agonizing manner. The Romans invented this form of execution that was the means of Christ's death many years later.

GLOSSARY

Use your "eye" Latin to discern the meaning of the underlined words.

Capuae	at Capua
lanista, ae, m.	trainer of gladiators
Thrācius, a, um, adj.	Thracian, pertaining to Thrace
ūnā cum	along with
sēditiō, sēditiōnis, f.	insurrection, mutiny
spīritus, ūs, m.	spirit, courage
Ītalōs.	Italian
fortissimī, superlative adj.	very strong, strongest
plūs, plūris, adj.	more
nēmō	no one
plēnus, a, um, adj.	full
spēs, speī, f.	hope
ūsque, adv.	up to, all the way up to
exercitus, exercitūs, m.	army
incipiō, incipere, incēpī, inceptum	to begin
vidēbātur	seemed
genū, genūs, n.	knees

Culture Corner

SLAVERY IN ANCIENT ROME

The institution of slavery long predated the American slave trade and Civil War. Slavery was quite common in antiquity. Unlike the slavery that existed in America, however, the slavery of ancient Rome was not based on race. Romans made slaves of criminals or those they captured in war. In Homer's *Iliad*, we read the heated arguments between the Greek hero Achilles and the warrior king Agamemnon over the slave girl Briseis, a captive who was the wife of King Mynes II of Lyrnessus, ally of Troy. Achilles sacked Lyrnessus, killed the king, and took Briseis as a slave. In the Book of Philemon, the Apostle Paul wrote to his friend on behalf of a slave who had run away, but now sought forgiveness for wronging his master. In both antiquity and *antebellum* America, however, people who became slaves lost all their rights, even their status as human beings. Slaves were regarded as nothing more than their master's property, and any children they bore were considered the master's property as well. The master had the power of life and death over all of this property, animals and slaves included. Some masters were kind and took care of their slaves. Sadly, there were others who treated them brutally.

The Latin word for a slave in general terms is *servus.* There were, however, many different types of slaves. Some slaves such as the *ancilla* and the *famulus* served the family in the house. The Romans depended upon a slave called *paedagōgus,* often a well-educated Greek, to serve as a tutor for their children. Some *medicī,* doctors, were also slaves. If a slave served his master well for many years, the master would sometimes give the slave his freedom. This act was known as *manūmissiō* (manumission), which literally means having been sent *(mittō)* from the hand *(manus)* of the master. Some slaves were allowed to work and earn wages outside their master's domain. In either event the former slave was now a freedman called a *lībertus.* The freedman was now a recognized person with some

For Discussion

What other comparisons can you make between slavery in Rome and in America?

civil rights. A freedman, however, was not allowed the full rights of a Roman citizen. History records that some freedmen, such as Trimalchio, became successful enough to acquire wealth and their own slaves.

Derivative Detective: Decoding the Gettysburg Address

Take another look at the Gettysburg Address. Each of the words in italics is a Latin derivative. Use an English dictionary to help you learn the Latin origin for each of the words. Make a list of the English derivatives, their Latin origin, and the meaning for both words.

Colloquāmur: Create Your Own Conversation

This chapter is full of great question words. Create a series of questions using the interrogative pronouns in this chapter as well as other question words. Then converse with your *amīcō/amīcā*.

Chapter 25 Teacher's Pages

Exercise 1

ag-nō-scō, ag-nō-sce-re, ag-nō-vī, ag-ni-tum

an-te-cē-dō, an-te-cē-de-re, an-te-ces-sī, an-te-ces-sum

re-fe-rō, re-fer-re, ret-tu-lī, re-lā-tum

a-li-quis, a-li-quid

quī, quae, quod

quis, quid

plē-nus, a, um

ul-ti-mus, a, um

post-quam

um-quam

tam

Exercise 2

that	proposition [line 2, 7th word]
who	those (the ones that "here gave their lives") [line 5, 5th word]
who	men (the braves ones "living and dead") [line 7, 7th word]
which	work (the "unfinished work") [line 9, 5th from the end]
who	they (the ones that "fought here") [line 9, 3rd from the end]
for which	cause (the one "for which they here gave the last full measure of devotion") [line 11, 6th word from the end]

Exercise 3

1. It was Spartacus whom the Romans feared.
   acc, sing, masc   quem Rōmānī timuērunt.

2. Crassus, who was a great general, went to fight the slaves.
   nom, sing, masc   quī erat dux magnus

3. The slaves, who were strong, did not fear Crassus.
   nom, pl, masc   quī erant fortēs

4. Crassus saw the man with whom Spartacus was speaking.
   abl, sing, masc   quōcum* Spartacus dīcēbat.

5. Caesar, who stayed in the city, did not fight Spartacus and his slave band.
   nom, sing, masc   quī in urbe mānsit

*quōcum = cum quō (with whom)

The preposition *cum* appears as a suffix when the object of the preposition is a pronoun. See the *Notā Bene* in Ch. 19, Section 51.

Exercise 4

      S   LV   Adj   PrN   P OP
1. Quī   sunt   illī   hominēs in viā?
    n/p/m 3/p/pr n/p/m n/p/m   ab/s/f
    Who are those men in the road?

      PPA   S   LV   P OP
2. Quōrum librī   sunt in mēnsā?
    g/p/m n/p/m 3/p/pr   ab/s/f
    Whose books are on the table?

a

```
         S      LV   PrN   P  OP
 3. Quis  erat  vir  in  ātriō?
    n/s/m 3/s/i n/s/m   ab/s/n
    Who was the man in the atrium?
```

```
        IO    DO    S+V
 4. Cui flōrēs dedistī?
    d/s ac/p/m 2/s/perf
    To whom did you give the flowers?
```

```
       P+OP      S+V
 5. Quibuscum ambulābās?
      ab/p       2/s/i
    With whom were you walking?
    Quibuscum = cum quibus
```

```
       S     LV   PrN     P+OP
 6. Quae erant puellae tēcum?
    n/p/f 3/p/i n/p/f    ab/s
    Who were the girls with you?
```

```
       PPA     S    LV
 7. Quārum pūpae sunt?
    g/p/f  n/p/f 3/p/pr
    Whose dolls are they?
```

```
      P+OP      S+V
 8. Quōcum  dīxistis?
    ab/s/m  2/p/perf
    With whom did you speak?
```

```
       S   LV   P  OP   P   OP
 9. Quis est  in casā cum familiā?
    n/s 3/s/pr ab/s/f   ab/s/f
    Who is in the house with the family?
```

```
        DO      S+V    P   OP
10. Quem  vīdistī  ad  lūdōs?
    ac/s/m 2/s/perf    ac/p/m
    Whom did you see at the games?
```

Translation

There was at Capua a trainer of gladiators named/by the name [of] Lentulus Batiatus. One of the gladiators of Lentulus was Spartacus, who was a Thracian. Some say that Spartacus had been a soldier who had deserted. Spartacus, along with many others in the school of Lentulus, did not like the life of a gladiator because gladiators were slaves. Spartacus, therefore, led the gladiators of Lentulus into a rebellion.

In 73 BC, Spartacus and two hundred other gladiators from the school of Lentulus tried to escape. Spartacus and seventy eight [others] were lucky. These men seized arms and went to Mt. Vesuvius. They attacked the towns near Vesuvius and found food in these towns. They took food from the citizens of the towns. Many said about Spartacus, "Spartacus was a man of great courage, great spirit, [and] great strength. He was also gentle."

This man so gentle and so strong encouraged all the Italian slaves to be free. He called all these slaves to arms. Soon he had 70,000 men. These were men who wished to be free. The slaves under Spartacus made their own weapons. They learned to fight. These slaves were very strong: for several years, nobody was able to overcome them. The rich men of Italy were full of fear/filled with fear on account of the victories of Spartacus and his slaves. For the same reason, the slaves of Italy were full of/filled with hope. Up to 120,000 slaves joined themselves to Spartacus, but Spartacus did not accept them because he was not able to care for them or to provide food to them. Spartacus and his army marched/made a journey to the

Alps. He wanted his men to cross the Alps and to leave [the army] and have a free life.

The men, however, said no. They were not prepared to obey Spartacus. They began to attack towns near the Alps. Several Roman armies attacked Spartacus and his men. Spartacus overcame the army of Crassus. Then he turned his route to the city [Rome]. Who is able to overcome Spartacus? Nobody seemed to be able to overcome Spartacus. Marcus Licinius [Crassus] and [his] soldiers finally overcame Spartacus and [his] army of slaves. Pompey helped Crassus. Spartacus himself was wounded in the final battle of the war, and he died fighting on his knees after he killed two centurions. Nobody was ever able to recognize [i.e., identify] the body of Spartacus, but Crassus crucified many men on the Appian Way.

Derivative Detective

four: not technically a Latin derivative; from the Old English *feower* but akin to the Latin word *quattor* (four)

seven: not technically a Latin derivative; from the Old English *seofon* but akin to the Latin word *septem* (seven)

continent: a large contiguous landmass partially or completely surrounded by water, which is generally also considered to include nearby islands on its continental shelf; from the Latin *continēre* (to hold together)

nation: a group of people who share a common language, territory and/or identity; from the Latin *nātiō* (nation/race/birth) and from *nātus* (born)

conceived: to develop or understand and idea; from the Latin *concipere* (to take together) and from *con* (together) + *cipere* (to take) = to take together

in: not technically a Latin derivative since it comes from the Old English *in*, but identical to the Latin *in* with the same meaning.

liberty: the condition of being free from outside or undue restrictions or restraints; from the Latin *lībertās* (freedom) and from the adjective *līber* (free)

dedicated: devoted or consecrated; from the Latin *de* (away or from) + *dicare* (to proclaim) and from the stem *dicere* (to say)

proposition: something offered for consideration or discussion; from the Latin *prōpositiōnem* (a setting forth or statement), the noun form of *proponere* (to offer something to be done), a compound of *pro* (before) + *ponere* (to put or place) = *proponere* (to place before [for consideration])

created: made; from the Latin *creāre* (to create)

equal: uniform, identical, just; from the Latin *aequālis* (the quality of being uniform, identical, equal) and from the adjective *aequus* (even, just, level)

civil: relating to public life or citizens; from the Latin *cīvīlis* (relating to a citizen or public life) and from *cīvis* (citizen, townsmen)

testing: challenging, trying; from the Latin *testum* (the lid of an earthen vessel, especially one used to test metals), made into the verb *testāre* (to test)

long: not technically a Latin derivative since it comes from the Old English *lang*, but akin to the Latin *longus, -a, -um* (long)

endure: to persevere in spite of hardships or difficulties; from the Latin *indūrāre* (to make hard or harden [the heart] against) and from *in* (in) + *dūrāre* (to harden) = to make hard [on the] in[side] which in turn ultimately derives from *dūrus* (hard)

portion: a part or specific amount; from the Latin *portiō, portiōnis* (part, portion) which is related to the Latin *pars, partis* (part)

final: the last, ending, or ultimate; from the Latin adjective *fīnālis* (final) and from the Latin noun *fīnis* (end)

resting-place: "resting" may not be a Latin derivative since there is an Old English (and thus Germanic) derivation in the word *raeste/reste* (rest, bed, peace), but it may derive from the Latin *rē* (back) + *stāre*, (to stand) = to stand back or remain; likewise, "place" has both an Old English derivation, *plaece* (open area) and a Latin derivation of *platēa* (plaza, wide street)

proper: suitable, acceptable, correct; from the Latin *prōprius* of the same meaning

larger: of greater size or extent; comparative form of "large" from the Latin *largus* of largely the same meaning

sense: 1) to see, hear, smell, taste, touch and/or be aware of by some undefined other ("6th sense") means; 2) meaning; from the Latin *sēnsus* (sense, feeling, meaning) and, in turn, from *sentīre* (to sense, perceive, feel, know)

consecrate: to make or declare something holy, usually in a group ceremony; from the Latin *com* (together) + *sacrāre* (to make holy) = to make holy together, and from *sacrum*, "holy"

poor: 1) having little money; 2) of low quality; from the Latin *pauper* (poor) which may come from *paucus parāre* (to get or prepare little)

power: the ability to do, control or influence; from the Latin *potēns* (powerful) from the Latin verb *potīrī* (to be powerful) and possibly related to the common Latin irregular verb *possum, posse, potuī* (to be able)

add: to increase; from the Latin *addere* (to add to/join) formed by a compound of *ad* (to/toward) + *dare* (to give) = to give to/toward

detract: to take away; from the Latin *dētractum*, the past participle of *dētrahere*, formed by a compound of *dē* (away) + *trahere* (to draw) = to draw away

note: to mark, sign or remark upon; this might be from a Germanic word, from the Old English *notu* (use, profit, utility) or a Latin derivative from *nota* (note, sign, letter, mark)

remember: to bring to mind again. It is probably a derivative from the Latin *rememorāri*, formed by a compound of *re*, "again" + *memor*, "to be mindful of," which comes from the adjective *memor*, "mindful." However, there is a Germanic derivation as well in the Old English *mimor*, "mindful.")

unfinished: not complete; formed by a compound of "un," and anglicizing of the Latin *in* (not) + *fīnere* (to limit, set bounds, finish) which, in turn, derives from the Latin noun *fīnis* (limit, boundary, end)

nobly: the adverb form of noble, having the qualities of being worthy of honor or respect; from the Latin *nōbilis* (well-known, famous, renowned, or of superior birth)

remaining: to stay; from the Latin *remanēre*, formed by a compound of *re* (back or again) + *manēre* (to stay) = to stay back

increased: grown in number or amount; from the Latin *increscere*, formed of the compound *in* (in) + *crescere* (to grow) = to grow in or into

devotion: dedication to a cause or principle; from the Latin *dēvōtiōnem*, noun formed from *dēvovēre* (to dedicate by vow), formed by a compound of *dē* (away or from) + *vovēre* (to vow) = to vow from)

cause: a source, reason, goal, aim, or principle; from the Latin *causa* (reason, sake, cause)

measure: a quantity or amount; from the Latin *mēnsūra* (a measure, a rule, something to measure by), from *mēnsus*, the past participle of the Latin verb *mētīrī* (to measure)

resolve: to find a solution or to solve again; from the Latin *resolvere* (to loosen, undue, settle) formed of a compound of *re* (again)—or simply an intensive prefix—and *solvere* (to loosen, untie, dissolve); the sense in which it is found here is actually more along the lines of "to make a firm decision about," and this meaning goes back to the 16th century.

government: an institution or administration with the power to make and enforce laws for a region or nation; from the Latin *gubernātiō* (government)

people: a group of human beings; from the Latin *populus* (people)

perish: to pass away or die; from the Latin *perīre* (to pass away, die)

Dum spīrō, spērō.
While I breathe, I hope.
—South Carolina state motto ᴬ

This quotation from Cicero was also the motto for the Irish Viscounts Dillion.

Chapter 26

- adverbs
- formation of adverbs

VOCABULARY

NOUNS		
*classis, classis, f.	fleet	(class)
fortitūdō, fortitūdinis, f.	courage, strength	(fortitude)
imperium, ī, n.	power, command	(empire, imperial)
modestia, ae, f.	temperance; humility	(modesty)
triumphus, ī, m.	triumphal procession	(triumphant)
ADJECTIVES		
modestus, a, um	well-behaved; humble, modest	(modest)
integer, integra, integrum	upright	(integrity)
CONJUNCTION		
antequam	before	
ADVERBS		
magnopere	greatly	
sincērē	honestly	(sincerely)
tamen	nevertheless, however	
vērē	truly	(verily)

*i-stem noun

TE **Exercise 1.** Using the rules for syllabication and accent that you have learned, write out the syllables and accents for the vocabulary words above. Then practice pronouncing them aloud.

195

SECTION 69. Adverbs

An adjective modifies or describes a noun or pronoun. An adverb, in both English and Latin, modifies or describes a verb, an adjective, another adverb, or in some cases even a whole sentence. Adverbs generally answer the questions: when? where? how? how much? The best thing about Latin adverbs is that like prepositions and most cardinal numerals they are indeclinable. One form fits all!

TE **Exercise 2.** Read the following English passage and identify all of the adverbs.

Once upon a time there was a boy named Marcus. Marcus lived happily with his mother, father, and sister in an unusually large house on a very short street in Rome. Marcus and his family always liked to eat dinner together, but sometimes they were not able to because Marcus' father often worked very late in his shop. Fortunately, Marcus' mother did not work outside the home, and she was usually able to eat with Marcus and his sister. These three sadly wished that the father could be there, but they always gratefully thanked the gods for their goods and their family and ate heartily while kindly saving some food for the father of the family.

Most adverbs in Latin are easily recognizable by the endings -*e* or -*ter*. There are other very common adverbs, however, that do not use these endings. Many of these you have already seen throughout the previous chapters.

nōn	**not**	ubi	**where**
semper	**always**	statim	**immediately**
saepe	**often**	subitō	**suddenly**
ibi	**there**	tandem	**finally**

SECTION 70. Formation of Adverbs

Many adverbs are formed from their adjective counterparts. Look at the following examples. Can you determine a rule for the formation of English adverbs?

Marcus is *humble.*   Julia is *beautiful.*   The soldiers are *ferocious.*
Marcus spoke *humbly.*   Julia sings *beautifully.*   The soldiers fight *ferociously.*

Adverbs in Latin, unlike adjectives, are indeclinable. That means they have only one ending. As in English most adverbs are formed from their adjective counterparts. Can you determine a rule for the formation of Latin adverbs based on the following sentences?
Hint: These are the same sentences as the English ones that you just read.

Marcus est *modestus.*   Iūlia est *pulchra.*   Mīlitēs sunt *ferōcēs.*
Marcus dīxit *modestē.*   Iūlia cantat *pulchrē.*   Mīlitēs pugnant *ferōciter.*

You can form an adverb from a first and second declension adjective. Simply replace the common ending with a long -*e*. For third declension adjectives replace the ending with -*iter*. For adjectives with a stem ending in -*nt*, just add -*er*.

TE **Exercise 3.** Using the examples above, form adverbs from the following Latin adjectives. Translate the adverbs.
          Example: lātus, lāta, lātum   lātē, widely

1. laetus, laeta, laetum
2. īrātus, īrāta, īrātum
3. fidēlis, fidēle
4. miser, misera, miserum

5. ingēns, ingentis
6. celer, celeris, celere
7. timidus, timida, timidum
8. fortis, forte
9. avārus, avāra, avārum
10. brevis, breve

Exercise 4. Parse, diagram, and translate the following sentences.

1. Dux erat bene nōtus.

2. Classem pīrātārum magnopere timēbāmus.

3. Rēx sincērē bonum prō populō petīvit.

4. Mīlitēs in pugnā semper fortiter pugnāvērunt.

5. You were running quickly through the fields.

6. Cincinnatus happily left behind power.

7. Truly I will now be king and have great power.

8. Many women were sincerely loving him for his courage.

Chapter Reading

POMPEIUS MAGNUS – Pompey the Great

CHARACTERS:

Gnaeus Pompeius – Gnaeus Pompey
Sulla – Roman general and dictator
Crassus – served as consul alongside Pompey
Julius Caesar – political ally of Pompey and Crassus

Gn. Pompēius *nātus est* ante diem iii Kalendās Octōbrēs AUC DCXLVIII. Gnaeus erat vir propter fortitūdinem et modestiam bene nōtus. Bene ēgit omnibus in **lūdīs** et in bellō. Omnēs Gnaeum magnopere amābant.

Inimīcōs Sullae ex Āfricā expulit. **Victōriīs et spīritū** Sulla eum iuvenem appellāvit nōmine "Magnus." Dīxērunt hominēs, "Gnaeus fāmam et triumphum habet antequam habet *barbam*." Gnaeus, nunc Pompēius Magnus, erat pulcherrimus. Multae fēminae eum vērē amābant, sed is erat semper modestus et semper dīxit timidē. Multōs post annōs, ubi senior erat, etiam erat modestus; sed quoque erat *obēsus*. Hae duae *rēs* **erant impedītiō Pompēiō**. Erat semper vir integer. Sincērē bonum prō populō petīvit, sed quoque suum bonum petīvit *vehementer*. Culpa ēius maxima erat *vānitās*. Sē rogāvit, "Cūr Rōmānī *haesitāvērunt* mē rēgem creāre *tam diū*?"

Pompēius et Crassus erant *eōdem annō* cōnsulēs. Cōnsulēs potestātem *tribūnōrum* laetē **retulērunt**. Senātus Pompēiō *negōtium* dedit. Necesse erat Pompēiō celeriter oppugnāre pīrātās *Ciliciae*. Trēs annōs Pompēius imperium tōtīus classis Rōmānae habēbit. Caesar in hāc *rē* Pompēium *ardenter* adiuvābat. (**In tempore futūrō** Caesar, Crassus, et Pompēius magnum imperium et magnam potestātem inter sē habēbunt.) Vērē Pompēius nunc erat rēx in omnibus *rēbus praeter* nōmen. Post longam vītam Pompēius, quī ōlim fīliam Caesaris in mātrimōnium dūxit, periit ante diem iv Kalendās Octōbrēs AUC DCCVII.

───────────────

Gn. Pompēius = Gnaeus Pompey (Always read aloud and translate Gn. as Gnaeus.)
lūdīs = sports
Victōriīs et spīritū = because of his victories and courage/spirit
erant impedītiō Pompēiō = were a hindrance to Pompey
retulērunt = restored
In tempore futūrō = in a time to be, in the future

GLOSSARY

nātus est	was born
barba, barbae, f.	beard
obēsus, obēsa, obēsum, adj.	fat
rēs, reī, f.	thing, matter
vehementer, adv.	enthusiastically
vānitās, vānitātis, f.	vanity
haesitō, āre, āvī, ātum	to be stuck; to hesitate
tam diū	so long, for so long
eōdem annō	in the same year
tribūnus, ī, m.	tribune (Roman official)
negōtium, negōtiī, n.	duty, job
Cilicia, ae, f.	Cilicia, country in S. Asia Minor, infamous for piracy
ardenter, adv.	eagerly
vērē, adv.	truly
praeter, prep. + acc.	except

Respondē Latīnē!

 1. Quōmodo Pompēius agēbat in lūdīs?

2. Quis Gnaeum "Magnum" appellāvit?

3. Quālis vir erat Pompēius senior?

4. Quid est culpa maxima Pompēiī?

5. Quis cōnsul erat cum Pompēiō?

ANSWER IN ENGLISH!

1. What good qualities did Pompey have?

2. What was Pompey's greatest fault?

3. Pompey wondered why the Romans had hesitated to do what?

4. Who in the selection ardently supported the appointment of Pompey to head all the Roman fleet?

5. Whom did Pompey marry?

Culture Corner

The earliest Romans designated a year by naming the two consuls for that year in a construction called the ablative absolute. Later Romans, including Varro, came up with the more convenient method of designating years: he and others began to designate a year as how long that year had been from the founding of Rome. They also fixed what we now call 753 BC as the year in which Rome was founded. Since there was no zero year, 753 BC was AUC 1 (*ab urbe condita* = from the founding of the city), 752 BC was AUC 2, and so on. If you know the date BC and want to find the date AUC, subtract the number of the year you know from 754. That method "cancels out" the zero year. In this way, 70 BC is AUC 684. It is much easier to convert a year we designate with AD. We simply add the AD year to 753. In that way, AD 30 is AUC 783.

More on the State Seal:

In addition to the quotation from Cicero there are three more Latin phrases on the State Seal of South Carolina.

meliōrem lāpsā locāvit "He has placed better than what has fallen"
animīs opibusque parātī "ready in soul and resource," Vergil's Aeneid, Book II, Line 799

Another reads *Quis sēparābit?* Use the interrogative pronouns that you learned in chapter 24 to translate this phrase.

Exercise 1

clas-sis, clas-sis, f.
for-ti-tū-dō, for-ti-tū-di-nis, f.
im-per-i-um, ī, n.
mo-des-ti-a, ae, f.
tri-um-phus, ī, m.
mo-des-tus, a, um

in-te-ger, in-te-gra, in-te-grum
an-te-quam
mag-no-pe-re
sin-cē-rē
ta-men
vē-rē

Exercise 2

once	very	sometimes	late	there	gratefully
happily	always	often	fortunately	always	heartily
unusually	together	very	usually	sadly	kindly

Exercise 3

1. laetus, laeta, laetum — laetē, happily
2. īrātus, īrāta, īrātum — īrātē, angrily
3. fidēlis, fidēle — fidēliter, faithfully
4. miser, misera, miserum — miserē, miserably
5. ingēns, ingentis — ingenter, greatly

6. celer, celeris, celere — celeriter, quickly
7. timidus, timida, timidum — timidē, timidly
8. fortis, forte — fortiter, bravely
9. avārus, avāra, avārum — avārē, greedily
10. brevis, breve — breviter, briefly

Exercise 4

```
      S    LV  Adv  Adj
1. Dux  erat  bene  nōtus.
   n/s/m 3/s/i       n/s/m
   The leader was well known.
```

```
      DO      PNA      Adv        S+V
2. Classem pīrātārum magnopere timēbāmus.
   ac/s/f     g/p/m              1/p/i
   We were greatly fearing the fleet of pirates.
```

```
      S   Adv  S Adj  P   OP     V
3. Rēx sincērē bonum prō populō petīvit.
      n/s/m   ac/s/m  ab/s/m 3/s/perf
   The king sincerely sought good for [his] people.
   A substantive adjective such as bonum (S.Adj.) stands alone without a noun.
```

```
      S    P   OP   Adv   Adv      V
4. Mīlitēs in pugnā semper fortiter pugnāvērunt.
   n/p/m    ab/s/f                3/p/perf
   The soldiers always fought bravely in battle.
```

```
     S   HV   V    Adv    P     OP
5. You were running quickly through the fields.
          2/s/i                ac/p/m
   Per agrōs celeriter currēbās.
```

```
     S       Adv      V      DO
6. Cincinnatus happily left behind power.
   n/s/m              3/s/perf  ac/s/n
   Cincinnātus laetē relīquit imperium.
```

```
       Adv  S HV  Adv LV  PrN  C   V   Adj   DO
```
7. Truly I will now be king and have great power.
```
        1/s/f              n/s/m    *1/s/f ac/s/n ac/s/n
```
   Vērē erō nunc rēx et habēbō magnum imperium.
```
       Adj   S   HV   Adv    V   DO  P PNA  OP
```
8. Many women were sincerely loving him for his courage.
```
   n/p/f  n/p/f  3/p/i           ac/s/m        ac/s/f
```
   Multae fēminae eum vērē amābant propter [ēius] fortitudinem.
   "His" (ēius) is implied and need not be used.

Translation

Gnaeus Pompeius was born September 29 in the six hundred forty-eighth year from the founding of the city (106 BC). Gnaeus was a man well noted for [his] bravery/strength and modesty. He did well in all sports and in war. Everybody loved Gnaeus greatly.

He drove the enemies of Sulla out of Africa. Because of his victories and courage, Sulla called the young man by the name of "Magnus" (the Great). People said, "Gnaeus had fame and a triumph before he had a beard." Gnaeus, now Pompey the Great, was very handsome. Many women truly loved him, but he was always modest and always spoke timidly. After many years, when he was older, he was still modest; but he was also fat. These two things were a hindrance to Pompey. He was always a man of integrity. He sincerely sought good for his people, but he also enthusiastically sought his own good. His greatest fault was vanity. He asked himself, "Why have the Romans hesitated so long to make me king?"

Pompey and Crassus were consuls in the same year. The consuls happily restored the power of the tribunes. The senate gave Pompey [another] job. It was necessary to attack quickly the pirates of Cilicia. For three years Pompey will have the imperium of the whole Roman fleet. Caesar ardently supported Pompey in this matter. (In a time to be/In the future, Caesar, Crassus and Pompey will have imperium and great power among them.) Indeed, now Pompey was king in all things except name. After a long life, Pompey, who once married the daughter of Caesar, died on September 28 in the seven-hundred-seventh year from the founding of the city (47 BC).

Respondē Latīnē!

1. Quōmodo Pompēius agēbat in lūdīs?
   Bene ēgit omnibus in lūdīs.

   How was Pompey doing in games?
   He was doing well in games.

2. Quis Gnaeum "Magnum" appellāvit?
   Sulla Gnaeum nōmine "Magnus" appellāvit.

   Who called Gnaeus "Great"?
   Sulla called Gnaeus the Great.

3. Quālis vir erat Pompēius senior?
   Erat semper modestus et semper dīxit timidē; quoque erat obēsus.

   What kind of man was the older Pompey?
   He was always modest and always spoke timidly; he was also fat.

4. Quid est culpa maxima Pompēiī?
   Culpa ēius maxima est vānitās.

   What is Pompey's greatest fault?
   His greatest fault was vanity.

5. Quis cōnsul erat cum Pompēiō?
   Crassus erat cōnsul cum Pompēiō.

   Who was consul with Pompey?
   Crassus was consul with Pompey.

ANSWER IN ENGLISH!

1. What good qualities did Pompey have?
   Bravery, strength, modesty

2. What was Pompey's greatest fault?
   vanity

3. Pompey wondered why the Romans had hesitated to do what?
   He wondered why they hesitated to make him king.

4. Who in the selection ardently supported the appointment of Pompey to head all the Roman fleet?
   Julius Caesar

5. Whom did Pompey marry?
   Julia, the daughter of Julius Caesar

Unit 6 Reading

Reading and Review for Chapters 22–26

POLITICS IN THE FIRST TRIUMVIRATE
Christopher Schlect

M. Calpurnius Bibulus was on his way to the Forum when someone dumped a vessel of manure on his head. Is this any way to treat one of Rome's consuls? Perhaps Bibulus deserved a crown of dung, for just a short time earlier he had tried to deceive the Popular Assembly into thinking that the gods were on his side when he concocted a story about birds in the heavens. Such were the ugly politics in Rome in 59 BC.

We don't know who fouled Bibulus. It was likely an ordinary citizen, perhaps a former soldier. Whoever it was, the person interrupted Bibulus as he prepared to oppose a law that was proposed by Rome's other consul that year, C. Julius Caesar. Caesar had a knack for inspiring the common people to help him get what he wanted. In this case, the common people used human waste to drive Caesar's opponent from the Forum. Bibulus ran home and hid there for the remainder of his term as consul.

Why did Caesar want this law passed? He was returning a favor to the man who had helped him become consul, Pompey the Great. Pompey had conquered the eastern Mediterranean, bringing more new territory under Roman rule than anyone had before him. Leaders in the Senate worried that Pompey was growing too powerful, so they refused to pass the laws that Pompey wanted for organizing all the territory he had conquered. So Pompey looked to Caesar for help and supported him to become Consul. Once in office, Caesar used his influence with the people to pass through the Popular Assembly the very laws that Pompey could not pass through the Senate. In the process, Bibulus wore a hat of fertilizer.

In league with Pompey and Caesar was their third associate, Crassus, a businessman who wanted to expand trade in the lands Pompey had conquered. Crassus set aside his former hatred of Pompey because he now stood to grow wealthy by taking up Pompey's cause. These three men, Caesar, Crassus and Pompey, formed an alliance that historians later named the "First Triumvirate." Each needed the help of the other two in order to advance his own career.

Using his popularity to his advantage, in 58 BC Caesar secured for himself a new military command in Gaul, the barbarian territories north of Italy corresponding to what we now call France. Over the next eight years Caesar conquered the Gauls in brilliant campaigns and distinguished himself, like Pompey, as one of history's greatest military leaders. While he waged war against the barbarians, Caesar's fellow triumvirs were busy advancing their own careers. When famine afflicted Rome, the desperate Romans granted to Pompey an unusual measure of authority so he could relieve the emergency. And Crassus, not wanting to be outdone by the others, took up a military command in Parthia. Unlike Pompey and Caesar, Crassus did not fare well. He lost both his army and his life.

Crassus' death set the triumvirate out of balance. Pompey worried that Caesar and his army were becoming too powerful. Caesar, in turn, feared Pompey's great influence back in Rome. Tensions mounted between these two, once friends and allies, who had helped one another become powerful. Pompey forced a standoff when he led the Senate to order Caesar to retire from his command in Gaul. But Caesar refused to leave his army. Instead, he marched them out of Gaul, across the Rubicon River and into Italy. This was an act of war. For the third time in the century, a Roman army marched upon Rome itself, and Rome descended into civil war.

GAIUS JULIUS CAESAR: THE EARLY YEARS [A]

CHARACTERS:

Gaius Iulius Caesar– a courageous and adventurous young man
Iulus (Ascanius)– son of Aeneas, founder of Alba Longa
Aeneas– Trojan prince, ancestor of the Roman race
Venus– goddess of love, mother of Aeneas
Catiline– Roman conspirator
Nicomedes– king of Bithynia, an ancient kingdom in modern-day Turkey
Cossutia– first wife of Caesar
Cornelia– second wife of Caesar

1.   Gāius Iūlius Caesar vir *insignis genere* et *animō* erat. **Ut fāma est**, ūnus *ē maiōribus*
2. Caesaris erat Iūlus. Hic Iūlus fīlius Aenēae erat, et Aenēās ipse fīlius Veneris erat. Venus
3. ipsa fīlia Iovis erat. Caesar, igitur, vērē erat *optimātum*. Sīcut Catilīna, tamen, Caesar erat
4. pauper. Familia in **Subūrā** habitābat.
5.   Gāius Iūlius *nātus est* circā DCLIII AUC, *aliter* C annōs ante Chrīstum. Māter
6. Caesaris erat Aurēlia, fēmina *insignis* familiā suā. Caesar **puer artī dīcendī** studēbat
7. cum *Gallō*. **Nōndum sciēns** Gāius bellō *Gallicō* parābat. *Adulēscēns* mīlitābat
8. cum Mārcō Thermō in Āsiā. Caesar quoque erat in Bīthyniā, ubi Nīcomēdēs erat rēx.
9. Quandō Gāius XVIII annōs habuit, Rōmam revēnit, ibi prīmam uxōrem, Cossutia, **in**
10. **mātrimōnium dūxit** quod illa patrī Gāiī placuit. **Patre mortuō** Iūlius Caesar
11. Cossutiam *repudiāvit* et Cornēliam **in mātrimōnium dūxit**. Ubi Sulla imperium et
12. potestātem obtinuit, Caesarem iussit Cornēliam *repudiāre*, sed Caesar *recūsāvit*.
13. Caesar Ītaliam effūgit et sē coniūnxit *exercituī* in *Ciliciā*. **Sullā mortuō**, Caesar
14. Rōmam revertit. *Quoniam* inimīcī Caesaris imperium habēbant, Caesar **profectus**
15. **est** ad Āsiam.
16.   In itinere ad Āsiam, *pīrātae* Caesarem cēpērunt. Eum tenēbant in īnsulā. Sī
17. amīcī Caesaris pecūniam *dederint*, Caesar līber erit. Postulābant pīrātae XX **talenta.**
18. Caesar rīdēbat et dīxit *pīrātīs*, "Postulāte L talenta." Caesar *pīrātās stultōs barbarōs*
19. appellāvit. Dīxit Caesar *pīrātīs*, "Revertam et vōs *crucibus adfīgam*." Amīcī
20. pecūniam *pīrātīs* dedērunt. Caesar discessit sed revertit et omnēs *pīrātās*
21. *crucibus adfīxit*.

---

ut fāma est = so the story goes
Subūra = the Subura, a very unfashionable part of Rome, almost a slum
puer = as a boy
artī dīcendī = the art of speaking (in the dative as the object of *studēbat*)
nōndum sciēns = not yet knowing; i.e., unconsciously
in mātrimōnium dūxit = he married (lit. he led into marriage)
patre mortuō = [his] father having died; i.e., after his father died
Sullā mortuō = This is the same construction as *patre mortuō*; how would you translate this one?
profectus est = set out
talenta = talents (large unit of Greek money)
The Greek talent was worth 6,000 drachma. A drachma was the equivalent of the Roman sesterce.

[A]The students should follow these steps to success for this reading comprehension exercise.
• Read the English title. (It is often a clue to the theme or content of the reading.)
• Read the Latin text all the way through without any attempt at translation.
• Read the questions in order to know what to look for in the reading.
• Read the selection again.
• Go back and begin answering the questions.

A single talent, therefore, was a large sum of money. How many sesterces would be the equivalent of Caesar's ransom?

GLOSSARY:

īnsignis, īnsignis, adj.	distinguished
īnsignis genere	distinguished by his ancestry/family
animus, ī	spirit, courage
maiōrēs, maiōrum, m. pl.	ancestors
optimātum	best translated here as "aristocracy" (the upper class of Rome)
nātus est	was born
aliter, adv.	otherwise
Gallus, ī, m.	a Gaul (The Gauls inhabited primarily what is today France.)
Gallicus, a, um, adj.	Gallic, pertaining to Gaul (modern day France)
adulēscēns, adulēscentis, m/f.	youth, young man/woman
repudiō, āre, āvī, ātum	to refuse, (wife) to divorce
recūsō, āre, āvī, ātum	to refuse
exercitus, exercitūs, m.	army
Cilicia, ae, f.	Cilicia, country in S. Asia Minor, infamous for piracy
quoniam, conj.	since, because
pīrāta, ae, m.	pirate
dederint	they will have given
stultus, a, um	stupid
barbarus, ī, m	barbarians
crucibus adfīgam	I will crucify (lit. I will fasten to crosses) Crucifixion was a means of execution reserved for the worst criminals. The victims were either nailed or tied down to a wooden cross. The hanging weight of their body caused them to slowly suffocate in a very agonizing manner. The Romans invented this form of execution that was the means of Christ's death many years later.

Question & Answer

1. According to line 1, Caesar was distinguished through what?
   a. his ancestry and writings
   b. his military skill and courage
   c. his ancestry and courage
   d. his wealth and courage

2. From what god was the Julian clan descended?
   a. Venus
   b. Aeneas
   c. Iulus
   d. Jupiter

3. According to line 4, Caesar was ___.
   a. courageous
   b. poor
   c. very intelligent
   d. living in the suburbs of Rome

4. Which of the following do lines 5 and 6 not tell us?
    a. that Aurelia herself was from a distinguished family
    b. that Gaius Julius Caesar was born about 100 BC
    c. that Gaius Julius Caesar studied public speaking
    (d.) that Caesar began to prepare early for the conquest of Gaul

5. Who was Caesar's first wife?
    a. Cornelia
    b. a Gaul
    (c.) Cossutia
    d. a relative of Sulla

6. Why did Caesar set out for Asia?
    a. because Sulla had died
    b. because Sulla ordered him to
    (c.) because his enemies were in power
    d. because it would please his father

7. The tense of *erit* in line 17 is ___.
    a. perfect
    (b.) future
    c. pluperfect
    d. present

8. What is the gender of *talenta* in line 17?
    a. masculine
    b. feminine
    (c.) neuter
    d. common

9. What is the case of *stultōs barbarōs* in line 18 and why?
    (a.) accusative object of *appellāvit* in line 19
    b. accusative object of *rīdēbat* in line 18
    c. dative indirect object of *dīxit* in line 18
    d. Greek nominative subject of *appellāvit* in line 19

10. What is the tense of *discessit* and *revertit* in line 20?
    a. historical present
    b. imperfect
    c. pluperfect
    (d.) perfect

TRANSLATION:

Gaius Julius Caesar was a man distinguished by his ancestry and courage. One of the ancestors of Caesar was Iulus, as the story goes. This Iulus was the son of Aeneas, and Aeneas himself was the son of Venus. Venus herself was the daughter of Jupiter. Caesar, therefore, was surely an aristocrat. Just as Catiline, however, Caesar was poor. [His] family lived in the Subura.

Gaius Julius was born about 653 years from the founding of the city, or [about] 100 BC. Caesar's mother was Aurelia, a woman distinguished by her own family. As a boy, Caesar studied rhetoric with a Gaul. Unconsciously, Gaius was preparing for the Gallic War. As a young man/youth, he served in the army/military with Marcus Thermus in Asia. Caesar also was in Bithynia, where Nicomedes was king. When Gaius was eighteen, he returned to Rome. There he married his first wife, Cossutia, because she was pleasing to his father. When his father died, Julius Caesar divorced Cossutia and married Cornelia. When Sulla came to power, he ordered Caesar to divorce Cornelia, but Caesar refused [to do so]. Caesar fled Italy and joined the army in Cilicia. When Sulla died, Caesar returned to Rome. Since enemies of Caesar were in power, he set out for Asia.

On the way to Asia, pirates captured Caesar. They held him on an island. If the friends of Caesar will have given money, Caesar will be free. The pirates demanded twenty talents. Caesar laughed and said to the pirates, "Demand fifty talents." Caesar called the pirates stupid barbarians. Caesar said to the pirates, "I shall return and crucify you." Friends gave the money to the pirates. Caesar departed but returned and crucified all the pirates.

Suggested Project:

We know an immense amount of information about the Romans in part because of the literature they left behind, such as the histories of Livy. Archaeology has also contributed a great amount to our knowledge of Roman culture. In an appendix to this book you will find an archaeology project for students. This project will help them better understand the important work of archaeologists by creating their own archaeological dig.

AVirginia adopted this seal at her Constitutional Convention in 1776. George Wythe, founding father and signer of the Declaration of Independence, led a design committee which also included George Mason, Robert Carter Nicholas, and Richard Henry Lee.

Sīc Semper Tyrannīs
Thus Always to Tyrants
—Virginia state motto[A]

This seal may claim Rome as her inspiration more so than any other. In the center the goddess Virtus (courage, valor) stands dressed as an Amazon. She clutches a spear in her right hand and a sheathed sword in her left. On her head she wears a helmet that may be reminiscent of Minerva, goddess of wisdom and war. She stands triumphant over a fallen king dressed in traditional Roman garb with his fallen crown lying nearby. The scene and the Latin phrase beneath it vividly remind us of the reason the Romans lost their taste for kings. It points to the great distaste Virginia had developed for the British monarchy in the late 1700's. Interestingly, this seal also appeared just a century later on battle flags carried against the North in the Civil War. Today, the attack submarine USS Virginia proudly wears this seal, Amazon and all, on her side.

Chapter 27

- fourth conjugation
- perfect system
  - pluperfect
  - future perfect

VOCABULARY

NOUNS

auctōritās, auctōritātis, f.	authority	(author)
gēns, gentis, f.	tribe, nation	(gentile)
gubernātor, gubernātōris, m.	governor	(gubernatorial)

VERBS

audiō, audīre, audīvī/audiī, audītum	to hear, listen	(audio, auditory)
cōnsentiō, cōnsentīre, cōnsēnsī, cōnsēnsum	to agree	(consent, consensus)
cōnscrībō, cōnscrībere, cōnscrīpsī, cōnscrīptum	to enlist, enroll; write up	(conscription)
reveniō, revenīre, revēnī, reventum	to come back, return	
sciō, scīre, scīvī/sciī, scītum	to know	(science)
sentiō, sentīre, sēnsī, sēnsum	to perceive, feel; sense	(sensible)
spērō, āre, āvī, ātum	to hope	(desperate)
veniō, venīre, vēnī, ventum	to come	(advent, venture)

TE **Exercise 1.** Using the rules for syllabication and accent that you have learned, write out the syllables and accents for the vocabulary words above. Then practice pronouncing them aloud.

SECTION 71. Fourth Conjugation, Present System

At last we have arrived at the fourth and final verb conjugation in Latin. This group of verbs is distinguishable from the other conjugations by its own unique infinitive, which ends in **-īre**. You can identify the stem for fourth conjugation verbs using the same formula as for all other conjugations.

2nd principal part – re = verb stem
                1st conjugation   amā/re = amā
                2nd conjugation   vidē/re = vidē
                3rd conjugation   mitte/re = mitte
                4th conjugation   audī /re = audī

Exercise 2. Identify the stem and conjugation of each of the verbs in the vocabulary list of this chapter.

The fourth conjugation follows the same patterns for conjugating as the third conjugation. It should remind you in particular of the third conjugation -io verbs that you learned in chapter 16, since fourth conjugation has an *i* throughout its tenses.**B**

PRESENT		IMPERFECT		FUTURE	
SINGULAR	PLURAL	SINGULAR	PLURAL	SINGULAR	PLURAL
audiō	audīmus	audiēbam	audiēbāmus	audiam	audiēmus
audīs	audītis	audiēbās	audiēbātis	audiēs	audiētis
audit	audiunt	audiēbat	audiēbant	audiet	audient

Notā Bene:

Notice that although the fourth conjugation stem ends in a long *ī*, this stem vowel shortens when it appears in front of another vowel. It is rare in Latin that you will see two long vowels next to each other.

Caveat Discipulus:

Be careful that you do not confuse third conjugation -io verbs with fourth conjugation. Remember that when uncertain, you can always identify a verb's conjugation by the infinitive.

Exercise 3. Following the example of *audīre,* conjugate the verbs *scīre* and *venīre* in all three tenses of the present system. Include the English translations.

Exercise 4. Identify the person, number, and tense of the underlined verb phrases in the following sentences. Translate the underlined phrases only.

1. I will listen to my teacher carefully.
2. We know when you are arriving.
3. Will we agree on a solution?
4. I kept on listening to you even though I was working.
5. Caesar knew that Marc Antony was his friend.
6. They were coming to see us, but the storm prevented them from doing so.
7. You girls always listened well.
8. The boys have enlisted in Caesar's army.

Section 72. The Perfect System

In chapter 8 you learned that the third principal part provides the stem for the perfect tense (Section 27). There are two other tenses in the perfect system that also use this same stem.

a. Pluperfect or Past Perfect Tense

We derive the name of this tense from the Latin phrase **plūs quam perfectus,** meaning more than perfect. Thus, the pluperfect tense shows action that happens *before* the perfect. We use this tense in English, just as the Romans did, to show a sequence of events. The only way to translate the pluperfect tense (sometimes called the past perfect) is with the helping verb "had."

Example:
Caesar multās pugnās **vīcerat** (pluperfect) antequam **vēnit** (perfect) ad Galliam.
Caesar **had won** many battles before **he came** to Gaul.

To form the pluperfect tense simply add the pluperfect endings in bold type to the perfect stem. Where have you seen these endings before?

Person	Singular	Plural
1	amāv-**eram** I had loved	amāv-**erāmus** We had loved
2	amāv-**erās** You had loved	amāv-**erātis** You (pl.) had loved
3	amāv-**erat** He/she/it had loved	amāv-**erant** They had loved

Notā Bene:
- The pluperfect endings are identical to the imperfect tense of *esse* (Section 24).
- Irregular verbs such as *eō, īre,* and *ferre* follow this same pattern.

b. Future Perfect Tense

We derive the name of this tense from the Latin phrase **futūrus perfectus,** meaning th future. The future perfect tense is probably the least common of the tenses in either English or Latin. This tense indicates an action that has not yet happened, but will have happened by a certain point of time. We often use this tense when our parents ask us about our chores.

Mom: Have you finished your work?
Māter: Perfēcistīne labōrem?

Son: No, but **I will have finished** in one hour.
Fīlius: Minimē, sed ūnā hōrā **perfēcerō.**

This tense also shows the earlier of two future actions.

Marcus **will have left** before Publius will arrive.
Mārcus **abīverit** ante Publius adveniet.

To form the future perfect tense add the future perfect endings to the perfect stem. The future perfect endings are almost identical to the future tense of *esse* (Section 24). Where do these endings differ from the future of *esse*? Why do you think it differs?

Person	Singular	Plural
1	amāv-**erō** I will have loved	amāv-**erimus** We will have loved
2	amāv-**eris** You will have loved	amāv-**eritis** You (pl.) will have loved
3	amāv-**erit** He/she/it will have loved	amāv-**erint** They will have loved

Notā Bene:
- The future perfect endings are identical to the future tense of *esse* (Section 24) except in the third person plural.
- If the third person plural was *-ērunt*, it might easily be confused with the perfect tense (Section 27).
- Irregular verbs such as *eō, īre,* and *ferre* follow this same pattern.

Exercise 5. Following the previous examples of *amāre* conjugate the verbs *vidēre, discēdere, audīre,* and *ferre* in all three tenses of the perfect system in both Latin and English.

Exercise 6. Parse each of the following verbs identifying their tense, person, and number. Then translate.

LATIN	PERSON	NUMBER	TENSE	TRANSLATION
mittēbam	1	Sing.	Imp.	I used to send
cōnsentit				
vīderis				
audiēmus				
rettulistī				
dūxerant				
petīvit				
				He will seize
				We perceived
				You (sing.) had hoped
				They had overcome
				They will have come
				You (pl.) knew
				I had returned

Exercise 7. Parse, diagram, and translate the following sentences.

1. Rēx mīlitēs in Galliam dūxerat.

2. Tribus mēnsibus lēgātī ā multīs gentibus ad ducem vēnērunt.

3. Nunc ad nostram terram revenīre cōnsēnsimus.

4. Mīlitēs Rōmānī multōs Germānōs mox necāverint.

5. All were hoping to conquer the enemy.

6. One nation out of many had asked them to return.

7. Many soldiers will soon have perished by (means of) the sword.

8. Had he heard the messenger before he returned?

Chapter Reading

CAESAR IN GAUL

CHARACTERS:
Gaius Julius Caesar – a Roman general and statesman
Ariovistus – a German king
Aedui – a Gallic tribe
Helvetii – a Gallic tribe, whose leader (not mentioned in the reading) was Orgetorix

Annō DCXCVI AUC, *aliter* LVIII ante Chrīstum, Caesar erat gubernātor in **Galliā Cisalpīnā** et in illīs partibus quae sunt *quibusdam* in partibus Ītaliae. Multōs annōs ante, Ariovistus, rēx Germānōrum, mīlitēs in Galliam dūxerat quod ūna gēns ē Gallīs eum rogāverat **sīc agere**. Ariovistus Galliam nōn relīquerat. Ūna gēns, Aeduī, petīvit auxilium ā Rōmānīs. Multī Germānī sē Ariovistō, quī eō tempore erat trāns *Rhēnum*, adiūnxērunt. Hī omnēs vincere tōtam Galliam spērābant.

Eōdem tempore Helvētiī, altera gēns Gallica, quī circum *Lacum Lemannum* habitābat, incēpērunt **iter facere ad sōlis occāsum**. **Caesar sēcum**, "Hī Helvētiī *trānsībunt* terram Rōmānam." Suā pecūniā et sine *auctōritāte senātūs*, Caesar IV legiōnēs cōnscrīpsit. Nūntium ad Ariovistum mīsit. Caesar dīcere cum rēge Germānō voluit. Ariovistus, tamen, cum Caesare dīcere nōn voluit. Nūntium **nōn amīcum** ad Caesarem mīsit. Nūntius erat, "*Nēmō* mēcum sine suā *perniciē* contendit." Nunc lēgātī ā multīs gentibus auxilium *petentibus* ad Caesarem vēnērunt. Caesar **bellum intulit** contrā Helvētiōs et Germānōs. Circum oppidum nōmine *Bibracte*, Rōmānī sub Caesare Helvētiōs superāvērunt. Helvētiī nunc ad suam terram revenīre voluērunt. Caesar cōnsēnsit. Dīxit, tamen, "Necesse est omnibus Helvētiīs sub imperiō Rōmānōrum vīvere." Tum prope Rhēnum Caesar cum Germānīs pugnāvit. Rōmānī mīlitēs multōs Germānōs necāvērunt, sed Ariovistus effūgit. Ariovistus etiam paulō post perierit.

Galliā Cisalpīnā = Cisalpine Gaul, which was that part of Gaul on the Italian side of the Alps
sīc agere = to act thus, to do this
eōdem tempore = at this same time
iter facere = to travel or journey (lit. to make a journey)
ad sōlis occāsum = toward the falling of the sun, i.e., westward
Caesar sēcum = Caesar sēcum (dīxit)
nōn amīcus = not friendly
bellum intulit = brought war upon, declared war upon
paulō post = a little later

GLOSSARY
aliter, adv. .... otherwise
quibusdam.. certain (adj. modifying *partibus*)
Rhēnus, ī, m. .... Rhine (a large and important river in Germany)
adiungō, adiungere, adiūnxī, adiūnctum........ to yoke, attach
Lacum Lemannum .... Lake Geneva
trānsībunt .... *trāns + īre*
senātus, ūs, m. .... senate
nēmō, nūllīus, pron.. nobody
perniciēs, perniciēī, f. .... destruction
petentibus .... seeking (modifies *gentibus*)
Bibracte .... Bibracte, a fortified city and perhaps the most important hillfort in Gaul, capital of the Aedui (The ancient town is near modern day Autun in Burgundy, France).

Respondē Latīnē!

 1. Quis mīlitēs Germānōs in Galliam dūxerat?

2. Quae gēns auxilium ā Rōmānīs petīvit?

3. Ubi habitābant Helvētiī?

4. Quō iter faciēbant Helvētiī?

5. Ubi pugnābat Caesar cum mīlitibus suīs Germānōs?

ANSWER IN ENGLISH!

1. What Gallic tribe asked the Romans for help?

2. What was the wish of Ariovistus and the Gauls who had joined him?

3. When Caesar sent a message to Ariovistus asking him to discuss the matter at hand, what did Ariovistus reply? (Give his whole answer.)

4. After the battle at Bribacte, what did the Helvetians want to do?

5. What was Caesar's condition concerning allowing them to do as they wished?

An Advanced Skill

In **Caesar sēcum, "Hī Helvētiī trānsībunt terram Rōmānam,** *dīxit* is understood. This stylistic device is an ellipsis. As you continue studying Latin, you will see many occasions of ellipsis. Often the elliptical element is some form of *sum*. Writers of the Advanced Placement Exam in Latin and other exams of advanced skills will expect you to interpret ellipses and to supply the missing word in your translations.

What Else Caesar Did in Gaul

VERCINGETORIX
DEPICTED ON COIN

Caesar believed that the freeing of Gaul from the German threat was a conquest of Gaul. He began to organize the society of the Gauls along Roman lines. He said that he had brought about this organization because he could not protect Gaul from the Germans in any other way. Several Gallic tribes rebelled against Roman rule. These rebellious tribes asked for help from the Belgians. The Belgians, Caesar has told us, were the bravest or strongest of all the Gauls. (*. . . fortissimī sunt Belgae.*) Caesar called Gaul a Roman province. The senate agreed with him and officially proclaimed Gaul as a province. Trouble, however, continued brewing in Gaul. A young Gallic prince named Vercingetorix proved especially troublesome to Caesar. The story of Vercingetorix is a sad one. Though he held out in a besieged town against Caesar for a long time, he was finally captured and taken to Rome. He appeared in Caesar's triumph in Rome. The Romans then executed him. The Gauls, however, and the French centuries later, always counted Vercingetorix as a great leader. They regarded him as a symbol of liberty.

Colloquāmur

Use the following questions and responses to review the parsing exercise above. Use some "eye" Latin to figure out what the responses mean.

interrogātiō:	Cūius est numerī?	What number is it?
respōnsum:	Singulāriter est.	
	Plūrāliter est.	
interrogātiō:	Cūius est persōnae?	What person is it?
respōnsum:	Est prīmae persōnae.	
	Est secundae persōnae.	
	Est tertiae persōnae.	
interrogātiō:	Cūius est temporis?	What tense (time) is it?
respōnsum:	Est praesentis.	
	Est imperfectī.	
	Est futūrī.	
	Est perfectī.	
	Est plūs quam perfectī	
	Est futūrī perfectī	

interrogātiō:	Cūius est coniugātiōnis?	What conjugation is it?
respōnsum:	Est prīmae coniugātiōnis.	
	Est secundae coniugātiōnis.	
	Est tertiae coniugātiōnis.	
	Est quartae coniugātiōnis.	

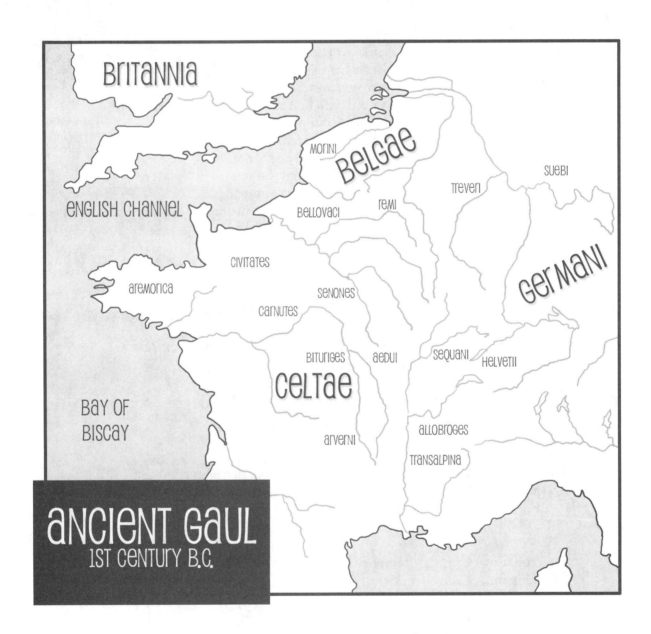

Chapter 27 Teacher's Pages

Exercise 1

auc-tō-ri-tās, auc-tō-ri-tā-tis, f.
gēns, gen-tis, f.
gu-ber-nā-tor, gu-ber-nā-tō-ris, m.
au-di-ō, au-dī-re, au-dī-vī/au-di-ī, au-di-tum
cōn-sen-ti-ō, cōn-sen-tī-re, cōn-sēn-sī, cōn-sēn-sum
con-scrī-bō, con-scrī-be-re, con-scrip-sī, con-scrip-tum

re-ve-ni-ō, re-ve-nī-re, re-vē-nī, re-ven-tum
sci-ō, scī-re, scī-vī/sci-ī, sci-tum
sen-ti-ō, sen-tī-re, sēn-sī, sēn-sum
spe-rō, ā-re, ā-vī, ā-tum
ve-ni-ō, ve-nī-re, vē-nī, ven-tum

Exercise 2

audiō, audīre, audīvī, audītum — audī, 4th
cōnsentiō, cōnsentīre, cōnsēnsī, cōnsēnsum — cōnsentī, 4th
conscrībō, conscrībere, conscrīpsī, conscrīptum — conscrībe, 3rd
reveniō, revenīre, revēnī, reventum — revenī, 4th
sciō, scīre, scīvī/ sciī, scītum — scī, 4th
sentiō, sentīre, sēnsī, sēnsum — sentī, 4th
spērō, spērāre, spērāvī, spērātum — spērā, 1st
veniō, venīre, vēnī, ventum — venī, 4th

Exercise 3

Person	scīre		venīre	
	Singular	Plural	Singular	Plural
Present Tense				
1st	sciō / I know	scīmus / we know	veniō / I come	venīmus / we come
2nd	scīs / you know	scītis / you (pl.) know	venīs / you come	venītis / you (pl.) come
3rd	scit / he/she/it knows	sciunt / they know	venit / he/she/it comes	veniunt / they come
Imperfect Tense				
1st	sciēbam / I was knowing	sciēbāmus / we were knowing	veniēbam / I was coming	veniēbāmus / we were coming
2nd	sciēbās / you were knowing	sciēbātis / you (pl.) were knowing	veniēbās / you were coming	veniēbātis / you (pl.) were coming
3rd	sciēbat / he/she/it was knowing	sciēbant / they were knowing	veniēbat / he/she/it was coming	veniēbant / they were coming
Future Tense				
1st	sciam / I will know	sciēmus / we will know	veniam / I will come	veniēmus / we will come
2nd	sciēs / you will know	sciētis / you (pl.) will know	veniēs / you will come	veniētis / you (pl.) will come
3rd	sciet / he/she/it will know	scient / they will know	veniet / he/she/it will come	venient / they will come

Exercise 4

1. I <u>will listen</u> to my teacher carefully.   1/S/F   audiam
2. We <u>know</u> when you are arriving.   1/P/Pr   scīmus
3. <u>Will we agree</u> on a solution?   1/P/F   cōnsentiēmusne
4. I <u>kept on listening</u> to you even though I was working.   1/S/I   audiēbam
5. Caesar <u>knew</u> that Marc Antony was his friend.   3/S/Pf   scīvit/sciit
6. They <u>were coming</u> to see us, but the storm prevented them from doing so.   3/P/I   veniēbant
7. You girls always <u>listened</u> well.   2/P/Pf   audīvistis
8. The boys <u>have enlisted</u> in Caesar's army.   3/P/Pf   cōnscrīpsērunt

Exercise 5

Person	videō, vidēre, vīdī, vīsum		discēdō, discēdere, discessī, discessum	
	Singular	Plural	Singular	Plural
Perfect Tense				
1st	vīdī — I saw	vīdimus — we saw	discessī — I departed	discessimus — we departed
2nd	vīdistī — you saw	vīdistis — you (pl.) saw	discessīsti — you departed	discessistis — you (pl.) departed
3rd	vīdit — he/she/it saw	vīdērunt — they saw	discessit — he/she/it departed	discessērunt — they departed
Pluperfect Tense				
1st	vīderam — I had seen	vīderāmus — we had seen	discesseram — I had departed	discesserāmus — we had departed
2nd	vīderās — you had seen	vīderātis — you (pl.) had seen	discesserās — you had departed	discesserātis — you (pl.) had departed
3rd	vīderat — he/she/it had seen	vīderant — they had seen	discesserat — he/she/it had departed	discesserant — they had departed
Future Perfect Tense				
1st	vīderō — I will have seen	vīderimus — we will have seen	discesserō — I will have departed	discesserimus — we will have departed
2nd	vīderis — you will have seen	vīderitis — you (pl.) will have seen	discesseris — you will have departed	discesseritis — you (pl.) will have departed
3rd	vīderit — he/she/it will have seen	vīderint — they will have seen	discesserit — he/she/it will have departed	discesserint — they will have departed

Person	audiō, audīre, audīvī, audītum		ferō, ferre, tulī, lātum	
	Singular	Plural	Singular	Plural
Perfect Tense				
1st	audīvī — I heard	audīvimus — we heard	tulī — I carried	tulimus — we carried
2nd	audīvistī — you heard	audīvistis — you (pl.) heard	tulistī — you carried	tulistis — you (pl.) carried
3rd	audīvit — he/she/it heard	audīvērunt — they heard	tulit — he/she/it carried	tulērunt — they carried
Pluperfect Tense				
1st	audīveram — I had heard	audīverāmus — we had heard	tuleram — I had carried	tulerāmus — we had carried
2nd	audīverās — you had heard	audīverātis — you (pl.) had heard	tulerās — you had carried	tulerātis — you (pl.) had carried
3rd	audīverat — he/she/it had heard	audīverant — they had heard	tulerat — he/she/it had carried	tulerant — they had carried

	FUTURE PERFECT TENSE			
1st	*audīverō* I will have heard	*audīverimus* we will have heard	*tulerō* I will have carried	*tulerimus* we will have carried
2nd	*audīveris* you will have heard	*audīveritis* you (pl.) will have heard	*tuleris* you will have carried	*tuleritis* you (pl.) will have carried
3rd	*audīverit* he/she/it will have heard	*audīverint* they will have heard	*tulerit* he/she/it will have carried	*tulerint* they will have carried

Exercise 6

LATIN	PERSON	NUMBER	TENSE	TRANSLATION
mittēbam	**1**	**Sing.**	**Imp.**	**I used to send**
cōnsentit	3	Sing.	Pres.	He agrees
vīderis	2	Sing.	Fut. Perf.	You will have seen
audiēmus	1	Pl.	Fut.	We will listen
rettulistī	2	Sing.	Perf.	You brought back
dūxerant	3	Pl.	Pluperf.	They had led
petīvit	3	Sing.	Perf.	He sought
capiet	3	Sing.	Fut.	He will seize
sēnsimus	1	Pl.	Perf.	We perceived
spērāverās	2	Sing.	Pluperf.	You (sing.) had hoped
superāverant	3	Pl.	Pluperf.	They had overcome
vēnerint	3	Pl.	Fut. Perf.	They will have come
scīvistis	2	Pl.	Perf.	You (pl.) knew
reverteram	1	Sing.	Pluperf.	I had returned

Exercise 7

```
      S       DO    P     OP      V
1. Rēx    mīlitēs  in Galliam  dūxerat.
   n/s/m   ac/p/m      ac/s/f   3/s/pp
   The king had led soldiers into Gaul.
```

```
      Adj      AbT      S    P   Adj     OP     P   OP      V
2. Tribus mēnsibus lēgātī ā multīs gentibus ad ducem vēnērunt.
   ab/p/m   ab/p/m   n/p/m  ab/p/f  ab/p/f      ac/s/m  3/p/per
   In 3 months the delegates have come/came from many nations/tribes to the leader/general.
```

```
      Adv   P   Adj    OP      Inf      S+V
3. Nunc ad nostram terram revenīre cōnsēnsimus.
               ac/s/f   ac/s/f         1/p/perf
   Now we agreed to return to our own land.
```

```
      S      Adj      Adj     DO     Adv      V
4. Mīlitēs Rōmānī multōs Germānōs mox necāverint.
   n/p/m   n/p/m   ac/p/m   ac/p/m        3/p/fp
   The Roman soldiers will soon have killed many Germans.
```

```
      S   HV    V      CoInf        DO
5. All were hoping to conquer the enemy.
   Omnēs spērābant superāre hostem.
   n/p/m   3/p/i            ac/s/m
```

```
      Adj   S    PG      HV    V   DO    CoInf
6. One nation out of many had asked them to return.
   Ūna  gēns  ē  multīs rogāverat eōs  revertere/revenīre.
   n/s/f n/s/f    ab/p/f  3/s/pp  ac/p/m
```

```
      Adj    S    HV  Adv HV   V                Ab Means
```
7. Many soldiers will soon have perished by (means of) the sword.
```
   Multī  mīlitēs mox perīverint gladiō.
   n/p/m  n/p/m       3/p/fp   ab/s/m
      HV    S    V         DO      Adv      V
```
8. Had he heard the messenger before he returned?
```
   Audīveratne  nūntium  ante  revēnit?
     3/s/pp      ac/s/m         3/s/per
```

Translation

In the year 696 A.U.C. (since the founding of the city), otherwise 58 before Christ, Caesar was governor in Cisalpine Gaul and in those parts which are in certain parts of Italy. Many years before, Ariovistus, king of the Germans, had led soldiers into Gaul because one tribe of the Gauls asked him to do thus. Ariovistus had not left Gaul. One tribe, the Aedui, sought aid from the Romans. Many Germans joined themselves to Ariovistus, who was at that time across the Rhine. All these were hoping to conquer all of Gaul.

At the same time the Helvetians, another Gallic tribe, who were living around Lake Geneva, were beginning to make a journey westward. Caesar (spoke) with himself (i.e. said to himself) "These Helvetians will go across into Roman land." With his own money and without the authority from the senate, Caesar enlisted four legions. He sent a messenger to Ariovistus. Caesar wished to speak with the German king. Ariovistus however did not wish to speak with Caesar. He sent a messenger not friendly to Caesar. The message was, "No one contends with me without his own destruction." Now delegates came to Caesar from many tribes seeking aid. Caesar declared war upon the Helvetians and the Germans. Around a town called Bribactus, the Romans under Caesar overcame the Helvetians. The Helvetians now wished to return to their own land. Caesar agreed. He said, however, "It is necessary for all Helvetians to live under the rule of the Romans." Then Caesar fought with the Germans near the Rhine. The Roman soldiers killed many Germans, but Ariovistus fled. After a little while Ariovistus will also have died.

Respondē Latīnē!

1. Quis mīlitēs Germānōs in Galliam dūxerat?
   Ariovistus, rēx Germanōrum, mīlitēs in Galliam dūxerat.

   Who had led the German soldiers into Gaul?
   Ariovistus, king of the Germans, led the soldier into Gaul.

2. Quae gēns auxilium ā Rōmānīs petīvit?
   Aeduī petīvērunt auxilium ā Rōmānīs.

   What tribe sought help from the Romans?
   The Aedui sought help from the Romans.

3. Ubi habitābant Helvētiī?
   Helvētiī circum Lacum Lemannum habitābant.

   Where were the Helvetians living?
   The Helvetians were living around Lake Geneva.

4. Quō iter faciēbant Helvētiī?
   Incēpērunt iter facere ad sōlis occāsum.

   Where were the Helvetians journeying?
   They began to make a journey to the west.

5. Ubi pugnābat Caesar cum mīlitibus suīs Germānōs?
   Prope Rhēnum Germānōs pugnābat.

   Where was Caesar fighting the Germans with his soldiers?
   He was fighting them near the Rhine.

ANSWER IN ENGLISH!

1. What Gallic tribe asked the Romans for help?
   The Aedui

2. What was the wish of Ariovistus and the Gauls who had joined him?
   They wished to conquer Gaul.

3. When Caesar sent a message to Ariovistus asking him to discuss the matter at hand, what did Ariovistus reply? (Give his whole answer.)
   "No one contends with me without his own destruction."

4. After the battle at Bribacte, what did the Helvetians want to do?
   They wished to return to their own land.

5. What was Caesar's condition concerning allowing them to do as they wished?
   They must live under Roman rule.

Montanī Semper Līberī
Mountaineers are Always Free
—West Virginia state motto^A

Chapter 28

- fourth declension
  - domus
- principal part study
  - formation of adjectives and nouns from supine

VOCABULARY

Nouns			
cornū, ūs, n.	wing (of an army); horn	(cornucopia, cornet, unicorn)
domus, ūs, f.	house, home	(domicile, domestic)
exercitus, ūs, m.	army	
frūctus, ūs, m.	fruit, profit, benefit	(fructose, frugal)
genū, ūs, n.	knee	(genuflect)
hiems, hiemis, f.	winter	(hiemal)
impetus, ūs, m.	attack; charge; impulse	(impetuous)
manus, ūs, f.	hand; band (of men)	(manual, manumit)
nix, nivis, f.	snow	(snow)
passus, ūs, m.	pace, footstep	(pace)
mīlle passūs, mīlia passuum	miles (1000 paces)	
rūs, rūris, n.	country (as opposed to city)	(rural, rusticate)
senātus, ūs, m.	senate; body of elders	(senate, senatorial)
vultus, vultūs, m.	face, visage	
Verbs		
adveniō, advenīre, advēnī, adventum	to arrive, come to	(advent)
carpō, carpere, carpsī, carptum	to seize, pluck	(carpal)
iungō, iungere, iūnxī, iūnctum	to join, unite	(conjunction)

Exercise 1. Using the rules for syllabication and accent that you have learned, write out the syllables and accents for the vocabulary words above. Then practice pronouncing them aloud.

The fourth declension endings are very similar in some ways to the third declension; they differ in that the vowel *u* is featured in every form. Compare the following chart to that of third declension nouns in chapter 10 (Section 29). How are these declensions alike? How are they different?

CASE	ENDINGS		MASCULINE & FEMININE	
	SING.	PLURAL	SING.	PLURAL
Nominative	-us	-ūs	frūctus	frūctūs
Genitive	-ūs	-uum	frūctūs	frūctuum
Dative	-uī	-ibus	frūctuī	frūctibus
Accusative	-um	-ūs	frūctum	frūctūs
Ablative	-ū	-ibus	frūctū	frūctibus

Notā Bene:
- The masculine and feminine forms are the same.
- The nominative and accusative endings are similar to third, replacing the *e* with a *u*.
- The genitive plural still ends in *um*, as it has for every declension thus far: *ā*rum, *ō*rum, um, *u*um.
- The dative and ablative plural are identical to third declension.
- The ablative singular ends in a single vowel, as it has for every declension.

Caveat Discipulus: **Domus** is a fourth declension feminine noun, but it does use the accusative plural form *(domōs)* and the ablative singular form *(domō)* from the second declension.

TE **Exercise 2.** Following the example of *frūctus*, decline *manus* and *impetus*. Decline *domus* using the *caveat* above.[B]

> [B]It has been some time since the text has introduced a noun declension. Teachers may want to use the declension worksheet to review the patterns for the first three declensions as well.

SECTION 74: More on Place Expressions

In chapter 11 you learned how to express place in Latin with prepositional phrases. Do you remember which cases the following place expressions use? Identify the appropriate case for each of these expressions.

> place where: ablative
> place to which: accusative
> place from which: ablative

There is a small group of Latin nouns that do not use prepositional phrases for place expressions. Instead the noun appears in the appropriate case as listed above without a preposition for "place to which" and "place from which." The expression of "place where" uses a special case known as the locative, which you will learn in Latin Alive Book II. Memorize the following rule to help you remember which nouns do NOT use a preposition to express place.

The names of cities, towns, small islands in the Mediterranean, and the nouns *domus, humus* and *rūs* do NOT use prepositions for expressions of place.

In the case of *domus* this is not unlike English. Think about how you use the word "home" when referring to a place. Most people often omit the preposition they would normally use with other nouns.

> I want to go **to the house.**   **Ad casam** īre volō.
> I want to go **home.**   **Domum** īre volō.

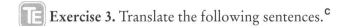

Exercise 3. Translate the following sentences.[c]

1. Caesar Crētam nōn nāvigāvit.
2. Vōs domō nocte nōn dēbētis īre.
3. Illī puerī in magnā urbe habitābant.
4. Eae puellae humō flōrēs carpsērunt.
5. He went to the country.
6. We lived in the town.
7. Caesar led his soldiers to Britain.
8. You (pl.) had gone away from Rome.

> [c]For additional practice on these new place expressions, have students compose their own Latin sentences demonstrating "place to which" and "place from which" using the following words: *oppidum*, *īnsula*, *terra*, *casa*, *Ītalia*, *Rōma*, *Corsica*, *domus*, *humus*, *rūs*. Before you begin, identify together which nouns will use prepositions and which nouns will not. (The first five will use prepositions, the rest will not.)

SECTION 75. Fourth Declension – Neuter

Most nouns in the fourth declension are masculine. The few feminine and neuter exceptions that do exist, however, are quite common.

FEMININE		NEUTER	
domus, ūs	house	cornū, ūs	wing (of an army); horn
manus, ūs	hand; band (of men)	genū, ūs	knee

The feminine nouns share the same endings as the masculine, but the neuter have their own unique set of endings. The singular forms should be very easy for you to memorize. The plural are nearly identical to those for masculine and feminine, but notice that the short *a* makes its usual appearance in the nominative and accusative plural.

	ENDINGS		NEUTER	
CASE	SING.	PLURAL	SING.	PLURAL
Nominative	-ū	-ua	genū	genua
Genitive	-ūs	-uum	genūs	genuum
Dative	-ū	-ibus	genū	genibus
Accusative	-ū	-ua	genū	genua
Ablative	-ū	-ibus	genū	genibus

Exercise 4. Following the example of *genū*, decline *cornū*.

Exercise 5. Identify the declension, gender, number, and case for each of the following nouns. Provide all possibilities.

Example: frūctūs – fourth declension; masculine; nominative plural, genitive singular, accusative plural

1. cornū
2. domōs
3. frūctuum
4. ducibus
5. genūs
6. impetibus
7. dōnum
8. manū
9. auxilia
10. passus

So far you have learned a use for the first three principal parts listed with each verb. Here is a brief review:

First principal part *(videō)* – dictionary entry; first person, singular, present tense
Second principal part *(vidēre)* – infinitive, provides the stem for the present system
Third principal part *(vīdī)* – first person, singular, perfect tense; provides the stem for the perfect system.

That leaves only the fourth principal part *(vīsum)*. This form is the equivalent to the perfect passive participle in English, "having been seen, seen." We will learn more about the perfect passive participle in the sequel to this text. For now, we will look at another great benefit to knowing your fourth principal part. It is from this form that Latin derives many adjectives and fourth declension nouns.

Example:
videō, vidēre, vīdī, vīsum, to see   *vīsus, vīsūs, m. sight, seeing*
parō, parāre, parāvī, parātum, to prepare   *parātus, -a,-um, adj. prepared*

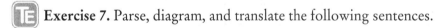 **Exercise 6.** Discern the meaning of each of the following nouns and adjectives based on the verb from which they are derived. Use your Latin dictionary to check your answers.

1. metus (metuō)
2. amātus (amō)
3. spīritus (spīrō)
4. adventus (adveniō)
5. vīsus (videō)
6. dictum (dīcō)
7. narrātus (narrō)
8. vulgātus (vulgō)

Exercise 7. Parse, diagram, and translate the following sentences.

1. Eō tempore, nūntius ad Caesarem advēnit.

2. Ā Germāniā ad Galliam iterum revertet.

3. Caesar ipse cum aliīs cōpiīs ad Ītaliam iter fēcerat.

4. Hiems erat et erat alta nix.

5. Hī paucī ex exercitū Rōmānō oppidum cēpērunt.

Chapter Reading

CAESAR IN BRITAIN AND BEYOND

CHARACTERS:
Gaius Julius Caesar – a Roman general and statesman
Cassivelaunus – a British chieftain
Vercingetorix – a young Gallic chieftain, a great hero to the Gauls then and to the French now

Nōn scīmus **cūr Caesar ad Britanniam prōcesserit.** *Fortasse* <u>rūmōrēs</u> audīverat dē aurō et *margarītīs* aut ferrum et *stannum* capere voluit. *Fortasse* gentēs <u>Britanniae</u> Caesar **molestē tulit** quod multum auxilium Gallīs dederant. Annō LV ante Chrīstum Caesar parvō cum *numerō* mīlitum mare *angustum* trānsiit et *Britannōs*, quī nōn parātōs erant, vīcit. Post ūnum annum Caesar iterum ad <u>Britanniam</u> nāvigāvit. Illō tempore *Britannī* sub Cassivelaunō pugnābant. Caesar impetum fēcit. Ducem Cassivelaunum et *reliquōs Britannōs* vīcit. *Ūsque* ad *Tamesis* flūmen processit. Postulāvit *tribūtum* ē *Britannīs.* Tum ad Galliam revertit.

Deinde Caesar exercitum suum in Germāniam duxit. Ā Germāniā ad Galliam iterum revertit. Exercitus Rōmānus in Galliā mānsit, sed Caesar ipse cum aliīs cōpiīs ad Ītaliam iter fēcit. Hiemābant in Ītaliā. Eō tempore, nūntius ad Caesarem advēnit et dīxit, "Vercingetorix, prīnceps magnus Gallōrum, omnēs gentēs Gallicās iūnxit. Vercingetorix *paene* omnēs Gallōs **hortātus est** pugnāre prō lībertāte." Caesar magnā difficultāte in Galliam iter fēcit. *Hiems* erat; erat alta *nix.* Hic dux magnus Rōmānus—**in aliēnā veste occultus**—paucīs cum *equitibus,* trāns Galliam *equitāvit.* Tandem hī paucī ex exercitū Rōmānō oppidum in quō Vercingetorix erant cēpērunt. Vercingetorigem quoque cēpērunt et eum *paulō* post Rōmam mīsērunt. Erat in triumphō Caesaris ante mortem suam **manibus Rōmānīs.** Quid Caesar nunc faciet? Nunc Caesar domum revertet.

---

cūr Caesar ad Britanniam prōcesserit = why Caesar went to Britain
(This is an advanced construction called indirect question. The verb is in the perfect subjunctive, which you will learn in *Latin Alive! Book III.*)
molestē tulit = he resented
in aliēnā veste occultus – disguised (literally, "hidden in the clothes of someone else")
hortātus est = has encouraged
manibus Rōmānīs = at Roman hands, by the Romans

GLOSSARY
Use your "eye" Latin to discern the meanings of the underlined words.

fortasse, adv. .... perhaps
margarīta, ae, f. .... pearl
stannum, ī, n. .... tin
angustus, a, um, adj. .... narrow
numerus, ī, m. .... number
Britannī, ōrum, m. .... Britains
reliquus, a, um, adj. .... remaining [the] rest [of]
ūsque, adv. .... all the way (to, from)
Tamesis .... Thames, major river flowing through Southern England (The river flows through modern day London, Oxford, and Windsor.)
tribūtum, ī, n. .... tribute, payment, a type of tax levied upon a conquered people
hiemābant .... they were wintering, spending the winter
iter fēcit .... made a journey, traveled, marched
paene, adv. .... almost
eques, equitis, m. .... horseman, (pl.) cavalry
equitō, āre, āvī, ātum .... to ride (a horse)
paulō, adv. .... a short while

Respondē Latīnē!

 1. Quās rēs Caesar in Britannia fortasse capere voluit?

2. Quāle erat mare inter Galliam et Britanniam?

3. Illō tempore quis erat dux Britannōrum?

4. Ad quod flūmen īvit Caesar?

5. Quōmodo Caesar iter fēcit ab Ītaliā ad Galliam?

ANSWER IN ENGLISH!
1. How much time passed between Caesar's two trips to Britain?

2. Where did Caesar leave some of his troops when he went to Italy?

3. Who, according to a messenger, had encouraged almost all the Gauls to rebel against the Romans to gain their freedom?

4. Where did the Romans transport Vercingetorix?

5. How did Vercingetorix die?

GRAMMAR EXERCISE
Make the following singular nouns plural, keeping the same case.
1. rūmor
2. margarīta
3. gēns
4. annus
5. mare
6. Britannus
7. Gallus
8. lībertās

Colloquāmur

Use the following questions and responses to review the nouns in the sentences above. Use some "eye" Latin to figure out what the responses mean.

interrogātiō:	Cūius est numerī?	What number is it?
respōnsum:	Singulāriter est.	
	Plūrāliter est.	

interrogātiō:	Quō est cāsū?	In what case is it?
respōnsum:	Cāsū nōminātīvō est.	
	Cāsū accūsātīvō est.	
	Cāsū datīvō est.	
	Cāsū ablātīvō est.	
	Cāsū genitīvō est.	

respōnsum:	Est virīlis.
	Est muliebris.
	Est neutrālis.

Latin as a Mother Language

Latin is the mother of the Romance or Romanic languages. These languages are Italian, Spanish, Catalan, Ladino, Portuguese, French, Provençal and Romanian. The reading above contains many words that entered one or more Romance languages in nearly direct ways. Below are some of these words with their Romance language equivalents. There are also some explanations of certain patterns the changes followed.

Latin	Romance Language	English
margarīta	margarita (Spanish)	pearl
multum	mucho (Spanish)	much

When a Latin word had "lt," the Spanish word has "ch" in the same position. Also, an "um" in Latin becomes an "o" in Spanish. Another example of this phonetic change is obvious in how *auscultō* became *escucho*. Both mean "I listen."

Latin	Romance Language	English
numerus	número (Spanish)	number
mare	mar (Spanish) mer (French)	sea
facere	hacer (Spanish) faire (French)	make

An "f" in Latin becomes an "h" in Spanish. It stays an "f" in French. Thus the Latin *factum* becomes *hecho* in Spanish. Both mean "made."

This information is only the proverbial tip of the iceberg; however, you can begin to see why people say that knowing Latin helps in learning other languages.

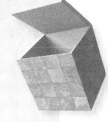

Challenge Box

Find out where people spoke or still speak Ladino.

Who were or are those people?

Chapter 28 Teacher's Pages

Exercise 1

cor-nū, ūs, n.
do-mus, ūs, f.
ex-er-ci-tus, ūs, m.
frūc-tus, ūs, m.
ge-nū, ūs, n.
hi-ems, hi-e-mis, f.
im-pe-tus, ūs, m.
ma-nus, ūs, f.
nix, ni-vis, f.

pas-sus, ūs, m.
mīl-le pas-sūs, mī-li-a pas-suum,
rūs, rū-ris, f.
se-nā-tus, ūs, m.
vul-tus, vul-tūs, m.
ad-ve-ni-ō, ad-ve-nī-re, ad-vē-nī, ad-ven-tum
car-pō, car-pe-re, carp-sī, carp-tum
iun-gō, iun-ge-re, iūn-xī, iūnc-tum

Exercise 2

CASE	manus		impetus		domus	
	SINGULAR	PLURAL	SINGULAR	PLURAL	SINGULAR	PLURAL
NOMINATIVE	manus	manūs	impetus	impetūs	domus	domūs
GENITIVE	manūs	manuum	impetūs	impetuum	domūs	domuum
DATIVE	manuī	manibus	impetuī	impetibus	domuī	domibus
ACCUSATIVE	manum	manūs	impetum	impetūs	domum	domōs
ABLATIVE	manū	manibus	impetū	impetibus	domō	domibus

Exercise 3

1. Caesar Crētam nōn nāvigāvit.   Caesar did not sail to Crete.
2. Vōs domō nocte nōn dēbētis īre.   You ought not to go away from home at night.
3. Illī puerī in magnā urbe habitābant. Those boys were living in a great city.
4. Eae puellae humō flōrēs carpsērunt.   Those girls plucked flowers from the ground.
5. He went to the country.   Rūs [is] īvit.
6. We lived in the town.   In oppidō [nōs] habitāvimus.
7. Caesar led his soldiers to Britain.   Caesar mīlitēs ad Britanniam dūxit.
8. You (pl.) had gone away from Rome.   Rōmā [vōs] abīverātis.

Exercise 4

CASE	cornū	
	SINGULAR	PLURAL
NOMINATIVE	cornū	cornua
GENITIVE	cornūs	cornuum
DATIVE	cornuī	cornibus
ACCUSATIVE	cornū	cornua
ABLATIVE	cornū	cornibus

Exercise 5

1. cornū — 4th decl; neuter, sing, nom/dat/acc/abl
2. domōs — 4th decl; fem, pl, acc
3. frūctuum — 4th decl; masc, pl, gen
4. ducibus — 3rd decl; masc, pl, dat/abl
5. genūs — 4th decl; neuter, sing, gen
6. impetibus — 4th decl; masc, pl, dat/abl
7. dōnum — 2nd decl; neuter, sing, nom/acc
8. manū — 4th decl; fem, sing, abl
9. auxilia — 2nd decl; neuter, pl, nom/acc
10. passus — 4th decl; masc, sing, nom

Exercise 6

1. metus (metuō) — fear, alarm, anxiety
2. amātus (amō) — beloved
3. spīritus (spīrō) — breath, breathing; spirit
4. adventus (adveniō) — arrival, approach
5. vīsus (videō) — sight, vision
6. dictum (dīcō) — saying, word, proverb
7. narrātus (narrō) — narrative
8. vulgātus (vulgō) — common, generally known; notorious

Exercise 7

    Adj   AbT   S   P   OP   V

1. Eō tempore, nūntius ad Caesarem advēnit.
   a/s/n a/s/n n/s/m   ac/s/m 3/s/per
   At that time, the messenger came to Caesar.

    P   OP   P   OP   Adv   V

2. Ā Germāniā ad Galliam iterum revertet.
    a/s/f   ac/s/f   3/s/f
   He will return from Germany to Gaul/France again.

    S   Adj P Adj OP P OP DO V

3. Caesar ipse cum aliīs cōpiīs ad ītaliam iter fēcerat.
   n/s/m n/s/m   ab/p/f ab/p/f   ac/s/f ac/s/n 3/s/pp
   Caesar himself had made a journey (traveled) with other troops to Italy.

    S   LV C LV Adj PrN

4. Hiems erat et erat alta nix.
   n/s/f 3/s/i   3/s/i n/s/f n/s/f
   It was winter and there was deep snow.

    Adj   Adj P OP   Adj   DO   V

5. Hī paucī ex exercitū Rōmānō oppidum cēpērunt.
   n/p/m n/p/m   ab/s/m ab/s/m ac/s/n 3/p/perf
   These few seized the town from the Roman army.

Translation

We do not know why Caesar went to Britain. Perhaps he had heard rumors about gold and pearls or he wanted to get iron and tin. Perhaps Caesar resented the tribes of Britain because they had given much help to the Gauls. In 55 BC Caesar, with a small number of soldiers, crossed the narrow sea and conquered the Britons, who were not prepared. After one year, Caesar again sailed to Britain. At that time, the Britons were fighting under Cassivelaunus. Caesar made an attack. He conquered the leader Cassivelaunus and the rest of the Britons. He went all the way [up to] the River Thames. He demanded tribute from the Britons. Then he returned to Gaul.

Then/next Caesar led his army into Germany. From Germany he returned again to Gaul. The Roman army stayed in Gaul, but Caesar himself with other troops traveled to Italy. They spent the winter in Italy. At that time, a messenger came to Caesar and said, "Vercingetorix, a great chieftain of the Gauls, has united all the Gallic tribes. Vercingetorix has encouraged almost all the Gauls to fight for freedom." Caesar traveled/marched into Gaul with great difficulty. It was winter; the snow was high. This great Roman general – disguised – with a few horsemen/knights rode horseback across Gaul. Finally, these few out of the army seized the town in which Vercingetorix was. They also seized Vercingetorix and a little later transported him to Rome. He was in Caesar's triumph before his death at the hands of the Romans. What will Caesar do now? Now Caesar will return home.

Respondē Latīnē!

1. Quās rēs Caesar in Britannia fortasse capere voluit?
Fortasse ferrum et stannum capere voluit.
What things did Caesar perhaps want to get in Britain?
Perhaps he wanted to get tin and iron.

2. Quāle erat mare inter Galliam et Britanniam?
Mare erat angustum.
What kind of sea was between Gaul and Britain?
The sea was narrow.

3. Illō tempore quis erat dux Britannōrum?
Dux erat Cassivelaunus.
At that time, who was the leader of the Britons?
The leader was Cassivelaunus.

4. Ad quod flūmen īvit Caesar?
Īvit ad flumen Thamesem.
To what river did Caesar go?
He went toward the Thames River.

5. Quōmodo Caesar iter fēcit ab Ītaliā ad Galliam?
Iter fēcit magnā cum difficultāte.
How [in what manne] did Caesar travel from Italy to Gaul?
He made the journey with great difficulty.

ANSWER IN ENGLISH!

1. How much time passed between Caesar's two trips to Britain?
one year

2. Where did Caesar leave some of his troops when he went to Italy?
in Gaul

3. Who, according to a messenger, had encouraged almost all the Gauls to rebel against the Romans to gain their freedom?
Vercingetorix

4. Where did the Romans transport Vercingetorix?
to Rome

5. How did Vercingetorix die?
at the hands of the Romans

GRAMMAR EXERCISE

1. rūmor — rūmōrēs
2. margarīta — margarītae
3. gēns — gentēs
4. annus — annī
5. mare — maria
6. Britannus — Britannī
7. Gallus — Gallī
8. lībertās — lībertātēs

Notes

Cēdant Arma Togae
Let arms yield to the toga
—Wyoming state motto[A]

This motto is taken from Cicero's Dē Officiīs, Book I, Chapter 22, Line 41.

[A]A woman draped in Roman clothing stands in the center. She holds a staff with a banner bearing the phrase "equal rights." When Wyoming joined the U.S. in 1890, women's suffrage was under great debate. Wyoming was among those who advocated equal rights for women. On either side of the woman are two ancient pillars with oil lamps representing knowledge. Scrolls around each pillar proclaim the state's economic resources: oil, mines, livestock, and grain. The cowboy and the miner also represent Wyoming's main industries. Below the trio is a shield surmounted by an American eagle. The number 44 on the shield indicates Wyoming's place as the 44th state in the Union. The date 1869 (left) is the date Wyoming became a territory. The date 1890 (right) is the year she gained statehood.

Chapter 29

• fifth declension

VOCABULARY

NOUNS		
diēs, diēī, m/f.	day (feminine used for an appointed or set day)	(diurnal, modern)
faciēs, faciēī, f.	face, appearance	(facial)
fidēs, fideī, f.	faith, trust	(fidelity)
rēs, reī, f.	thing, matter, affair; state	(Republic)
rēs pūblica, reī pūblicae, f.	state, republic	
spēs, speī, f.	hope	(desperate)
voluntās, voluntātis, f.	will, wish	(voluntary)
VERBS		
agō, agere, ēgī, āctum	to do, drive, act	(agent, action)
dīmittō, dīmittere, dīmīsī, dīmissum	to send away, dismiss	(dismiss, dismissal)
permittō, permittere, permīsī, permissum	to permit, allow	(permission)
ADJECTIVES		
cīvīlis, cīvīle	civil	(civil)
dignus, a, um	worthy	(dignified)
fessus, fessa, fessum	tired	

Exercise 1. Using the rules for syllabication and accent that you have learned, write out the syllables and accents for the vocabulary words above. Then practice pronouncing them aloud.

The fifth declension is the smallest of all declensions. The words that belong to this group are few, but some of these words are among the most common in the Latin language. So, be diligent to learn this last set of declension endings.

Whereas the fourth declension endings are characterized by a *u*, the fifth declension endings are characterized by an *e*. Whereas the fourth declension consisted of predominantly masculine nouns, the fifth declension consists only of the feminine. The exception to this rule of gender is the noun *diēs (day)*, which can be either masculine or feminine. Some of the endings for this new declension may seem very different, but some should also be quite familiar.

	ENDINGS		FEMININE	
CASE	SING.	PLURAL	SING.	PLURAL
Nominative	-ēs	-ēs	diēs	diēs
Genitive	-ēī, -eī	-ērum	diēī	diērum
Dative	-ēī, eī	-ēbus	diēī	diēbus
Accusative	-em	-ēs	diem	diēs
Ablative	-ē	-ēbus	diē	diēbus

Notā Bene:
- The nominative and accusative endings are similar to third declension.
- The genitive plural still ends in *um*, as it has for every declension thus far: *ā*rum, *ō*rum, um, *u*um, *ē*rum.
- The dative and ablative plural are similar to third declension -*ibus*.
- The ablative singular ends in a single vowel, as it has for every declension.

Caveat Discipulus:
There are two alternate endings for the genitive and dative singular. In the first both vowels are long; in the second the *e* is short. The combination of two long vowels side-by-side is unusual in Latin. It occurs in the fifth declension when the stem of the noun ends in a vowel. If the stem ends in a consonant, then use the short *e*.

> diēs, diēī – stem = di / ēī - vowel stem
>
> spēs, speī – stem = sp / eī - consonant stem

Exercise 2. Following the example of *diēs*, decline *rēs* and *faciēs*. Be careful to determine whether nouns will have -*ēī* or -*eī* in the genitive and dative singular.

Exercise 3. Identify the case, number, and gender of the underlined nouns. Translate underlined phrases.

1. Give us <u>this day</u> our daily bread.

2. I wash <u>my face</u> every morning.

3. We place <u>our faith</u> in God.

4. <u>Our hopes</u> were high!

5. The beginning <u>of that affair</u> caused the war.

Exercise 4. Parse, diagram, and translate the following sentences.

1. Tū eris hostis sī cōpiās tuās nōn dīmīseris.

2. Caesar contrā voluntātēs senātūs aget.

3. Quod cōpiās suās ūnus dux nōn dīmīsit, alter dux quoque copiās suās tenuit.

4. Erit dē factō bellum cīvīle, et nūlla spēs pācī.

5. Do not permit him to go across the river! (Hint: see Section 57)

6. Who wishes to guard the republic?

7. The leader sailed across the sea with his army.

8. At that time the senate dismissed all hope.

Chapter Reading ᵀᴱ

CAESAR CROSSES THE RUBICON

CHARACTERS:

Gaius Julius Caesar – a Roman general and statesman, soon to be dictator for life
Marcus Marcellus – a Roman against Caesar
Cato the Younger – a highly conservative Roman, against Caesar
Pompeius Magnus – Pompey the Great, a sometime friend, now enemy of Caesar
Titus Labienus – a former favorite lieutenant of Caesar, now on Pompey's side

Post Bellum Gallicum Caesar erat Galliae gubernātor. Caesar fessus est ob bellum, sed studet cōnsulātuī. Vult servīre reī pūblicae. *Rē vērā*, vult rem pūblicam servāre. Mārcus Mārcellus, tamen, dīxit, "Caesar, nōn *licet* tibi cōnsul esse." Catō **iūnior** dīxit Mārcellō et senātōribus, "Vōs *rēctē* dīcitis. Ego spērō vidēre istum Caesarem ex Ītaliā *expellī*." Tribūnī, tamen, *vōtō* suō Caesarem servāverant. Et Caesar et Pompēius Magnus ūnam legiōnem nunc in *Parthiam* mīsērunt. Amīcī Caesaris, tamen, eī dīcēbant, "Caesar, legiō tua nōn est in *Parthiā*; est *Capuae*." Hōc tempore Caesar senātum rogāvit, "Mē permittite, senātōrēs, esse *candidātum cōnsulātuī* in underline{absentiā}." Senātōrēs *recūsāvērunt*. Dīxērunt, "Caesar, tū nōn dēbēs *candidātus cōnsulātuī* esse. Cōpiās dīmitte!" Caesar cōnsēnsit. Necesse est quoque Pompēiō copiās suās dēmittere, sed Pompēius nōn vult sīc agere.

Tum quod cōpiās suās Pompēius nōn dīmīsit, Caesar quoque cōpiās suās tenuit. Senātus, igitur, dīxit, "Caesar, tū eris hostis reī pūblicae sī nōn cōpiās tuās dīmīseris." Senātus tum Pompēiō dedit **senātūs cōnsultum ultimum**. Dē factō, Pompēius nunc est dictātor. **Eōdem tempore** Caesar agnōscit Titum Labiēnum, quī cum Caesare in Galliā *fuisset* et quī optimus amīcus Caesarī *fuisset*, Pompēium nunc adiuvāre.

Caesar ad sē vocāvit Legiōnem XIII. Dīxit eīs, "**Commīlitōnēs!** Senātōrēs mē nōn audīvērunt. Mē *rēiēcērunt*! Istī senātōrēs et aliī *Rōmae* nōn sunt dignī **optimīs** reī pūblicae. Vultisne mē *sequī*?" Omnēs Caesarem *sequī* voluērunt. Nūllus homō Caesarem *recūsāvit*.

Certā diē, ante diem iv Īdūs Iānuāriās, annō DCCV AUC, aliter XLIX ante Chrīstum, Caesar cum ūnā legiōne, Rubicōnem trānsīvit. Rubicō erat *minimum* flūmen. Erat fīnis Galliae Cisalpīnae. Caesar nunc erat, contrā voluntātēs senātūs, in Ītaliā. Caesar dīxit hōc tempore, "**Ālea iacta est!**" Aliae legiōnēs nunc Caesarem iūnxērunt. Erit nunc dē factō bellum cīvīle inter Caesarem et Pompēium. Pompēius Rōmā discessit et cōpiās suās *Brundisium* dūxit et trāns mare nāvigāvit. Caesar Rōmam intrāvit. Hī quī Caesarem nōn adiuvābant effūgērunt. Mox Caesar underline{dictātor} erit et paulō post, **trīste dictū**, periet.

---

iūnior = the younger
(Cato the Younger as opposed to Cato the Elder, his great grandfather whom you read about in Chapter Reading 5 – we typically use the phrases "junior" and "senior" instead.)
senātūs cōnsultum ultimum – a decree by the senate charging someone to "see that no harm should come to the state." The person receiving this charge was virtually the dictator. Cicero had had this charge from the senate during the Catilinarian conspiracy.
eōdem tempore = at that same time
commīlitōnēs = fellow soldiers
optimīs = the best things
Ālea iacta est! = The die is/has been cast!
trīste dictū = sad to say

GLOSSARY
Use your "eye" Latin to discern the meaning of the underlined words.

cōnsulātus, cōnsulātūs, m. .... the consulship
rē vērā .... in truth, truly
nōn licet (+ dat.) .... it is not allowed to/for _____ (impersonal verb)
rectē, adv. .... rightly, correctly
expellī .... to be expelled, to be driven out
vōtum, ī, n. .... vote; vow
Parthia, Parthiae, f. .... Parthia, a country where Iran is today
Capua, Capuae, f. .... an Italian town
candidātus, candidātī, m. .... one wearing the *toga candida*, a candidate
fuisset .... was
recūsō, recūsāre, recūsāvī, recūsātum ... refuse
rēiciō, rēicere, rēiēcī, rēiectum .... to reject
Rōmae .... at Rome
sequī .... to follow
certus, a, um, adj. .... certain
minimus, minima, minimum, adj. .... smallest, very small
Brundisium, Brundisiī, n. .... an Italian port on the Adriatic Sea

A Special Note from the Authors

It would have been impossible for us in this brief Latin reading to present to you all the details leading up to the civil war, the awarding to Caesar of the dictatorship for life, and his death. One of the best accounts of all this is in *The Story of Civilization III: Caesar and Christ*, by Will Durant (pp. 180–197). If you are interested in this story, you should read this account or an account in some other scholarly work.

Respondē Latīnē!

1. Quam ob rem erat Caesar fessus?

2. Quis Caesarem expellī voluit?

3. Quā rē tribūnī Caesarem servāvērunt?

4. Ubi erat legiō Caesaris?

5. Quī amīcus Caesaris nunc Pompēium Magnum adiuvat?

ANSWER IN ENGLISH!

1. At one time, where did both Pompey and Caesar send their armies?

2. Under what condition did Caesar request that he be allowed to run for the consulship?

3. Why did Caesar not dismiss his troops?

4. What would be the effect of Caesar's addressing Legion XII as *commīlitōnēs* rather than as *mīlitēs*?

5. What action of Caesar brought about the civil war?

Colloquāmur

Use the following questions and responses to review the nouns in the sentences above. Use some "eye" Latin to figure out what the responses mean.

interrogātiō:	**Cūius est numerī?**	What number is it?
respōnsum:	**Singulāriter est.**	
	Plūrāliter est.	
interrogātiō:	**Quō est cāsū?**	In what case is it?
respōnsum:	**Cāsū nōminātīvō est.**	
	Cāsū accūsātīvō est.	
	Cāsū datīvō est.	
	Cāsū ablātīvō est.	
	Cāsū genitīvō est.	
interrogātiō:	**Cūius est generis?**	What gender is it?
respōnsum:	**Est virīlis.**	
	Est muliebris.	
	Est neutrālis.	

Chapter 29 Teacher's Pages

Exercise 1

di-ēs, di-ē-ī, m/f.
fa-ci-ēs, fa-ci-ē-ī, f.
fi-dēs, fi-de-ī, f.
rēs, re-ī f.
rēs pū-bli-ca, re-ī pū-bli-cae, f.
spēs, spe-ī, f.
vo-lun-tās, vo-lun-tā-tis, f.

a-gō, a-ge-re, ē-gī, ac-tum
dī-mit-tō, dī-mit-te-re, dī-mī-sī, dī-mis-sum
per-mit-tō, per-mit-tere, per-mī-sī, per-mis-sum
cī-vi-lis, cī-vi-le
dig-nus, a, um
fes-sus, fes-sa, fes-sum

Exercise 2

	rēs		*faciēs*	
CASE	SINGULAR	PLURAL	SINGULAR	PLURAL
NOMINATIVE	*rēs*	*rēs*	*faciēs*	*faciēs*
GENITIVE	*reī*	*rērum*	*faciēī*	*faciērum*
DATIVE	*reī*	*rēbus*	*faciēī*	*faciēbus*
ACCUSATIVE	*rem*	*rēs*	*faciem*	*faciēs*
ABLATIVE	*rē*	*rēbus*	*faciē*	*faciēbus*

Exercise 3

1. Give us this day our daily bread. — Abl, sing, fem. = hāc diē
2. I wash my face every morning. — Acc, sing, fem. = meam faciem
3. We place our faith in God. — Acc, sing, fem. = nostram fidem
4. Our hopes were high! — Nom, pl, fem. = nostrae spēs
5. The beginning of that affair caused the war. — Gen, sing, fem. = illīus/ēius reī

Exercise 4

   S   LV   PrN C DO   Adj Adv   V

1. Tū eris hostis sī cōpiās tuās nōn dīmīseris.
   n/s 2/s/f n/s/m   ac/p/f ac/p/f   2/s/fp
   You will be an enemy if you will not have sent away your troops.

      S   P   OP   PNA   V

2. Caesar contrā voluntātēs senātūs aget.
   n/s/m   ac/p/f   g/s/m 3/s/f
   Caesar will act against the wishes of the senate.

      C   DO Adj Adj S Adv V   Adj   S   C   DO   Adj   V

3. Quod cōpiās suās ūnus dux nōn dīmīsit, alter dux quoque cōpiās suās   tenuit.
   ac/p/f ac/p/f n/s/m   n/s/m   3/s/perf n/s/m n/s/m   ac/p/f ac/p/f 3/s/perf
   Because one leader/general did not send away his own troops, another leader/general also held his own troops.

       LV   P   OP   SN   Adj C Adj   S   DR

4. Erit dē factō bellum cīvīle, et nūlla spēs pācī.
   3/s/f   ab/s/n ac/s/n ac/s/n   n/s/f n/s/f d/s/f
   There will be civil war concerning the deed, and no hope for peace.

       HV Adv V   DO Inf   P   OP

5. Do not permit him to go across the river! (Hint: see Section 57)
   Nōlī permittere eum īre trāns flūmen(n)/rivum(m).
   2/s/p   imp   ac/s/m   ac/s/m,n

         S   V   Inf   DO

6. Who wishes to guard the republic?
   Quis   vult dēfendere/servāre rem pūblicam?
   n/s/m 3/s/p   ac/s/f

         S   V   P   OP P Adj OP

7. The leader sailed across the sea with his army.
   Dux   nāvigāvit trāns mare cum (ēius) exercitū.
   n/s/m 3/s/perf   ac/s/n   g/s/m ab/s/m

        AbT   S   V   Adj DO

8. At that time the senate dismissed all hope.
   Eō   tempore senātus dīmīsit omnem spem.
   ab/s/n ab/s/n   n/s/m 3/s/perf ac/s/f ac/s/f

Translation

    After the Gallic War, Caesar was governor of Gaul. Caesar is tired on account of the war, but he is eager for the consulship/consulate. He wants to serve the republic. Indeed, he wants to save the republic. Marcus Marcellus, however, said, "Caesar, it is not permitted to you to be consul/you may not be consul." Cato the younger said to Marcellus and the senators, "You are speaking correctly. I hope to see that Caesar driven out of Italy." The tribunes, however, had saved Caesar with their vote. Both Caesar and Pompey the Great now sent one legion [each] into Parthia. Friends of Caesar, however, were saying/ kept saying to him, "Caesar, your legion is not in Parthia; it is at Capua." At this time Caesar asked the senate, "Allow me, senators, to be a candidate for the consulship in absentia/while I am absent [i.e. am not in Italy]." The senators refused. They said, "Caesar, you must not/ought not be a candidate for the consulship. Dismiss your troops!" Caesar agreed. It is also necessary for Pompey to dismiss his troops, but Pompey does not with to act thus/to do this.

    Then because Pompey did not dismiss his troops, Caesar also held [on to] his own troops. The senate, therefore, said, "Caesar, you will be an enemy of the republic unless you will have dismissed your troops." The senate then gave Pompey the senātūs consultum ultimum. In fact, Pompey now is dictator. At that same time, Caesar found out that Titus Labienus, who had been with Caesar in Gaul and had been the best friend to Caesar, was now supporting Pompey.

    Caesar summoned Legion Thirteen to him. He said to them, "Fellow soldiers! The senators did not listen to me. They rejected me! Those senators and others at Rome are not worthy of the best things of the republic. Do you want to follow me?" All wanted to follow Caesar. Not any man refused Caesar.

    On a certain day, January 10 in the 705th year from the founding of the city, otherwise 49 BC, Caesar, with one legion, crossed the Rubicon. The Rubicon was a very small river. It was the boundary of Cisapline Gaul. Caesar was now, against the wishes of the senate, in Italy. Caesar said at this time, "Alea iacta est (The die is cast)." Other legions now joined Caesar. There will not be, in fact, a civil war between Caesar and Pompey. Pompey left Rome and led his troops to Brundisium and across the sea. Caesar entered Rome. Those who were not supporting Caesar fled. Soon Caesar will be dictator; a little while after that, sad to say, he will die.

Respondē Latīnē!

1. Quam ob rem erat Caesar fessus?
   Caesar fessus erat ob bellum.

   For what reason was Caesar tired?
   Caesar was tired on account of the war.

2. Quis Caesarem expellī voluit?
   Catō iūnior Caesarem expellī voluit.

   Who wished to expel Caesar?
   Cato the younger wanted Caesar expelled.

3. Quā rē tribūnī Caesarem servāvērunt?
   Vōtō tribūnī Caesarem servāvērunt.

   By what thing did the tribunes save Caesar?
   The tribunes saved Caesar by their vote.

4. Ubi erat legiō Caesaris?
   Legiō Caesaris erat Capuae.

   Where was Caesar's legion?
   Caesar's legion was at Capua.

5. Quī amīcus Caesaris nunc
   Pompēium Magnum adiuvat?
   Titus Labiēnus nunc Pompēium
   Magnum adiūvat.

   Which friend of Caesar now helps
   Pompey the Great?
   Titus Labienus now helped Pompey the Great.

ANSWER IN ENGLISH!

1. At one time, where did both Pompey and Caesar send their armies?
   to Parthia

2. Under what condition did Caesar request that he be allowed to run for the consulship?
   in absentia

3. Why did Caesar not dismiss his troops?
   Pompey refused to dismiss his troops.

4. What would be the effect of Caesar's addressing Legion XII as commīlitōnēs rather than as mīlitēs?
   They would feel that he was one of them; they would love and admire him even more than they already did.

5. What action of Caesar brought about the civil war?
   crossing the Rubicon

Notes

Unit 7 Reading

Reading and Review for Chapters 27–29

KING CAESAR?
By Christopher Schlect

We name things as a way of organizing our complicated world. We even name time. The Romans knew that humans do not rule over time, but rather are ruled by it, so they named the months after their gods. They named Iānuārius (January) after the god Iānus (Janus, the god of doors, who opened the year), Mārtius (March) after Mars, god of war, Iūnius (June) after Iūnō (Juno, wife of Jupiter), and so on. They named years after their great city, which held more majesty than any one person. Note, for example, how Livy dates a historical event: *"anno trecentēsimō decimō quam urbs Rōma condita"* (in the year 310 from the founding of Rome—Livy IV.7).

This changed in 44 BC, when a mere human being became larger even than time itself. In that year the Senate named time after a man who ruled over Rome and even over the calendar, a man they deemed equal to the gods. They renamed the month "Quīntīlis," and called it Iūlius (July), after Julius Caesar.

Caesar defeated his rival Pompey at the Battle of Pharsalus in 48 BC and chased him on to Egypt, where he found that Pompey had already been killed. While there, he grew enchanted with Queen Cleopatra and even fathered a child by her, despite the fact that he was still married to Calpurnia. Caesar even fought Cleopatra's wars for her, attacking her enemy Pharnaces of Pontus. When he achieved victory after just five days, Caesar proclaimed, "*Vēnī, vīdī, vīcī*" (I came, I saw, I conquered). Caesar seemed to act more and more like his new lover, like a Pharaoh of Egypt: above the law, above his marriage, and even above time itself— that is, like a god.

Caesar spent the next two years crisscrossing the Mediterranean and sweeping away the remnants of Pompey's supporters. Meanwhile, back in Rome, the Romans heaped unprecedented honors upon him. They dubbed him *Pater Pātriae*, "father of the fatherland"; put up a statue of him among those of Rome's ancient kings; placed his image in the temple of Quirinus; erected a new temple to his clemency and appointed a *flāmen* (priest) to serve there; and put his image on coinage—the first living person to be represented this way. The people loved Caesar, but many senators sensed that their influence, and the Republic itself, were slipping away.

Caesar received power that would ordinarily be held by a dozen separate people in the Roman Republic. He was consul continuously from the year 48 BC onward, and sole consul in 45 BC; he received the immunity of a tribune; and in 46 BC he received censorial powers as *Praefectus Mōrum* (Prefect of Morals) which enabled him to enlarge the Senate and fill it with his supporters. Most importantly, he became dictator in 49 BC, again in 47 BC, and in 46 BC they declared that he would serve in that office for ten consecutive

223

one-year terms. The dictatorship was an unusual office granted only in time of emergency, and only for the duration of the emergency—usually six months. The model for dictatorship had been the famous Cincinnatus, who received dictatorial power, led Rome out of an emergency, then surrendered his office and retired to his farm. Julius Caesar was no Cincinnatus. He used his dictatorship to enact sweeping reforms that bolstered his popularity with the people. He freed slaves, cancelled debts, gave pensions to veterans, opened new colonies to countless families, and gave away farmland, all of which gave fresh opportunities to countless Romans who started new lives for themselves. He rebuilt temples and other public buildings, and staged lavish games for the people's entertainment. He cleared Rome of the rabble-rousers who had terrorized elections. He extended Roman citizenship to Gauls, Spaniards and Africans, and made provisions for organizing these new territories. He even forgave those who had taken up arms against him. His most lasting reform altered time: he created a 365-day year with a leap day every fourth year.

When his friends in the senate named him *Dictātor Perpetuus* (Dictator for life), it was the last straw. By then Caesar had taken to wearing purple robes, red shoes and a gold laurel garland on his head, all symbols of kingship. More than once some actually tried to make him king, and one day the people placed a crown upon his statue. Though Caesar formally refused the title "*rēx*," the *Dictātor Perpetuus* was a king in all respects but the title. A handful of senators plotted to kill him and brought their plan to a dramatic conclusion on the *Ides* (middle, or 15th) of March, 44 BC Brutus, whom Caesar had named as heir in his will, helped devise the plan. On that day Caesar entered the Senate chamber and took his place under Pompey's statue. Those in on the plot surrounded him and each plunged at him with sword or dagger. Caesar's blood flowed out from his twenty-three wounds and covered the base of the statue, as if Pompey himself was presiding over the grisly assassination.

These assassins had no plan for what would become of Rome after they killed Caesar. If they thought the city would go back to the ways of the old Republic, they were sadly mistaken. Caesar's power did not return to the Senate and to the Roman People. Instead, strong men raised armies to win Caesar's power for themselves. Mark Antony along with Octavian, Caesar's nephew and heir, led armies in pursuit of Caesar's assassins. One again Rome erupted in civil war. Meanwhile, Caesar became even more popular in death than he had been in life, and the Senate officially declared him to be a god.

THE DEATH OF CAESAR [A] ASee p. 225 for this note.

CHARACTERS:

> Gaius Cassius – Roman senator and conspirator
> Marcus Brutus – Roman senator, descendant of Lucius Iunius Brutus who expelled Tarquinius Superbus (see reading chapter 2)
> Julius Caesar – Roman dictator
> Lucius Cotta – Roman senator, supporter of Caesar
> Calpurnia – Caesar's wife
> Pompeius Magnus – former member of the first triumvirate who opposed Caesar when he returned from the Gallic Wars

1.   Paulō post *Lupercālia* annō DCCX AUC, aliter XLIV ante Chrīstum, Gāius
2. Cassius ad Mārcum Brūtum *appropinquāvit* et dīxit, "Brūte, necesse est Caesarī
3. perīre. Necesse est nōbīs eum necāre. Multī senātōrēs hoc probant."
4. Brūtus erat *prōgnātus* illīus Brūtī quī Tarquiniōs ex urbe Rōmā expulerat. Erat vir
5. fortis sed timidus **in rē caedis** Caesaris, amīcī suī. Caesar rē vērā sīcut pater Brūtō
6. fuerat.
7.   Multī tamen ē Rōmānīs Brūtum necāre Caesarem voluērunt. Erant *Rōmae* multae
8. statuae Brūtī *antīquī*. Hominēs in statuās nūntiōs posuērunt. Verbīs sīcut
9. "**Mortuusne es**, Brūte" et "Tuī *prōgnātī* nōn dignī sunt tuī" Brūtum **hortātī sunt**.
10. Multī quoque ē *optimātibus* susurrāvērunt, "Īdibus Mārtiīs in senātū Lūcius Cotta
11. dīcet, '**Sit Caesar rēx. Sōlus rēx Parthōs vincēbit. Scrīptum est!**'"
12.   Caesar in suō *domiciliō* amīcōs rogāvit, "Quae est mors optima?" Sibi <u>respōnsum</u>
13. suum dedit: "Mors *subita*." *Māne,* nunc Īdibus Mārtiīs uxor Caesaris, Calpurnia, eum ad senātum īre nōn

14. vult. Caesar verba Calpurniae nōn audīvit, et domō discessit

15. *plūribus* cum amīcīs. In viā ad senātum Caesar *vātem* vīdit quī ōlim, "Cavē Īdūs

16. Mārtiās" Caesarī dīxerat. Caesar illī dīxit, "Īdūs Mārtiae advēnērunt." Et *vātēs*

17. Caesarī, "Sed nōn *abīvērunt*." Gāius Iūlius Caesar ad senātum prōcessit.

18.   Ubi Caesar in senātum intrāverat, *sēdit*. Multī Caesarem oppugnāvērunt. Ubi

19. Caesar Brūtum vīdit, dīxit Graecīs verbīs Latīnē <u>significantibus</u> "Et tū, *puer* **mī**?"

20. Caesar nōn iam *rēstitit* sed togā caput suum et vultum *tēxit*. Cecidit **sub statuam**

21. Pompēiī. Caesar voluntātem habuit. *Mortuus est subitō.*

---

in rē caedis = in the matter of murder
mortuusne es . . .? = Are you dead . . . ?
hortātī sunt = they encouraged
sit = let [Caesar] be
scrīptum est = It is written, It has been written
mī = my (This is the vocative case to agree with *puer*.)
sub statuam = at the foot of the statue

GLOSSARY
Use your "eye" Latin to discern the meaning of the underlined words.

Lupercālia	a feast for Pan, celebrated in February
appropinquō, appropinquāre,	
appropinquāvī, appropinquātum	to approach
prōgnātus, prōgnātī, m.	descendant
Rōmae	at Rome
antīquus, a, um, adj.	ancient
optimātes, m. pl.	optimates, one of the political factions in Rome
susurrāvērunt	they whispered
domicilium, ī, n.	residence, home
subitus, a, um, adj.	sudden, unexpected
mānē	in the morning
plūs, plūris, adj.	several
vātēs, vātis, m.	prophet, soothsayer
abīvērunt	*ab + īvērunt*
sedeō, sedēre, sēdī, sessum	to sit
puer	(best here) child
rēstō, rēstāre, rēstitī	to stand firm
tegō, tegere, tēxī, tēctum	to cover
Mortuus est	he died
subitō, adv.	suddenly

Circle the letter of the correct choice.

1. According to line 2, Cassius ___.
   a. was afraid to talk to Brutus.
   b. approached Brutus silently
   c. approached Brutus and talked to him
   d. wanted to talk to Brutus but did not

2. According to line 3, many senators ___.
   a. thought it was necessary for Caesar to die
   b. had little or no sympathy with Cassius' plans
   c. had little or no sympathy with Brutus' plans
   d. were unaware of Cassius' thoughts

3. An ancestor of Brutus had ___.
   a. been a supporter of the Tarquin kings
   b. had driven the Tarquin kings away from Rome
   c. left no male descendants
   d. not been memorialized in Rome

4. Which of the following was a message placed on a statue?
   a. Old Brutus is ashamed.
   b. Your descendants are not worthy of you.
   c. Another tyrant needs to die.
   d. Young Brutus is a coward.

5. What did many of the aristocrats believe?
   a. that Caesar should be king
   b. that Brutus should be king
   c. that Brutus should take no part in public affairs
   d. that Caesar would be offered a crown

6. What prophecy concerning the Parthians had been made?
   a. they could be defeated only by a king
   b. they would defeat Rome only if Rome had a king
   c. they posed no threat to Rome
   d. they would become allies with the Romans

7. According to lines 12 and 13 ___.
   a. Caesar asked a question
   b. Caesar answered himself
   c. Calpurnia gave Caesar a warning on March 15
   d. All of the above are true.

8. Which of the following is not an adverb?
   a. subita
   b. māne
   c. subitō
   d. ōlim

9. *Verbīs* in line 8 is ___.
   a. ablative of means
   b. dative indirect object
   c. dative direct object with an intransitive verb
   d. accusative of an i-stem noun

10. *Quī* in line 15 refers to ___.
   a. *vātem* in line 15
   b. *vātēs* in line 16
   c. *viā* in line 15
   d. *senātum* in line 15

Culture Corner

WHO WERE THE PARTHIANS?

The Parthians lived southeast of the Caspian Sea. The Parthian Kingdom covered all of what is modern Iran. In fact, the Persian word for Parthia is Pahlavi; and the Iranians chose that as a last name for their *shah* (king) in modern times. The Parthian Kingdom lasted from about 250 BC until AD 190. They posed a serious threat to Rome. Indeed, they defeated and slew Crassus in 53 BC. The Parthian army consisted chiefly of mounted archers, who would act as if retreating and then turn and fire an arrow. This practice gives us the term "Parthian shot." Trajan Antoninus and Caracalla finally defeated the Parthians.

Challenge Box

Write an essay of five paragraphs telling how today's world might be different if the Parthians had conquered the Roman Empire. With your teacher's permission, you may choose an alternative topic: How would today's world be different if the Carthaginians had conquered the Roman Empire. (You would probably need to do more research on the second topic than the first; the first could be more imaginative than the alternative.)

TRANSLATION:

A little after the Lupercalia in the 710th year from the founding of the city, otherwise 44 BC, Gaius Cassius approached Marcus Brutus and said, "Brutus, it is necessary for Caesar to die. It is necessary for us to kill him. Many senators approve of this." Brutus was the descendant of that Brutus who had driven the Tarquins from the city of Rome. He was a brave man but hesitant in the matter of the death of Caesar, his friend. Indeed, Caesar had been like a father to Brutus.

Many Romans, however, wanted Brutus to kill Caesar. There were in Rome many statues of old Brutus. Men placed messages onto the statues. With words such as "Are you dead, Brutus?" and "Your descendants are not worthy of you" they encouraged Brutus. Also, many of the aristocracy whispered, "On the Ides of March in the senate Lucius Cotta will say, 'Let Caesar be king. Only a king will conquer the Parthians. It is written.'"

Caesar in his house asked his friends, "What is the best death?" He gave the answer to himself: "A sudden death." In the morning, now the Ides of March, the wife of Caesar, Calpurnia, did not want him to go to the senate. Caesar did not listen to the words of Calpurnia, and he left the house with several friends. On the way to the senate, Caesar saw a soothsayer who once had said to Caesar, "Beware the Ides of March." Caesar said to him, "The Ides of March have come"; and the soothsayer said to Caesar, "But they have not gone." Gaius Julius Caesar proceeded to the senate.

When Caesar had entered into the senate, he sat. Many [men] attacked Caesar. When Caesar saw Brutus, he spoke with Greek words, meaning in Latin *"Et tū, puer mī**?" Caesar no longer resisted but covered his head and face with his toga. He fell at the foot of Pompey's statue. Caesar had his wish. He died suddenly.

*Greek: και συ τεκνον (kai su, teknon?) This means "even you, my child/son"; however teknon can also carry the connation of "punk" or "[young] thug." It is hardly likely that the idea posed centuries later that Caesar indeed was Brutus's father is valid. Though Caesar had an affair with Brutus's mother, Servilia, the affair was long after the birth of Brutus.

Reference

VOCABULARY BY CHAPTER

CHAPTER 2

VERBS

amō, amāre, amāvī, amātum	to love, like	(amorous)
cantō, cantāre, cantāvī, cantātum	to sing	(chant, cantata)
labōrō, labōrāre, labōrāvī, labōrātum	to work	(labor)
nāvigō, nāvigāre, nāvigāvī, nāvigātum	to sail	(navigate, navigation)
oppugnō, oppugnāre, oppugnāvī, oppugnātum	to attack	(pugnacious)

ADVERB

nōn	not	(nonsense)

CHAPTER 3

VERBS

ambulō, ambulāre, ambulāvī, ambulātum	to walk	(perambulator, ambulance)
arō, arāre, arāvī, arātum	to plow	(arable)
habitō, habitāre, habitāvī, habitātum	to live, dwell	(habitat)
portō, portāre, portāvī, portātum	to carry	(portable)
rogō, rogāre, rogāvī, rogātum	to ask	(interrogation)
rēgnō, rēgnāre, rēgnāvī, rēgnātum	to rule	(reign, regent)
vocō, vocāre, vocāvī, vocātum	to call	(vocal, vocation)

CONJUNCTIONS

et	and	(et cetera)
aut	or	

CHAPTER 4

NOUNS

agricola, agricolae, m.	farmer	(agriculture)
fēmina, fēminae, f.	woman	(feminine)

Graecia, Graeciae, f.	Greece	(Grecian)
incola, incolae, m.	settler	
īnsula, īnsulae, f.	island	(insulate)
nauta, nautae, m.	sailor	(nautical)
pātria, pātriae, f.	fatherland, country	(patriot)
poēta, poētae, m.	poet	(poet)
puella, puellae, f.	girl	
rēgīna, rēgīnae, f.	queen	
terra, terrae, f.	earth, land	(terrain)
Trōia, Trōiae, f.	Troy (a citystate in Asia Minor)	(Troy, Trojan)

ADJECTIVE

pulcher, pulchra, pulchrum	beautiful	(pulchritude)

CHAPTER 5

NOUNS

amīca, amīcae, f.	friend (female friend)	(amicable)
ancilla, ancillae, f.	maidservant	(ancillary)
cēna, cēnae, f.	dinner	(cenacle)
culīna, culīnae, f.	kitchen	(culinary)
fābula, fābulae, f.	story	(fable, fabulous)
fīlia, fīliae, f.	daughter	(filial)
pūpa, pūpae, f.	doll	(pupa)
rosa, rosae, f.	rose	(rose)
stella, stellae, f.	star	(stellar, constellation)

VERBS

aedificō, aedificāre, aedificāvī, aedificātum	to build	(edifice, edification)
spectō, spectāre, spectāvī, spectātum	to look at, watch	(spectator, spectacle)

CHAPTER 6

NOUNS

ager, agrī, m.	field	(agriculture, agrarian)
amīcus, amīcī, m.	friend (male friend)	(amicable, amigo)
auxilium, auxiliī, n.	aid, help	(auxiliary)
bellum, bellī, n.	war	(belligerent, bellicose)
dōnum, dōnī, n.	gift	(donation)
equus, equī, m.	horse	(equestrian, equine)
germānus, germānī, m.	brother	(German, germane)
humus, humī, f.	ground	(humus)
līberī, līberōrum, m. pl.	children	
oppidum, oppidī, n.	town	
puer, puerī, m.	boy	(puerile, puerperal)
socius, sociī, m.	ally	(social)
vir, virī, m.	man	(virile)

VERBS

dō, dare, dedī, datum	to give	(donate)

mōnstrō, mōnstrāre, mōnstrāvī, mōnstrātum	to show	(demonstration)
narrō, narrāre, narrāvī, narrātum	to tell	(narrate, narrator)
pugnō, pugnāre, pugnāvī, pugnātum	to fight	(pugnacious)
servō, servāre, servāvī, servātum	to take care of; guard, protect	(conserve)

Chapter 7

Nouns

deus, deī, m.	god	(deity)
flamma, flammae, f.	flame	(flammable, inflammatory)
scūtum, scūtī, n.	shield	(scutes)
signum, signī, n.	sign	(signal)
templum, templī, n.	temple	(temple, Knights Templar)

Verbs

creō, creāre, creāvī, creātum	to create, make	(creation, creator)
iuvō, iuvāre, iūvī, iūtum	to help	(aid, adjutant)
optō, optāre, optāvī, optātum	to wish for, desire	(option, opt)
saltō, saltāre, saltāvī, saltātum	to leap, dance	
sum, esse, fuī, futūrum	to be	(essence, future)

Adjectives

aēneus, aēnea, aēneum	bronze	
bonus, bona, bonum	good	(bonus, bonafide)
magnus, magna, magnum	big, great	(magnify, magnitude)
multus, multa, multum	many	(multiply, multitude)
pius, pia, pium	pious, devout (godfearing)	(pious, piety)
sacer, sacra, sacrum	sacred, holy	(sacred)
tūtus, tūta, tūtum	protected, safe	

Adverbs

dum	while	
tum	then	

Conjunction

quoque	also	

Chapter 8

Verbs

clāmō, āre, āvī, ātum	to shout	(clamor, exclaim)
dēsīderō, āre, āvī, ātum	to desire, wish	(desire)
exerceō, exercēre, exercuī, exercitum	to train	(exercise)
habeō, habēre, habuī, habitum	to have, hold; consider	(habit)
moneō, monēre, monuī, monitum	to warn	(admonish)
necō, āre, āvī, ātum	to kill	
parō, āre, āvī, ātum	to prepare, get ready	(preparation)
terreō, terrēre, terruī, territum	to scare, frighten	(terrify)
videō, vidēre, vīdī, vīsum	to see	(video, vision)
vulnerō, āre, āvī, ātum	to wound	(vulnerable)

ADJECTIVES			
laetus, a, um	happy	
validus, a, um	strong	(validity)
vīvus, a, um	living, alive	(vivacious)
vulnerātus, a, um	wounded	

ADVERBS			
deinde	then	
mox	soon	

CHAPTER 9

NOUNS

arma, armōrum, n. pl.	weapons, arms	(armor, arms)
carrus, carrī, m.	wagon, cart, chariot	(cart)
cōpiae, cōpiārum, f. pl.	troops	(copious)
frūmentum, frūmentī, n.	grain	
gaudium, gaudiī, n.	joy	
grātia, grātiae, f.	thanks, gratitude	(gratitude, grateful)
rēgia, rēgiae, f.	palace	(regal)
studium, studiī, n.	zeal, eagerness	(studious)

VERBS

careō, carēre, caruī, caritūrum (+ abl. of separation)	to be without, to be deprived of, want, lack; be free from	
līberō, līberāre, līberāvī, līberātum	to free	(liberate)
lūdificō, lūdificāre, lūdificāvī, lūdificātum	to fool	(ludicrous)
prohibeō, prohibēre, prohibuī, prohibitum	to keep (back), prevent	(prohibit)

ADJECTIVES

mortuus, a, um	dead	(mortuary)
optimus, a, um	best	(optimum)

ADVERBS

nunc	now	
ubī	when	

CHAPTER 10

NOUNS

aqua, ae, f	water	(aquatic)
corpus, corporis, n.	body	(corporal)
caput, capitis, n.	head	(capital, chapter)
ferrum, ferrī, n.	iron; sword	(ferric)
iter, itineris, n.	journey	(itinerary, itinerate)
iuvenis, iuvenis, m./f.	youth, young man	(juvenile)
māter, mātris, f.	mother	(maternal, maternity)
pater, patris, m.	father	(paternal, paternity)
rēx, rēgis, m.	king	(regent)
rīpa, ae, f.	river bank, shore	(riparian)
rīvus, ī, m.	brook, small stream	(rival)

uxor, uxōris, f.	wife	(uxorious)
tyrannus, ī, m.	king, tyrant	(tyranny)

VERBS		
dēleō, dēlēre, dēlēvī, dēlētum	to destroy	(delete)
nato, āre, āvī, ātum	to swim	
servō, āre, āvī, ātum	to guard, save	(preserve)
temptō, āre, āvī, ātum	to try, attempt	(tempt)
timeō, timēre, timuī	to be afraid, fear	(timid, timidity)

ADJECTIVES		
timidus, a, um	afraid	(timid, timidity)

ADVERBS		
etiam	also, even	

CHAPTER 11

NOUNS		
castra, castrōrum, n. pl.	camp	
mīles, mīlitis, m.	soldier	(military)
scrība, ae, m.	clerk; scribe	(scribe)
toga, togae, f.	toga	

VERBS		
currō, currere, cucurrī, cursum	to run	(current)
circumdō, circumdare, circumdedī, circumdatum	to surround	
dīcō, dīcere, dīxī, dictum	to speak, say, tell	(dictate)
gerō, gerere, gessī, gestum	to wear	
mittō, mittere, mīsī, missum	to send	(mission)
petō, petere, petīvī / petiī, petītum	to aim at, attack, seek	(petulant)
pōnō, pōnere, posuī, positum	to put, place	(position)
probō, āre, āvī, ātum	to approve	(probation)
teneō, tenēre, tenuī, tentum	to hold	(tenacious)

ADJECTIVES		
cārus, a, um	dear, expensive, costly	
dexter, dextra, dextrum	right; f. noun right hand	(dexterity)

CHAPTER 12

NOUNS		
dux, ducis, m.	leader	(conductor)
familia, ae, f.	family	(familial)
flūmen, flūminis, n.	river	(flume)
lēgātus, ī, m.	officer, lieutenant	(delegate)
obses, obsidis, m.	hostage	(obsess)
pāx, pācis, f.	peace	(pax, pacify)
perīculum, ī, n.	danger	(peril)
statua, ae, f.	statue	(statuesque)
virgō, virginis, f.	maiden	(Virginia)

Verbs

legō, legere, lēgī, lēctum	to read; choose, gather	(legible)
prōpōnō, prōpōnere, prōposuī, prōpositum	to put before; to propose	(proposition)
revertō, revertere, revertī, reversum	to turn back, return	(reverse)

Adjectives

cēterī, cēterōrum, m. pl.	the rest	
līber, lībera, līberum	free	(liberty)

Prepositions

circum (+ acc.)	around	(circumference)
prope (+ acc.)	near	

Conjunction

quod	because	

CHAPTER 13

Nouns

marītus, ī, m.	husband	(marital)
nūntius, ī, m.	messenger; message	(announcement)
vīlla, vīllae, f.	farmhouse	(village)
virtūs, virtūtis, f.	manhood, courage	(virtue)

Verbs

ascendō, ascendere, ascendī, ascēnsum	to climb, to go up	(ascension)
claudō, claudere, clausī, clausum	to shut, close; close off	(closure)
ēvādō, ēvādere, ēvāsī, ēvāsum	to come out, escape	(evasion)
induō, induere, induī, indūtum	to put on	
respondeō, respondēre, respondī, respōnsum	to reply, respond	(responsive)
vincō, vincere, vīcī, victum	to conquer	(vanquish)

Adjectives

nōtus, a, um	known	(notable)
squālidus, a, um	dirty	(squalid)

Adverbs

modo	only	
posteā	afterwards	

CHAPTER 14

Nouns

animal, animālis, n.	animal	(animal)
aurum, ī, n.	gold	(auric)
caelum, ī, n.	sky	(celestial)
collum, collī, n.	neck	(collar)
fīnis, fīnis, m.	end, boundary	(finish, finite)
homō, hominis, m.	human, man	(homo sapiens)
īnfāns, īnfantis, m./f.i.	baby	(infant)
mare, maris, n.	sea	(marine)
nāvis, nāvis, f.	ship	(naval)

nōmen, nōminis, n.	name, title	(nomination)
nox, noctis, f.	night; darkness	(nocturnal)
parēns, parentis, m/f.	parent	(parent)
pars, partis, f.	part	(particle, partition)
urbs, urbis, f.	city	(urbane, urban)

ADJECTIVES

parvus, a, um	little, small	
praecipuus, a, um	special; principal	

VERBS

appellō, āre, āvī, ātum	to speak to; call, name	(appellation)
dēdicō, āre, āvī, ātum	to consecrate, dedicate; declare	(dedicate)
iubeō, iubēre, iussī, iussum	to order, command	(jussive)

CONJUNCTION

sī	if	

CHAPTER 15

NOUNS

annus, ī, m.	year	(annual)
ēducātiō, ēducātiōnis, f.	upbringing, rearing; education	(education)
lūdus, ī, m.	school, game	(ludicrous)
mēnsa, mēnsae, f.	table	

VERBS

doceō, docēre, docuī, doctum	to teach	(doctrine)
discō, discere, didicī	to learn	(discern)
scrībō, scrībere, scrīpsī, scrīptum	to write	(scribble)

ADJECTIVES

ācer, ācris, ācre	sharp, eager; severe, fierce	(acrid, acrimony)
aptus, a, um	fitting, proper, apt, suitable	
brevis, breve	short, brief	(brevity)
celer, celeris, celere	swift, quick, rapid	(accelerate)
fortis, forte	strong, brave	(fortitude)
ingēns, ingentis	huge	
iuvenis, iuvenis	young, youthful	(juvenile)
omnis, omne	all, every	(omnibus, omnipresent)
pūblicus, a, um	public	(publicity)
senex, senis	old, aged; (as a noun) old man	(senate, senile)
gravis, grave	serious, important, weighty	(grave)

CHAPTER 16

NOUNS

camera, ae, f.	room	
flōs, flōris, m.	flower, blossom	(floral)
ignis, ignis, m.	fire	(igneous)
lectus, ī, m.	couch, bed; bier	
nux, nucis, f.	nut; nut tree	

VERBS		
accipiō, accipere, accēpī, acceptum	to receive	(accept)
capiō, capere, cēpī, captum	to take, seize; capture	(capture)
cōnspiciō, cōnspicere, cōnspexī, cōnspectum	to catch sight of	(conspicuous)
cōnsūmō, cōnsūmere, cōnsūmpsī, cōnsūmptum	to consume, eat	(consume)
iaciō, iacere, iēcī, iactum	to throw	(eject)
incipiō, incipere, incēpī, inceptum	to begin	(inception)
faciō, facere, fēcī, factum	to do, make	(fact)
ōrnō, āre, āvī, ātum	to decorate, adorn	(ornate)
surgō, surgere, surrēxī, surrēctum	rise, arise	(resurrection)
vīvō, vīvere, vīxī, vīctum	to live	(vivacious)

ADJECTIVES		
fēlīx, fēlīcis	happy	(felicity)
flammeus, a, um	fiery; flame covered as a neuter noun – bridal veil	(flammable)

CHAPTER 17

NOUNS		
honor, honōris, m.	honor	(honorable)
officium, ī, n.	office, duty	(officiate)
tempus, temporis, n.	time	(temporal)

VERBS		
administrō, āre, āvī, ātum	to manage	(administer)
faveō, favēre, fāvī, fautum (+ dat.)	to favor, to support	
noceō, nocēre, nocuī, nocitum (+ dat.)	to harm, to be harmful to	(innocuous)
pāreō, pārēre, pāruī, pāritum (+ dat.)	to obey, to be obedient to	
placeō, placēre, placuī, placitum (+ dat.)	to please, to be pleasing to	(placate)
stō, stāre, stetī, statum	to stand	(statute, statue)
studeō, studēre, studuī (+ dat.)	to study, to direct one's zeal to	(studious)

ADJECTIVES		
amīcus, a, um	friendly	(amicable)
cārus, a, um	dear (to)	
dissimilis, dissimile	unlike	(dissimilar)
fidēlis, fidēle	faithful, loyal (to)	(fidelity)
inimīcus, a, um	unfriendly	(inamicable)
pār, paris	equal (to)	(partial)
similis, simile	like, similar (to)	(similarity)

ADVERBS		
bene	well	
iterum	again	

CHAPTER 18

NOUNS		
captīvus, ī, m.	captive, prisoner of war	(captivity)
proelium, ī, n.	battle	
senātor, senātōris, m.	senator, member of the Roman senate	(senator)
verbum, ī, n.	word	(verbose)

235

Verbs

āmittō, āmittere, āmīsī, āmissum	to let go, lose	
dēbeō, dēbēre, dēbuī, dēbitum	ought, must	(debt)
eō, īre, iī/īvī, itum	to go	(exit)
ferō, ferre, tulī, lātum	to bring, carry	(ferry, transfer)
maneō, manēre, mānsī, mānsum	stay, remain	(mansion)
possum, posse, potuī	to be able, can	(possible)
prōcēdō, prōcēdere, prōcessī, prōcessum	to advance, proceed	(process)
superō, āre, āvī, ātum	to surpass, outdo; overcome	
reddō, reddere, reddidī, redditum	to give back, return	

Adjectives

potēns, potentis	able, capable; powerful	(potent)
vīcīnus, a, um	neighboring, nearby; (as a noun) neighbor	(vicinity)

Conjunction

apud, prep. + acc.	among	

Chapter 19

Nouns

amor, amōris, m.	love	(amorous)
corium, coriī, n.	skin, hide	(excoriate)
cōnsilium, cōnsiliī, n.	plan	
fātum, ī, n.	fate	(fatal)
frāter, frātris, m.	brother	(fraternal)
līnum, ī, n.	line, rope; thread	(linear)
prīnceps, prīncipis, m.	prince, leader	(principate)
soror, sorōris, f.	sister	(sorority)

Pronoun

ego	I	
is, ea, id	he, she, it	
nōs, nostrī/nostrum	we	
tū	you	

Verbs

adamō, āre, āvī, ātum	to fall in love with	
circumscrībō, scrībere, scrīpsī, scrīptum	to draw a line around	(circumscribe)
condō, condere, condidī, conditum	to found, establish	
crēdō, crēdere, crēdidī, crēditum (+ dat. of person, + acc. of thing)	to believe, trust	(creed, credulous)
effugiō, effugere, effūgī	to run away, escape	
relinquō, relinquere, relīquī, relictum	to leave behind	(relinquish)

Adjectives

crūdēlis, crūdēle	hardhearted, cruel	(crudelity)
miser, misera, miserum	unhappy, wretched, miserable	(miser)

Conjunctions

contrā, prep. + acc.	against	(contrary)
post, prep. + acc.	after	

Chapter 20

Nouns

iniūria, ae, f.	wrong, injury; insult	(injurious)
*hostis, hostis, m.	enemy	(hostile)
legiō, legiōnis, f.	legion (up to 6000 men); (pl) troops, army	(legionnaire)
*mōns, montis, m.	mountain	(montane)
odium, odiī, n.	hatred	(odious)
victōria, ae, f.	victory	(victorious)

Verbs

dēmōnstrō, dēmōnstrāre, dēmōnstrāvī, dēmōnstrātum	to point out, show	(demonstrate)
exspectō, āre, āvī, ātum	to wait for; to see, expect	(expect)
iūrō, āre, āvī, ātum	to swear, take an oath	(iurat)

Pronouns/Adjectives

hic, haec, hoc	this, these	
ille, illa, illud	that	
ipse, ipsa, ipsum	himself, herself	
iste, ista, istud	that (of yours/near you)	
parātus, a, um	prepared	(preparatory)

Adverbs

semper	always	
sīc	thus, so, in this way	

Chapter 21

Nouns

fortūna, ae, f.	fortune, luck	(fortunate)
ratiō, ratiōnis, f.	reason	(ration, rational)

Verbs

dēcipiō, dēcipere, dēcēpī, dēceptum	deceive	(deception)
intellegō, intellegere, intellēxī, intellēctum	understand	(intelligence)
metuō, metuere, metuī, metūtum	fear	
nōlō, nōlle, nōluī	to not wish, to be unwilling	
volō, velle, voluī	to wish, want, be willing	(volition, volunteer)

Adjectives

alius, alia, aliud	other, another	(alias, alibi)
alter, altera, alterum, alter . . . alter	the other (of two) one . . . the other	(alternative, alternate)
neuter, neutra, neutrum	neither	(neuter, neutral)
nūllus, nūlla, nūllum	no, none, not any	(nullify, annul)
sōlus, sōla, sōlum	alone, only	(solo, solitude)
tōtus, tōta, tōtum	whole, entire	(total)
ūllus, ūlla, ūllum	any	
ūnus, ūna, ūnum	one	(unify, union)
uter, utra, utrum	either, which (of two)	

Conjunction

igitur	therefore	

ob, prep. + acc.	in front of; on account of, for	(obvious)

ADVERBS

numquam	never	
sīcut	just as	

CHAPTER 22

NOUNS

dominus, ī, m.	master, lord	(domain)
epistula, ae, f.	letter	(epistle)
factum, ī, n.	deed	(fact)
lēx, lēgis, f.	law	(legal)
lībertus, ī, m	freedman (former slave who has been given freedom)	
litterae, litterārum, f. pl.	literature	(literature)
ōrātiō, ōrātiōnis, f.	speech	(oratory)

VERBS

discēdō, discēdere, discessī, discessum	go away, depart	
emō, emere, ēmī, emptum	to buy, procure	
mīlitō, āre, āvī, ātum	to serve as a soldier	(military)
obtruncō, āre, āvī, ātum	to slaughter	

ADJECTIVES

cardinālis, cardināle	that on which something turns, depends	(cardinal)
duo, duae, duo	two	(dual, duet)
trēs, tria	three	(trio, tricycle)

CONJUNCTION

ante, prep. + acc.	before	

CHAPTER 23

NOUNS

hōra, hōrae, f.	hour	(hour)
mēnsis, mēnsis, m.	month	
mors, mortis, f.	death	(mortician)
pecūnia, ae, f.	money	(pecuniary)
pretium, ī, n.	price	

VERBS

coniungō, coniungere, coniūnxī, coniūnctum	to unite, join together	(conjugate)
obtineō, obtinēre, obtinuī, obtentum	to hold on, possess	(obtain)
pereō, perīre, periī, peritum	to die	(perish)
stō, stāre, stetī, statum (price + dat.)	to cost	
vēndō, vēndere, vēndidī, vēnditum	to sell	(vendor)
vertō, vertere, vertī, versum	to turn	(convert)

ADJECTIVES

altus, a, um	high, deep	(altitude)
mīlle (pl. mīlia)	thousand	(mile)

minimus, a, um	least, very little	(minimal)
paucī, paucae, pauca, pl.	few, a few	(paucity)
pauper, pauperis	poor, a poor man	(poverty)
plūrimus, a, um	most, very much	(plural)
proximus, a, um	next, near	(approximate)
vīle	cheap	(vile, vilify)

CHAPTER 24

NOUNS

factiō, factiōnis, f.	political party, faction	(faction)
inimīcus, inimīcī, m.	personal enemy	(enmity)
iūs, iūris, n.	law	(jurisprudence)
ōs, ōris, n.	mouth	(oral)
praemium, ī, n.	reward; booty, loot	(premium)
vigil, vigilis, m.	watchman; (m.pl.) a fire brigade, firemen	(vigilant)

VERBS

exstinguō, exstinguere, extīnxī, extīnctum	to put out, extinguish	(extinct)
interficō, interficere, interfēcī, interfectum	to kill	
postulō, āre, āvī, ātum	to demand	(postulate)
reflectō, reflectere, reflexī, reflexum	to bend back	(reflect)

ADJECTIVES

dīves, dīvitis	rich	(dives)
meus, a, um	my, mine	
mītis, mīte	gentle	
noster, a, um	our	
senior, seniōris	older, elder	(seniority)
suus, a, um	his, her, its, their	(suicide)
tuus, a, um	your, yours	
vester, a, um	your (plural)	

CHAPTER 25

VERBS

agnōscō, agnōscere, agnōvī, agnitum	to know, understand, identify	
antecēdō, antecēdere, antecessī, antecessum	to precede, to surpass	(antecedent)
referō, referre, rettulī, relātum	to bring back, carry back; report	(relate, relative)

PRONOUNS

aliquis, aliquid	somebody, something	
quī, quae, quod, rel. pron.	who, which	
quis, quid, interrog. pron.	who, what	

ADJECTIVES

plēnus, a, um	full	(plenty)
ultimus, a, um	last	(ultimatum)

CONJUNCTION		
postquam	after	

ADVERBS		
umquam	ever, at any time	
tam	so	

CHAPTER 26

NOUNS		
classis, classis, f.	fleet	(class)
fortitūdō, fortitūdinis, f.	courage, strength	(fortitude)
imperium, ī, n.	power	(empire, imperial)
modestia, ae, f.	temperance; humility	(modesty)
triumphus, ī, m.	triumphal procession	(triumphant)

ADJECTIVES		
modestus, a, um	well-behaved; humble, modest	(modest)
integer, integra, integrum	upright	(integrity)

CONJUNCTION		
antequam	before	

ADVERBS		
magnopere	greatly	
sincērē	honestly	(sincerely)
tamen	nevertheless, however	
vērē	truly	(verily)

CHAPTER 27

NOUNS		
auctōritās, auctōritātis, f.	authority	(author)
gēns, gentis, f.	tribe, nation	(gentile)
gubernātor, gubernātōris, m.	governor	(gubernatorial)

VERBS		
audiō, audīre, audīvī/audiī, audītum	to hear, listen	(audio, auditory)
cōnsentiō, cōnsentīre, cōnsēnsī, cōnsēnsum	to agree	(consent, consensus)
cōnscrībō, cōnscrībere, cōnscrīpsī, cōnscrīptum	to enlist, enroll; write up	(conscription)
reveniō, revenīre, revēnī, reventum	to come back, return	
sciō, scīre, scīvī/sciī, scītum	to know	(science)
sentiō, sentīre, sēnsī, sēnsum	to perceive, feel; sense	(sensible)
sperō, āre, āvī, ātum	to hope	
veniō, venīre, vēnī, ventum	to come	(advent, venture)

CHAPTER 28

NOUNS		
cornū, ūs, n.	wing (of an army); horn	(cornucopia, cornet, unicorn)
domus, ūs, f.	house, home	(domicile, domestic)
exercitus, ūs, m.	army	

frūctus, ūs, m.	fruit, profit, benefit	(fructose, frugal)
genū, ūs, n.	knee	(genuflect)
hiems, hiemis, f.	winter	(hiemal)
impetus, ūs, m.	attack; charge; impulse	(impetuous)
manus, ūs, f.	hand; band (of men)	(manual, manumit)
nix, nivis, f.	snow	(snow)
passus, ūs, m.	pace, footstep	(pace)
mīlle passūs, mīlia passuum,	miles (1000 paces)	
rūs, rūris, n.	country (as opposed to city)	(rural, rusticate)
senātus, ūs, m.	senate; body of elders	(senate, sentorial)
vultus, vultūs, m.	face, visage	

Verbs

adveniō, advenīre, advēnī, adventum	to arrive, come to	(advent)
carpō, carpere, carpsī, carptum	to seize, pluck	
iungō, iungere, iūnxī, iūnctum	to join, unite	(conjunction)

CHAPTER 29

NOUNS

diēs, diēī, m/f.	day (feminine used for an appointed or set day)	(diurnal, modern)
faciēs, faciēī, f.	face, appearance	(facial)
fidēs, fideī, f.	faith, trust	(fidelity)
rēs, reī f.	thing, matter, affair; state	(Republic)
rēs pūblica, reī pūblicae, f.	state, republic	
spēs, speī, f.	hope	(desperate)
voluntās, voluntātis, f.	will, wish	(voluntary)

VERBS

agō, agere, ēgī, āctum	to do, drive, act	(agent, action)
dīmittō, dīmittere, dīmīsī, dīmissum	to send away, dismiss	(dismiss, dismissal)
permittō, permittere, permīsī, permissum	to permit, allow	(permission)

ADJECTIVES

cīvīlis, cīvīle	civil	(civil)
dignus, a, um	worthy	(dignified)
fessus, fessa, fessum	tired	

Reference

REFERENCE CHART

NOUNS

1ST DECL. (CH. 4)

CASE	1ST DECL. FEMININE	FĒMINA, FĒMINAE
Nom.	-a	*fēmin*a
Gen.	-ae	*fēmin*ae
Dat.	-ae	*fēmin*ae
Acc.	-am	*fēmin*am
Abl.	-ā	*fēmin*ā
Voc.	-a	*fēmin*a
Nom.	-ae	*fēmin*ae
Gen.	-ārum	*fēmin*ārum
Dat.	-īs	*fēmin*īs
Acc.	-ās	*fēmin*ās
Abl.	-īs	*fēmin*īs
Voc.	-ae	*fēmin*ae

2nd Decl. (Ch. 6)

Case	2ND DECL. MASCULINE	AMĪCUS, AMĪCĪ	AGER, AGRĪ	2ND DECL. NEUTER	DŌNUM, DŌNĪ
Nom.	-us, -r	amīcus	ager	-um	dōnum
Gen.	-ī	amīcī	agrī	-ī	dōnī
Dat.	-ō	amīcō	agrō	-ō	dōnō
Acc.	-um	amīcum	agrum	-um	dōnum
Abl.	-ō	amīcō	agrō	-ō	dōnō
Voc.	-e, -r	amīce	ager	-um	dōnum
Nom.	-ī	amīcī	agrī	-a	dōna
Gen.	-ōrum	amīcōrum	agrōrum	-ōrum	dōnōrum
Dat.	-īs	amīcīs	agrīs	-īs	dōnīs
Acc.	-ōs	amīcōs	agrōs	-a	dōna
Abl.	-īs	amīcīs	agrīs	-īs	dōnīs
Voc.	-ī	amīcī	agrī	-a	dōna

3rd Decl. (Ch. 10 & 14)

Case	3RD DECL. MASC./FEM.	REGULAR RĒX, RĒGIS	I-STEM URBS, URBIS	3RD DECL. NEUTER	REGULAR ITER, ITINERIS	I-STEM MARE, MARIS
Nom.	*	rēx	urbs	*	iter	mare
Gen.	-is	rēgis	urbis	-is	itineris	maris
Dat.	-ī	rēgī	urbī	-ī	itinerī	marī
Acc.	-em	rēgem	urbem	*	iter	mare
Abl.	-e	rēge	urbe	-e (-ī)	itinere	marī
Voc.	*	rēx	urbs	*	iter	mare
Nom.	-ēs	rēgēs	urbēs	-a (-ia)	itinera	maria
Gen.	-um (-ium)	rēgum	urbium	-um (-ium)	itinerum	marium
Dat.	-ibus	rēgibus	urbibus	-ibus	itineribus	maribus
Acc.	-ēs	rēgēs	urbēs	-a (-ia)	itinera	maria
Abl.	-ibus	rēgibus	urbibus	-ibus	itineribus	maribus
Voc.	-ēs	rēgēs	urbēs	-a (-ia)	itinera	maria

243

4th Decl. (Ch. 28)

Case	4th Decl. Masc./Fem.	Frūctus, Frūctūs	4th Decl. Neuter	Genū, Genūs
Nom.	-us	frūctus	-ū	genū
Gen.	-ūs	frūctūs	-ūs	genūs
Dat.	-uī	frūctuī	-ū	genū
Acc.	-um	frūctum	-ū	genū
Abl.	-ū	frūctū	-ū	genū
Voc.	-us	frūctus	-ū	genū
Nom.	-ūs	frūctūs	-ua	genua
Gen.	-uum	frūctuum	-uum	genuum
Dat.	-ibus	frūctibus	-ibus	genibus
Acc.	-ūs	frūctūs	-ua	genua
Abl.	-ibus	frūctibus	-ibus	genibus
Voc.	-ūs	frūctūs	-ua	genua

5th Decl. (Ch. 29)

Case	5th Decl. Masc./Fem.	Vowel Stem Diēs, Diēī	Consonant Stem Fidēs, Fideī
Nom.	-ēs	diēs	spēs
Gen.	-ēī, -eī	diēī	speī
Dat.	-ēī, -eī	diēī	speī
Acc.	-em	diem	spem
Abl.	-ē	diē	spē
Voc.	-ēs	diēs	spēs
Nom.	-ēs	diēs	spēs
Gen.	-ērum	diērum	spērum
Dat.	-ēbus	diēbus	spēbus
Acc.	-ēs	diēs	spēs
Abl.	-ēbus	diēbus	spēbus
Voc.	-ēs	diēs	spēs

ADJECTIVES
1st & 2nd Decl. (Ch. 7)

CASE	MASCULINE	FEMININE	NEUTER
Nom.	bon**us**	bon**a**	bon**um**
Gen.	bon**ī**	bon**ae**	bon**ī**
Dat.	bon**ō**	bon**ae**	bon**ō**
Acc.	bon**um**	bon**am**	bon**um**
Abl.	bon**ō**	bon**ā**	bon**ō**
Voc.	bon**e**	bon**a**	bon**um**
Nom.	bon**ī**	bon**ae**	bon**a**
Gen.	bon**ōrum**	bon**ārum**	bon**ōrum**
Dat.	bon**īs**	bon**īs**	bon**īs**
Acc.	bon**ōs**	bon**ās**	bon**a**
Abl.	bon**īs**	bon**īs**	bon**īs**
Voc.	bon**ī**	bon**ae**	bon**a**

3RD DECLENSION (CH. 15)

three termination: **celer, celeris, celere**

CASE	MASCULINE	FEMININE	NEUTER
Nom.	celer	celeris	celere
Gen.	celeris	celeris	celeris
Dat.	celerī	celerī	celerī
Acc.	celerem	celerem	celere
Abl.	celerī	celerī	celerī
Voc.	celer	celeris	celere
Nom.	celerēs	celerēs	celeria
Gen.	celerium	celerium	celerium
Dat.	celeribus	celeribus	celeribus
Acc.	celerēs	celerēs	celeria
Abl.	celeribus	celeribus	celeribus
Voc.	celerēs	celerēs	celeria

two termination: **omnis, omne**

CASE	MASC & FEM	NEUTER
Nom.	omnis	omne
Gen.	omnis	omnis
Dat.	omnī	omnī
Acc.	omnem	omne
Abl.	omnī	omnī
Voc.	omnis	omne

Nom.	omnēs	omnia
Gen.	omnium	omnium
Dat.	omnibus	omnibus
Acc.	omnēs	omnia
Abl.	omnibus	omnibus
Voc.	omnēs	omnia

one termination: **ingēns, ingentis**

CASE	MASC & FEM	NEUTER
Nom.	ingēns	ingēns
Gen.	ingentis	ingentis
Dat.	ingentī	ingentī
Acc.	ingentem	ingēns
Abl.	ingentī	ingentī
Voc.	ingēns	ingēns
Nom.	ingentēs	ingentia
Gen.	ingentium	ingentium
Dat.	ingentibus	ingentibus
Acc.	ingentēs	ingentia
Abl.	ingentibus	ingentibus
Voc.	ingentēs	ingentia

Special -*ius* adjectives (Ch. 21)

CASE	MASCULINE	FEMININE	NEUTER
Nom.	ūllus	ūlla	ūllum
Gen.	**ūllīus**	**ūllīus**	**ūllīus**
Dat.	**ūllī**	**ūllī**	**ūllī**
Acc.	ūllum	ūllam	ūllum
Abl.	ūllō	ūllā	ūllō
Voc.	ūlle	ūlla	ūllum
Nom.	ūllī	ūllae	ūlla
Gen.	ūllōrum	ūllārum	ūllōrum
Dat.	ūllīs	ūllīs	ūllīs
Acc.	ūllōs	ūllās	ūlla
Abl.	ūllīs	ūllīs	ūllīs
Voc.	ūllī	ūllae	ūlla

ILLE, ILLA, ILLUD (Ch. 20)
that, those

CASE	MASCULINE	FEMININE	NEUTER
Nom.	ille	illa	illud
Gen.	illīus	illīus	illīus
Dat.	illī	illī	illī
Acc.	illum	illam	illud
Abl.	illō	illā	illō
Nom.	illī	illae	illa
Gen.	illōrum	illārum	illōrum
Dat.	illīs	illīs	illīs
Acc.	illōs	illās	illa
Abl.	illīs	illīs	illīs

*iste declines the same as *ille.*

HIC, HAEC, HOC (Ch. 20)
this, these

CASE	MASCULINE	FEMININE	NEUTER
Nom.	hic	haec	hoc
Gen.	hūius	hūius	hūius
Dat.	huic	huic	huic
Acc.	hunc	hanc	hoc
Abl.	hōc	hāc	hōc
Nom.	hī	hae	haec
Gen.	hōrum	hārum	hōrum
Dat.	hīs	hīs	hīs
Acc.	hōs	hās	haec
Abl.	hīs	hīs	hīs

IS, EA, ID (Ch. 19)

This may be a demonstrative pronoun meaning "that," or a personal pronoun meaning "he," "she," or "it."

Case	Masculine	Feminine	Neuter
Nom.	is	ea	id
Gen.	ēius	ēius	ēius
Dat.	eī	eī	eī
Acc.	eum	eam	id
Abl.	eō	eā	eō
Nom.	eī	eae	ea
Gen.	eōrum	eārum	eōrum
Dat.	eīs	eīs	eīs
Acc.	eōs	eās	ea
Abl.	eīs	eīs	eīs

Personal Pronouns (Ch. 19)

Case	1st Person	2nd Person
Nom.	ego	tū
Gen.	meī	tuī
Dat.	mihi	tibi
Acc.	mē	tē
Abl.	mē	tē

Plural

Case	1st Person	2nd Person
Nom.	nōs	vōs
Gen.	nostrī, nostrum	vestrī, vestrum
Dat.	nōbīs	vōbīs
Acc.	nōs	vōs
Abl.	nōbīs	vōbīs

REFLEXIVE PRONOUNS (CH. 24)
myself, yourself, himself, . . .

CASE	1ST PERSON	2ND PERSON	3RD PERSON
Gen.	meī	tuī	suī
Dat.	mihi	tibi	sibi
Acc.	mē	tē	sē
Abl.	mē	tē	sē
Gen.	nostrī	vestrī	suī
Dat.	nōbīs	vōbīs	sibi
Acc.	nōs	vōs	sē
Abl.	nōbīs	vōbīs	sē

RELATIVE PRONOUN (CH. 25)
who, which

CASE	MASCULINE	FEMININE	NEUTER
Nominative	quī	quae	quod
Genitive	cūius	cūius	cūius
Dative	cui	cui	cui
Accusative	quem	quam	quod
Ablative	quō	quā	quō
Nominative	quī	quae	quae
Genitive	quōrum	quārum	quōrum
Dative	quibus	quibus	quibus
Accusative	quōs	quās	quae
Ablative	quibus	quibus	quibus

INTERROGATIVE PRONOUN (CH. 25)
Who? What?

CASE	MASC & FEM	NEUTER
Nominative	**quis**	**quid**
Genitive	cūius	cūius
Dative	cui	cui
Accusative	quem	quid
Ablative	quō	quō

The plural forms are the same as those of the relative pronoun.

Verbs — Regular Verbs
Imperative Mood (Ch. 16)

Positive Imperative

1st Conj.	2nd Conj.	3rd Conj.	3rd -io	4th Conj.
amā	vidē	mitte	cape	audī
amāte	vidēte	mittite	capite	audīte

Negative Imperative

1st Conj.	2nd Conj.	3rd Conj.	3rd -io	4th Conj.
nolī amāre	nolī vidēre	nolī mittere	nolī capere	nolī audīre
nolīte amāre	nolīte vidēre	nolīte mittere	nolīte capere	nolīte audīre

Indicative Mood
Present Tense (Ch. 2, 8, 11, 16, 27)

1st Conj.	2nd Conj.	3rd Conj.	3rd -io	4th Conj.
amō	videō	mittō	capiō	audiō
amās	vidēs	mittis	capis	audīs
amat	videt	mittit	capit	audit
amāmus	vidēmus	mittimus	capimus	audīmus
amātis	vidētis	mittitis	capitis	audītis
amant	vident	mittunt	capiunt	audiunt

Imperfect Tense (Ch. 3, 13, 27)

1st Conj.	2nd Conj.	3rd Conj.	3rd -io	4th Conj.
amābam	vidēbam	mittēbam	capiēbam	audiēbam
amābās	vidēbās	mittēbās	capiēbās	audiēbās
amābat	vidēbat	mittēbat	capiēbat	audiēbat
amābāmus	vidēbāmus	mittēbāmus	capiēbāmus	audiēbāmus
amābātis	vidēbātis	mittēbātis	capiēbātis	audiēbātis
amābant	vidēbant	mittēbant	capiēbant	audiēbant

Future Tense (Ch. 3, 13, 27)

1st Conj.	2nd Conj.	3rd Conj.	3rd -io	4th Conj.
amābō	vidēbō	mittam	capiam	audiam
amābis	vidēbis	mittēs	capiēs	audiēs
amābit	vidēbit	mittet	capiet	audiet
amābimus	vidēbimus	mittēmus	capiēmus	audiēmus
amābitis	vidēbitis	mittētis	capiētis	audiētis
amābunt	vidēbunt	mittent	capient	audient

Perfect Tense (Ch. 8, 27)

1st Conj.	2nd Conj.	3rd Conj.	3rd -io	4th Conj.
amāvī	vīdī	mīsī	cēpī	audīvī
amāvistī	vīdistī	mīsistī	cēpistī	audīvistī
amāvit	vīdit	mīsit	cēpit	audīvit
amāvimus	vīdimus	mīsimus	cēpimus	audīvimus
amāvistis	vīdistis	mīsistis	cēpistis	audīvistis
amāvērunt	vīdērunt	mīsērunt	cēpērunt	audīvērunt

Pluperfect Tense (Ch. 27)

1st Conj.	2nd Conj.	3rd Conj.	3rd -io	4th Conj.
amāveram	vīderam	mīseram	cēperam	audīveram
amāverās	vīderās	mīserās	cēperās	audīverās
amāverat	vīderat	mīserat	cēperat	audīverat
amāverāmus	vīderāmus	mīserāmus	cēperāmus	audīverāmus
amāverātis	vīderātis	mīserātis	cēperātis	audīverātis
amāverant	vīderant	mīserant	cēperant	audīverant

FUTURE PERFECT TENSE (CH. 27)

1ST CONJ.	2ND CONJ.	3RD CONJ.	3RD -IO	4TH CONJ.
amāverō	vīderō	mīserō	cēperō	audīverō
amāveris	vīderis	mīseris	cēperis	audīveris
amāverit	vīderit	mīserit	cēperit	audīverit
amāverimus	vīderimus	mīserimus	cēperimus	audīverimus
amāveritis	vīderitis	mīseritis	cēperitis	audīveritis
amāverint	vīderint	mīserint	cēperint	audīverint

IRREGULAR VERBS AND A COUPLE OF COMMON COMPOUNDS (CH. 7, 18, 21)

sum, esse, fuī, futūrum   ferō, ferre, tulī, lātum   volō, velle, voluī
possum, posse, potuī,   eō, īre, īvī/iī, itum   nōlō, nōlle, nōluī

IMPERATIVE MOOD
es	fer	ī	nōlī
este	ferte	īte	nōlīte

INDICATIVE MOOD

PRESENT TENSE

sum	possum	ferō	volō	nōlō	eō
es	potes	fers	vīs	nōn vīs	īs
est	potest	fert	vult	nōn vult	it
sumus	possumus	ferimus	volumus	nōlumus	īmus
estis	potestis	fertis	vultis	nōn vultis	ītis
sunt	possunt	ferunt	volunt	nōlunt	eunt

IMPERFECT TENSE

eram	poteram	ferēbam	volēbam	nōlēbam	ībam
erās	poterās	ferēbās	volēbās	nōlēbās	ībās
erat	poterat	ferēbat	volēbat	nōlēbat	ībat
erāmus	poterāmus	ferēbāmus	volēbāmus	nōlēbāmus	ībāmus
erātis	poterātis	ferēbātis	volēbātis	nōlēbātis	ībātis
erant	poterant	ferēbant	volēbant	nōlēbant	ībant

erō	poterō	feram	volam	nōlam	ībō
eris	poteris	ferēs	volēs	nōlēs	ībis
erit	poterit	feret	volet	nōlet	ībit
erimus	poterimus	ferēmus	volēmus	nōlēmus	ībimus
eritis	poteritis	ferētis	volētis	nōlētis	ībitis
erunt	poterunt	ferent	volent	nōlent	ībunt

* Irregular verbs form their perfect tenses in the same way as the regular verbs.

NUMBERS (CH. 22)

NUMERALS	CARDINAL	ORDINAL
I	ūnus, ūna, ūnum	prīmus, a, um
II	duo, duae, duo	secundus, a, um
III	trēs, tria	tertius, a, um
IV or IIII	quattuor	quārtus, a, um
V	quīnque	quīntus, a, um
VI	sex	sextus, a, um
VII	septem	septimus, a, um
VIII	octō	octāvus, a, um
IX	novem	nōnus, a, um
X	decem	decimus, a, um
XI	ūndecim	ūndecimus, a, um
XII	duodecim	duodecimus, a, um
XIII	tredecim	tertius decimus, a, um
XIV	quattuordecim	quārtus decimus, a, um
XV	quīndecim	quīntus decimus, a, um
XVI	sēdecim	sextus decimus, a, um
XVII	septendecim	septimus decimus, a, um
XVIII	duodēvīgintī	duodēvīcēsimus, a, um
XIX	ūndēvīgintī	ūndēvīcēsimus, a, um
XX	vīgintī	vīcēsimus, a, um
XXI	vīgintī ūnus, ūnus et vīgintī	vīcēsimus, a, um prīmus, a, um
XXX	trīgintā	trīcēsimus, a, um
XXXX or XL	quadrāgintā	quadrāgēsimus, a, um
L	quīnquāgintā	quīnquāgēsimus, a, um
LX	sexāgintā	sexāgēsimus, a, um

LXX	septuāgintā	septuāgēsimus, a, um
LXXX	octōgintā	octōgēsimus, a, um
LXXXX or XC	nōnāgintā	nōnāgēsimus, a, um
C	centum	centēsimus, a, um
CI	centum ūnus, a, um	centēsimus, a, um prīmus, a, um
CC	ducentī, ae, a	ducentēsimus, a, um
CCC	trecentī, ae, a	trecentēsimus, a, um
CCCC	quadringentī, ae, a	quadringentēsimus, a, um
D	quīngentī, ae, a	quīngentēsimus, a, um
DC	sescentī, ae, a	sescentēsimus, a, um
DCC	septingentī, ae, a	septingentēsimus, a, um
DCCC	octingentī, ae, a	octingentēsimus, a, um
DCCCC	nōngentī, ae, a	nōngentēsimus, a, um
M	mīlle	mīllēsimus, a, um
MM	duo mīlia	bis mīllēsimus, a, um

Cardinal numbers four through one hundred do not decline. Numbers two hundred and greater decline like first and second declension adjectives. The number *ūnus* declines as *ūllus* and the other special *-ius* adjectives. The numbers *duo* and *trēs* decline as follows.

DUO - TWO

CASE	MASCULINE	FEMININE	NEUTER
Nom.	duo	duae	duo
Gen.	duōrum	duārum	duōrum
Dat.	duōbus	duābus	duōbus
Acc.	duōs	duās	duo
Abl.	duōbus	duābus	duōbus

TRĒS - THREE

CASE	MASCULINE & FEMININE	NEUTER
Nom.	trēs	tria
Gen.	trium	trium
Dat.	tribus	tribus
Acc.	trēs	tria
Abl.	tribus	tribus

Glossary

VOCABULARY BY ALPHABET

LATIN	ENGLISH	DERIVATIVES
ad, prep + acc.	to, toward, against; at, near, by	
amō, amāre, amāvī, amātum	to love, like	(amorous)
accipiō, accipere, accēpī, acceptum	to receive	(accept)
ācer, ācris, ācre	sharp, eager; severe, fierce	(acrid, acrimony)
adamō, āre, āvī, ātum	to fall in love with	
adiuvō, āre, āvī, ātum	to help	
administrō, āre, āvī, ātum	to manage	(administer)
adveniō, advenīre, advēnī, adventum	to arrive, come to	(advent)
aedificō, aedificāre, aedificāvī, aedificātum	to build	(edifice, edification)
aēneus, aēnea, aēneum	bronze	
ager, agrī, m.	field	(agriculture, agrarian)
agnōscō, agnōscere, agnōvī, agnitum	to know, understand, identify	
agō, agere, ēgī, āctum	to do, drive, act	(agent, action)
agricola, agricolae, m.	farmer	(agriculture)
aliquis, aliquid	somebody, something	
alius, alia, aliud	other, another	(alias, alibi)
alter, altera, alterum alter . . . alter	the other (of two) one . . . the other	(alternative, alternate)
altus, a, um	high, deep	(altitude)
ambulō, ambulāre, ambulāvī, ambulātum	to walk	(perambulator, ambulance)

amīca, amīcae, f.	friend (female friend)	(amicable)
amīcus, a, um	friendly	(amicable)
amīcus, amīcī, m.	friend (male friend)	(amicable, amigo)
āmittō, āmittere, āmīsī, āmissum	to let go, lose	
amor, amōris, m.	love	(amorous)
ancilla, ancillae , f.	maid-servant	(ancillary)
animal, animālis, n.	animal	(animal)
annus, ī, m.	year	(annual)
ante, prep. + acc.	before	
antecēdō, antecēdere, antecessī, antecessum	to precede, to surpass	(antecedent)
antequam	before	
appellō, āre, āvī, ātum	to speak to; call, name	(appellation)
aptus, a, um	fitting, proper, apt, suitable	(apt)
apud, prep. + acc.	among	
aqua, ae, f.	water	(aquatic)
arbor, arboris	tree	(arboreal)
arma, armōrum, n. pl.	weapons, arms	(armor, arms)
arō, arāre, arāvī, arātum	to plow	(arable)
ascendō, ascendere, ascendī, ascēnsum	to climb, to go up	(ascension)
auctōritās, auctōritātis, f.	authority	(author)
audiō, audīre, audīvī/audiī, audītum,	to hear, listen	(audio, auditory)
aurum, ī, n.	gold	(auric)
aut	or	
auxilium, auxiliī, n.	aid, help	(auxiliary)
bellum, bellī, n.	war	(belligerent, bellicose)
bene	well	
bonus, bona, bonum	good	(bonus, bonafide)
brevis, breve	short, brief	(brevity)
caelum, ī, n.	sky	(celestial)
camera, ae, f.	room	
cantō, cantāre, cantāvī, cantātum	to sing	(chant, cantata)
capiō, capere, cēpī, captum	to take, seize; capture	(capture)
captīvus, ī, m.	captive, prisoner of war	(captivity)
caput, capitis, n.	head	(capital, chapter)
cardinālis, cardināle	that on which something turns, depends	(cardinal), (cardinal)
careō, carēre, caruī, caritūrum (+ abl. of separation)	to be without, to be deprived of, want, lack; be free from	
carpō, carpere, carpsī, carptum	to seize, pluck	(carpal)
carrus, carrī, m.	wagon, cart, chariot	(cart)

cārus, a, um	dear, expensive, costly	(caress)
castra, castrōrum, n. pl.	camp	
celer, celeris, celere	swift, quick, rapid	(accelerate)
cēna, cēnae, f.	dinner	(cenacle)
cēterī, cēterōrum, m. pl.	the rest	
circum (+ acc.)	around	(circumference)
circumdō, circumdare, circumdedī, circumdatum	to surround	
circumscrībō, -scrībere, -scrīpsī, -scrīptum	to draw a line around	(circumscribe)
cīvīlis, cīvīle	civil	(civil)
cīvis, cīvis, m.	citizen	
clāmō, āre, āvī, ātum	to shout	(clamor, exclaim)
classis, classis, f.	fleet	(class)
claudō, claudere, clausī, clausum	to shut, close; close off	(closure)
collum, collī, n.	neck	(collar)
condō, condere, condidī, conditum	to found, establish	
coniungō, coniungere, coniūnxī, coniūnctum	to unite, join together	(conjugate)
conscrībō, conscrībere, conscrīpsī, conscrīptum	to enlist, enroll; write up	(conscription)
cōnsentiō, cōnsentīre, cōnsēnsī, cōnsēnsum	to agree	(consent, consensus)
cōnsilium, cōnsiliī, n.	plan	
cōnspiciō, cōnspicere, cōnspexī, cōnspectum	to catch sight of	(conspicuous)
cōnsūmō, cōnsūmere, cōnsūmpsī, cōnsūmptum	to consume, eat	(consume)
contrā, prep. + acc.	against	(contrary)
cōpiae, cōpiārum, f. pl.	troops	(copious)
corium, coriī, n.	skin, hide	(excoriate)
cornū, ūs, n.	wing (of an army); horn	(cornucopia, cornet, unicorn)
corpus, corporis, n.	body	(corporal)
crēdō, crēdere, crēdidī, crēditum (+ dat. of person, + acc. of thing)	to believe, trust	(creed)
creō, creāre, creāvī, creātum	to create, make	(creation, creator)
crūdēlis, crūdēle	hard-hearted, cruel	(crudelity)
culīna, culīnae, f.	kitchen	(culinary)
cūrō, āre, āvī, ātum	to care for, take care of	
currō, currere, cucurrī, cursum	to run	(current)
dēbeō, dēbēre, dēbuī, dēbitum	ought, must	(debt)
dēcipiō, dēcipere, dēcēpī, dēceptum	to deceive	(deception)
dēdicō, āre, āvī, ātum	to consecrate, dedicate; declare	(dedicate)

deinde	then	
dēleō, dēlēre, dēlēvī, dēletum	to destroy	(delete)
dēmōnstrō, dēmōnstrāre, dēmōnstrāvī, dēmōnstrātum	to point out, show	(demonstrate)
desiderō, āre, āvī, ātum	to desire, wish	(desire)
deus, deī, m.	god	(deity)
dexter, dextra, dextrum	right; f. noun right hand	(dexterity)
dīcō, dīcere, dīxī, dictum	to speak, say, tell	(dictate)
diēs, diēī, m/f.	day (feminine used for an appointed or set day)	(diurnal, modern)
dignus, a, um	worthy	(dignified)
dīmittō, dīmittere, dīmīsī, dīmissum	to send away, dismiss	(dismiss, dismissal)
discēdō, discēdere, discēssī, discessum	go away, depart	
discō, discere, didicī	to learn	(discern)
dissimilis, dissimile	unlike	(dissimilar)
dīves, dīvitis	rich	
dō, dare, dedī, datum	to give	(donate)
doceō, docēre, docuī, doctum	to teach	(doctrine)
dominus, ī, m.	master, lord	(domain)
domus, ūs, f.	house, home	(domicile, domestic)
dōnum, dōnī, n.	gift	(donation)
dum	while	
duo, duae, duo	two	(dual, duet)
dux, ducis, m.	leader	(conductor)
ēducātiō, ēducātiōnis, f.	upbringing, rearing; education	(education)
effugiō, effugere, effūgī	to run away, escape	
ego	I	(egocentric)
emō, emere, ēmī, emptum	to buy, procure	
eō, īre, iī/īvī, itum	to go	(exit)
epistula, ae, f.	letter	(epistle)
equus, equī, m.	horse	(equestrian, equine)
et	and	(et cetera)
etiam	also, even	
ēvādō, ēvādere, ēvāsī, ēvāsum	to come out, escape	(evasion)
exerceō, exercēre, exercuī, exercitum	to train	(exercise)
exercitus, ūs, m.	army	
exspectō, āre, āvī, ātum	to wait for; to see, expect	(expect)
exstinguō, exstinguere, extinxī, extinctum	to put out, extinguish	(extinct)
fābula, fābulae, f.	story	(fable, fabulous)
faciēs, faciēī, f.	face, appearance	(facial)
faciō, facere, fēcī, factum	to do, make	(fact)

factiō, factiōnis, f.	political party, faction	(faction)
factum, ī, n.	deed	(fact)
familia, ae, f.	family	(familial)
fātum, ī, n.	fate	(fatal)
faveō, favēre, fāvī, fautum (+ dat.)	to favor	
fēlix, fēlīcis	happy	(felicity)
fēmina, fēminae, f.	woman	(feminine)
ferō, ferre, tulī, lātum	to bring, carry	(ferry, transfer)
ferrum, ferrī, n.	iron; sword	(ferric)
fessus, fessa, fessum	tired	
fidēlis, fidēle	faithful, loyal (to)	(fidelity)
fidēs, fideī, f.	faith, trust	(fidelity)
fīlia, fīliae, f.	daughter	(filial)
fīlius, fīliī, m.	son	
fīnis, fīnis, m.	end, boundary	(finish, finite)
flamma, flammae, f.	flame	(flammable, inflammatory)
flammeus, a, um	fiery; flame covered, as a neuter noun – bridal veil	(flammable)
flōs, flōris, m.	flower, blossom	(floral)
flūmen, flūminis, n.	river	(flume)
fortis, forte	strong, brave	(fortitude)
fortitūdinō, fortitūdinis, f.	courage, strength	(fortitude)
fortūna, ae, f.	fortune, luck	(fortunate)
frāter, frātris, m.	brother	(fraternal)
frūctus, ūs, m.	fruit, profit, benefit	(fructose, frugal)
frūmentum, frūmentī, n.	grain	
gaudium, gaudiī, n.	joy	
gēns, gentis, f.	tribe, nation	(gentile)
genū, ūs, n.	knee	(genuflect)
germānus, germānī, m.	brother	(German, germane)
gerō, gerere, gessī, gestum	to wear	
gladius, gladiī, m.	sword	(gladiator)
Graecia, Graeciae, f.	Greece	(Grecian)
grātia, grātiae, f.	thanks, gratitude	(gratitude, grateful)
gravis, grave	serious, important, weighty	(grave)
gubernātor, gubernātōris, m.	governor	(gubernatorial)
habeō, habēre, habuī, habitum	to have, hold; consider	(habit)
habitō, habitāre, habitāvī, habitātum	to live, dwell	(habitat)
hic, haec, hoc	this, these	
hiems, hiemis, f.	winter	(hiemal)
homō, hominis, m.	human, man	(homo sapiens)

honor, honōris, m.	honor	(honorable)
hōra, hōrae, f.	hour	(hour)
hostis, hostis, m.	enemy	(hostile)
humus, humī, f.	ground	(humus)
iaciō, iacere, iēcī, iactum	to throw	(eject)
igitur	therefore	
ignis, ignis, m.	fire	(igneous)
ille, illa, illud	that	
imperium, ī, n.	power	(empire, imperial)
impetus, ūs, m.	attack; charge; impulse	(impetuous)
incipiō, incipere, incēpī, inceptum	to begin	(inception)
incola, incolae, m.	settler	
induō, induere, induī, indūtum	to put on	
īnfāns, īnfantis, m./f.i.	baby	(infant)
ingēns, ingentis	huge	
inimīcus, a, um	unfriendly	(inamicable)
inimīcus, inimīcī, m.	personal enemy	(enmity)
iniūria, ae, f.	wrong, injury; insult	(injurious)
īnsula, īnsulae, f.	island	(insulate)
integer, integra, integrum	upright	(integrity)
intellegō, intellegere, intellēxī, intellēctum	understand	(intelligence)
interficiō, interficere, interfēcī, interfectum	to kill	
ipse, ipsa, ipsum	himself, herself	
is, ea, id	he, she, it	
iste, ista, istud	that (of yours/near you)	
iter, itineris, n.	journey	(itinerary, itinerate)
iterum	again	
iubeō, iubēre, iussī, iussum	to order, command	(jussive)
iungō, iungere, iūnxī, iūnctum	to join, unite	(conjunction)
iūrō, āre, āvī, ātum	to swear, take an oath	(jurat)
iūs, iūris, n.	law	(jurisprudence)
iuvenis, iuvenis	young, youthful	(juvenile)
iuvenis, iuvenis, m./f.	youth, young man	(juvenile)
iuvō, iuvāre, iūvī, iūtum	to help	(aid, adjutant)
labōrō, labōrāre, labōrāvī, labōrātum	to work	(labor)
laetus, a, um	happy	
lectus, ī, m.	couch, bed; bier	
lēgātus, ī, m.	officer, lieutenant	(delegate)
legiō, legiōnis, f.	legion (up to 6000 men); (pl.) troops, army	(legionnaire)

legō, legere, lēgī, lēctum	to read; choose, gather	(legible)
lēx, lēgis, f.	law	(legal)
līber, lībera, līberum	free	(liberty)
līberī, līberōrum, m. pl.	children	
līberō, līberāre, līberāvī, līberātum	to free	(liberate)
lībertus, ī, m	freedman (former slave who has been given freedom)	
līnum, ī, n.	line, rope; thread	(linear)
litterae, litterārum, f. pl.	literature	(literature)
lūdificō, lūdificāre, lūdificāvī, lūdificātum	to fool	(ludicrous)
lūdus, ī, m.	school, game	(ludicrous)
magnopere	greatly	
magnus, magna, magnum	big, great	(magnify, magnitude)
malus, mala, malum, adj.	bad, evil	
maneō, manēre, mānsī, mānsum	to stay, remain	(mansion)
manus, ūs, f.	hand; band (of men)	(manual, manumit)
mare, maris, n.	sea	(marine)
marītus, ī, m.	husband	(marital)
māter, mātris, f.	mother	(maternal, maternity)
mēnsa, mēnsae, f.	table	
mēnsis, mēnsis, m.	month	
metuō, metuere, metuī, metūtum	fear	
meus, a, um	my, mine	
mīles, mīlitis, m.	soldier	(military)
mīlitō, āre, āvī, ātum	to serve as a soldier	(military)
mīlle passūs, mīlia passuum	miles (1000 paces)	
mīlle (pl. mīlia)	thousand	(mile)
minimus, a, um	least, very little	(minimal)
miser, misera, miserum	unhappy, wretched, miserable	(miser)
mītis, mīte	gentle	
mittō, mittere, mīsī, missum	to send	(mission)
modestia, ae, f.	temperance; humility	(modesty)
modestus, a, um	well-behaved; humble, modest	(modest)
modo	only	
moneō, monēre, monuī, monitum	to warn	(admonish)
mōns, montis, m.	mountain	(montane)
mōnstrō, mōnstrāre, mōnstrāvī, mōnstrātum	to show	(demonstration)
mors, mortis, f.	death	(mortician)
mortuus, a, um	dead	(mortuary)
mox	soon	
multus, multa, multum	many	(multiply, multitude)

narrō, narrāre, narrāvī, narrātum	to tell	(narrate, narrator)
natō, āre, āvī, ātum	to swim	(natatorium)
nauta, nautae, m.	sailor	(nautical)
nāvigō, nāvigāre, nāvigāvī, nāvigātum	to sail	(navigate, navigation)
nāvis, nāvis, f.	ship	(naval)
necō, āre, āvī, ātum	to kill	
neuter, neutra, neutrum	neither	(neuter, neutral)
nix, nivis, f.	snow	(snow)
noceō, nocēre, nocuī, nocitum (+ dat.)	to harm, to be harmful to	(innocuous)
nōlō, nōlle, nōluī	to not wish, to be unwilling	
nōmen, nōminis, n.	name, title	(nomination)
nōn	not	(nonsense)
nōs, nostrī/nostrum	we	
noster, a, um	our	
notā bene	phrase: "note well"	
nōtus, a, um	known	(notable)
nox, noctis, f.	night; darkness	(nocturnal)
nūbes, nūbis, m.	cloud	
nūllus, nūlla, nūllum	no, none, not any	(nullify, annul)
numquam, adv.	never	
nunc	now	
nūntius, ī, m.	messenger; message	(announcement)
nux, nucis, f.	nut; nut tree	
ob, prep. + acc.	in front of; on account of, for	(obvious)
obses, obsidis, m.	hostage	(obsess)
obtineō, obtinēre, obtinuī, obtentum	to hold on, possess	(obtain)
obtruncō, āre, āvī, ātum	to slaughter	
odium, odiī, n.	hatred	(odious)
officium, ī, n.	office, duty	(officiate)
omnis, omne	all, every	(omnibus, omnipresent)
oppidum, oppidī, n.	town	
oppugnō, oppugnāre, oppugnāvī, oppugnātum	to attack	(pugnacious)
optimus, a, um	best	(optimum)
optō, optāre, optāvī, optātum	to wish for, desire	(option, opt)
ōrātiō, ōrātiōnis, f.	speech	(oratory)
ōrnō, āre, āvī, ātum	to decorate, adorn	(ornate)
ōs, ōris, n.	mouth	(oral)
pār, paris	equal (to)	(partial)
parātus, a, um	prepared	(preparatory)

parēns, parentis, m/f.	parent	(parent)
pāreō, pārēre, pāruī, pāritum (+ dat.)	to obey, to be obedient to	
parō, āre, āvī, ātum	to prepare, get ready	(preparation)
pars, partis, f.	part	(particle, partition)
parvus, a, um	little, small	
passus, ūs, m.	pace, footstep	(pace)
pater, patris, m.	father	(paternal, paternity)
pātria, pātriae, f.	fatherland, country	(patriot)
paucī, paucae, pauca, pl.	few, a few	(paucity)
pauper, pauperis	poor, a poor man	(poverty)
pāx, pācis, f.	peace	(pax, pacify)
pecūnia, ae, f.	money	(pecuniary)
pereō, perīre, periī, peritum	to die	(perish)
perīculum, ī, n.	danger	(peril)
permittō, permittere, permīsī, permissum	to permit, allow	(permission)
petō, petere, petīvī / petiī, petītum	to aim at, attack, seek	(petulant)
pius, pia, pium	pious, devout (god-fearing)	(pious, piety)
placeō, placēre, placuī, placitum (+ dat.)	to please, to be pleasing to	(placate)
plēnus, a, um	full	(plenty)
plūrimus, a, um	most, very much	(plural)
poēta, poētae, m.	poet	(poet)
pōnō, pōnere, posuī, positum	to put, place	(position)
portō, portāre, portāvī, portātum	to carry	(portable)
possum, posse, potuī	to be able, can	(possible)
post, prep. + acc.	after	
posteā	afterwards	
postquam, conj.	after	
postulō, āre, āvī, ātum	to demand	(postulate)
potēns, potentis	able, capable; powerful	(potent)
praecipuus, a, um	special; principal	
praemium, ī, n.	reward; booty, loot	(premium)
pretium, ī, n.	price	
prīnceps, prīncipis, m.	prince, leader	(principate)
probō, āre, āvī, ātum	to approve	(probation)
prōcēdō, prōcēdere, prōcessī, prōcessum	to advance, proceed	(process)
proelium, ī, n.	battle	
prohibeō, prohibēre, prohibuī, prohibitum	to keep (back), prevent	(prohibit)
prope (+ acc.)	near	
prōpōnō, prōpōnere, prōposuī, prōpositum	to put before; to propose	(proposition)

proximus, a, um	next, near	(approximate)
pūblicus, a, um	public	(publicity)
puella, puellae, f.	girl	
puer, puerī, m.	boy	(puerile, puerperal)
pugnō, pugnāre, pugnāvī, pugnātum	to fight	(pugnacious)
pulcher, pulchra, pulchrum	beautiful	(pulchritude)
pūpa, pūpae, f.	doll	(pupa)
quaerō, quaerere, quaesīvī/quaesiī, quaesītum	to seek, ask	
quī, quae, quod, rel. pron.	who, which	
quis, quid, interrog. pron.	who, what	
quod	because	
quoque	also	
ratiō, ratiōnis, f.	reason	(ration, rational)
reddō, reddere, reddidī, redditum	to give back, return	
referō, referre, rettulī, relātum	to bring back, carry back; report	(relate, relative)
reflectō, reflectere, reflexī, reflexum	to bend back	(reflect)
rēgia, rēgiae, f.	palace	(regal)
rēgīna, rēgīnae, f.	queen	
rēgnō, rēgnāre, rēgnāvī, rēgnātum	to rule	(reign, regent)
relinquō, relinquere, relīquī, relictum	to leave behind	(relinquish)
rēs pūblica, reī pūblicae, f.	state, republic	
rēs, reī f.	thing, matter; state	(Republic)
respondeō, respondēre, respondī, respōnsum	to reply, respond	(responsive)
reveniō, revenīre, revēnī, reventum,	to come back, return	
revertō, revertere, revertī, reversum	to turn back, return	(reverse)
rēx, rēgis, m.	king	(regent)
rīpa, ae, f.	river bank, shore	(riparian, riptide)
rīvus, ī, m.	brook, small stream	(rival)
rogō, rogāre, rogāvī, rogātum	to ask	(interrogation)
rosa, rosae, f.	rose	(rose)
rūs, rūris, f.	country (as opposed to city)	(rural, rusticate)
sacer, sacra, sacrum	sacred, holy	(sacred)
saltō, saltāre, saltāvī, saltātum	to leap, dance	
sciō, scīre, scīvī / sciī, scītum	to know	(science)
scrība, ae, m.	clerk; scribe	(scribe)
scrībō, scrībere, scrīpsī, scrīptum	to write	(scribble)
scūtum, scūtī, n.	shield	(scutes)
semper	always	
senātor, senātōris, m.	senator, member of the Roman senate	(senator)

senātus, ūs, m.	senate; body of elders	(senate, senatorial)
senex, senis	old, aged; (as a noun) old man	(senate, senile)
senior, seniōris	older, elder	
sentiō, sentīre, sēnsī, sēnsum	to perceive, feel; sense	(sensible)
servō, servāre, servāvī, servātum	to take care of; guard, protect, save	(conserve, preserve)
sī	if	
sīc	thus, so, in this way	
sīcut, adv.	just as	
signum, signī, n.	sign	(signal)
similis, simile	like, similar (to)	(similarity)
sincērē	honestly	(sincerely)
socius, sociī, m.	ally	(social)
sōlus, sōla, sōlum	alone, only	(solo, solitude)
soror, sorōris, f.	sister	(sorority)
spectō, spectāre, spectāvī, spectātum	to look at, watch	(spectator, spectacle)
spērō, āre, āvī, ātum	to hope	
spēs, speī, f.	hope	(desperate)
squālidus, a, um	dirty	(squalid)
statua, ae, f.	statue	(statuesque)
stella, stellae , f.	star	(stellar, constellation)
stō, stāre, stetī, statum	to stand; (+ dat.) to cost	(statue, statute, from "to stand")
studeō, studēre, studuī (+ dat.)	to study, to direct one's zeal to	(studious)
studium, studiī, n.	zeal, eagerness	(studious)
sum, esse, fuī, futūrum	to be	(essence, future)
superō, āre, āvī, ātum	to surpass, outdo; overcome	
surgō, surgere, surrēxī, surrēctum	to rise, arise	(resurrection)
suus, a, um	his, her, its, their own	
tam	so	
tamen	nevertheless, however	
templum, templī, n.	temple	(temple, Knights Templar)
temptō, āre, āvī, ātum	to try, attempt	(tempt)
tempus, temporis, n.	time	(temporal)
teneō, tenēre, tenuī, tentum	to hold	(tenacious)
terra, terrae, f.	earth, land	(terrain)
terreō, terrēre, terruī, territum	to scare, frighten	(terrify)
timeō, timēre, timuī	to be afraid, fear	(timid, timidity)
timidus, a, um	afraid, fearful; hesitant	(timid, timidity)
toga, togae, f.	toga	
tōtus, tōta, tōtum	whole, entire	(total)
trēs, tria	three	(trio, tricycle)
triumphus, ī, m.	triumphal procession	(triumphant)
Trōia, Trōiae, f.	Troy (a city-state in Asia Minor)	(Troy, Trojan)
tū	you	

tum	then	
tūtus, tūta, tūtum	protected, safe	
tuus, a, um	your, yours	
tyrannus, ī, m.	king, tyrant	(tyranny)
ubī	when	
ūllus, ūlla, ūllum	any	
ultimus, a, um	last	(ultimatum)
umquam	ever, at any time	
ūnus, ūna, ūnum	one	(unify, union)
urbs, urbis, f.	city	(urbane, urban)
uter, utra, utrum	either, which (of two)	
uxor, uxōris, f.	wife	(uxorious)
validus, a, um	strong	(validity)
vēndō, vēndere, vēndidī, vēnditum	to sell	(vendor)
veniō, venīre, vēnī, ventum	to come	(advent, venture)
verbum, ī, n.	word	(verbose)
vērē	truly	(verily)
vertō, vertere, vertī, versum	to turn	(convert)
vester, a, um	your (plural)	
vīcīnus, a, um	neighboring, nearby; (as a noun) neighbor	(vicinity)
victōria, ae, f.	victory	(victorious)
videō, vidēre, vīdī, vīsum	to see	(video, vision)
vigil, vigilis, m.	watchman; (m.pl.) a fire brigade, firemen	(vigilant)
vīlis, vīle	cheap	(vile, vilify)
vīlla, vīllae, f.	farmhouse	(village)
vincō, vincere, vīcī, victum	to conquer	(vanquish)
vir, virī, m.	man	(virile)
virgō, virginis, f.	maiden	(Virginia)
virtūs, virtūtis, f.	manhood, courage	(virtue)
vīvō, vīvere, vīxī, vīctum	to live	(vivacious)
vīvus, a, um	living, alive	(vivacious)
vocō, vocāre, vocāvī, vocātum	to call	(vocal, vocation)
volō, velle, voluī	to wish, want, be willing	
voluntās, voluntātis, f.	will, wish	(voluntary)
vulnerātus, a, um	wounded	
vulnerō, āre, āvī, ātum	to wound	(vulnerable)
vultus, vultūs, m.	face, visage	

Reference

l	locative
LV	linking verb
m	masculine
n	neuter *or* nominative
OP	object of the preposition
p	plural *or* passive
pl.	plural (see also p)
P	preposition
part. abl.	partitive ablative
part. gen.	partitive genitive
pf	perfect
PfW	place from which
PNA	possessive noun adjective
PPA	possessive pronoun adjective
ppf	pluperfect
part	participle
pr	present
PrAc	predicate accusative
PrAdj	predicate adjective
PrN	predicate nominative
pro	pronoun
PW	place where
refl. pro.	reflexive pronoun
s	singular
sing	singular (see also s)
S.	subject
SbAdj.	substantive adjective
sem. dep.	semi-deponent
SpAdj	superlative adjective
SpAdv	superlative adverb
SPr	subject pronoun
SV	subject and verb (a verb containing the subject for the sentence)
V	verb
voc	vocative

Teacher's Extras

nomen: _____   datum: _____

Early Roman Calendar

Rome was founded in the year _____. At that time Rome was a small village made up of _____. The people measured time and determined dates according to the cycle of their crops. According to tradition, Romulus, the first _____ of Rome, created the Early Roman Calendar to help his people as they took care of their crops and fields. The calendar he created was lunar, which means the days and months were measured according to the phases of the _____. Romulus' calendar had only 10 months. They were named:

1. Mārtius = _____

2. Āprīlis = _____

3. Māius = _____

4. Iūnius = _____

5. Quīnctīlis = _____

6. Sextīlis = _____

7. September = _____

8. Octōber = _____

9. November = _____

10. December = _____

The first month, Martius, began with the arrival of _____ and the new planting season. The last month, December, ended with the harvesting and storing away of the _____. In between these two months was a _____ _____, when the fields rested. The Romans did not measure this period of rest. The local pontifices (_____) would decide when it was time for the new year to begin. Romulus' calendar consisted of _____ months that had a total of _____ days.

This winter gap in the calendar, however, could cause some confusion. So, Numa Pomplilius, the second king of Rome, added two months after December.

11. Iānuārius = _____

12. Februārius = _____

This updated calendar now had _____ months and lasted a total of _____ days.

The Romans did not have a seven day week, and they did not have weekends. Instead they had three festival days each month. The phase of the moon determined each one of them. The Kalends (*Kalendae*) fell on the _____ day of each month. The Ides (*Īdūs*) fell on the _____ in the short months and the _____ in the long months. The Ides celebrated the full moon. The Nones (*Nōnae*) came _____ days before the Ides. The Nones, therefore, fell on the _____ in short months and the _____ in long months. The Romans numbered the rest of the days by counting down to these festival days, much like we count down to _____.

©2008, Classical Academic Press • All rights reserved.

The Roman Calendar

270

This new system worked out fine for a while, but eventually the farmers realized the seasons were not coming out quite right. The year was still too short. So, Tarquinius Priscus, the _____ king of Rome, added a new month at the end of Februarius. The Romans called this month the "Intercalans" because it was placed _____ (*inter*) the last and first months of the year. This 13th month did not come every year. The pontifices (_____), who were in charge of the calendar, decided which years should add the new month. The intercalans became a kind of "leap month."

The Julian Calendar

This latest version of the calendar seemed to work well for several centuries. Over time, however, the old calendar system still had problems, and the priests sometimes abused their power to control it. In 45 BC _____ Caesar became the new Pontifex Maximus (_____ _____). He decided to completely reform the calendar. He saw that Egypt had a solar calendar, determined by the _____. He hired Sosigenes, an Egyptian _____, to help him create a new solar calendar for Rome. Caesar changed the first month of the calendar from Martius to _____. He gave the months alternating lengths of 30 or 31 days, but left Februarius with only 29. He also created an extra day called the Bissextile, which was the very first _____ _____. The bissextile day came once every 4 years. In those years, February would have 30 days. This gave the new Julian Calendar, named for Julius Caesar, 365.25 days.

On March 15, _____ Julius Caesar was murdered. The Roman Senate renamed the month Quinctilis "_____" in honor of Caesar. In 31 BC, Octavian, Caesar's nephew, became the first emperor of Rome. He persuaded the Senate to rename the month Sextīlis "_____" in honor of his new title Augustus Caesar. The emperor's new month had only 30 days, so he took a day from Februarius and added it to his own month. Now the month of August has _____ days, but Februarius has only _____.

Days of the Week

Strange as it may seem to us, the Romans did not have a seven-day week. They relied solely on the numbering system that revolved around the festival days. It was the Emperor Constantine (AD _____ – _____) who introduced the seven-day week. Constantine had converted to _____ shortly before becoming the Roman Emperor. He believed that God had granted him his rule and, therefore, was deeply interested in the Judeo-Christian Religion. In the ninth year of his reign he issued an edict creating the seven-day week based on that of the _____ Calendar. He gave each of the seven days a name according to the _____ bodies that rose in the sky. These names have remained a part of our calendar until this day, although some use the Norse version of the name instead.

Diēs Sōlis = _____

Diēs Lūnae = _____

Diēs Mārtis = _____   Norse Mythology: Tyr, _____

Diēs Mercuriī = _____   Norse Mythology: Woden, _____

Diēs Iovis = _____   Norse Mythology: Thor, _____

Diēs Veneris = _____   Norse Mythology: Freya, _____

Diēs Sāturnī = _____

The Gregorian Calendar

The Julian Calendar worked very well for more than a thousand years. In the 16th century AD, however, the Church began to realize that something was terribly wrong. The _____ Holiday, whose date is determined by the stars and _____, was off by _____ days. At the Council of Trent in AD _____ Pope Gregory XIII determined to fix this problem. He commissioned _____Christopher Clavis and Luigi Lilio to reform the calendar. They discovered that the Julian Calendar was off by _____ minutes and _____ seconds! That is a difference of just .0078 days! In order to fix the problem they moved leap day (the bissextile) to the last day of February, and created the Century Leap Year Rule:

Three out of every four centennial years (a year divisible by _____) are "common." No centennial year, however, can be a leap year IF it is divisible by _____.

Because of this rule the year 2000 was not a leap year, even though 1996 and 2004 were leap years. What year will the century leap year rule next effect?

CREATE YOUR OWN ROMAN CALENDAR

Step One: Decide which month you would like to create and see how many days it has.

Step Two: Determine when the Kalends, Nones and Ides will occur.

"In October, July, March and May the Nones fall on the 7th day!"

Step Three: Count backwards from these festival days until you run into a preceding festival day. The day before a holiday is the *prīdiē*, and the day before that will always begin *a.d. iii.* When counting backwards, the Romans always counted the holiday itself as day #1.

Step Four: Find other holidays for your month (modern or ancient) and decorate your calendar.

Important Notations for the Roman Calendar

Kalendae	Kal.	1st of every month
Nōnae	Non.	5th or 7th of the month
Īdūs	Id.	13th or 15th of the month
Prīdiē	Prid.	day immediately preceding a festival day
ante diem	AD	other days leading up to a festival day

Sample Calendar

September MMVII

Diēs Sōlis	Diēs Lūnae	Diēs Mārtis	Diēs Mercuriī	Diēs Iovis	Diēs Veneris	Diēs Saturnī
			Kal.	a.d.iv Non.	a.d.iii Non.	Prid. Non.
Non.	a.d. viii Id.	a.d. vii Id.	a.d. vi Id.	a.d. v Id.	a.d. iv Id.	a.d. iii Id.
Prid. Id.	Id.	a.d. xviii Kal.	a.d. xvii Kal.	a.d. xvi Kal.	a.d. xv Kal.	a.d. xiv Kal.
a.d. xiii Kal.	a.d. xii Kal.	a.d. xi Kal.	a.d. x Kal.	a.d. ix Kal.	a.d. viii Kal.	a.d. vii Kal.
a.d. vi Kal.	a.d. v Kal.	a.d. iv Kal.	a.d. iii Kal.	Prid. Kal.		

The Roman Calendar

Early Roman Calendar

Rome was founded in the year __753 BC__ . At that time Rome was a small village made up of ____farmers____ . The people measured time and determined dates according to the cycle of their crops. According to tradition, Romulus, the first ___king___ of Rome, created the Early Roman Calendar to help his people as they took care of their crops and fields. The calendar he created was lunar, which means the days and months were measured according to the phases of the ___moon___ . Romulus' calendar had only 10 months. They were named:

1. Mārtius = __Mars, god of war (legendary father of Romulus)__
2. Āprīlis = __Aphrilis (a Greek name for Venus, godess of love, mother of Aeneas)__
3. Māius = __Maia, star in Pleiades (mother of Mercury)__
4. Iūnius = __Juno, queen of gods, goddess of marriage__
5. Quīnctīlis = __fifth__
6. Sextīlis = __sixth__
7. September = __seven__
8. Octōber = __eight__
9. November = __nine__
10. December = __ten__

The first month, Martius, began with the arrival of ___Spring___ and the new planting season. The last month, December, ended with the harvesting and storing away of the ___crops___ . In between these two months was a ___winter___ ___gap___ , when the fields rested. The Romans did not measure this period of rest. The local pontifices (___priests___) would decide when it was time for the new year to begin. Romulus' calendar consisted of _____ months that had a total of __304__ days.

This winter gap in the calendar, however, could cause some confusion. So, Numa Pomplilius, the second king of Rome, added two months after December.

11. Iānuārius = __Ianus, god of doorways, beginnings and endings__
12. Februārius = __a purification festival that took place during this month__

This updated calendar now had __12__ months and lasted a total of __355__ days.

The Romans did not have a seven day week, and they did not have weekends. Instead they had three festival days each month. The phase of the moon determined each one of them. The Kalends (*Kalendae*) fell on the ___first___ day of each month. The Ides (*Īdūs*) fell on the __13th__ in the short months and the __15th__ in the long months. The Ides celebrated the full moon. The Nones (*Nōnae*) came __9__ days before the Ides. The Nones, therefore, fell on the __5th__ in short months and the __7th__ in long months. The Romans numbered the rest of the days by counting down to these festival days, much like we count down to _____(name favorite holiday)_____ .

This new system worked out fine for a while, but eventually the farmers realized the seasons were not coming out quite right. The year was still too short. So, Tarquinius Priscus, the _5th_ king of Rome, added a new month at the end of Februarius. The Romans called this month the "Intercalans" because it was placed ___between___ (*inter*) the last and first months of the year. This 13th month did not come every year. The pontifices (___priests___), who were in charge of the calendar, decided which years should add the new month. The intercalans became a kind of "leap month."

THE JULIAN CALENDAR

This latest version of the calendar seemed to work well for several centuries. Over time, however, the old calendar system still had problems, and the priests sometimes abused their power to control it. In 45 BC ___Julius___ Caesar became the new Pontifex Maximus (___High___ ___Priest___). He decided to completely reform the calendar. He saw that Egypt had a solar calendar, determined by the _sun_. He hired Sosigenes, an Egyptian ___astronomer___, to help him create a new solar calendar for Rome. Caesar changed the first month of the calendar from Martius to ___Iānuārius___. He gave the months alternating lengths of 30 or 31 days, but left Februarius with only 29. He also created an extra day called the Bissextile, which was the very first ___leap___ ___day___. The bissextile day came once every 4 years. In those years, February would have 30 days. This gave the new Julian Calendar, named for Julius Caesar, 365.25 days.

On March 15, ___44 BC___ Julius Caesar was murdered. The Roman Senate renamed the month Quinctilis "___Iulius___" in honor of Caesar. In 31 BC, Octavian, Caesar's nephew, became the first emperor of Rome. He persuaded the Senate to rename the month Sextīlis "___Augustus___" in honor of his new title Augustus Caesar. The emperor's new month had only 30 days, so he took a day from Februarius and added it to his own month. Now the month of August has _31_ days, but Februarius has only _28_.

The Roman Calendar ANSWERS

Days of the Week

Strange as it may seem to us, the Romans did not have a seven-day week. They relied solely on the numbering system that revolved around the festival days. It was the Emperor Constantine (AD __313__ – __337__) who introduced the seven-day week. Constantine had converted to ____Christianity____ shortly before becoming the Roman Emperor. He believed that God had granted him his rule and, therefore, was deeply interested in the Judeo-Christian Religion. In the ninth year of his reign he issued an edict creating the seven-day week based on that of the __Jewish__ Calendar. He gave each of the seven days a name according to the __heavenly__ bodies that rose in the sky. These names have remained a part of our calendar until this day, although some use the Norse version of the name instead.

Diēs Sōlis = __Sun's Day__

Diēs Lūnae = __Moon's Day__

Diēs Mārtis = __Mars' Day__   Norse Mythology: Tyr, __god of war__

Diēs Mercuriī = __Mercury's Day__   Norse Mythology: Woden, __god of wisdom, death__

Diēs Iovis = __Iove's Day (Jupiter)__   Norse Mythology: Thor, __god of thunder__

Diēs Veneris = __Venus' Day__   Norse Mythology: Freya, __goddess of love__

Diēs Sāturnī = __Saturn's Day__

The Gregorian Calendar

The Julian Calendar worked very well for more than a thousand years. In the 16th century AD, however, the Church began to realize that something was terribly wrong. The ____Easter____ Holiday, whose date is determined by the stars and __moon__, was off by __10__ days. At the Council of Trent in AD __1545__ Pope Gregory XIII determined to fix this problem. He commissioned ____astronomers____ Christopher Clavis and Luigi Lilio to reform the calendar. They discovered that the Julian Calendar was off by __11__ minutes and __14__ seconds! That is a difference of just .0078 days! In order to fix the problem they moved leap day (the bissextile) to the last day of February, and created the Century Leap Year Rule:

Three out of every four centennial years (a year divisible by __100__) are "common." No centennial year, however, can be a leap year IF it is divisible by __400__.

Because of this rule the year 2000 was not a leap year, even though 1996 and 2004 were leap years. What year will the century leap year rule next effect?

CREATE YOUR OWN ROMAN CALENDAR

Step One: Decide which month you would like to create and see how many days it has.

Step Two: Determine when the Kalends, Nones and Ides will occur.

   "In October, July, March and May the Nones fall on the 7th day!"

Step Three: Count backwards from these festival days until you run into a preceding festival day. The day before a holiday is the *prīdiē* the day before that will always begin *a.d. III*. When counting backwards, the Romans always counted the holiday itself as day #1.

Step Four: Find other holidays for your month (modern or ancient) and decorate your calendar.

Important Notations for the Roman Calendar

Kalendae	Kal.	1st of every month
Nōnae	Non.	5th or 7th of the month
Īdūs	Id.	13th or 15th of the month
Prīdiē	Prid.	day immediately preceding a festival day
ante diem	a.d.	other days leading up to a festival day

It would be wise to use abbreviations for festival days and months within the calendar. This is easier and less confusing for the students. If you choose to write out the days in full, then please be aware of the following:
- The festival day should be in the ablative case (ablative of time when).
- The days preceding the festival day will follow the phrase "*ante diem*" or "*prīdiē*." These days should be in the accusative case (accusative of duration of time).

Sample Calendar

September MMVII

Diēs Sōlis	Diēs Lūnae	Diēs Mārtis	Diēs Mercuriī	Diēs Iovis	Diēs Veneris	Diēs Saturnī
			Kal.	a.d.iv Non.	a.d.iii Non.	Prid. Non.
Non.	a.d. viii Id.	a.d. vii Id.	a.d. vi Id.	a.d. v Id.	a.d.iv Id.	a.d. iii Id.
Prid. Id.	Id.	a.d. xviii Kal.	a.d. xvii Kal.	a.d. xvi Kal.	a.d. xv Kal.	a.d. xiv Kal.
a.d. xiii Kal.	a.d. xii Kal.	a.d. xi Kal.	a.d. x Kal.	a.d. ix Kal.	a.d. viii Kal.	a.d. vii Kal.
a.d. vi Kal.	a.d. v Kal.	a.d. iv Kal.	a.d. iii Kal.	Prid. Kal.		

The Roman Calendar ANSWERS

nōmen: _____   datum: _____

Unit 1 Test

Use this passage to answer the questions that follow.

1.   Rhēa Silvia est fīlia *rēgis*. *Quoque* ancilla deae Vestae est. Mars Rhēam Silviam
2.   *vīsitat*, et *mox* fēmina puerōs *geminōs parit*. *Pātruus Rhēae Silviae* iubet servum
3.   puerōs *in rīvum pōnere*. *Rīvus altus* est, et puerī *in* terram nāvigant. Lupa līberōs
4.   servat. Tum servus puerōs spectat et *ad casam* puerōs portat. Servus et
5.   *marīta* puerōs in *casā cūrant*.
6.   *Ubī* puerī sunt virī, oppidum **aedificāre volunt**. Rōmulus mūrum aedificat.
7.   <u>Rōmulus Remō mūrum mōnstrat. Remus *rīdet*. Rōmulus est *īrātus*. Rōmulus</u>
8.   <u>Remum necat.</u> Rōmulus oppidum aedificat. Rōmulus oppidum Rōmam *appellat*.
9.   Nunc Rōmulus est *rēx*.

———————

Notā Bene:
aedificāre volunt = they wish to build

GLOSSARY

rēgis	of a king
quoque, adv.	also
vīsitō, vīsitāre	to visit
mox, adv.	soon
geminus, -ī, m.	twin
pareō, parēre	to give birth to
pātruus, pātruī, m.	paternal uncle (father's brother)
Rheae Silviae	of Rhea Silvia
iubeō, iubēre	to order
in	into
rīvus, -ī, m.	river, stream
pōnere	to put, to place
altus, a, um, adj.	deep
lupa, -ae, f.	a female wolf
ad, preposition + accusative	to
casa, -ae, f.	house
marīta, marītae, f.	wife
cūrō, cūrāre	to care for
ubi, adv.	when
mūrus, mūrī, m.	wall
rīdeō, rīdēre	to laugh
īrātus	angry
necō, necāre	to kill
nunc, adv.	now
appellō, appellāre	to call, name
rēx, nominative, sing., m.	king

1. Provide the form specified in ( ) for each of the following verbs that appear in the passage above, then translate.

    a. Vīsitāre (1, S, Pres.)

    b. Nāvigāre (3, Pl., Imp.)

    c. Aedificāre (2, S., Fut.)

    d. Mōnstrāre (1, Pl. Pres.)

    e. Necāre (2, Pl., Imp.)

2. Identify the case, number, and gender of the following nouns as they appear in the passage.

    a. Deae (ln. 1)

    b. Fēmina (ln. 2)

    c. Puerōs (ln. 4)

    d. Virī (ln. 6)

    e. Rēmō (ln. 7)

    f. Oppidum (ln. 8)

3. Identify the noun job for each word in #2. (i.e. subject, predicate, direct object, etc.)

    a.

    b.

    c.

    d.

    e.

    f.

4. Translate the underlined portion of the passage as literally as possible.

5. Using the story above as your guide, briefly describe how each of the following characters is related to Romulus, the founder of Rome.

    a. Rhea Silvia

    b. Mars

    c. Remus

    d. "Patruus"

Bonus: Who is Numitor and how is he related to Romulus?

UNIT 1 TEST ANSWERS

1. Provide the form specified in ( ) for each of the following verbs that appear in the passage above, then translate.

    a. Vīsitāre (1, S, Pres.)   vīsitō   I visit

    b. Nāvigāre (3, Pl., Imp.)   nāvigābant   they were sailing

    c. Aedificāre (2, S., Fut.)   aedificābis   you will build

    d. Mōnstrāre (1, Pl. Pres.)   mōnstrāmus   we show

    e. Necāre (2, Pl., Imp.)   necābātis   you were killing

2. Identify the case, number, and gender of the following nouns as they appear in the passage.

    a. Deae (ln. 1)   dative, singular, feminine

    b. Fēmina (ln. 2)   nominative, singular, feminine

    c. Puerōs (ln. 4)   accusative, plural, masculine

    d. Virī (ln. 6)   nominative, plural, masculine

    e. Rēmō (ln. 7)   dative, singular, masculine

    f. Oppidum (ln. 8)   accusative, singular, neuter

3. Identify the noun job for each word in #2. (i.e. subject, predicate, direct object, etc.)

    a. reference

    b. subject

    c. direct object

    d. predicate nominative

    e. indirect object

    f. direct object

4. Translate the underlined portion of the passage as literally as possible.

    Romulus builds a wall. Romulus shows the wall to Remus. Remus laughs. Romulus is angry. Romulus kills Remus.

5. Using the story above as your guide, briefly describe how each of the following characters is related to Romulus, the founder of Rome.

    a. Rhea Silvia   Romulus' mother

    b. Mars   Romulus' father

    c. Remus   Romulus' brother

    d. "Patruus"   Romulus' great uncle (Rhea Silvia's uncle)

Bonus: Who is Numitor and how is he related to Romulus?

    Numitor is Romulus' grandfather, father to Rhea Silvia.

Unit 2 Test

Use this passage to answer the questions that follow.

1.   *Ultimus tyrannus* Rōmae erat Tarquinius Superbus. Quod fīlius *tyrannī*, Sextus
2.   Tarquinius, fēminae bonae, Lūcrētiae, *nocuit*, Rōmānī īrātī *tyrannum cum* familiā *ex*
3.   oppidō armīs *expulērunt*. Rōmānī Sextum *Gabiī* necāvērunt, sed *pater* et germānī Sextī
4.   *fūgērunt* ad alium oppidum. *Duo* virī, Brūtus et Collātīnus, erant nunc *cōnsulēs*.
5.   Tarquinius Superbus oppugnāvit Rōmānōs *prope* Silvam Arsiam. Pugna *minimē*
6.   *significāns* erat. Tarquinius, *igitur, appropinquāvit* Larem Porsennam, *rēgem Clūsiō*.
7.   <u>Porsenna tyrannum adiuvābat. Rōmam nōn *cēpērunt* Tarquinius Superbus et Lars</u>
8.   <u>Porsenna. Horātius, Mūcius, et Cloelia, *iuvenēs* Rōmānī, Rōmam servāre adiuvērunt.</u>
9.   Quod Rōmānī Ētruscōs *ex* oppidō *expulērunt*, populī *aliī* in Ītaliā expellere Etruscōs
10. *temptābant. Fortūna* erat bona: Etruscōs *ex* oppidīs *expulērunt*. **Quā dē causā** *populī*
11. *quī* in Italiā habitābant erant validī.
12.   Tarquinius Superbus, *tamen, etiam vīvit! Fūgit tyrannus ad* Mamilium Octāvium.
13. Mamilius erat marītus *fīliae tyrannī*. Etruscī *cum* Tarquiniō et Mamiliō *prope* Lacum
14. Rēgillum magnō studiō pugnāvērunt. Latīnī adiuvābant Etruscōs in pugnā. Rōmānī
15. *superāvērunt*. Castor et Pollux, deī, Rōmānōs ad Rēgillum adiūvērunt. *Paucōs annōs*
16. *post* Tarquinius Superbus mortuus erat. *Post* Tarquinium Superbum, *ultimum*
17. *tyrannum* Rōmae, Rōmānī *propter scelera semper verbum* "tyrannus" aut "rēx"
18. dēplōrāvērunt; et *numquam iterum* erat rēx *Rōmae*.

_____

Notā Bene:
Quā dē causā = for this reason

GLOSSARY

expellō, expellere, expulī, expulsum.. to drive out, expel
Gabiī .... at Gabia (town)
pater, nom., sing. m. .... father
fugiō, fugere, fūgī, fugitum .... to flee
ad prep. + acc. .... to, toward
alius, a, ud, adj. .... other
duo, numerical adj. .... two
cōnsulēs, nom., pl., m. .... consuls (highest elected official)
appropīnquō, āre, āvī, ātum .... to approach
capiō, capere, cēpī, captum .... to sieze
iuvenēs, nom., pl., m./f. .... youth, young people
temptō, āre, āvī, ātum .... to try

1. Identify the noun that each of the following adjectives modifies.

    a. īrātī (ln 2)

    b. bona (ln 10)

    c. validī (ln 11)

    d. ultimum(ln 16)

2. Provide the form specified in parentheses for each of the following verbs that appear in the passage above, then translate.

    a. necāre (2,P, Present)

    b. habēre (3, Pl, Perfect)

    c. habitāre (1, Sing., Imperfect)

    d. pugnāre (2, Sing., Future)

3. Identify the jobs or uses of the following words or phrases as they appear in the passage. (i.e. subject, direct object, ablative of means, etc.)

    a. fīlius (ln 1)

    b. armīs (ln 3)

    c. bona (ln 10)

    d. marītus (ln 13)

    e. magnō studiō (ln 14)

4. Translate the underlined portion of the passage as literally as possible.

5. According to the passage, why did the Romans expel the Tarquins?

Bonus: Romulus was the first king of Rome, Tarquinius Superbus was the last. Name, in chronological order, the five who came in the middle.

UNIT 2 TEST ANSWERS

1. Identify the noun that each of the following adjectives modifies.

    a. īrātī (ln 2)   *Rōmānī*

    b. bona (ln 10)   *Fortūna*

    c. validī (ln 11)   *populī*

    d. ultimum(ln 16)   *tyrannum*

2. Provide the form specified in parentheses for each of the following verbs that appear in the passage above, then translate.

    a. necāre (2,P, Present)   necātis

    b. habēre (3, Pl, Perfect)   habuērunt

    c. habitāre (1, Sing., Imperfect)   habitābam

    d. pugnāre (2, Sing., Future)   pugnābis

3. Identify the jobs or uses of the following words or phrases as they appear in the passage. (i.e. subject, direct object, ablative of means, etc.)

    a. fīlius (ln 1)   subject

    b. armīs (ln 3)   ablative of means

    c. bona (ln 10)   predicate nominative/adjective

    d. marītus (ln 13)   predicate nominative

    e. magnō studiō (ln 14) ablative of manner

4. Translate the underlined portion of the passage as literally as possible.

    Porsenna was helping the tyrant. Tarquinius Superbus and Lars Porsenna did not seize Rome. Horatius, Mucius, and Cloelia, Roman youths, helped to save Rome.

5. According to the passage, why did the Romans expel the Tarquins?

    Sextus Tarquinius, the son of Tarquinius Superbus, harmed Lucretia.

Bonus: Romulus was the first king of Rome, Tarquinius Superbus was the last. Name, in chronological order, the five who came in the middle.

    Numa Pompilius, Tullus Hostilius, Ancus Marcius, Tarquinius Priscus, Servius Tullius

    Notā Bene: If you find that students are struggling with the reading and need some additional help with the italicized words, feel free to point them to pages 65–66, where the reading and its full glossary appear.

©2008, Classical Academic Press • All rights reserved.

Unit 3 Test

Use this passage to answer the questions that follow.

1.   *Ōlim* lēgātī ad Rōmānōs ex oppidō Clūsiō *appropinquāvērunt.* Sēnōnēs, populus
2. Gallicus, Clūsium oppugnābant. Tum Rōmānī monuērunt Sēnōnēs: "*Nōlīte*
3. *oppugnāre* amīcōs Rōmānōrum!" Ubī pugna *incēpit,* lēgātī Rōmānī, contrā *lēgem*
4. *pātriārum,* arma *cēpērunt* et populum *urbis* Clūsiī adiuvābant. Posteā Gallī
5. *compēnsātiōnem* ē Rōmānīs *postulāvērunt.* Rōmānī *recūsāvērunt.*
6. Gallī, igitur, Rōmam petīvērunt.
7.   Gallī prope flūmen nōmine Allia vīcērunt. <u>Multī mīlitēs Rōmānī ad Vēiōs</u>
8. <u>*fūgērunt.* Multī aliī Rōmānī ad urbem Rōmam *fūgērunt.* Portās nōn etiam</u>
9. <u>*clausērunt,* sed cum uxōribus *līberīsque* ad *arcem fūgērunt. Ibi* manēbant.</u>
10.   Gallī *aedificia* et casās *urbis cremābant.* Etiam *arcem* oppugnābant! Rōmānī
11. *tamen* in *arce* manēbant et *dēsuper* Gallōs oppugnābant. Pars Gallōrum in agrīs
12. frūmentum petīvērunt.
13.   **Dum haec geruntur** Rōmānī in *urbe* magnō in perīculō erant. *Nocte* Gallī
14. montem ascendērunt. Ascendērunt magnō cum *silentiō. Nē quidem*
15. *canēs lātrābant! Nōtitiam, tamen, ānserum* sacrōrum deae Iūnōnī nōn *ēvādērunt.*
16. *Somnus* Manlium, *clārum* ducem, tenēbat. Ānserēs Manlium *excitāvērunt. Ālās*
17. et *vōcēs ānserum notāvit* Manlius. Manlius ūnum ex Gallīs, **quī erat in summō**
18. **monte,** *dēiēcit.* Cēterī Rōmānī armīs *saxīsque ūnā cum* Manliō hostēs *fūgāvērunt.*
19. Gallī cucurrērunt dē monte **magnā cum celeritāte.** Rōmam *ānserēs* servāvērunt!

Notā Bene:
Dum haec geruntur = while these things are being done (Best translation:
                        "While these things were going on . . . .")
quī erat in summō monte = who was on the top of the mountain
magnā cum celeritāte = with great speed

GLOSSARY

fugiō, fugere, fūgī, fugitum .... to flee
līberī, līberōrum, m. pl. .... [free born] children
crēmō, āre, āvī, ātum .... to burn
arx, arcis, f. .... citadel (The citadel is the highest geographical or
                                natural point in a city.)
ibi, adv. .... there
silentium, ī, n. .... silence

1. Identify the case and use of the following nouns as they appear in the passage.

      a. Sēnōnēs (ln 1)

      b. flūmen (ln 7)

      c. urbis (ln 10)

      d. armīs (ln 18)

      e. hostēs (ln 18)

2. Provide the form specified in parentheses for each of the following verbs that appear in the Latin passage, then translate.

      a. oppugnāre (2nd person, plural, present)

      b. petere (3rd person, plural, imperfect)

      c. vincere (1st person, singular, future)

      d. manēre (2nd person, singular, perfect)

      e. ascendere (1st person, plural, perfect)

      f. servāre (3rd person, singular, future)

3. Identify and translate the following constructions as they appear in the passsage.

      a. ad Vēiōs (ln 7)

      b. cum uxōribus (ln 9)

      c. in agrīs (ln 11)

      d. magnō cum *silentiō* (ln 14)

      e. dē monte (ln 19)

4. Translate the underlined portion of the passage as literally as possible.

5. In your own words, briefly tell how Manlius saved Rome. Quote and translate as literally as possible at least one sentence from the story to prove one or more of your points. Enclose your Latin sentence in quotation marks and your translation in square brackets.

Bonus: This story takes place on the Capitoline Hill. Name the other six hills of Rome.

Unit 3 Test ANSWERS

1. Identify the case and use of the following nouns as they appear in the passage.

    a. Sēnōnēs (ln 1)   nominative, subject

    b. flūmen (ln 7)   accusative, place

    c. urbis (ln 10)   genitive, possession

    d. armīs (ln 18)   ablative, means

    e. hostēs (ln 18)   accusative, direct object

2. Provide the form specified in parentheses for each of the following verbs that appear in the passage above, then translate.

    a. oppugnāre (2nd person, plural, present)   oppugnātis

    b. petere (3rd person, plural, imperfect)   petēbant

    c. vincere (1st person, singular, future)   vincam

    d. manēre (2nd person, singular, perfect)   mānsistī

    e. ascendere (1st person, plural, perfect)   ascendimus

    f. servāre (3rd person, singular, future)   servābit

3. Identify and translate the following constructions as they appear in the passsage.

    a. ad Vēiōs (ln 7)   accusative of place to which, to the Veii

    b. cum uxōribus (ln 9)   ablative of accompaniment, with the wives

    c. in agrīs (ln 11)   ablative of place where, in the fields

    d. magnō cum *silentiō* (ln 14)   ablative of manner, with great silence

    e. dē monte (ln 19)   ablative of place from which, from/down from the mountain

4. Translate the underlined portion of the passage as literally as possible.

    Many Roman soldiers fled to Veii. Many other Romans fled to the city Rome. They did not even shut the gates, but with their wives and children fled to the arc. They were staying there.

5. In your own words, briefly tell how Manlius saved Rome. Quote and translate as literally as possible at least one sentence from the story to prove one or more of your points. Enclose your Latin sentence in quotation marks and your translation in square brackets.

    The Romans had helped the town Clusium when the Senones attacked them. The Senones later demanded compensation from Rome for aiding Clusium. Rome refused.

Bonus: This story takes place on the Capitoline Hill. Name the other six hills of Rome.

    Aventine, Palatine, Caelian, Esquiline, Viminal, Quirinal

Unit 4 Test

Use this passage to answer the questions that follow.

THE DEATH AND FUNERAL OF THE FATHER OF MARCUS AND CORNELIA

1. **Miserum dictū**, pater Mārcī et Cornēliae, vir *grandaevus*, mortuus est. Mārcus prope
2. lectum patris stābat cum Cornēliā et mātre. Mārcus *sē inclīnāvit suprā* patrem et
3. patris nōmen clāmāvit. Pater nōn respondit. <u>Mārcus tum "*Conclāmātum*" dīxit "*est.*"</u>
4. <u>Pater *enim* vīxit. Mārcus *oculōs* patris clausit. Corpus patris *togātum* tum in *ātriō*</u>
5. <u>posuērunt servī.</u> Flōrēs circum corpus posuērunt.
6. *Paucīs diēbus* patrī *fūnus* erat. Erat *processiō*. In *processiōne* erant familia, *vīcīnī*,
7. amīcī, et *mūsicī*. Mārcus et amīcī patris corpus in *humerīs* portāvērunt. *Ante*
8. *processiōnem* ambulāvērunt hominēs *quī* patrem mortuum *laudāvērunt. Imāginēs*
9. *cēreās remōtās* ab *ātriō actōrēs* gerēbant. *Actōrēs* quoque *vestēs antīquōs* gerēbant.
10. *Vidēbantur māiōrēs* vīvere et ambulāre in viā et virum mortuum ad *īnferōs* dūcere.
11. Virī *facēs ferentēs* erant *ultimī* hominēs in *processiōne. Processiō* stetit in *forō*
12. *Rōmānō* et Mārcus *laudātiōnem aliter ōrātiōnem* habuit. Mārcus omnia bona dē
13. patre dīxit.
14. *Processiō* tum *processit extrā* urbem ad Viam *Appiam*. Prope Viam *Appiam* erat
15. *sepulcrum* patris. Ad *sepulcrum* erat *rogus. Aliquis condīmenta* et *odōrem* et dōna in
16. corpus iēcit. Tum corpus *cremāvērunt*. Ignem *exstīnxērunt vīnō* et aquā. Omnēs
17. "*Valē!*" clāmāvērunt. *Aliquis* omnēs aquā *sparsit.* Omnēs *praeter* familiam
18. *abīvērunt.* Familia *suem sacrificāvit. Sacrificium locum* sacrum facit. Omnis
19. familia *silicernium* cōnsūmpsit. Tum familia *domum* revertit. *Domī, Laribus*
20. *oblātum offerēbant. Fūneris* fīnis erat.

_____

Miserum dictū = sad to say

GLOSSARY

grandaevus, a, um, adj. .... old, aged
inclīnō, āre, āvī, ātus .... bend
    with *sē* .... bent
suprā , prep. + acc. .... over
conclāmātum est .... it [his name] has been called
enim, adv. .... indeed, truly
vīxit .... he has lived, meaning has lived but does not live now;
    i.e., he has died
oculus, ī, n. .... eye
togātum .... clad in a toga
fūnus, fūneris, n. .... funeral
processiō, processiōnis, f. .... procession
antīquus, a, um, adj. .... ancient, old

1. Identify the case and use of the following nouns as they appear in the passage. (e.g. nominative, subject, dative, possession)

    a. Cornēliae (ln 1)

    b. mātre (ln 2)

    c. nōmen (ln 3)

    d. flōrēs (ln 5)

    e. patris (ln 7)

    f. corpus (ln 16)

2. Identify the noun that each of the following adjectives modify.

    a. mortuus (ln 1)

    b. *antīquōs* (ln 9)

    c. omnis (ln 18)

3. Using the vocabulary provided, translate the following sentences into Latin as directed.

    a. Cornelius is the father of Marcus and Cornelia.
      (genitive of possession)

    b. The father's name is Cornelius.
      (dative of possession)

    c. The family of Cornelius had great honor.
      (genitive & dative of possession)

    d. Is a Roman funeral similar to an American (*Americānus*) funeral?
      (dative with adjective)

4. Translate the underlined portion of the passage as literally as possible.

5. Name three elements of a traditional Roman funeral that are mentioned in the passage.

Bonus: According to Roman mythology, who were Clotho, Lachesis, and Atropos? What did they do?

Unit 4 Test ANSWERS

1. Identify the case and use of the following nouns as they appear in the passage. (e.g. nominative, subject, dative, possession)

      a. Cornēliae (ln 1)   genitive, possession

      b. mātre (ln 2)   ablative, accompaniment

      c. nōmen (ln 3)   accusative, direct object

      d. flōrēs (ln 5)   accusative, direct object

      e. patris (ln 7)   genitive, possession

      f. corpus (ln 16)   accusative, place to which

2. Identify the noun that each of the following adjectives modify.

      a. mortuus (ln 1)   pater

      b. *antīquōs* (ln 9)   *vestēs*

      c. omnis (ln 18)   familia

3. Using the vocabulary provided, translate the following sentences into Latin as directed.

      a. Cornelius is the father of Marcus and Cornelia.
      (genitive of possession)   Cornēlius est pater Mārcī et Cornēliae.

      b. The father's name is Cornelius.
      (dative of possession)   Patrī nōmen est Cornēlius.

      c. The family of Cornelius had great honor.
      (genitive & dative of possession)   Familiae Cornēliī est magnus honor.

      d. Is a Roman funeral similar to an American (*Americānus*) funeral?
      (dative with adjective)   Estne Rōmānum fūnus simile fūnerī Americānō?

4. Translate the underlined portion of the passage as literally as possible.

    Marcus then said, "It has been called." Truly the father lived. Marcus closed his father's eyes. Then the slaves placed the father's body clad in a toga in the atrium.

5. Name three elements of a traditional Roman funeral that are mentioned in the passage.

    The family and friends carried the body in a procession.

    Men walked in front of the procession praising the dead person.

    Images of deceased ancestors were carried in the procession.

    Actors wore ancient garments.

Bonus: According to Roman mythology, who were Clotho, Lachesis, and Atropos? What did they do?

    They were the Fates. They determined the length of a mortal person's life.

UNIT 5 TEST

Use this passage to answer the questions that follow.

M. PORCIUS CATO INSTIGATES THE THIRD PUNIC WAR

1.   Secundum post Bellum Pūnicum multī senātōrēs pācem cum Poenīs volēbant.
2. Etiam Scīpiōnēs pācem dēsīderābant. Sed aliī Poenī Hannibalem *adiuvāre*
3. nōlēbant. P. Scīpiō Nāsīca *vērē* prō Hannibale et Carthāgine in *senātū* dīxit. Populus
4. Rōmānus, *tamen*, Hannibalem *etiamnunc* metuēbant. Parentēs līberīs *saepe*
5. dīcēbant, "Hannibal ad portās!"
6.   M. Porcius Catō populum Rōmānum et aliōs *quī* Hannibalem *odērunt* et timēbant
7. *adiuvābat.* Catō erat vir *īnsignis gravitāte* et virtūte. *Odit* **lūcrum malē partum**
8. sed amābat *lūcrum quod obtineat* ūllō *modō* bonō. Aliī *putābant* **Catōnem dīvitiās**
9. **Poenās obtinēre velle**, sed *rē vērā* Poenās *maximē* metuēbat. Catō, *mīles* Secundō in
10. Bellō Pūnicō, perīcula **factōrum priōrum** Hannibalis intellēxit. Nōn probābat ūllam
11. pācem cum Poenīs aut cum Hannibale. Nūllum *foedus* probābat. Omnēs *quī*
12. pācem cum hīs dēsīderābant *dēnūntiābat.* Omnem ōrātiōnem in *senātū fīniēbat* verbīs
13. **"Carthāgō dēlenda est!"** Senātōrēs Catōnī *cessērunt*, et *Tertium* Bellum Pūnicum
14. **secūtum est.** *Postquam* mīlitēs Rōmānī et sociī in Āfricā Poenōs vīcērunt, Poenī
15. Rōmānīs sociīsque *sē* in *dēditiōnem* dedērunt. *Tandem* Rōmānī, **secundum** *voluntātēs*
16. *senātūs*, Poenōs ex urbe *suā* ēgērunt. Deinde, terram circum Carthāginem *sale sēvērunt.*

---

lūcrum malē partum = ill-gotten gains, filthy lucre
Catōnem dīvitiās Poenās obtinēre velle = that he wanted to obtain Punic wealth
factōrum priōrum = of the former deeds
Carthāgō dēlenda est! = Carthage must be destroyed!
secundum (prep. + acc.) = in accordance with, according to
secūtum est = followed

GLOSSARY

adiuvō, āre	to support
vērē, adv...................................	truly
senātū, ablative, sing., m.	the senate
senātus, senātūs	the senate
etiamnunc, adv.	still, even now
saepe, adv..................................	often
putō, putāre.............................	to think
ōrātiō, ōrātiōnis, f.	speech, oration
fīniō, fīnīre..............................	to end
cēdo, cēdere, cessi, cessus.....................	to yield
tertius, a, um, adj.	third
postquam, adv.	after, afterwards
sē, accusative pronoun	themselves
dēditiō, dēditiōnis, f....................	surrender
tandem, adv..............................	finally
sāl, salis, m..............................	salt
sale seruērunt	they sowed . . . with salt

1. Identify the case and use of the following words as they appear in the passage. (e.g. nominative, subject; ablative, accompaniment)

    a. aliī (ln 2)

    b. vir (ln 7)

    c. perīcula (ln 10)

    d. omnēs (ln 11)

    e. hīs (ln 12)

    f. Rōmānīs (ln 15)

2. Identify 5 uses of the "naughty nine" adjectives in this passage. Parse each example identifying its case, number, and gender.

3. Replace the underlined noun in each sentence with the correct form of the pronoun in parentheses.

    a. Post Bellum <u>Pūnicum</u> multī senātōres pācem cum Poenīs volēbant. (ille)

    b. Parentēs <u>līberīs</u> dīcēbant, "Hannibal ad portās!" (tū)

    c. Catō perīcula **factōrum** <u>Hannibalis</u> intellēxit. (is)

    d. Omnem *ōrātiōnem* in *senātū fīniēbat* <u>verbīs</u> **"Carthāgō dēlenda est!" (hic)**

    e. Poenī <u>Rōmae</u> *sē* in *dēditiōnem* dedērunt. (hic)

    f. Terram circum <u>Carthāginem</u> *sale sēvērunt.* (iste)

4. Translate the underlined portion of the passage as literally as possible.

5. According to the passage, what did the Romans do to Carthage after she surrendered in the Third Punic War?

Bonus: Name the three islands that Rome took as a result of the First Punic War.

Unit 5 Test ANSWERS

1. Identify the case and use of the following words as they appear in the passage. (e.g. nominative, subject; ablative, accompaniment)

    a. aliī (ln 2)   nominative, adjective modifying Poeni

    b. vir (ln 7)   nominative, predicate nominatiave

    c. perīcula (ln 10)   accusative, direct object

    d. omnēs (ln 11)   accusative, direct object

    e. hīs (ln 12)   ablative, accompaniment

    f. Rōmānīs (ln 15)   dative, indirect object

2. Identify 5 uses of the "naughty nine" adjectives in this passage. Parse each example identifying its case, number, and gender.

    aliī – nominative, plural, masculine

    aliōs – accusative, plural, masculine

    ūllō – ablative, singular, masculine

    ūllam – accusative, singular, feminine

    nullum – nominative, singular, neuter

3. Replace the underlined noun in each sentence with the correct form of the pronoun in parentheses.

    a. Post Bellum <u>Pūnicum</u> multī senātōres pācem cum Poenīs volēbant. (ille)   illud

    b. Parentēs <u>līberīs</u> dīcēbant, "Hannibal ad portās!" (tū)   vōbīs

    c. Catō perīcula **factōrum** <u>Hannibalis</u> intellēxit. (is)   ēius

    d. **Omnem** *ōrātiōnem* in *senātū fīniēbat* <u>verbīs</u> "**Carthāgō dēlenda est!**" (hic)   hīs

    e. Poenī <u>Rōmae</u> *sē* in *dēditiōnem* dedērunt. (hic)   huic

    f. Terram circum <u>Carthāginem</u> *sale seruērunt.* (iste)   istam

4. Translate the underlined portion of the passage as literally as possible.

    After the Second Punic War many senators were wanting peace with the Carthaginians. Even the Scipios were desiring peace. But some Carthaginians were not wanting to support Hannibal. Publius Scipio Nasica truly spoke on behalf of Hannibal and Carthage in the senate. The Roman people however were still fearing Hannibal.

5. According to the passage, what did the Romans do to Carthage after she surrendered in the Third Punic War?

    They drove the Carthaginians from the city and sewed the ground with salt.

Bonus: Name the three islands that Rome took as a result of the First Punic War.

    Sicily, Corsica, Sardinia

Unit 6 Test

Use this passage to answer the questions that follow.

GAIUS JULIUS CAESAR: THE EARLY YEARS

1.   Gāius Iūlius Caesar vir *īnsignis genere* et *animō* erat. **Ut fāma est**, ūnus *ē māiōribus*
2.   Caesaris erat Iūlus. Hic Iūlus fīlius Aenēae erat, et Aenēās ipse fīlius Veneris erat. Venus
3.   ipsa fīlia Iovis erat. Caesar, igitur, vērē erat *optimātum*. Sīcut Catilīna, tamen, Caesar erat
4.   pauper. Familia in **Subūrā** habitābat.
5.   Gāius Iūlius *nātus est* circā DCLIII AUC, *aliter* C annōs ante Chrīstum. Māter
6.   Caesaris erat Aurēlia, fēmina *īnsignis* familiā suā. Caesar **puer artī dīcendī** studēbat
7.   cum *Gallō*. **Nōndum sciēns** Gāius bellō *Gallicō* parābat. *Adulēscēns* mīlitābat
8.   cum Mārcō Thermō in Āsiā. Caesar quoque erat in Bīthȳniā, ubi Nīcomēdēs erat rēx.
9.   Quandō Gāius XVIII annōs habuit, Rōmam revēnit, ibi prīmam uxōrem, Cossutia, **in**
10.   **mātrimōnium dūxit** quod illa patrī Gāiī placuit. **Patre mortuō** Iūlius Caesar
11.   Cossutiam *repudiāvit* et Cornēliam **in mātrimōnium dūxit**. Ubi Sulla imperium et
12.   potestātem obtinuit, Caesarem iussit Cornēliam *repudiāre*, sed Caesar *recūsāvit*.
13.   Caesar Ītaliam effūgit et sē coniūnxit *exercituī* in *Ciliciā*. **Sullā mortuō**, Caesar
14.   Rōmam revertit. *Quoniam* inimīcī Caesaris imperium habēbant, Caesar **profectus**
15.   **est** ad Āsiam.
16.   In itinere ad Āsiam, *pīrātae* Caesarem cēpērunt. Eum tenēbant in īnsulā. Sī
17.   amīcī Caesaris pecūniam *dederint*, Caesar līber erit. Postulābant pīrātae XX **talenta.**
18.   Caesar rīdēbat et dīxit *pīrātīs*, "Postulāte L talenta." Caesar *pīrātās stultōs barbarōs*
19.   appellāvit. Dīxit Caesar *pīrātīs*, "Revertam et vōs *crucibus adfīgam*." Amīcī
20.   pecūniam *pīrātīs* dedērunt. Caesar discessit sed revertit et omnēs *pīrātās*
21.   *crucibus adfīxit.*

———————

ut fāma est = so the story goes
Subūra = the Subura, a very unfashionable part of Rome, almost a slum
puer = as a boy
artī dīcendī = the art of speaking (in the dative as the object of *studēbat*)
nōndum sciēns = not yet knowing; i.e., unconsciously
in mātrimōnium dūxit = he married (lit. he led into marriage)
patre mortuō = [his] father having died; i.e., after his father died
Sullā mortuō = This is the same construction as *patre mortuō*; how would you translate this one?
profectus est = set out
talenta = talents (large unit of Greek money)

GLOSSARY

īnsignis, īnsignis, adj......................	distinguished
īnsignis genere	distinguished by his ancestry/family
nātus est	was born
aliter, adv...	otherwise
Gallus, ī, m...	a Gaul (The Gauls inhabited primarily what is today France.)
Gallicus, a, um, adj............................	Gallic, pertaining to Gaul (modern day France)
adulēscēns, adulēscentis, m/f............	youth, young man/woman
repudiō, āre, āvī, ātum	to refuse, (wife) to divorce

1. Identify examples of the following constructions in the passage, then translate.

     a. ablative with cardinal number

     b. ablative place where

     c. dative of reference

     d. ordinal number

     e. demonstrative pronoun

     f. dative with special intransitive verb

     g. ablative of accompaniment

     h. reflexive pronoun

     i. dative indirect object

     j. imperative verb

     k. personal pronoun

2. Parse and translate the following verbs as they appear in the passage above.

     a. erat (ln 6)

     b. revēnit (ln 9)

     c. habēbant (ln 14)

     d. erit (ln 17)

     e. *adfīgam* (ln 19)

     f. revertit (ln 20)

3. Identify and translate three adverbs in the passage.

4. Translate the underlined portion of the passage as literally as possible.

Bonus: Name the three members of the first triumvirate.

UNIT 6 TEST ANSWERS

1. Identify examples of the following constructions in the passage, then translate.
   - a. ablative with cardinal number — ūnus ē *maiōribus, one of the ancestors*
   - b. ablative place where — in Subūrā, in Subura
   - c. dative of reference — bellō *Gallicō,* for the Gallic war
   - d. ordinal number — prīmam, first
   - e. demonstrative pronoun — illa, she
   - f. dative with special intransitive verb — patrī placuit, she pleased the father
   - g. ablative of accompaniment — cum Mārcō, with Marcus OR cum *Gallō,* with a Gaul
   - h. reflexive pronoun — se, himself
   - i. dative indirect object — *pīrātīs,* to the pirates
   - j. imperative verb — Postulāte, demand
   - k. personal pronoun — vōs, you

2. Parse and translate the following verbs as they appear in the passage above.
   - a. erat (ln 6) — 3, S, Imp - he was
   - b. revēnit (ln 9) — 3, S, Perf – he returned
   - c. habēbant (ln 14) — 3, P, Imp – they were having
   - d. erit (ln 17) — 3, S, F – he will be
   - e. *adfīgam* (ln 19) — 1, S, F, - I will fix
   - f. revertit (ln 20) — 3, S, Pr – he returns

3. Identify and translate three adverbs in the passage.
   - Ubi, when
   - Ibi, there
   - Tamen, nevertheless, however

4. Translate the underlined portion of the passage as literally as possible.
   Gaius Julius was born around 658 A.U.C., otherwise 100 years before Christ. The mother of Caesar was Aurelia, a woman distinguished by her family. The boy Caesar was studying the art of speaking with a Gaul. Not yet knowing Gaius was preparing for the Gallic War.

Bonus: Name the three members of the first triumvirate.
   Caesar, Pompey, Crassus

Unit 7 Test

Use this passage to answer the questions that follow.

THE DEATH OF CAESAR

1.   Paulō post *Lupercālia* annō DCCX AUC, aliter XLIV ante Chrīstum, Gāius
2. Cassius ad Mārcum Brūtum *appropinquāvit* et dīxit, "Brūte, necesse est Caesarī
3. perīre. Necesse est nōbīs eum necāre. Multī senātōrēs hoc probant."
4. Brūtus erat *prōgnātus* illīus Brūtī quī Tarquiniōs ex urbe Rōmā expulerat. Erat vir
5. fortis sed timidus **in rē caedis** Caesaris, amīcī suī. Caesar rē vērē sīcut pater Brūtō
6. fuerat.
7.   Multī tamen ē Rōmānīs Brūtum necāre Caesarem voluērunt. Erant *Rōmae* multae
8. statuae Brūtī *antīquī*. Hominēs in statuās nūntiōs posuērunt. Verbīs sīcut
9. "**Mortuusne es**, Brūte" et "Tuī *prōgnātī* nōn dignī esse tuī" Brūtum **hortātī sunt**.
10. Multī quoque ē *optimātibus susurrāvērunt*, "Īdibus Mārtiīs in senātū Lūcius Cotta
11. dīcet, 'Sit Caesar rēx. Sōlus rēx Parthiōs vincēbit. **Scrīptum est!**'"
12.   Caesar in suō *domiciliō* amīcōs rogāvit, "Quae est mors optima?" Sibi <u>respōnsum</u>
13. suum dedit: "Mors *subita*." *Māne*, nunc Īdibus Mārtiīs uxor Caesaris, Calpurnia, eum ad senātum īre nōn
14. vult. Caesar verba Calpurniae nōn audīvit, et domō discessit
15. *plūribus* cum amīcīs. In viā ad senātum Caesar *vātem* vīdit quī ōlim, "Cavē Īdūs
16. Mārtiās" Caesarī dīxerat. Caesar illī dīxit, "Īdūs Mārtiae advēnērunt." Et *vātēs*
17. Caesarī, "Sed nōn *abīvērunt*." Gāius Iūlius Caesar ad senātum prōcessit.
18.   Ubi Caesar in senātum intrāverat, *sēdit*. Multī Caesarem oppugnāvērunt. Ubi
19. Caesar Brūtum vīdit, dīxit Graecīs verbīs Latīnē <u>significantibus</u> "Et tū, *puer* **mī**?"
20. Caesar nōn iam *rēstitit* sed togā caput suum et vultum *tēxit*. Cecidit **sub statuam**
21. Pompēiī. Caesar voluntātem habuit. *Mortuus est subitō*.

---

in rē caedis = in the matter of murder
mortuusne es . . .? = Are you dead . . . ?
hortātī sunt = they encouraged
sit = let [Caesar] be
scrīptum est = It is written, It has been written
mī = my (This is the vocative case to agree with *puer*.)
sub statuam = at the foot of the statu

GLOSSARY
Use your "eye" Latin to discern the meaning of the underlined words.
Lupercālia ....a feast for Pan, celebrated in February
appropinquō, appropinquāre,
appropinquāvī, appropinquātus...................to approach
prōgnātus, prōgnātī, m. ....descendant
antīquus, a, um, adj. ....ancient
optimātes, m.pl.......................................optimates, one of the political factions in Rome
susurrāvērunt ....they whispered
subitus, a, um, adj.................................sudden, unexpected
māne ....in the morning

1. Identify examples of the following constructions in the passage, then translate.
   a. ablative of time when
   b. complementary infinitive
   c. relative clause
   d. dative of possession
   e. partitive ablative
   f. reflexive possessive adjective
   g. interrogative pronoun
   h. imperative

2. Identify the case and function of the following words as they appear in the passage.
   a. Brūte (ln 2)
   b. illīus (ln 4)
   c. fortis (ln 5)
   d. Īdibus Mārtiīs (ln 10)
   e. senātum (ln 14)
   f. verba (ln 14)
   g. illī (ln 16)
   h. Graecīs verbīs (ln 19)
   i. togā (ln 20)

3. Identify the conjugation of the following verbs (I = irregular), parse and translate.
   a. probant
   b. expuleram
   c. fuerat
   d. es
   e. dīcet
   f. vincēbis
   g. dedit
   h. nōn vult
   i. audīvimus
   j. oppugnāvērunt
   k. habueritis

4. Translate the underlined portion of the passage as literally as possible.

Bonus: Give the date (day, month, year) of Julius Caesar's assasination. What is the Roman name for this particular day of the month?

Unit 7 Test ANSWERS

1. Identify examples of the following constructions in the passage, then translate.

    a. ablative of time when   annō, in the year

    b. complementary infinitive   perīre, to die OR necāre to kill

    c. relative clause   quī Tarquiniōs ex urbe Rōmā expulerat, who had expelled

    d. dative of possession   Brūtō, Brutus'   the Tarquins from the city Rome

    e. partitive ablative   Multī ē Rōmānīs, many of the Romans

    f. reflexive possessive adjective   sibi, to himself OR suum, his own OR suī, his own

    g. interrogative pronoun   Quid, what

    h. imperative   Cavē, beware

2. Identify the case and function of the following words as they appear in the passage.

    a. Brūte (ln 2)   vocative, direct address

    b. illīus (ln 4)   genitive, possession

    c. fortis (ln 5)   nominative adjective modifying vir

    d. Īdibus Mārtiīs (ln 10)   ablative of time when

    e. senātum (ln 14)   accusative, place to which

    f. verba (ln 14)   accusative, direct object

    g. illī (ln 16)   dative, indirect object

    h. Graecīs verbīs (ln 19)   ablative of means

    i. togā (ln 20)   ablative of means

3. Identify the conjugation of the following verbs (I = irregular), parse and translate.

    a. probant   1; 3, P, Imp; they were approving

    b. expuleram   2; 1, S, PP; I had expelled

    c. fuerat   I; 3, S, PP; he had been

    d. es   I; 2, S, Pr; you are

    e. dīcet   3; 3, S, F; he will say

    f. vincēbis   3; 2, S, F; you will conquer

    g. dedit   1; 3, S, Pf; he gave

    h. nōn vult   I; 3, S, P; he does not wish

    i. audīvimus   4; 1, P, Pf; we heard

    j. oppugnāvērunt   1; 3, P, Pf; they attacked

    k. habueritis   2; 2, P, FP; you will have had

4. Translate the underlined portion of the passage as literally as possible.

    Brutus, it is necessary for Caesar to die. It is necessary for us to kill him. Many senators approve this. Brutus was the descendent of that Brutus who had expelled Tarquinius from the city Rome. He was a brave man but afraid in the matter of murder of Caesar, his own friend.

Bonus: Give the date (day, month, year) of Julius Caesar's assasination. What is the Roman name for this particular day of the month?

    March 15, 44 BC

    Ides

Latin Across America

Half of the states in the U.S. have Latin mottoes. Write down the Latin motto for each state and its translation. Then, label the state on the U.S. map

1. Alabama: _____

2. Arizona: _____

3. Arkansas: _____

4. California: _____

5. Colorado: _____

6. Connecticut: _____

7. Idaho: _____

8. Kansas: _____

9. Kentucky: _____

10. Maine: _____

11. Maryland: _____

12. Massachusetts: _____

13. Michigan: _____

14. Mississippi: _____

15. Missouri: _____

16. New Mexico: _____

17. New York: _____

18. North Carolina: _____

19. Ohio: _____

20. Oklahoma: _____

21. Oregon: _____

22. South Carolina: _____

23. Virginia: _____

24. West Virginia: _____

25. Wyoming: _____

The other states in the U.S. have mottoes of various languages; some are English, some European, and some Native American. Find the mottoes for the remaining 25 states, and then label them on your map as well. What do these mottoes say about the states they represent?

1. Alaska: _____

2. Delaware: _____

3. Florida: _____

4. Georgia: _____

5. Hawaii: _____

6. Illinois: _____

7. Indiana: _____

8. Iowa: _____

9. Louisiana: _____

10. Minnesota: _____

11. Montana: _____

12. Nebraska: _____

13. Nevada: _____

14. New Hampshire: _____

15. New Jersey: _____

16. North Dakota: _____

17. Pennsylvania: _____

18. Rhode Island: _____

19. South Dakota: _____

20. Tennessee: _____

21. Texas: _____

22. Utah: _____

23. Vermont: _____

24. Washington: _____

25. Wisconsin: _____

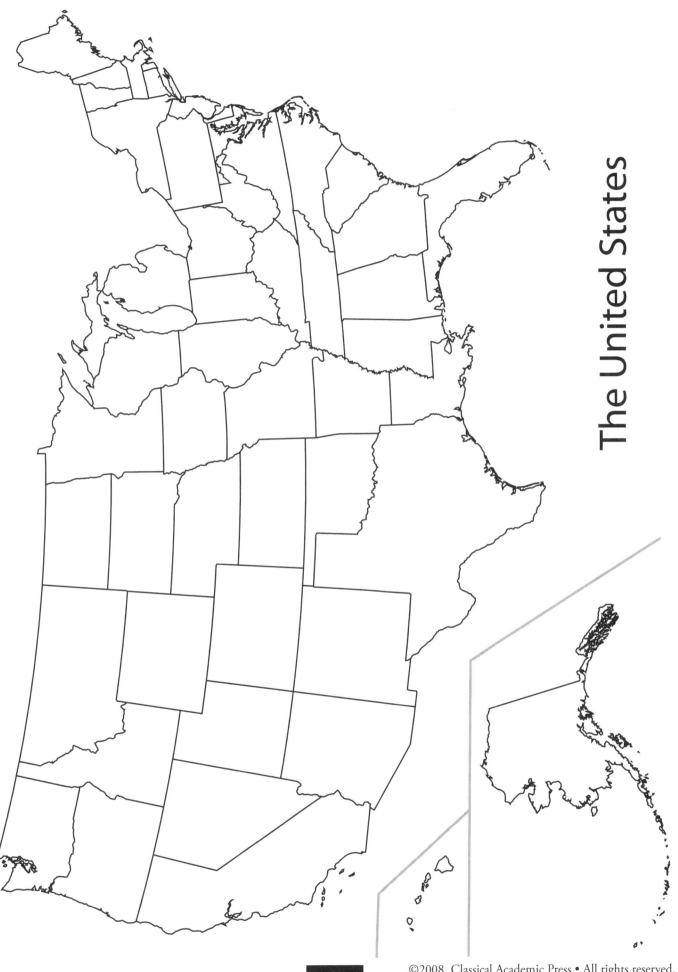

The United States

Latin Across America

Half of the states in the U.S. have Latin mottoes. Write down the Latin motto for each state and its translation. Then, label the state on the U.S. map

1. Alabama: *Audēmus jūra nostra dēfendere* – We dare to defend our rights

2. Arizona: *Dītat Deus* – God enriches

3. Arkansas: *Regnat populus* – The people rule

4. California: *Eureka* – I found it

5. Colorado: *Nīl sine nūmine* – Nothing without divine will

6. Connecticut: *Quī trānstulit sustinet* – He who transplants sustains

7. Idaho: *Estō perpetua* – May thou endure forever

8. Kansas: *Ad astra per aspera* – To the stars through difficulties

9. Kentucky: *Deō grātiam habeāmus* – Let us be grateful to God

10. Maine: *Dīrigō* – I direct

11. Maryland: *Scūtō bonae voluntātis tuae corōnāstī nōs* – With the shield of Your good will You have encircled us

12. Massachusetts: *Ēnse petit placidam sub lībertāte quiētem* – With a sword she seeks peaceful quiet with liberty

13. Michigan: *Sī quaeris paenīnsulam amoenam circumspice* – If you seek a pleasant peninsula, look about you

14. Mississippi: *Virtūte et armīs* – By virtue and arms

15. Missouri: *Salūs populī suprēma lēx estō* – The welfare of the people shall be the supreme law

16. New Mexico: *Crēscit eundō* – It grows as it goes

17. New York: *Excelsior* – Ever higher

18. North Carolina: *Esse quam vidērī* – To be rather than to seem

19. Ohio: *Imperium in imperiō* – An empire in an empire

20. Oklahoma: *Labor omnia vincit* – Work conquers all

21. Oregon: *Ālīs volat prōpriīs* – She flies with her own wings

22. South Carolina: *Dum spīrō spērō* – While I breathe I hope *Animīs opibusque parātī* – Ready in soul and resource

23. Virginia: *Sīc semper tyrannīs* – Thus always to tyrants

24. West Virginia: *Montanī semper līberī* – Mountain men are always free

25. Wyoming: *Cēdant arma togae* – Let arms yield to the toga

The other states in the U.S. have mottoes of various languages; some are English, some European, and some Native American. Find the mottoes for the remaining 25 states, and then label them on your map as well. What do these mottoes say about the states they represent?

1. Alaska: North to the future

2. Delaware: Liberty and independence

3. Florida: In God We Trust

4. Georgia: Wisdom, justice, and moderation

5. Hawaii: *Ua Mau ke Ea o ka 'Aina i ka Pono* (Hawaiian) – The life of the land is perpetuated in righteousness

6. Illinois: State sovereignty, national union

7. Indiana: The crossroads of America

8. Iowa: Our liberties we prize and our rights we will maintain

9. Louisiana: *Union, justice, et confiance* (French) – Union, justice, and confidence

10. Minnesota: *L'étoile du Nord* (French) – The star of the North

11. Montana: *Oro y plata* (Spanish) – Gold and silver

12. Nebraska: Equality before the law

13. Nevada: All for our country

14. New Hampshire: Live Free or Die

15. New Jersey: Liberty and prosperity

16. North Dakota: Liberty and union, now and forever, one and inseparable; Strength from the soil

17. Pennsylvania: Virtue, Liberty, and Independence

18. Rhode Island: Hope

19. South Dakota: Under God the people rule

20. Tennessee: Agriculture and commerce

21. Texas: Friendship

22. Utah: Industry

23. Vermont: Freedom and Unity

24. Washington: (Unofficial) *Al-ki* (Chinook) – By and by

25. Wisconsin: Forward

Latin Across America ANSWERS

Archaeology Project

Praenōmina et Cognōmina: _____

    In the summer of 2006, I (Gaylan Dubose) attended the American Classical League Institute in Philadelphia. While there, I attended a workshop given by a fellow Latin teacher who suggested that since we have learned much about Roman history (and Latin) by means of archeology, we therefore should give students a first-hand experience in the field of archeology. She suggested an "archeology project" in which students mimicked an archeological dig, by first burying a collection of artifacts and then digging them up six weeks later. Of course six weeks can hardly equate to six hundred years, but the brief experiment still helps students see the effects of time and burial on various materials. In this modified project, I have selected a six month burial to better show the effects of time.

    My students have had fun deciding what to bury and digging the holes (one for each of the three fifth grade Latin classes at our school). There was much amusement on my part, too. For example, one boy brought a bottle of turquoise-blue Gatorade. Another boy opened it and took a sip. The original boy was distraught, so I bought another bottle of that turquoise-blue Gatorade, and we buried it. Six months later, we found the Gatorade apparently in its pristine state. I resisted the temptation to let the boy who buried it take a drink. All in all, this activity was very instructive to these classes, as they were able to discern the effect that time and burial had on various objects, except perhaps on the Gatorade. They also derived a more concrete understanding of how archeology works and its importance for imparting to us an understanding of the past.

PART ONE

Either by going to resources on the internet or by consulting printed resources (such as a dictionary or encyclopedia), answer the following questions.

What is an archaeologist?

_____

_____

_____

What is archaeology?

_____

_____

_____

How do archaeologists work?

_____

_____

_____

Part Two

Discuss with your partner or class what types of things you want to bury. Consider materials and shapes. Remember that the items must be small.

Make a preliminary list of at least ten items.

1. _____

2. _____

3. _____

4. _____

5. _____

6. _____

7. _____

8. _____

9. _____

10. _____

After discussion, narrow your list down to five or six items.

1. _____

2. _____

3. _____

4. _____

5. _____

6. _____

Write down what items on your list you think will last for six months buried in the ground. Why do you think each item will last or why not? You will check in six months to see how right you were!

_____

_____

_____

_____

Archaeology Project

PART THREE

Devise a plan to record the weather at the school every school day for six months and each Saturday, Sunday, or holiday at your home. Divide the work up by weeks or months so that the same person does not do the observation and recording every day. (I suggest you do your recording on a calendar.) After six months, list below what items lasted, what items did not, and how you think the weather affected the condition of your articles. Finally, offer further observations on the condition of each object and a summary of what you have learned about the value of archaeology.

1. Which objects lasted well?

_____

_____

2. Which objects did not last well or not at all?

_____

_____

3. What effects do you think the weather had on the objects?

_____

_____

4. Write out your observations on the condition of each object.

_____

_____

5. What might an archaeologist have learned about your school by examing the objects you recovered?

_____

_____

_____

6. Write what you have learned about the value of archaeology for understanding the past.

_____

_____

_____

_____

Tempus Fugit!

Each reading in this book tells a story about the history of the Roman Republic. As you complete each unit, build a timeline in your classroom to help you review all of these important events in Rome's history.

> Step 1: Fill in the outlines provided below using clues from the chapter readings and information from other sources.
>
> Step 2: Make a history card for each person or event.
>
> Step 3: Create a timeline on your wall and arrange your cards in chronological order.
>
> Hint: Extra-wide ribbon works really well for a timeline.

You will need:

- thick ribbon for timeline
- card stock cut to your preferred size
- staples, thumbtacks, or other adhesives to mount on timeline on walls
- art supplies for cutting and decorating event cards
    - scissors
    - rulers
    - drawing materials

Caveat Discipulus: Not all the events and people mentioned are included in this text. You will need to do some extra research elsewhere to complete the timeline of important events.

Unit 2: The Roman Monarchy

Founding of Rome: 753 BC

Romulus, 1st king: c. _____

     Hint: chapter 7 reading (p. 47)

     Important people & events: _____

Numa Pompilius, 2nd king: c. _____

     Hint: chapter 7 reading (p. 47)

     Important people & events: _____

Tullus Hostilius, 3rd king: c. _____

     Hint: chapter 8 reading (p. 55)

     Important people & events: _____

Ancus Marcius, 4th king: c. _____

     Hint: chapter 9 reading (p. 60)

     Important people & events: _____

Tarquinius Priscus, 5th king: c. _____

      Hint: unit 2 reading (p. 63)

      Important people & events: _____

Servius Tullius, 6th king: c. _____

      Hint: chapter 9 reading (p. 60) & unit 2 reading (p. 63)

      Important people & events: _____

Tarquinius Superbus, 7th king: c. _____

      Hint: chapter 9 reading (p. 60) & unit 2 reading (p. 63)

      Important people & events: _____

Unit 3: Early Heroes of Rome

Wars against Tarquinius Superbus and Lars Porsenna (chapters 10-12 readings, pp. 70, 78, 83)

      Dates: c. _____

      Important heroes/events: _____

Cincinnatus (chapter 13 reading, p. 88)

      Date: _____

      Event: _____

Gallic Invasion (unit 3 reading, p. 91)

      Date: _____

      Important heroes: _____

      Event: _____

First Samnite War

      Date: _____

      Important heroes/leaders: _____

      Events: _____

      Results: _____

Latin Wars

      Date: _____

      Important heroes/leaders: _____

      Events: _____

      Results: _____

Second Samnite War

    Date: _____

    Important heroes/leaders: _____

    Events: _____

    Results: _____

Third Samnite War

    Date: _____

    Important heroes/leaders: _____

    Events: _____

    Results: _____

Unit 5: The Punic Wars

1st Punic War (chapter 19 reading, p. 141)

    Dates: _____

    Important leaders/heroes: _____

    Results: _____

2nd Punic War (chapters 20 & 21 readings, pp. 147, 155)

    Dates: _____

    Important leaders/heroes: _____

    Important battles: _____

    Results: _____

1st Macedonian War

    Dates: _____

    Important generals/leaders: _____

    Results: _____

2nd Macedonian War

    Dates: _____

    Important generals/leaders: _____

    Important battles: _____

    Results: _____

Timeline Project

Seleucid War

    Dates: _____

    Important generals/leaders: _____

    Important battles: _____

    Results: _____

3rd Macedonian War

    Dates: _____

    Important generals/leaders: _____

    Important battles: _____

    Results: _____

4th Macedonian War

    Dates: _____

    Important generals/leaders: _____

    Results: _____

3rd Punic War (unit 5 reading, p. 159)

    Dates: _____

    Important generals/leaders: _____

    Results: _____

Unit 6

Gracchan Revolution

    Dates: c. _____

    Tiberius Gracchus: _____

    Gaius Gracchus: _____

Jugurthine War

    Dates: _____

    Important leaders/heroes: _____

    Results: _____

Dictatorship of Sulla

    Dates: _____

    Events: _____

Third Servile War

    Date: _____

    Important heroes/leaders: _____

    Results: _____

Catalinarian Conspiracy

    Dates: _____

    Event: _____

First Triumvirate

    Date formed: _____

    Members: _____

Gallic Wars

    Dates: _____

    Important heroes/leaders: _____

    Results: _____

Invasion of Britain

    Dates: _____

    Important leaders: _____

    Results: _____

Dictatorship of Julius Caesar

    Dates: _____

    Events: _____

    Death: _____

Timeline Project

Unit 2: The Roman Monarchy

Founding of Rome: 753 BC

Romulus, 1st king: c. 753–716 BC
> Hint: chapter 7 reading (p. 47)
> Important people & events:
> Built the walls of Rome, established first Senate

Numa Pompilius, 2nd king: c. 716 BC–673 BC
> Hint: chapter 7 reading (p. 47)
> Important people & events:
> Built the Temple of Janus, Created Roman Calendar, Created the Vestal Virgins
> and priests for the god Mars.

Tullus Hostilius, 3rd king: c. 672–641 BC
> Hint: chapter 8 reading (p. 55)
> Important people & events:
> War with Albans (king Gaius Cluilius)
> Battle of the Horatii and Curiatii

Ancus Marcius, 4th king: c. 642–617 BC
> Hint: chapter 9 reading (p. 60)
> Important people & events:
> Overcame the Latin tribe.
> He built the first prison known as the Mamertine.
> Built the Pons Sublicius across the Tiber River.
> Founded the port city of Ostia.

Tarquinius Priscus, 5th king: c. 617 - 579 BC
> Hint: unit 2 reading (p. 63)
> Important people & events:
> Built the Circus Maximus between the Aventine and Palatine hills.
> Constructed the Cloaca Maxima (great sewer) to drain the valley between the hills
> in order to create the Roman Forum.
> Began construction on the great temple to Jupiter Optimus on the Capitoline Hill.

Servius Tullius, 6th king: c. 579–535 BC
> Hint: chapter 9 reading (p. 60) & unit 2 reading (p. 63)
> Important people & events:
> Tullius' daughters married the sons of Tarquinius Priscus.
> Servius is credited with taking the first census of Rome.

Tarquinius Superbus, 7th king: c. 535–510 BC
> Hint: chapter 9 reading (p. 60) & unit 2 reading (p. 63)
> Important people & events:
> Expulsion of Tarquinius and end of monarchy
> Lucius Iunius Brutus & Tarquinius Collatinus (first consuls): c. 509 BC

Unit 3: Early Heroes of Rome

Wars against Tarquinius Superbus and Lars Porsenna (chapters 10-12 readings, pp. 70, 78, 83)
> Dates: c. 500 BC
> Important heroes/events:
> Mucius Scaevola, Cloelia, Horatius

Cincinnatus (chapter 13 reading, p. 88)
> Date: Roman dictator in 458 BC (and again in 439 BC)
> Event: Assisted in the defeat of the Aequi and Volscians

Gallic Invasion (unit 3 reading, p. 91)
> Date: 390 BC
> Heroes: Marcus Manlius Capitolinus
> Event: The Senones, a Gallic tribe, attack Rome and lay siege to the Capitoline

First Samnite War:
> Date: 343–341 BC
> Heroes/Leaders: Marcus Valerius Corvus
> Events: Battle of Mt. Gaurus
> Results: Rome obtains the region of Campania

Latin Wars:
> Date: 340–388 BC
> Heroes/Leaders: Decius Mus, Manlius Torquatus Imperiosus
> Events: Battle of Vesuvius
> Results: Latin towns become Romanized; some become Roman colonies

Second Samnite War:
> Date: 326–304 BC
> Important heroes/leaders: Pontius (Samnite leader)
> Events: Battle of Caudine Forks
> Results: Rome extends territory into Etruria and Umbria

Third Samnite War:
> Date: 298–290 BC
> Important heroes/leaders: Fabius Maximus Rullianus
> Events: Battle of Sentinum
> Results: Rome dominates all of the Italian peninsula except the extreme south and Po valley

Unit 5: The Punic Wars

1st Punic War (chapter 19 reading, p. 141)
        Dates: 264–241 BC
        Important leaders/heroes: Regulus, Hamilcar Barca
        Results: Rome obtains the islands of Sicily, Sardinia, and Corsica

2nd Punic War (chapters 20 & 21 readings, pp. 147, 155)
        Dates: 218–201 BC
        Important heroes/leaders: Hannibal, Hasdrubal
        Quintus Fabius Maximus, Scipio Africanus
        Important battles: Battle of Cannae, Battle of Zama
        Results: Carthage stripped of colonies, forbidden to own large army or navy

1st Macedonian War
        Dates: 215–205 BC
        Important generals/leaders:
        Philip V (ally of Hannibal)
        Results: Treaty of Phoenice

2nd Macedonian War
        Dates: 200–196 BC
        Important generals/leaders:
        Philip V and Antiochus III
        Important battles:
        Battle of Cynoscephalae, 197 BC
        Results: Liberation of Greece, 194 BC; Philip V forbidden to wage war
        outside of his borders

Seleucid War
        Dates: 192–188 BC
        Important generals/leaders:
        Antiochus III and AetolianLeague
        Scipio Africanus
        Important battles: Battle of Thermopylae, 191; Magnesia, 190
        Results: Seleucid Empire divided between Rome and Pergamon

3rd Macedonian War
        Dates: 172–168 BC
        Important generals/leaders:
        Perseus, son of Philip V
        Important battles: Battle of Pydna
        Results: Macedonia divided into 4 "puppet" republics

4th Macedonian War
> Dates: 150–148 BC
> Important generals/leaders:
> Andrisius (alleged son of Perseus)
> Results: Greece becomes a province of Rome, Corinth destroyed in 146

3rd Punic War (unit 5 reading, p. 159)
> Dates: 149–146 BC
> Important generals/leaders:
> Cato the Elder, Scipio Aemilianus (also called Scipio Africanus Minor)
> Results: Carthage utterly destroyed in 146

Unit 6

Gracchan Revolution
> Dates: c.133–121 BC
> Tiberius Gracchus: tribune in 133 BC
> Gaius Gracchus: tribune in 123 and 122 BC

Jugurthine War (takes place in Numidia)
> Dates: 112–105 BC
> Important heroes/leaders: Jugurtha, Gaius Marius (uncle to Julius Caesar),
> Lucius Cornelius Sulla
> Results: revealed growing corruption within Rome

Dictatorship of Sulla
> Dates: 82–79 BC
> Events: introduced a "reign of terror" through proscriptions
> doubled size of Senate and increased its power
> reformed court system

Third Servile War
> Date: 73 - 71 BC
> Important heroes/leaders: Spartacus, Marcus Licinius Crassus, Gnaeus Pompeius
> Results: 6,600 slaves were crucified along the Via Appia from Rome to Brundisium

Catalinarian Conspiracy
> Dates: 63 BC (first conspiracy in 65 BC)
> Event: Cicero uncovers a conspiracy by Cataline to seize power in Rome

First Triumvirate
> Date formed: 60 BC
> Members: Julius Caesar, Gnaeus Pompeius Magnus, Marcus Licinius Crassus

Timeline Project ANSWERS

Gallic Wars

    Dates: 58–51 BC

    Important heroes/leaders: Julius Caesar, Vercingetorix, Ariovistus, Orgetorix

    Results: Roman rule expanded over whole of Gaul

    Caesar gains great power and popularity

    Caesar crosses Rubicon and marches army into Rome

Invasion of Britain

    Dates: 55 & 54 BC

    Important leaders: Julius Caesar, Cassivellaunus

    Results: nominal victory, Rome receives tribute from some tribes in Britain

Dictatorship of Julius Caesar

    Dates: 49–44 BC

    Events: civil war that ended with defeat of Pompey's armies in Egypt

    established new reforms

    enlarged Senate

    created Julian calendar with Sosigenes of Egypt

    named dictator for life in 44 BC

    Death: assassinated on March 15, 44 BC

Declining Worksheets

1. Choose 6 nouns from chapter(s) _____.   2. Find the stem of each noun.
3. Decline the noun.   4. Translate the box marked *.

1. stem: _____

CASE	SINGULAR	PLURAL
	*	

* _____

2. stem: _____

CASE	SINGULAR	PLURAL
		*

* _____

3. stem: _____

CASE	SINGULAR	PLURAL
	*	

* _____

Declining Worksheet

4. stem: _____

CASE	SINGULAR	PLURAL
		*

* _____

5. stem: _____

CASE	SINGULAR	PLURAL
	*	

* _____

6. stem: _____

CASE	SINGULAR	PLURAL
		*

* _____

Declining Worksheet

Verb Conjugating Worksheets

1. Choose 6 verbs from chapter(s) _____.
2. Find the stem of each verb.
3. Conjugate the verb in the tense requested.
4. Translate the box marked * in two different ways.

1. tense: _____   stem: _____

*		

* _____

_____

2. tense: _____   stem: _____

		*

* _____

_____

3. tense: _____   stem: _____

*		

* _____

_____

4. tense: _____   stem: _____

		*

* _____

_____

5. tense: _____   stem: _____

*		

* _____

_____

6. tense: _____   stem: _____

		*

* _____

_____

Verb Conjugating Worksheet

nōmen: _____   datum: _____

Verb Parsing Worksheet

VERB	TENSE	PERSON	NUMBER	TRANSLATION

Roman Timeline Outline

BC	EVENT
753	Rome founded; reign of Romulus begins
716–673	Reign of Numa Pompilius
672–641	Reign of Tullus Hostilius
642–617	Reign of Ancus Marcius
616	Reign of Tarquinius Priscus begins
c. 600	Tarquinius Priscus drains the forum; Earliest known Latin inscriptions
579	Reign of Servius Tullius
543	Reign of Tarquinius Superbus
509	Expulsion of Tarquins (monarchy comes to an end); wars with Etruscans
c. 500	Wars with Lars Porsenna
494	Class struggle between plebeians and patricians begins
458	Dictatorship of Cincinnatus
450	First Roman code of law: The Twelve Tables
390	Gallic Invasion
343–341	1st Samnite War
340–338	Latin Wars
326–304	2nd Samnite War
312	Appian Way (*rēgīna longārum viārum*) constructed
298–290	3rd Samnite War
287	Class struggle between plebeians and patricians comes to an end
282–272	Wars with Pyrrhus
c. 280	First known coinage
272	Rome wins control of Italy
264–241	1st Punic War; Rome wins Sicily, Corsica, and Sardinia
247	Birth of Hannibal Barca
236	Birth of Publius Cornelius Scipio
228	Death of Hamilcar Barca
218	2nd Punic War begins
December 17, 217	Saturnalia festival is established
215–205	1st Macedonian War
214–212	Siege of Syracuse; Archimedes Death Ray
October 19, 202	Battle of Zama
201	2nd Punic War ends; Spain becomes a Roman province

Roman Timeline Outline

BC	EVENT
200–196	2nd Macedonian War
192–188	Seleucid War
172–168	3rd Macedonian War
150	4th and final Macedonian War begins
149	3rd Punic War begins
148	Macedonia becomes a Roman Province; end of 4th Macedonian War
February, 146	Rome destroys Carthage and Corinth on the same day. This brings the Punic Wars and the Macedonian Wars to a final end.
135–132	1st Servile War (slave revolt)
133	Tiberius Gracchus becomes tribune
123–122	Gaius Gracchus conducts reforms as tribune
112–105	Jugurthine Wars
107–86	Marius elected consul 7 times
100	Julius Caesar born
91–87	Social War; Rome extends Roman citizenship to all of Italy
88–85	1st Mithridatic War
82–79	Dictatorship of Sulla
73–71	Spartacus leads the 3rd Servile War
73–63	3rd Mithridatic War
64	Pompey captures Jerusalem
63	Cicero wins consulship; Conspiracy of Cataline
60	1st Triumvirate formed: Caesar, Pompey, Crassus
58–50	Gallic Wars
55	Theatre of Pompey built
55 & 54	Caesar's expeditions to Britain
October 2, 52	Final battle for Alesia; defeat of Vercingetorix
49–45	Rome's Civil War; dictatorship of Julius Caesar
August, 48	Caesar defeats Pompey at Battle of Pharsalus
September, 48	Caesar arrives in Egypt
June 23, 47	Birth of Caesarion (Ptolemy XV), son of Caesar and Cleopatra, Queen of Egypt
46	Caesar's forum built
46–44	Cleopatra lives at Caesar's estate in Rome
44	Caesar appointed Dictator for Life
March 15, 44	Caesar assassinated in Theatre of Pompey

Roman Timeline Outline

CLASSICALU
TEACHER TRAINING

We created ClassicalU with *you* in mind. We are confident this resource will inspire educators in schools, home-schools, and co-ops to dig deep into the richness of learning, no matter where you find yourself on your journey in classical education.

What You Get by Subscribing

✓ **New Content Regularly**
Whether it's new courses, conversations, or interviews, we are always releasing new content to help you grow.

★ **Ambrose Curriculum Guide**
View more than 250 documents, including course guides for every class in a K–12 school or homeschool.

⬇ **Downloadable Resources**
Download notes, articles, recommended resources, and other files associated with our courses.

💬 **ClassicalU Community**
Engage other educators and administrators in conversation and share ideas and resources.

🎞 **Promotional Videos**
Access professionally designed videos that promote classical education to grow your school or co-op.

🔖 **Over 35 Self-Paced Courses!**

COURSE LEVELS

1 **2** **3** **L**

Level 1: Apprentice
Begin your journey toward mastery.

Level 2: Journeyman
Continue your journey toward mastery.

Level 3: Master
Train to mentor and lead other teachers.

Level L: Leader
Grow as a leader or administrator.

Visit www.ClassicalU.com
to see free previews of every course.